Property Insolvency

Property Insolvency

Peter Levaggi, Joint Head of Property Litigation Group, Charles Russell LLP

Roger Elford, Joint Head of Property Insolvency Group, Charles Russell LLP

JORDANS

Published by
Jordan Publishing Limited
21 St Thomas Street, Bristol BS1 6JS

British Library Cataloguing-in-Publication Data

A catalogue record for this book is available from the British Library.

ISBN 978 1 84661 151 3

Typeset by Letterpart Ltd, Reigate, Surrey

Printed in Great Britain by Antony Rowe Limited, Chippenham, Wiltshire

FOREWORD

It is conventional, or at least not unusual, for a foreword to a new legal publication to describe the work as 'timely'. In this case, the description could not be more accurate.

During the last quarter of 2007 and the first and, possibly, the second quarters of 2008, the global downturn still appeared, at least at first blush, to be confined to the financial sector. True it was that the seeds of that downturn were sub-prime lending on property in the United States and elsewhere. However, during this period, the focus of attention was very much upon the effects of the downturn on banks, structured investment vehicles, hedge funds and other financial institutions, and the immediate concern of practitioners was to understand the nature of the occasionally arcane-seeming products which comprised those institutions' assets and liabilities and to formulate mechanisms by which they could (if at all) be restructured. By the early autumn of 2008, however, the downturn had spread with a vengeance from the City to the so-called 'real' economy. There is now no sector of the economy which appears to be immune from the downturn. Whatever the business – whether in the service, manufacturing, retail or property sectors – there are none now which appear immune to the consequences of the downturn. It is plain that many will follow those which have already been forced into formal insolvency proceedings; still others will require some form of restructuring. As with businesses, so with individuals. With the labour market contracting at a time of very significant personal debt, it is inevitable that the instances of individual insolvency will rise at an alarming rate as the recession gathers pace and deepens.

At such a time as this, the work of practitioners involved in restructuring and insolvency is crucial. With swift and effective assistance, a business and jobs may be saved; at worst, a return can be achieved for creditors which can properly be regarded as being the best reasonably achievable in the circumstances. For many businesses and individuals, it remains the case that a significant source of a debtor's assets and liabilities will be or will be derived from freehold or leasehold property owned by that debtor. Accordingly, the giving of such assistance will require a detailed understanding, not only of the ordinary rights and obligations which flow from the property in question, but also of the effect of insolvency on those rights and obligations. What is true of those practising in the field of restructuring and insolvency is no less true for those practising or specialising in other fields. No one seeking to advise or assist a party in respect of a property related matter in which the other, or another, party is or may be insolvent can properly do so without considering the effect of that insolvency.

Property Insolvency is a new and specialised publication which fills an existing gap in an area raising issues of considerable legal and practical complexity. It has been written by two practitioners who are eminent in this area and who have, individually and collectively, very many years of relevant experience. In an intellectually rigorous and authoritative but nevertheless accessible manner, which will be invaluable to every practitioner having to address property issues in an insolvency context, it identifies the main issues which are likely to arise, explains the consequences of the different insolvency processes and offers sensible and practical guidance. Where appropriate, the editors have not shrunk from setting out the general legal principles and relevant case-law which form the background to a particular topic; see, for example, the helpful summary of the law relating to forfeiture in the opening paragraphs of chapter 4. The book covers all of the relevant legislation and is generous in its citation of authorities. In both respects, it is completely up to date. Thus, for example, the provisions of the Tribunals and Enforcement Act 2007 which, amongst other things, abolish distress and introduce the new commercial rent arrears recovery procedure are covered in depth; so also are the important judgments of the Court of Appeal in *Innovate Logistics Ltd v Sunberry Properties Ltd* [2008] EWCA Civ 1261, a case which will provide much comfort for insolvency practitioners, but rather less for landlords and their advisers. The controversial question of pre-packaged administrations is also covered, with references to the forthcoming SIP 16 and the accompanying guidance notes, and there is extensive consideration of the difficult issues which arise in the context of voluntary arrangements, with a careful consideration of Lord Neuberger's judgment in the under-reported case of *Thomas v Ken Thomas Ltd* [2007] BLR 429 as well as the issues which underlie, and still remain following, the *Powerhouse* litigation.

This is, therefore, truly a 'timely' publication and one which, by virtue of its content, will be a thoroughly welcome and invaluable tool for those practising in the fields of insolvency and property alike.

Peter Arden QC
Enterprise Chambers
Lincoln's Inn
January 2009

PREFACE

The purpose of this book is to give a full account of the modern law relating to property insolvency. Perhaps there could be no better moment to produce a work on this subject, given that the current economic crisis is largely driven by the collapse of mortgage lending and property prices. The current issues involving property and insolvency have reached a level of complexity that has never been seen before. The loss of confidence in interbank credit arrangements can be directly linked with the high level of defaulting mortgagors and tenants (albeit the link is partially hidden by the fact that property portfolios and mortgage funds have been shuffled and traded through obscure securitisation vehicles). The time is right for a book dedicated solely to property insolvency.

Activity across all sectors of the commercial property market is severely depressed with most of the headline indicators deteriorating. The severe market downturn in 2008 has hit confidence worldwide with many jurisdictions in a broad based recession. The Royal Institute of Chartered Surveyors (RICS) has noted that occupier demand has declined at the fastest pace in its survey's history whilst the amount of available space for occupation has increased at the fastest pace ever recorded. This has proved to be a potent cocktail with increased property supply accentuated by severely reduced demand. In the investment market, activity remains depressed with investment demand for prime property falling dramatically. The economic downturn has hit all areas of the property sector. Office (part completed, new, ageing and obsolete), retail, residential and industrial property values are under intense downward pressure.

For developers, the worsening market conditions have left low demand for completed projects and a sharp rise in insolvency within the construction industry (with the only exception being infrastructure and publicly funded projects).

The aim of this book is to provide a comprehensive and practical guide for lawyers, property and insolvency professionals (together with those interested generally in the subject). The book reviews the legal mechanisms which underpin the treatment of property in formal and informal insolvent arrangements and covers everything from the Statute of Marlborough 1267 to the Statement of Insolvency Practice 16 (published January 2009).

Although investing in property across the world has been a winning proposition for years, there is now a huge constituency of at risk investors (including individuals, banks, property companies, and trust funds) attempting to navigate their way through the toughest of market conditions.

Our thanks are due to Peter Arden QC, Kiran Goss (a tolerant, benevolent driving force), Phillipa Broadhurst (who produced an earlier version of the tax chapter and was a valuable sounding board for parts of the text), Hazel Shearing (the loudest voice in the house!), Molly Lucia (great at tables), Julian Fenn (the original inspiration), James Hyne (for his insights into the vagaries of insolvency practice), Tony Murphy (the law maker and the chief protagonist in a number of influential recently reported cases), Cheryl Prophett, Jess Lorimer, Liz Rourke and Rhianne Martin. Brian Johnson, Gary Burns and Tony Farrant for excellent technical advice. Peter Mooney for his immense contribution to the distress/CRAR chapter, Tarl Lall for his substantial contribution to the tax chapter and Corrinn Buland. Finally, we would like to thank Maureen Hanley, Peter Elford and Jill Elford for all their support, assistance and encouragement over the years.

The law is stated as at January 2009.

Peter Levaggi
Roger Elford

Contributors
Tarl Lall (Partner, Charles Russell LLP) – Chapter 20 (Tax)
Peter Mooney (Managing Director of County Bailiff Group) – Chapter 3
(Distress for Rent and Commercial Rent Arrears Recovery)

CONTENTS

Part 1
Tenant's Insolvency

Chapter 2
Liability for Rent and Other Obligations Under a Lease   33

TABLE OF CASES

References are to paragraph numbers.

Property Insolvency

TABLE OF STATUTES

References are to paragraph numbers.

TABLE OF STATUTORY INSTRUMENTS

References are to paragraph numbers.

TABLE OF ABBREVIATIONS

AGA	authorised guarantee agreement
AJA 1970/1973	Administration of Justice Act 1970/1973
AST	assured shorthold tenancy
CAB	Citizens Advice Bureau
CCA 1974	Consumer Credit Act 1974
CGT	Capital Gains Tax
CPR	Civil Procedure Rules
CRAR	Commercial Rent Arrears Recovery
CVA	company voluntary arrangement
ECHR	European Convention on Human Rights
ER	entrepreneurs' relief
FA 2003	Finance Act 2003
HMRC	Her Majesty's Revenue and Customs
IA 1986	Insolvency Act 1986
ICTA 1988	Income and Corporation Taxes Act 1988
IR 1986	Insolvency Rules 1986, SI 1986/1925
ITA 2007	Income Tax Act 2007
IVA	individual voluntary arrangement
JCT	Joint Contracts Tribunal
LLP	Limited Liability Partnership
LPA 1925	Law of Property Act 1925
LTA 1954	Landlord and Tenants Act 1954
NICs	national insurance contributions
NSP	notice seeking possession
ROT	retention of title
SCPC	Standard commercial property conditions
SDLT	Stamp Duty Land Tax
TCC	Technology and Construction Court
TCEA 2007	Tribunals, Courts and Enforcement Act 2007
TCGA 1992	Taxation of Chargeable Gains Act 1992
the 1908 Act	Law of Distress Amendment Act 1908
the Covenants Act	Landlord and Tenant (Covenants) Act 1995
TLATA 1996	Trusts of Land and Appointment of Trustees Act 1996
TOGC	transfer of going concern
VA	voluntary arrangement

VAT	Value Added Tax
VATA 1994	Value Added Tax Act 1994
VAT Regs 1995	Value Added Tax Regulations 1995, SI 1995/2518

Chapter 1

INTRODUCTION

PROPERTY INSOLVENCY – OVERVIEW

A brief history

1.1 The law of property was, until the far reaching reforms of the nineteenth and twentieth centuries, based on a highly evolved feudal system. The residue of this system survives to this day with all estates of land ultimately deriving from the Crown or one of the Royal Duchies. These origins still have practical consequences (see chapter 11 in relation to escheat). In fact all land is owned by the Crown. A small part is occupied by the Crown (or one of its agencies) and the remaining land is let through various forms of direct or indirect tenures from the Crown. There are no areas which have a 'Passport to Pimlico' style independence, there is no land without a lord (*nulle terre sans seigneur*).

1.2 Under the Crown, there are three ways to own land, freehold, leasehold and commonhold. Each has its advantages and disadvantages in particular circumstances. Freehold comes closest to absolute ownership. Leasehold confers ownership for a temporary period, subject to terms and conditions contained in the contract, or lease. Commonhold is a new form of property ownership which combines aspects of both freehold and leasehold estates. It was introduced by Part I of the Commonhold and Leasehold Reform Act 2002, which came into force on 27 September 2004, and is still rare.

1.3 Land interests usually represent the single most valuable asset or investment for the vast majority of adults (whether this is bound up in home ownership or property investment). The late twentieth century saw a mass democratisation of home ownership; however investment has always been concentrated in property rights. Capital and security have since time immemorial driven the ancient connection between property, solvency and debt. One of the earliest examples of statutory regulation in the form of the Statute of Marlborough 1267 was inspired by this trinity (the precursor to all moratoriums/restrictions and the ancestral mother of the Rent Acts, the Insolvency Acts and the law of distress). This is not an esoteric point. The statute remains in force and has real effect today. It has even survived the sweeping reforms made by the Tribunals, Courts and Enforcement Act 2007 (which will abolish the ancient law of distress; see chapter 3). The statute protects the occupiers of land from the excessive demands of debt collectors and elegantly provides:

'Whereas at the time of a commotion late stirred up within this realm, and also sithence, many great men, and divers other, refusing to be justified by the King and his court, like as they ought and were wont in time of the King's noble progenitors, and also in his time; but took great revenges and distresses of their neighbours, and of other, until they had amends and fines at their own pleasure; and further, some of them would not be justified by the King's officers, nor would suffer them to make delivery of such distresses as they had taken of their own authority; it is provided, agreed, and granted, that all persons, as well of high as of low estate, shall receive justice in the King's court; and none from henceforth shall take any such revenge or distress of his own authority, without award of our court, though he have damage or injury, whereby he would have amends of his neighbour either higher or lower.'

1.4   Over time the justice in the king's court has been supplemented so that property rights are highly regulated. The purpose of the regulation has always been (in varying degrees) to restrict landowners from:

- taking the tenants goods in distress without due process (from the Distress for Rent Act 1689 to the Tribunals, Courts and Enforcement Act 2007); and

- preventing a wrongful forfeiture and securing the tenant's occupation/ tenure (through the evolution of leasehold interests in the thirteenth century to the statutory protection created in the twentieth century).

1.5   Insolvency law has developed in parallel with property law. The Bankruptcy Act 1542 and the earlier doctrine of Law Merchant created the underlying principles that govern much of the modern legislation. Through a modern lens the original doctrine may seem cruel. The fate of debtors in early times was grim. However, even the early legislation was actually put in place to protect debtors from what otherwise would have been a Hobbesian nightmare of creditors and landowners taking the law into their own hands.

Modern property insolvency

1.6   Almost all forms of property rights are now regulated. Landowners, mortgagees, landlords and licensors are restricted by a complex raft of common law principles and statutory control. Residential tenants have the protection of the myriad of housing and rent acts. Commercial tenants have the benefit of the Landlord and Tenant Act 1954 and numerous other statutory provisions.

1.7   The Insolvency Act 1986 created a sea change with the introduction of corporate rescue structures. The Insolvency Act 2000 supplemented this and was followed by the reforming and controversial Enterprise Act 2002. The Act relaxed the law of bankruptcy (see **1.94**) and boosted corporate rescue with new style administrations (see **1.67**) with the objective of boosting the entrepreneur and the enterprise culture. The Enterprise Act 2002 was controversial with commentators calling it a bankrupt's charter. This was summed up by Boris Johnson in 2002:

> 'Of course much of this may be a function of worsening economic conditions, and excessive household debt. But it is also clear that by encouraging bankruptcy – literally – the Government is encouraging some people to take the money and run, and to conclude that they are better off being dead than in the red, especially when they can be born again almost immediately, with bankruptcy discharged after only a year.
>
> Yes, we need an enterprise culture, but you should bring it about first by reuniting effort and reward, and cutting taxes, not encouraging shysters to go bankrupt at the drop of a hat.'

1.8　Perhaps these comments were prescient. The last few years have seen record numbers of people being caught in the debt trap. In 2006 the Citizens Advice Bureau (CAB) dealt with 6,500 new cases of debt every day, a rise of more than 30% on the figures in 2004 and 1.7 million people needed help with money problems. Between 2006 and 2008 county court judgments rose by 42% (the Registry Trust). The number of Individual Voluntary Arrangements rose between 1998 and 2006 by 900%. In this period the number of bankruptcies rose by 320%.

1.9　The year 2008 saw the collapse of Lehman Brothers and a host of banks failing or being subject to takeovers (including Dawnay Day, HBOS, Merrill Lynch, and the list goes on). The failure of these institutions has been attributed to their exposure to the ailing real estate market (driven by a boom which saw average house prices increase from £101,000 in 2001 to £221,000 in 2007). The credit crunch was a turbulent time for property lenders. Retail companies were also hit hard with insolvencies up by 48% from 2005 to 2008.

1.10　Property interests are invariably one of the most important components in the realisation of the insolvent estate. As a consequence of the increasing uncertainty in the property market there has been close interest in the development of property insolvency cases in recent years. Perhaps the most significant example of this came with the *Powerhouse* case which combined the potent mix of property insolvency and retail turbulence (see **5.82**). The case was summed up in a headline in the *Estates Gazette* as 'Test case threatens "Armageddon"' (6 May 2006). Following the credit crunch and the strong connection to the property market there is likely to be continued interest in the development of property insolvency issues.

Human rights

1.11　The law relating to property insolvency is required to strike a balance between upholding the rights of the most vulnerable and weak tenants and mortgagors who are unable to pay their debts whilst providing effective remedies against hardened and recalcitrant tenants who refuse to pay theirs.

These groups of debtors were classified into 'can't pay' and 'won't pay' by a research paper published by the Lord Chancellor's Department in March 2003 ('Effective Enforcement') which was used in the consultation process for the Tribunals, Courts and Enforcement Act 2007. The process recognised the rights of both creditors and debtors and the fine balance which must be struck. The Human Rights Act 1998 gave direct effect in the UK to the European Convention on Human Rights and Fundamental Freedoms (ECHR). Although still controversial the changes made by the Tribunals Act (see **3.11**) and the Enterprise Act 2002 create a modern system of regulation which is more ECHR compliant. However, it should not be forgotten that landlords, mortgagees and creditors also have rights under the ECHR to peacefully enjoy their property/assets (if they are individuals).

1.12 In this book the Insolvency Act 1986 will be abbreviated to IA 1986, and the Insolvency Rules 1986, SI 1986/1925, will be IR 1986.

INSOLVENCY – OVERVIEW

Immediate considerations and signs that a tenant may be or may become insolvent

1.13 Often creditors (both corporate and individuals) are unaware of a debtor's insolvency until they receive notification from the insolvency practitioner, charged with dealing with the debtor's insolvency, that the debtor has entered a formal insolvency regime. There are often signs that should alert creditors to the possibility that one of their debtors is facing financial difficulties:

- debtors may make redundancies in relation to its workforce or seek to come to an informal arrangement with the creditor to improve their cash flow;

- a tenant of commercial premises may seek the landlord's agreement to pay rent on a monthly basis rather than a quarterly basis in order to improve cash flow;

- a dishonoured cheque should send immediate warning signs to the creditor;

- an unsubstantiated dispute may arise in relation to service charges or other payments which may be a ploy to delay payment;

- the diversification of the debtor's business into new products and territories may be an indication that its core business is failing;

- the debtor may have granted new security to a creditor other than the debtor's usual bank, which may be indicative of commercial pressure being placed upon the debtor to do so;

- the insolvency of one of tenant's suppliers or major customers may cause a sudden and unforeseen deterioration in the tenant's financial circumstances;

- certain industry sectors may be experiencing endemic problems which may substantially affect their immediate or long-term viability (such as for estate agents in times of recession).

1.14 There are disadvantages for a corporate debtor in dealing with creditors on an individual and piecemeal basis. Whilst a particular creditor may be placated, an arrangement reached with that creditor will not restrict the rights of other creditors to take action against the debtor for the recovery of the sums owed to them. The advantage of insolvency legislation is to ensure (so far as possible) that creditors of equal standing are treated equally and the creditors' remedies are carried out by an officeholder acting collectively. There are safeguards in place to ensure that debtors do not unfairly prefer some creditors' claims in the lead up to insolvency (see IA 1986, ss 239 and 340).

1.15 Landlords are often important for the success or failure of any insolvency. If the officeholder wishes to retain a leased property for the benefit of the insolvent estate then he has to deal with the landlord. The collective insolvency process has a number of measures in place to assist this process.

1.16 In the case of companies and limited liability partnerships, where the directors know or ought to conclude that there is no reasonable prospect that the company would avoid going into insolvent liquidation (see IA 1986, s 214), then there is a duty to:

- cease trading the business; or

- take appropriate steps such as placing the company into administration or liquidation; or

- proceed with the consent of the company's creditors (using a formal method such as a voluntary arrangement or for listed companies the formal 'work out' process some times known as the 'London approach').

A director of a company can be made personally liable for any additional debts that the company incurred after the date he ought to have concluded that there was no reasonable prospect that the company could avoid insolvent liquidation.

Pre-insolvency action by directors

1.17   Taking the example of an insolvent retailer with multiple sites (which has become increasingly common in recent years), the directors will be typically faced with the following factors:

- some stores may be trading well (ie are profitable) whilst others are failing. The directors should carry out a store-by-store audit to reflect the viability of each store;

- there may be a core business of successful trading stores which is salvageable. This is likely to depend on whether the business can be downsized so as to diminish the effect of the unsuccessful stores. The core business may have a well-known brand name together with goodwill;

- before considering insolvency the company will have attempted to market each and every site to attempt to find an assignee (for that store). Unfortunately, poorer performing stores are usually difficult to dispose of with a lack of potential assignees. Conversely, the company may wish to retain attractive sites where an assignment may be possible (but not wanted);

- the stock value for many retailers is often low. Whatever stock in the company's possession is likely to be subject to a *retention of title* (ROT) clause held by a supplier. Directors should consider the ROT position carefully and perhaps go to the length of putting together a schedule;

- where there is a core business it is essential to look after trade creditors and credit insurers. Their support is essential for any viable business going forward;

- landlords do not usually behave in a concerted way but the company must review the risk of forfeiture or distress (soon to be Commercial Rent Arrears Recovery); and

- potential buyers of the business should be investigated to explore the advantages of a *pre-packaged* sale of the core business (see chapter 8).

1.18   There is always a balancing act to perform in advising directors in these circumstances. The business may need to:

- downsize (shed some stores) to survive as a going concern;

- close down completely in a structured way, maximising its assets; or

- obtain a breathing space to trade on or to do one of the above.

1.19 Generally the directors will need to keep major creditors on side including the banks. There may be listing issues, the directors may have to go through a formal workout (eg the London Approach) or an informal workout. There may be indecision and disagreement between the directors as to which way they should go. This is the time for the directors and the board to take great care to minute the reasons for their decisions and involve an insolvency practitioner at an early stage. Directors are usually fully aware of the dangers they face (wrongful and fraudulent trading and general misfeasance). Listing requirements regarding notifications need to be reviewed. Also director and officer insurance cover should be reviewed to ensure no steps are taken that could invalidate the directors' insurance.

1.20 As well as the general company review a specific urgent review should be undertaken in relation to each property, to include:

• an analysis of the profit and costs of that store including management accounts;

• a stock analysis (including ROT position) for that store;

• a review of the lease including the rent position, deposits, dilapidations, service charges and rent review;

• a review of all facilities and guarantees;

• a review of sub-franchises/sub-tenancies;

• short and medium-term cash flow projections; and

• budgeting including capital expenditure.

1.21 One of the purposes of the insolvency legislation is to prevent debtors from taking on new liabilities where it becomes clear or ought to be clear that they will not be able to satisfy those liabilities. Against this backdrop, this chapter will provide a short overview of the various formal insolvency procedures under the IA 1986 and their implications for creditors who are primarily concerned with property occupied by the debtor.

When is a company insolvent?

1.22 Under the IA 1986, a company may be adjudged as being insolvent in two distinct cases: (i) where it is demonstrated that the company is unable to pay its debts; or (ii) where it is proved that the value of the company's assets is less than the amount of its liabilities (taking into account its contingent and prospective liabilities) (IA 1986, s 123(2)). The fact that a company is unable to pay its debts is a ground upon which a creditor may present a petition to the court for a winding-up order, so as to place the company into compulsory liquidation (IA 1986, s 123(1) and (2) – see below).

Determining the insolvency of an individual debtor

1.23 The test for solvency (or otherwise) in relation to individuals is similar to that of companies, namely that the individual is unable to pay his debts as they fall due. Where bankruptcy proceedings are instigated by a creditor against an individual debtor he must demonstrate to the court that he has served a statutory demand on the debtor for the payment of a debt exceeding £750 and at least 3 weeks have elapsed without the debtor making payment or applying to the court to set aside the statutory demand. Alternatively, a judgment creditor can also petition for the debtor's bankruptcy where execution (or other enforcement method) issued in respect of the creditor's debt on a judgment has been returned unsatisfied in whole or in part (IA 1986, s 268(1)(b)).

Voluntary arrangements

1.24 In essence, a voluntary arrangement is a statutory compromise between the debtor and his creditors. A debtor will make a proposal to his creditors in order to discharge his liabilities to his creditors, either in full or at a reduced rate over a period of time dictated by the terms of the arrangement. The effect of the voluntary arrangement will usually be that it will provide a better return to the debtor's creditors than they could expect to achieve on the winding up or bankruptcy of the debtor.

1.25 Voluntary arrangements are available to companies (known as Company Voluntary Arrangements or CVAs) and to individuals (Individual Voluntary Arrangements or IVAs). It is also possible for partnerships and limited liability partnerships to propose voluntary arrangements.

Individual voluntary arrangements (IVAs)

1.26 There are a number of reasons why an insolvent debtor will wish to avoid bankruptcy. It may be that the debtor has a profession that he would be unable to continue if he is made bankrupt. For example, it is unlawful for an undischarged bankrupt to be a director of a company or be involved in the management of a company without the leave of the court (IR 1986, r 6.235). An undischarged bankrupt cannot practise as a solicitor or act as the trustee of a charity.

1.27 The debtor may have significant assets but may be unable to realise or liquidate those assets within a short enough period of time to satisfy the demands of his creditors (who may be instigating bankruptcy proceedings against him). Voluntary arrangements provide the debtor with a possible alternative to bankruptcy (under IA 1986, Part VIII).

1.28 An IVA is flexible as to how it will operate and enables the debtor 'to make a proposal to his creditors for a composition in satisfaction of his debts or a scheme of arrangement of his affairs' (IA 1986, s 253(1)).

1.29 Prior to the implementation of the Insolvency Act 2000 it was a necessary prerequisite to any IVA that the debtor obtain an interim order prior to putting a proposal to his creditors (*Fletcher v Vooght* [2000] BPIR 435). The effect of the interim order is to create a moratorium over the debtor's assets and prevents creditors from taking action against the debtor and his property pending the meeting of the debtor's creditors to consider his proposal. The debtor may proceed to make a proposal for a voluntary arrangement with or without first obtaining an interim order (IA 1986, s 253). Whilst an interim order is in force, no bankruptcy petition may be presented or proceeded with against the debtor, no landlord may exercise any right to forfeiture by peaceable re-entry and no other proceedings or execution or other legal process may be commenced or continued without the court's permission (see chapter 7). Further, a landlord may not commence or continue any distraint against the debtor's property, again without the leave of the court (IA 1986, s 252(2) and see **3.32**). IA 1986, s 254 provides that the restriction on creditors' rights comes into force immediately the application for an interim order is made. The restrictions are released if the interim order is not granted.

1.30 The court will only make an interim order where it is satisfied that:

- the debtor intends to make a proposal for an IVA;

- at the time the application is made, the debtor was either an undischarged bankrupt or was able to petition for his own bankruptcy;

- the debtor has made no previous application for an interim order in the period of 12 months ending with the date of the application; and

- the nominee under the debtor's proposal is willing to act in relation to the proposal (IA 1986, s 255(1)(a)–(d)).

1.31 The debtor's nominee will be a licensed insolvency practitioner who will also act (usually) as the debtor's supervisor in the event that his IVA is approved. The nominee should satisfy himself that the arrangement which the debtor is proposing has a 'reasonable prospect of being approved and implemented' (IA 1986, s 256(1)) and where the debtor has obtained an interim order, then the nominee must prepare a report on the debtor's proposal prior to the interim order coming to an end, confirming whether a meeting of the debtor's creditors should be summoned and when and where that meeting should take place (IA 1986, s 256(1)). On the question of the nominee's responsibilities when considering the proposal see *Greystoke v Hamilton-Smith* [1997] BPIR 24; and *Shah v Cooper* [2003] BPIR 1018 and finally *Prosser v Castle-Sanderson (a Firm)* [2002] EWCA Civ 1140, [2002] BPIR 1163.

1.32 The debtor may not require an interim order. He may be satisfied that there is no immediate pressure from creditors taking action. The debtor can proceed to make a proposal to his creditors without first obtaining an interim order. In such cases, the nominee must prepare the report within 14 days of receiving the proposals from the debtor (IA 1986, s 256A(3)). The interim order will cease at the end of 14 days unless extended (IA 1986, s 255). In practice the nominee will help the debtor to draft the proposals.

1.33 Upon the nominee being satisfied that the debtor's proposal is 'fit, feasible and fair' (IR 1986, r 5.11(3)), the nominee will summon a meeting of the debtor's creditors for the purposes of considering the debtor's proposal. The rules relating to the conduct of such meetings are contained at IR 1986, rr 5.17–5.24.

1.34 A proposal will not be approved unless in excess of 75% in value of the creditors present at the meeting (in person or by proxy) vote in favour to approve the proposal (and any modifications that are proposed to it) (IR 1986, r 5.23(1)). There is a further safeguard in place where part of the debtor's total unsecured debts is owed to a person who is an associate including (IA 1986, s 435(2)):

- the debtor's husband, wife or civil partner;

- a relative of the debtor or the debtor's husband, wife or civil partner;

- the husband, wife or civil partner of a relative of the debtor or the debtor's husband, wife or civil partner;

- a person with whom the debtor is in partnership;

- a person who is employed by the debtor or by whom he is employed.

Where at least one of the debtor's creditors is an associate of the debtor, then IR 1986, r 5.43(3) provides that in addition to the requirement for more than 75% of the creditors to approve the arrangement, at least 50% of those creditors voting in favour of the proposal must not be associates.

1.35 In the event that any party wishes to propose modifications to the debtor's proposal, then any modifications must be approved by more than 75% in value of the creditors voting and, importantly, any modification must be approved by the debtor himself. If it is not, then the IVA will be a nullity (see *Re Plummer* [2004] BPIR 767 and *Reid v Hamblin* [2001] BPIR 929).

Secured creditors

1.36 A meeting of the debtor's creditors cannot approve any proposal (or modification) which affects the right of a secured creditor to enforce his security unless the secure creditor consents to his being bound in this way. In *Khan v Permayer* [2001] BPIR 95 the secured creditor was taken to have waived his security in favour of receiving a dividend in the debtor's IVA. In *Re a Debtor (No 10 of 1992)* [1995] BCC 525, the Court noted that a creditor with the benefit of a charge, mortgage or lien would be a secured creditor for these purposes. This also included where an enforcement agent had taken control of goods in execution by *walking possession*.

1.37 Under IA 1986, s 258(5) the position is identical in relation to preferential creditors. Following the abolition of Crown preference by the Enterprise Act 2002, the categories of preferential debt are now significantly narrower and will usually relate only to claims by the debtor's employees up to a statutory maximum.

The effect of approval of the IVA

1.38 Where a meeting of the debtor's creditors approves the debtor's proposal, the chairman of the meeting (usually the nominee) must immediately report the decision of that meeting to the court (IA 1986, s 259(1)). Where a meeting fails to approve a proposal, it is possible (upon 50% of the creditors voting in favour) for the chairman to adjourn the meeting for up to 14 days (IR 1986, r 5.24(3)). It is possible to have more than one creditors' meeting but the final adjourned meeting must not be more than 14 days after the initial meeting was held.

1.39 The chairman's report must be filed within 4 days of the meeting being held (IR 1986, r 5.27(3)). A landlord with a right to forfeit has been held not to be a secured creditor for the purposes of these rules (*Razzaq v Pala* [1997] 1 WLR 1336 and *March Estates v Gunmark* [1996] 2 EGLR 38). The position of landlords in voluntary arrangements is considered in more detail at **4.85**.

Level of voting rights

1.40 Where the debtor is a tenant and is in arrears of rent, then the landlord will be entitled to vote in respect of the value of those arrears. However, the position in relation to future rents and any dilapidations existing at the date of the creditors' meeting is treated differently. The leading authorities in this area are *Doorbar v Alltime Securities Ltd* [1996] 1 WLR 456 and *Re Newlands (Seaford) Educational Trust* [2007] BCC 195. Essentially, a creditor may vote in respect of a debt that is either unliquidated or not ascertained at the date of the meeting but that claim will be valued at £1 unless the chairman of the meeting agrees to put a high value on it (IR 1986, r 5.21(3)). In *Doorbar*, a landlord's future rent claim was held to be unliquidated and unascertained. Given the uncertainty of dilapidations claims, a chairman will almost certainly always be justified in ascribing the claim with £1 (see *Re Newlands*).

1.41 Where the creditor's claim is neither unliquidated nor unascertained, but the chairman is in doubt as to whether the claim should be admitted or rejected, he must mark it as 'objected to' and allow the vote to be cast in respect of it. This provision is subject to such votes being subsequently discounted in the event that the chairman's objection to the claim is sustained (IR 1986, r 5.22(4)).

Implementation of the IVA

1.42 Once approved, the nominee of a debtor's proposal will usually become the supervisor of the debtor's IVA (but see IR 1986, r 5.25(2)).

1.43 The supervisor must notify the court within 4 days of the meeting being held. His report must contain the following information (IR 1986, r 5.27(2)):

- whether the proposal was approved or rejected (and if approved, with what (if any) modifications);

- the resolutions which were taken at the meeting and the decision on each one;

- a list of the creditors (with their respective values) who were present or represented at the meeting and how they voted on each resolution;

- whether in the opinion of the supervisor, the EC regulation on insolvency proceedings applies to the voluntary arrangement, and if so, whether the proceedings are main proceedings or territorial proceedings; and

- any such further information as the chairman thinks is appropriate to make known to the court.

1.44 The level or calculation of the nominee's and supervisor's fees will often be included as a proposal in the voluntary arrangement for the approval of the debtor's creditors. In the event that they are not approved in this way, the fees, costs, charges and expenses incurred in relation to a voluntary arrangement are payable in the same way that they would be in the event of the debtor's bankruptcy (IR 1986, r 5.33(b)(II)).

1.45 The supervisor will be responsible for collecting the debtor's assets that are to be subject to the voluntary arrangement. This may include collecting monthly or annual contributions from the debtor and will subsequently make distributions to the individual's creditors in accordance with the arrangement. As the terms of the voluntary arrangement are entirely flexible, the duration of the voluntary arrangement is not fixed. However, voluntary arrangements typically do not last longer than 5 years and it is current HM Revenue and Customs (HMRC) policy (where they are a creditor in the arrangement) to not vote in favour of any voluntary arrangement that proposes a longer duration than 5 years.

Default by the debtor

1.46 The terms of the voluntary arrangement will usually provide a framework for what is to happen in the event that the debtor fails to comply with his obligations under his IVA:

- the supervisor is often given discretion under the proposals as to whether or not to extend the IVA in order to give the debtor an opportunity to complete his compliance with his obligations under the IVA;

- the supervisor may issue a certificate of non-compliance and seek the creditors' instructions as to whether or not they wish the supervisor to present a bankruptcy petition for the debtor's bankruptcy; or

- the supervisor can take no action but simply fail the IVA, which would then enable the debtor's creditors to take further enforcement action against the debtor should they wish to do so.

Company voluntary arrangements (CVAs)

1.47 Voluntary arrangements of companies operate in an almost identical way to IVAs. The rules and procedure for the conduct of CVAs are set out in IA 1986, ss 1–7 and IR 1986, rr 1.1–1.29. A company may make a proposal in a similar way to an individual debtor and the provisions relating to voting at creditors' meetings and the quantification of those votes is mirrored in the rules relating to CVAs (IR 1986, r 1.17). Where an administrator of a company in administration believes that a CVA could be used to achieve one (or more) of the purposes of the administration, then an administrator has the power to propose a voluntary arrangement to the company's creditors (IA 1986, s 1(3)). Similarly, a proposal for a voluntary arrangement may also be made by the liquidator of a company in liquidation (IA 1986, s 1(3)(b)).

1.48 Some companies are eligible to apply for a moratorium (similar to the interim order in IVA cases). This right is reserved to companies that are deemed to be 'small companies' and 'eligible companies'. A company will be a small company if it satisfies the requirements for small companies pursuant to the Companies Act 2006 (for the effect of the moratorium see **3.35**).

1.49 As with IVAs, the requisite majority of creditors voting in value must be in excess of 75% in value (voting by proxy or in person). Therefore, it is not the number of creditors but how much debt they account for which counts. In addition, 50% of those creditors voting in favour of the proposal must not be 'connected with the company' for the purposes of IA 1986, s 249. A creditor will be connected if he is a director or shadow director of the company or is an associate of the director or shadow director of the company, or alternatively, the creditor is an associate of the company for the purposes of IA 1986, s 435. This will include companies or individuals having control of the debtor company or being part of the same group of companies.

1.50 There is also an obligation to hold a meeting of the company's members, at least 50% of whom (voting in person or by proxy) in value must approve a resolution for the arrangement.

1.51 Upon the CVA being approved by the requisite majority of the company's creditors and members, the chairman of the meeting must report to the court within 4 days of the meeting being held and must also notify the registrar of companies at Companies House (IR 1986, r 1.24).

The effect of the approval of the voluntary arrangement

1.52 In relation to both CVAs and IVAs the effect of a proposal for a voluntary arrangement being passed by the requisite majority of creditors (and members in the case of CVAs) is that voluntary arrangements bind every person who in accordance with IA 1986 and IR 1986 was:

'(i)   entitled to vote at that meeting (whether or not he was present or represented at it); or
(ii)   would have been so entitled if he had had notice of it,

as if he were a party to the voluntary arrangement.'

1.53 Prior to the coming into force of the Insolvency Act 2000, it was the position that a creditor who was not given notice of a creditors' meeting could not be bound by it. However, the position now is that a creditor will be bound by the arrangement even if he did not receive notice of the meeting (although a failure to give a particular creditor's notice of a creditors' meeting extends the period of challenge for the purposes of IA 1986, s 6 (CVA) and s 262 (IVA)).

Challenging voluntary arrangements

1.54 In the case of both CVAs and IVAs, the IA 1986 and accompanying rules provided a mechanism for creditors to challenge the decision on the grounds of unfair prejudice or material irregularity.

1.55 It is inherent in any CVA that there is likely to be a degree of prejudice to most, if not all, of the debtor's creditors. The creditors are prejudiced by being asked to accept less than they are owed, or to wait for a longer period before being paid what they are owed. The question is whether that prejudice can be said to be 'unfair' for the purposes of IA 1986. The question of unfair prejudice in relation to the attempted release of third-party obligations under a CVA is discussed in more detail at **5.66**. There is no statutory definition of what will constitute unfair prejudice. It is for the applicant who seeks relief, under IA 1986, s 6 or s 262, to demonstrate that the voluntary arrangement which he is challenging unfairly prejudices his interests. In *IRC v Wimbledon Football Club Ltd* [2005] 1 BCLC 66, Lightman J stated that to constitute a good challenge:

•   the unfair prejudice complained of must be caused by the terms of the arrangement itself;

- the existence of unequal or differential treatment of creditors of the same class will not of itself constitute unfairness, but may leave cause to enquire and require an explanation;

- in determining whether or not there is unfairness, it is necessary to consider all of the circumstances including, as alternatives to the arrangement proposed, not only liquidation but the possibility of a different fairer scheme;

- depending on the circumstances, differential treatment may be necessary to ensure fairness; and

- differential treatment may be necessary to secure the continuation of the company's business which underlies the arrangement (consider *Re Business City Express Ltd* [1997] 2 BCLC 510).

1.56 Lightman J's analysis of the previous authorities on unfair prejudice was cited with approval by Warren J in his lengthy judgment in the widely reported case of *Sisu Capital Fund Ltd and Others v Tucker and Others* [2005] EWHC 2170 (Ch). For an example of a case where a class of creditors was successful in demonstrating unfair prejudice, see *Prudential Assurances Co Ltd v PRG Powerhouse Ltd* [2007] EWHC 1002, which is discussed in more detail at **5.82**.

Material irregularity

1.57 A creditor may also mount a challenge to the voluntary arrangement where there has been some material irregularity at the meeting of creditors or at the meeting of members (in the case of CVAs; IA 1986, s 6(1)(b) (CVA) and s 262(1)(b) (IVA)). As with unfair prejudice, there is no statutory definition of what will constitute a 'material irregularity'. It has been left to the courts to consider the scope and extent of conduct or events that would give rise to a successful challenge to a disgruntled creditor. It is first necessary to establish that there has been an irregularity and if there has, that the irregularity was material (as per Warren J in *Sisu*). An irregularity may be an omission by the debtor or the nominee of certain information that may have influenced the creditors' decision to vote either in favour of or against the debtor's proposal. In *Re Trident Fashions plc (in administration)* [2004] 2 BCLC 35, Lewison J, relying on the test in *Somji v Cadbury Schweppes plc* [2001] 1 BCLC 498, stated:

'I do not consider that is the same as asking: would the meeting have been adjourned? It seems to me the real question is: would the revelation of the truth have made a material difference to the way in which the creditors would have considered the terms of the CVA itself? The word "likely" is used in a variety of different ways. It does not necessarily mean that there is more than a 50% chance. It seems to me, therefore, that the right test is whether there was a substantial chance that the creditors would not have approved the CVA in the form in which it was presented.'

This test was cited with approval by Warren J in *Sisu*. The court is unlikely to find that there has been a material irregularity unless the irregularity complained of, if remedied, would have had an appreciable effect on the creditors' decision to approve the voluntary arrangement. For a case concerning alleged irregularities over the quantification of a landlord's claim in a voluntary arrangement, see *Re Newlands (Seaford) Educational Trust* [2006] BC 6 195, [2006] BPIR 1230.

1.58 Finally, there have been cases where creditors have sought to challenge the binding nature of voluntary arrangements on the basis that the terms of the voluntary arrangement went beyond the scope of what a voluntary arrangement was entitled to do under the provisions of IA 1986 and in particular, of s 1 (in relation to companies). For an analysis of this in relation to voluntary arrangements that seek to discharge co-debtor and third-party obligations, see **5.79**.

Time-limited for challenge

1.59 The IA 1986 imposes strict time-limits on applications to challenge voluntary arrangements on grounds of unfair prejudice and/or material irregularity. IA 1986, s 6(3) provides that any application under s 6 must be made within 28 days beginning with the first day on which the chairman filed his report pursuant to s 4(6) (referred to above) at court, or in the case of a person who has not given notice of the creditors' meeting, after the end of the period of 28 days, beginning with the day on which he became aware that the meeting had taken place (s 6(3)(b)). These provisions are mirrored by IA 1986, s 262(3) in relation to IVAs. This time-limit is mandatory and case-law has confirmed that the court has no power to extend these time-limits (see *Re Bournemouth and Boscombe PFC Co Ltd* [1998] BPIR 183). Where a voluntary arrangement unfairly prejudices a creditor and the 28-day limitation is missed he will be bound by its terms.

The court's power on making a finding of unfair prejudice or material irregularity

1.60 Where the court is satisfied that the debtor's voluntary arrangement is unfairly prejudicial or that there has been a material irregularity the court has a wide discretion as to how to deal with the voluntary arrangement (under IA 1986, s 6(4) (CVAs) and s 262(4) (IVAs)). The court may revoke or suspend the voluntary arrangement or may give directions for a further meeting of creditors to consider a revised proposal, on the basis that such a proposal would remedy any unfair prejudice or material irregularity. It should be noted that the court has no power to make modifications to a voluntary arrangement and so if the debtor is unwilling or unable to put forward a revised proposal to creditors, then the court's likely order will be to revoke the voluntary arrangement in full.

Variation of voluntary arrangement

1.61 IA 1986 does not include any provision enabling a voluntary arrangement to be varied once it has been approved. However, the arrangements themselves will often include an express provision permitting variations to be made to the voluntary arrangement and such provisions have been held to be valid (see *Re a Debtor (No 368 of 1994)* (1998) *The Times*, December 3). However, such a provision will not be implied into a voluntary arrangement (see *Raja v Rubin* [2000] Ch 274, CA). In practice though, it is open to a debtor to agree variations to the voluntary arrangement with all of his creditors. Any such variation will not be binding on a creditor who does not expressly agree to be bound by that variation (see *Raja v Rubin* (above)).

Administrative receivership

1.62 The holder of a debenture that contains a floating charge over the whole or substantially the whole of the company's undertaking had the ability to appoint an administrative receiver over the company's undertaking in the event of default by the company (this is now being phased out by the Enterprise Act 2002). The duties of receivers (including administrative receivers) are covered in chapter 17. The administrative receiver owes duties predominantly to the debenture holder who appoints him. He acts as an agent of the debtor company. He owes no express duty to the company's other creditors or to the company itself. This perceived advantage to debenture holders at the expense of the company and its remaining creditors was considered by many to be unjust and in need of redress, in favour of a more collective approach to the realisations of a company's assets. Administrative receivers would act so as to maximise recoveries for their appointer but once that process was complete, and the administrative receiver vacated office, there was only a limited duty to maximise the residual estate for the benefit of unsecured creditors. The effect of the administrative receivership was perceived to cripple the company's business resulting in almost certain liquidation.

1.63 The Enterprise Act 2002 brought in further reforms designed to promote a rescue culture and to encourage legitimate entrepreneurial risk taking. On the corporate side, the Enterprise Act 2002 amended IA 1986 so as to abolish a debenture holder's right to appoint an administrative receiver in relation to any debenture created on or after 15 September 2003. The holder of a pre-15 September 2003 debenture, which contains a floating charge(s) over the whole or substantially the whole of the company's undertaking is still entitled to appoint an administrative receiver and the right to appoint an administrative receiver has been retained in relation to certain debentures in the case of certain capital market transactions.

1.64 Unlike administration, the administrative receiver's only objective is to realise property in order to make a distribution to his appointing debenture holder.

Administrations

1.65 Until the implementation of the reforms brought in by the Enterprise Act 2002, administration was rarely used as the insolvency procedure of choice for companies and those advising them. Banks still retained the ability to appoint administrative receivers who would act predominantly to maximise recoveries to their appointing chargeholder and so banks preferred the appointment of administrative receivers. The administration procedure was expensive to implement because it required the preparation of a substantial report detailing the financial status of the company, accompanied by an application to the court by the company, its directors, or by one of its creditors. On such an application, the court had to be satisfied on the balance of probabilities that the company was, or was likely to become 'unable to pay its debts' in accordance with the definition contained in IA 1986, s 123 (see *Re Colt Telecom Group plc (No 2)* [2002] EWHC 2815 (Ch), [2003] BPIR 324).

1.66 However, in relation to the vast majority of cases, it is no longer possible to create a debenture giving the debenture holder the power to appoint an administrative receiver. Any such provision in a debenture is to be construed as a power to appoint an administrator (IA 1986, Sch B1, para 14(2)).

1.67 Whilst abolishing the ability to appoint an administrative receiver, the Enterprise Act 2002 reforms also brought in sweeping reforms to the process of administration. These reforms are contained in IA 1986, Sch B1 and the new set of rules from IR 1986, rr 2.1–2.132.

1.68 The reforms preserved the ability of the company, its directors or a creditor of the company to apply to the court for an administration order. However, they also gave the directors of the company and the holder of a 'qualifying floating charge' the ability to appoint an administrator over the company's undertaking without the need to obtain a court order.

1.69 Accordingly, a person may be appointed as an administrator of a company by:

• administration order of the court under IA 1986, Sch B1, para 10;

• the holder of a floating charge under IA 1986, Sch B1, para 14;

• the company or its directors under IA 1986, Sch B1, para 22.

1.70 Irrespective of the route into administration, the administrator (who must be a licensed insolvency practitioner) must perform his functions with the aim of achieving one of three hierarchical objectives (IA 1986, Sch B1, para 3(1)). He must:

(1) consider whether the administration could rescue the company as a going concern;

(2) in the event that it is not reasonably practical to achieve that objective, consider whether the administration would achieve a better result for the company's creditors as a whole than would be likely if the company were wound up (without first being in administration); and

(3) if he does not consider that either of these objectives is achievable, conduct the administration with the objective of realising property in order to make a distribution to one or more secured or preferential creditors. Provided, that in doing so, he does not unnecessarily harm the interests of the creditors of the company as a whole (IA 1986, Sch B1, para 3(4)(b)).

This position should be contrasted with administrative receivership where the administrative receiver's only objective is to realise property in order to make a distribution to his appointing debenture holder. The provisions of IA 1986, Sch B1, para 3 introduce a new landscape for insolvency practitioners to operate in.

Administration order

1.71 Where an application is made for an administration order the court's powers are now subject to IA 1986, Sch B1, para 39 that give the holder of debenture that predates 15 September 2003 the ability to veto the appointment of an administrator. This provision provides that where an administrative receiver is already in office, the court must dismiss an administration application (except in limited circumstances). Where it is still possible to appoint an administrative receiver after the making of the administration application, the administrative receiver will displace any administrator in office (IA 1986, Sch B1, para 39(2)).

Appointment of administrator by holder of qualifying floating charge out of court

1.72 The holder of a 'qualifying floating charge' may appoint an administrator of the company by filing a Notice of Appointment at court (IA 1986, Sch B1, para 14(1)). A floating charge will qualify if it is created by an instrument which:

• states that Sch B1, para 14 applies to the floating charge;

• purports to empower the holder of the floating charge to appoint an administrator of the company;

• purports to empower the holder of the floating charge to make an appointment which would be the appointment of an administrative receiver within the meaning given by IA 1986, s 29(2); or

- purports to empower the holder of a floating charge in Scotland to appoint a receiver who on appointment would be an administrative receiver.

1.73 A person will be the holder of a qualifying floating charge if he holds one or more debentures of the company secured:

- by a qualifying floating charge which relates to the whole or substantially the whole of the company's property; or

- by a number of qualifying floating charges which together relate to the whole or substantially the whole of the company's property; or

- by charges and other forms of security which together relate to the whole or substantially the whole of the company's property and at least one of which is a qualifying floating charge.

1.74 The only restriction on the holder of a qualifying floating charge from appointing an administrator by filing a Notice of Appointment at court is that he must give at least 2 business days' written notice to the holder of any floating charge that has priority to his own. This will be the case either where priority arises by virtue of the fact that the other party's debenture was created first, or where another party's debenture has been given priority pursuant to an agreement reached between the holders of the floating charges (IA 1986, Sch B1, para 15(2)).

1.75 It should be noted that there is no requirement for the qualifying floating chargeholder to demonstrate that the company is insolvent and the only restriction is that an administrator may not be appointed under para 14 while the floating charge is not yet enforceable (IA 1986, Sch B1, para 16).

1.76 Finally, an administrator may not be appointed under para 14 if a provisional liquidator is in office under IA 1986, s 135 or an administrative receiver of the company is in office (see above).

1.77 The Notice of Appointment must include a statutory declaration by or on behalf of the person making the appointment that the person is the holder of a qualifying floating charge in effect of the company's property, that the floating charge(s) relied upon has become enforceable and that the appointment is being made in accordance with IA 1986, Sch B1.

Appointment of administrator by company or its directors

1.78 The directors of a company may appoint an administrator without the need to first obtain a court order. However the directors of the company cannot appoint an administrator out of court where:

- there is an outstanding petition for the winding up of the company in place that has not yet been disposed of; or

- an administration application has been made and has not yet been disposed of (IA 1986, Sch B1, para 25); or

- an administrative receiver of the company is in office.

1.79 Where any person may be entitled to appoint an administrator pursuant to para 14 (usually the company's bank), then the directors of the company must give any such person(s) at least 5 business days' written notice of their intention to appoint an administrator. The notice must be in the prescribed form (Form 2.8B) and must identify the name of the proposed administrator. The directors must file with the court the notice accompanied by a copy of the record of the directors' decision to appoint an administrator as soon as reasonably practicable. The notice must include a statutory declaration made by or on behalf of the directors or company as follows:

- that the company is or is likely to become unable to pay this debt;

- that the company is not in liquidation;

- that, so far as the person making the statement is able to ascertain, the appointment is not prevented by paras 23–25; and

- any such additional information that may be prescribed.

The statutory declaration must be in Form 2.8B. The directors must then either wait the 5 business days without the floating chargeholder responding or obtain written consent from each qualifying floating chargeholder to the appointment before proceeding to file a Notice of Appointment.

1.80 Under IA 1986, Sch B1, para 28(2), the directors may not appoint an administrator after the period of 10 business days beginning with the date on which the Notice of Intention to Appoint is filed. However, whilst most administrators consider the practice to be less than ideal, there is nothing in the legislation preventing directors from filing successive notices of intention to appoint in the event that they are not in a position (logistically) to appoint the administrator on the expiry of the first (or successive) period of 10 business days, in order to take advantage of the interim moratorium imposed by IA 1986, Sch B1, para 44 (see **1.86**). It may though be possible on the facts of a particular case for a creditor to argue that such action by directors constitutes abuse of process.

1.81 On the basis that the qualifying floating chargeholders provide their consent to the appointment or fail to respond to the Notice of Intention to Appoint within the requisite 5-business-day period, then the directors may proceed to file a Notice of Appointment at court.

1.82 The appointment of the administrator takes effect on filing the Notice of Appointment (and accompanying documents) with the court. Where a qualifying floating chargeholder objects to the directors' choice of administrator, then it may appoint its own choice of administrator, thereby trumping the directors' choice. The holder of the qualifying floating charge cannot prevent the company's entry into administration but can ensure that their choice of administrator is appointed.

The status of the administrator

1.83 An administrator is an officer of the court (irrespective of the method of appointment) and as such is subject to the ruling in *ex-parte James* (1874) LR 9 Ch App 609. This imposes an obligation on the administrator to act both honorably and fairly (IA 1986, Sch B1, para 5). In addition to having to have regard to the interests of the creditors of the company as a whole, the administrator is also under an express duty to perform his functions as quickly and efficiently as is reasonably practicable (IA 1986, Sch B1, para 4).

1.84 Upon taking office, the administrator must prepare and circulate his proposals to the company's creditors within 8 weeks of his appointment, detailing the steps he proposes to take (or has taken) which have the aim of achieving the purpose of the administration (IA 1986, Sch B1, para 49). Creditors who continue to be involved with the company (such as landlords of commercial premises) should review the administrator's proposals in detail to ascertain the effect those proposals will have on them. The administrator's liability (or otherwise) to continue to pay creditors during the administration is dealt with in detail at **2.80**.

1.85 In conducting the administration, an administrator has the powers contained in IA 1986, Sch 1.

The effect of administration

1.86 Where the court makes an administration order under IA 1986, Sch B1, para 12 any petition for the winding up of the company subsisting at the time shall be dismissed and where the appointment is made by the holder of a qualifying floating charge out of court, shall be suspended while the company is in administration (IA 1986, Sch B1, para 40(1)) (save in the case of winding-up petitions presented on public interest grounds under IA 1986, s 124A).

1.87 Whilst the company is in administration, no resolution may be passed by the members of the company for the winding up of the company and no order may be made for the winding up of the company (IA 1986, Sch B1, para 42).

1.88 Most importantly, once the company is in administration, a comprehensive moratorium arises that cocoons the company and its assets from actions by creditors. The moratorium is designed to provide the administrator of the company with a breathing space in which to consider how best to deal with the company's assets and to formulate his proposals. During the administration, a creditor is prohibited (without the administrator's consent or the court's permission) from:

- taking steps to enforce his security over the company's property (see **3.27**);

- repossessing goods in the company's possession under a higher purchase agreement;

- exercising a right of forfeiture by peaceable re-entry in relation to premises let to the company(see **4.95**);

- instituting or continuing any legal process (including legal proceedings, execution, distress and diligence against the company or its property except with the consent of the administrator or with the permission of the court) (see **3.54**).

The effect of the moratorium under IA 1986, Sch B1, para 43 is discussed further in chapters 3 and 4.

1.89 IA 1986, Sch B1, para 44 provides that when an administration application is pending or where a Notice of Intention to Appoint an administrator is still alive, then the provisions of paras 42 and 43 of Sch B1 (the moratorium provisions) apply on an interim basis.

1.90 The interim moratorium is controversial and has been used by unscrupulous directors as a fast and effective way of thwarting attempts by landlords to levy distress. Landlords are often faced with a Notice of Intention to Appoint an administrator shortly after they have started to levy.

1.91 The moratorium provisions apply for the entire duration of the administration.

The duration of the administration

1.92 An administration will automatically come to an end at the end of the period of one year beginning with the date on which the administration took effect (IA 1986, Sch B1, para 76(1)). There is scope to extend the administration with the consent of the court or the company's creditors (under IA 1986, Sch B1, paras 76–78). However, that administration is now intended (post-Enterprise Act 2002) to be a temporary procedure and the administrator will have to exit the administration in one of four main ways:

- return the company to the shareholders in a solvent state;

- apply for the company to be dissolved on the basis that there will be no returns to the company's unsecured creditors;

- exit via a company voluntary arrangement (discussed above); or

- exit to a liquidation.

1.93 An administrator is unable to distribute assets to the company's unsecured creditors without a court order and so where there is likely to be a return to the company's unsecured creditors he will invariably exit to a creditors' voluntary liquidation for this purpose. A liquidator also has certain powers that are not available to an administrator, such as the ability to pursue directors and former directors of the company for wrongful or fraudulent trading pursuant to IA 1986, ss 213 and 214. Since the introduction of the *prescribed part* for unsecured creditors under IA 1986, s 176A there will increasingly be returns to a company's unsecured creditors (see **2.82**).

Bankruptcy and individual insolvency

1.94 Where an individual is insolvent and an individual voluntary arrangement is either not appropriate or possible, the insolvent individual will often be faced with bankruptcy. The bankruptcy process is designed to wind up the individual's estate whilst also releasing the individual from the debts he has incurred up to the date he is adjudged bankrupt. The law relating to bankruptcy is contained in IA 1986 and the accompanying IR 1986.

1.95 A bankruptcy order is made following the presentation of a bankruptcy petition to the court. A petition may be presented by:

- the debtor himself;

- the supervisor of a voluntary arrangement (in the event of non-compliance);

- any person who is at the time being bound by a voluntary arrangement (in the event of non-compliance, see *Clarke v Birkin* [2006] EWHC 340 (Ch), [2006] BPIR 632); or

- a creditor who is owed more than £750 and who does not hold security for the entirety of his debt (IA 1986, s 264).

Debtor's petition

1.96 An individual may decide to petition for his own bankruptcy where he is facing severe financial difficulty, his debts exceed his liabilities and he is unable to discharge his obligations to his creditors as they fall due. This is the only ground on which an individual can present a bankruptcy petition (IA 1986, s 272). The court retains a discretion to determine whether or not the individual is able to pay his debts or not (IA 1986, s 264 and see *Re a Debtor, ex p Debtor v Allen (No 17 of 1966)* [1967] Ch 590).

Creditor's petition

1.97 A creditor who is owed a liquidated sum of at least £750 may present a bankruptcy petition to the court where he can demonstrate that the debtor is unable to pay the debt or has no reasonable prospects of paying that debt (IA 1986, s 267). A secured creditor is unable to petition for the debtor's bankruptcy in this way unless there is a shortfall in the value of his security of more than £750 or if the secured creditor is willing to waive his security in relation to that amount. In these circumstances, the creditor will only be able to petition for the unsecured balance (IA 1986, s 269).

1.98 The debt must be a liquidated debt. Accordingly, a creditor should act with caution before proceeding to present a bankruptcy petition based on an unascertained debt, such as a claim for breach of covenant under a lease or for unpaid solicitors' fees (where the client is entitled to have those fees assessed by reference to a numeration certificate).

1.99 In addition to being a liquidated debt, the petitioning creditor must also be able to demonstrate that the debtor is unable to pay his debts (IA 1986, s 268). The petitioner must satisfy one of two tests in this regard, namely:

- that he has served on the debtor a demand in the prescribed form (known as a 'statutory demand') requiring the debtor to pay the debt or to provide security to the creditor's satisfaction and at least have elapsed without the debtor having made payment, or having made a 3 weeks application to the court to set aside the statutory demand; or

- the creditor has taken steps to enforce a judgment obtained against the debtor by means of execution or other process and that execution or other process has been returned by the court unsatisfied in whole or in part (see *Skarzyuski v Chalford Property Co Ltd* [2001] BPIR 673).

1.100 The procedural requirements for the service of the statutory demand and the subsequent bankruptcy petition contained in IR 1986, rr 6.1–6.34 contain a number of pitfalls. Creditors should be vigilant in complying with these rules in order to ensure that their statutory demand or petition is not set aside or dismissed on technical grounds.

1.101 Once the debtor has been served with a statutory demand (and this must usually be effected by personal service (IR 1986, r 6.3(2)), the debtor has a period of 18 days in which to apply to the court for an order setting aside the statutory demand. The court has the power to set aside a statutory demand under the four grounds contained in IR 1986, r 6.5(4) as follows:

- the debtor appears to have a counterclaim, set-off or cross-demand which equals or exceeds the amount of the debt or debts specified in the statutory demand (see *Hofer v Strawson* [1999] BPIR 501 and *Re a Debtor*

(No 87 of 1999) [2000] BPIR 589 (cross-claims); on the question of cross-demands see *Popely v Popely* [2004] EWCR Civ 463); or

- the debt is disputed on grounds which appear to the court to be substantial (see *Re a Debtor (No 11 of 1987)* (1998) *The Independent*, March 28 and *Cale v Assiudoman KPS (Harrow) Ltd* [1996] BPIR 245. See also *Kellar v BPR Graphic Engineers Ltd* [2002] BPIR 54); or

- it appears that the creditor holds some security in respect of the debt claimed by the demand, and either r 6.15(5) is not complied with in respect of it, or the court is satisfied that the value of the security equals or exceeds the full amount of the debt; or

- the court is satisfied, on other counts that the demand ought to be set aside.

The bankruptcy petition

1.102 Where the debtor fails to comply with the statutory demand and/or is unsuccessful in having the statutory demand set aside, then the creditor is entitled to present a petition to the court for the bankruptcy of the individual debtor. The presentation of a petition does not create an automatic moratorium but an application can be made to the court to stay any action, execution or other legal process against the property of the debtor (IA 1986, s 285(1)).

1.103 Any disposition of property made by the individual during the period between the presentation of the petition and the appointment of a trustee in bankruptcy following the making of a bankruptcy order is void pursuant to IA 1986, s 284. The recipient of any such property will only be protected if he can demonstrate that he received the property before the commencement of the bankruptcy in good faith, for value and without notice that the petition had been presented (IA 1986, s 284(1)).

1.104 Dispositions made between the date the bankruptcy petition is presented and the order are void if made (IA 1986, s 284):

- without the court's permission or subsequent ratification;

- to anyone other than a purchaser acting in good faith, without notice of the petition and for value.

Action following making of bankruptcy order

1.105 In the first instance, the official receiver will act as receiver and manager of the bankrupt's estate pending the appointment of a trustee in bankruptcy (IA 1986, s 287). The official receiver's role is not to realise the bankrupt's estate but to take such steps as are necessary for protecting any property which may be claimed for the estate and generally preserving the bankrupt's assets. This may include the sale or disposal of any perishable goods comprised in the estate and end with any other goods which may face a diminution in value in the short term if not sold immediately (IA 1986, s 287(2)).

1.106 Once the bankruptcy order is made no creditor with a provable debt (as defined by IR 1986, r 12.3) may have any remedy against the property of the bankrupt in respect of that debt or commence any action or other legal proceedings against the bankrupt except with the leave of court (IA 1986, s 285(3)). It should be noted that debts that are secured are expressly precluded from being provable debts (IA 1986, s 285(4)) and these restrictions will not apply to secured creditors.

1.107 Where there are assets capable of realisation in the debtor's estate, then it is usual for a trustee in bankruptcy to be appointed following a resolution of the bankrupt's creditors or by appointment by the Secretary of State (usually on a request by one of the bankrupt's significant creditors). The trustee in bankruptcy will be a licensed insolvency practitioner. Upon his appointment, the bankruptcy estate will vest in the trustee in bankruptcy without conveyance, assignment or transfer (IA 1986, s 306(2)). It has been held that the bankrupt has no interest in the bankruptcy estate until such time as a surplus (if any) has been determined (see *Ram v Ram (No 2)* [2004] EWCA Civ 1684, [2005] BPIR 628).

1.108 The trustee's role is to ascertain the extent of the bankruptcy estate and then realise it for the benefit of the bankrupt's creditors. This will include any interest the bankrupt had in any land prior to the making of the bankruptcy order and this is considered in more detail in chapter 18.

Liquidation

1.109 Where there is little prospect of selling an insolvent business as a going concern or where it is considered necessary to liquidate the assets of the company in order to effect a distribution to its creditors and/or members, then liquidation is the means of effecting such a winding up. There are three types of liquidation:

(1) *Compulsory liquidation* – This is where the company enters liquidation pursuant to a court order following the presentation of a petition to wind up the company by the directors, members, creditors or contributors of the company.

(2) *Creditors' Voluntary Liquidation* – The members of an insolvent company may resolve to wind up the company by resolving to do so. Following the passing of this resolution, a meeting of the company's creditors will be called pursuant to IA 1986, s 98, who will vote on the choice of liquidator with reference to the value of their claim.

(3) *Members' Voluntary Liquidation* – Where the directors of the company are prepared to make a statutory declaration of solvency under IA 1986, s 89, then the winding up will be a members voluntary winding up (IA 1986, s 90). The contents of the declaration of solvency must be to the effect that the company will be able to pay its debts within a period not exceeding 12 months. A members' voluntary liquidation is therefore a solvent liquidation and the role of the liquidator will be to discharge the debts of the company in full, before distributing any surplus to the members of the company either by realising the company's assets and paying them a cash dividend, or alternatively by distributing the assets (or some of them) 'in specie'.

1.110 Where it becomes apparent to the liquidator that the company will not be able to pay its debts in full within the period stated in the directors' declaration of solvency, the liquidator has a duty to summon a meeting of the company's creditors within 28 days for the purposes of converting the members' voluntary winding up into a creditors' voluntary winding up.

Voluntary liquidation

1.111 When a company enters voluntary liquidation, there is no automatic stay on proceedings being continued or commenced against the company or its property. A landlord, for example, is still entitled to levy distress and there is no prohibition on him forfeiting the lease by peaceable re-entry (this is discussed in more detail at **3.51**). This is subject to the liquidator's ability to apply to the court for an order pursuant to IA 1986, s 112 for a direction that the creditors' voluntary liquidation ought to be subject to the same restrictions and powers that the court might exercise if the company were being wound up by the court (see *Stetzel Thomson & Co Ltd, Re* (1998) 4 BCC 75 and *Re Movitex Ltd* [1992] BCC 101). The decision to grant relief remains at the discretion of the court and no rules have been prescribed to assist the court in determining how to exercise that discretion.

1.112 The liquidator is empowered by IA 1986, s 165(3) to exercise the powers set out in IA 1986, Sch 4. Schedule 4 is divided into three subcategories of powers, namely:

(1) powers exercisable with sanction;

(2) powers exercisable without sanction in the voluntary winding up but with sanction in a winding up by the court;

(3) powers exercisable without sanction in any winding up.

Compulsory winding up by the court

1.113 Compulsory liquidation usually follows the presentation of a petition by one of the company's creditors who is owed an undisputed debt of more than £750. However, it is also possible for a winding-up petition to be presented by the company, its directors or even its shareholders (in limited circumstances see IA 1986, s 124).

1.114 A creditor will almost always petition on the ground that the company is unable to pay its debts. The definition of the company's inability to pay these debts is contained at IA 1986, s 123(1) and (in relation to England and Wales) there are three circumstances where a company will be taken to be unable to pay its debts:

(1) failure to comply with a statutory demand within 3 weeks of service on the company;

(2) execution or other process issued on a judgment obtained by the creditor from the court is returned unsatisfied in whole or in part; or

(3) it is proved to the satisfaction of the court that the company is unable to pay its debts as they fall due.

1.115 Creditors who petition for the winding up of the company will not always serve a statutory demand as a precursor to presenting a winding-up petition and will often rely on an unpaid invoice to demonstrate that the company is unable to pay its debts as they fall due.

1.116 It is an abuse of process to present a winding-up petition in circumstances where the creditor is aware that the debt is the subject of a genuine dispute (*Favermead Ltd v FPD Savills Ltd* [2005] EWHC 626 (Ch), [2005] BPIR 715). The debtor may seek to oppose the making of a winding-up order on grounds that either the debt is disputed or that the debtor has a counterclaim or cross-claim equal to or exceeding the value of the petition debt (*Penwith DC v VP Developments Ltd* [2005] EWHC 259 (Ch), [2005] BPIR 607).

1.117 The winding-up procedure should not be used where the debt is the subject of a genuine dispute and in such circumstances, a creditor ought to issue proceedings and obtain judgment before proceeding to attempt to wind up the company.

Effect of presentation of a winding-up petition

1.118 Whilst a winding-up petition is pending and has not been heard by the court, any disposition of the company's property (including any transfer of shares or alteration in the status of the company's members) is void unless the court orders otherwise (IA 1986, s 127).

1.119 Where the company is of the view that the intended disposition of its property to a third party will not have a detrimental effect on its creditors or would actually improve the position of the creditors, it may apply to the court for an order validating the disposition. An application may also be made by the purchaser of the property (see *Re Argentum Reductions (UK) Ltd* [1975] 1 WLR 186). In exercising its discretion in determining whether or not to validate a proposed disposition, the leading case is *Re Gray's Inn Construction Co Ltd* [1980] 1 WLR 711.

1.120 The ability of a creditor to take action against a company in a compulsory liquidation is discussed in detail at **3.36** and **4.112**.

Partnerships and limited liability partnerships

1.121 A partnership may be wound up by presenting bankruptcy petitions against all of the individual partners or by seeking to wind up the partnership as an unincorporated association (with or without concurrent petitions being presented for the bankruptcy of the partners).

1.122 The insolvency of partnerships is governed by the Insolvent Partnerships Order 1994, SI 1994/2421, which directs those provisions of IA 1986 that will apply to the particular method being used to wind up the partnership. In respect of limited liability partnerships, most of the provisions that apply to companies will apply (with some modifications) to limited liability partnerships pursuant to the Limited Liability Partnership Act 2000.

Part 1

TENANT'S INSOLVENCY

Chapter 2

LIABILITY FOR RENT AND OTHER OBLIGATIONS UNDER A LEASE

2.1   Once a tenant becomes insolvent the landlord's first concern is whether rent arrears will be paid and whether rent will be paid going forward. This chapter reviews the landlord's position and remedies following insolvency. The landlord must review the prospects of recovery in relation to rent liability, together with claims arising in relation to other lease obligations such as service charges, insurance payments and damages claims (such as liability for disrepair). The chapter will deal with how a landlord seeking payment of rent may submit a *proof* for a debt during the insolvency process or otherwise claim. It should not be forgotten that landlords have additional rights (in line with all lessors of chattels, whose property is in possession of the insolvent company or individual). Landlords have proprietary rights that can often be exercised regardless of the insolvency of the tenant. Although the insolvency process may affect these rights (to a varying extent), such rights often place a landlord in a better position than ordinary unsecured creditors. These rights are to levy distress (or exercise Commercial Rent Arrears Recovery) and to effect forfeiture by peaceable re-entry or legal proceedings.

2.2   Proprietary rights are not absolutely prohibited by any insolvency process. Accordingly, there is a close correlation between a landlord's ability to levy distress or forfeit and the prospect of receiving ongoing payment of rent as an expense of the insolvency process. The position of the landlord during the insolvency process in relation to proprietary rights is dealt with in chapters 3 and 4. Depending on the insolvency process, these rights are sometimes conditional upon the landlord making an application to the court for permission to continue with the remedy (or legal proceedings). The position is summarised in the table at Appendix 1.

RECEIVERSHIPS – RENT AND LIABILITIES

2.3   The expression *receiver* in this section applies to administrative receivers and fixed charge receivers. An insolvent tenant may have one or more creditors possessing security (either in the form of a debenture or mortgage). Receivership is a remedy solely available to creditors possessing security. If a creditor has a fixed charge over the lease then a fixed charge receiver may be appointed (see chapter 17). Creditors with a debenture which contains a floating charge created prior to 15 September 2003 may appoint an administrative receiver (IA 1986, s 29) (although this process is being phased out under the reforms introduced by the Enterprise Act 2002; see **17.35**). Whereas administrative receivership is dwindling the appointment of fixed charge receivers is increasing (see **17.2**).

2.4   At face value receivership has little effect on liability. There is no moratorium and no restriction of any kind on creditors. Landlords' rights largely remain intact during a receivership. The nature of receivership is distinct from the collective insolvency remedies. Whereas receivership is only available to secured creditors, the insolvency regimes (administration, liquidation, bankruptcy and voluntary arrangements) are available to all creditors. This essential difference sets receivership apart from insolvency procedures (for an overview of receivership, see **1.62**). The main restrictions which apply to the collective treatment of creditors under insolvency regimes do not have any role in receivership. The result is that a receiver has no immediate statutory power to prevent claims made by a landlord.

2.5   The tenant in receivership remains liable for the ongoing rent in the usual way (as and when sums fall due). Actually the tenant's position in relation to all liabilities arising under the terms of a lease is unaltered. Unfortunately for landlords this does not mean payment will be made in full (or at all). Receivership is an indication of serious financial difficulty and usually a precursor to formal insolvency (liquidation is the most common outcome with 91% of companies entering receivership going into liquidation within 12 months). The landlord's prospect of receiving payment from the tenant in receivership is dramatically diminished. With this knowledge landlords sometimes mistakenly treat a receivership as if its tenant was automatically in liquidation. Often a landlord will have little indication that the tenant is in financial difficulty until he receives formal notice of the receivership (administrative receivers must send a Notice of Appointment to the landlord pursuant to IR 1986, r 3.2). On receipt of this notice a well-advised landlord will act quickly to appraise the position and take appropriate action. It is often worthwhile levying distress or moving to forfeit the lease (see chapters 3 and 4).

Where the receiver has use for the property (or there is value)

2.6   The demised premises may be a prized asset of the company in receivership, or the receiver may need the premises for the purposes of the receivership (eg to facilitate the sale of stock or plant). However, the receiver has no enhanced power to resist distress for rent (or Commercial Rent Arrears Recovery (CRAR)) or prevent forfeiture (see **3.22**). In practice this means that if the receiver wishes to retain the property it must be paid for. Liabilities of all kinds must be met to avoid the risk of prematurely losing possession of the property or assets.

2.7   If the tenant company is in administrative receivership, the receiver should quickly determine which of the tenant's properties (where there are a number of leases) have value. The value may arise in four ways:

(1)   short-term value, where the receiver requires the premises for storage of the tenant's assets pending a sale;

(2)   in the sale, the receiver may need to include a promise to use reasonable endeavors to procure an assignment of the lease to a purchaser of the tenant's business;

(3)   if the rent under the lease is significantly over the market rate and there is no pending rent review then there may be a premium value on assignment;

(4)   if the lease is of a property in a highly sought after location (eg a top pitch in a primary shopping centre) then there may be a premium value on an assignment.

Where the receiver has no use for the property (and there is no value)

2.8   The demised premises may be a liability for the receivership. A receiver has no power to disclaim onerous property. He cannot force the landlord to accept a surrender. Where the tenant in receivership has no real use for the property it will usually be left vacant by the receiver and a surrender offered to the landlord. If this happens whilst the landlord is able to take action to attempt to make a recovery he may decide it is not commercial to do so. The choice for landlords is often reduced to:

•   waiting to see what happens in the receivership and perhaps an eventual voluntary liquidation; or

•   accelerating the inevitable outcome by presenting a petition for the compulsory winding up of the company; or

•   forfeiture.

Where the landlord appoints a receiver

2.9   Some landlords have the benefit of a charge over a tenant's lease or a debenture over all (or a substantial part) of the tenant's assets. In relation to rent and other liabilities this provides the landlord with an enhanced position with additional remedies. If the landlord has the benefit of a properly constituted charge he may well have the following advantages:

•   The charge provides a landlord with the additional remedy of being able to appoint his own receiver. Although administrative receiverships are being 'phased out', if the landlord has a fixed charge then he will be able to appoint a fixed charge receiver even for a post-Enterprise Act 2002 charge (see **17.2**).

- If the landlord has a qualifying floating charge (as defined by IA 1986, Sch B1, para 14) he will be able to prevent the directors of a tenant company from appointing an administrator without the landlord's consent.

- The landlord will be able to appoint an administrator (subject to IA 1986, Sch B1, para 15) (an administrator acts on behalf of all creditors and a prior qualifying floating chargeholder could veto the landlord's choice).

- Where the landlord has a fixed charge and where the directors appoint an administrator no proposal can be made by the administrator which would affect the landlord's rights as a secured creditor (IA 1986, Sch B1, para 73).

- If the landlord also has the benefit of a charge he may be able to defeat the rights of a creditor with a court judgment even where an enforcement agent (High Court or county court) has already seized goods. This puts the landlord in a better position than where he is attempting to levy distress. (The Tribunals Courts and Enforcement Act 2007 will remove the priority that a landlord's distress enjoys over the rights of a judgment creditor's bailiff; see **3.22**.)

- The landlord would be entitled to enforce its security notwithstanding the existence of a voluntary arrangement (IA 1986, s 4(3)) unless there is a small company moratorium (IA 1986, Sch A1, para 12).

Is a receiver personally liable to pay rent?

2.10 Receivers (including administrative receivers) are deemed to be merely the agents of the tenant pursuant to the Law of Property Act 1925, s 109 and IA 1986, s 44. They do not usually have personal liability for pre-receivership contracts they adopt unless there is bad faith or the receiver acts outside his authority (*Lathia v Dronsfield Bros Ltd* [1987] BCLC 321). Accordingly the landlord cannot pursue a receiver personally for rent or in relation to other obligations in a lease. As agent for the tenant company there is no liability arising for existing contracts or the existing lease. One exception to this arises where the receiver enters into a new tenancy or contract when carrying out his functions. Unless the contract expressly excludes the liability (which would usually be the case) the receiver is entitled to an indemnity from the company's assets (IA 1986, s 44(1)(c) and *Hill Samuel & Co Ltd v Laing* (1988) 4 BCC 9, Sc).

2.11 However, in relation to the receiver's role, the normal rules of agency apply. Accordingly there are limited circumstances where the receiver may become liable if, for example, he does not disclose his position (as receiver/agent) and does not have ostensible authority.

2.12 An administrative receiver is deemed to be the company's agent unless or until the company goes into liquidation.

2.13 Where the receiver enters into a new lease then he may incur liabilities (as it represents a new contract to be carried out by the receiver in relation to the carrying out of his functions). However, an administrative receiver will, as a matter of course, insist upon the inclusion of an express contractual provision excluding personal liability when entering into any new contract (including a lease). This contractual exclusion should also be included in any agreement to surrender a lease (a point which is sometimes forgotten by practitioners). In addition to this if the receiver enters into any material variation of the fundamental terms of the lease this may be the equivalent of a surrender and regrant (see the case of *Friends' Provident Life Office v British Railways Board* [1995] 2 EGLR 55). Accordingly, if the receiver wants to avoid personal liability he must ensure that liability is excluded in relation to all such transactions.

2.14 Where an administrative receiver is appointed over a tenant that is liable to complete an agreement for lease the prospective landlord may be able to obtain an order for specific performance to force the tenant to execute the lease (*Freevale Ltd v Metrostore Holdings Ltd* [1984] Ch 199 and *AMEC Properties Ltd v Planning Research and Systems plc* [1992] BCLC 1149). In such circumstances it might be possible to obtain an order that the receiver be excluded from personal liability, given the lease obligations would arise from a pre-receivership contract.

2.15 The continuing liability in receiverships therefore has two consequences:

(1) all the ongoing liabilities under the terms of a lease continue. Landlords are still entitled to claim rent and enforce lease obligations. They continue to enjoy their proprietary rights of forfeiture and distress for rent (however, this might not be the position in relation to CRAR see **3.22**); and

(2) if the administrative receiver wishes to preserve the property then he may have no option but to ensure that all obligations continue to be complied with (including the payment of rent arrears – including pre-receivership arrears). In practice if the company has no use for the property then the receiver may be happy to withhold payment of rent and continue in a position of non-compliance provoking the landlord to forfeit the lease (see **4.81**).

VOLUNTARY ARRANGEMENTS – RENT AND LIABILITIES

2.16 A tenant faced with severe financial constraints may seek to avoid entering into formal insolvency by proposing a voluntary arrangement (VA).

The nature and extent of VAs is explored in more depth at **3.28** in relation to companies (CVAs) and at **3.32** in relation to individuals (IVAs). In proposing a VA, the tenant will often (but not always) seek to compromise liability for:

- rent arrears due at the date of the creditors meeting;

- future rent liability;

- all other lease liabilities (incurred or to be incurred – eg liability for dilapidations); and

- third party liabilities (eg original tenant liability, authorised guarantee agreements and sureties – see chapter 5).

The tenant (if a company through its directors) may put forward proposals that affect each one of the above. This is subject to the rights of the creditors to vote against the VA or to challenge the VA process (in relation to the creditor's right to challenge see **5.66**).

2.17 In essence VAs have the nature of a contract/agreement reached between the company and its creditors. As a consequence of this the process is extremely flexible. Landlords are usually in the position of being unsecured creditors and if a VA is passed then landlords will be bound to the extent provided by the VA (in relation to the process and requirements for passing a VA see **4.144**). To a limited extent even the landlord's proprietary rights can be restricted by a VA (*Thomas v Ken Thomas Ltd* [2007] BLR 429, CA).

2.18 If a VA acts as a statutory compromise contract between the tenant and its creditors (including the landlord) it should not be forgotten that the express wording of the proposals have great importance. Arrangements are interpreted as if they were contractual documents. The courts have taken a very strict line when construing the terms and effect of a VA (eg see *Burford Midland Properties Ltd v Marley Extrusions Ltd* [1994] BCC 604).

2.19 It may be possible for a landlord to be estopped from taking certain steps after a VA has been approved on the basis of the factual matrix and representations made to the creditors' meeting (see *Re Millwall Football Club and Athletic Co (1985) plc* [1999] BCC 455). On the same basis it might be possible for the directors of the tenant proposing the CVA to be estopped from taking steps even if permissible under the terms of the proposals (also see remedies for misrepresentation and IA 1986, s 6A and see **1.24**). In the *Millwall* case a creditor made various representations that he would be bound on the express terms of the arrangement and was estopped from attempting to deny this.

2.20 Other than voting rights, the main boundary to the extensive flexibility of VAs is the creditor's right to challenge subject to IA 1986, s 6 (see **5.66**).

2.21   Accordingly, a VA may extensively restructure the liability owed to the landlord by the tenant (see **1.24**). The landlord may have a greater prospect of enhancing his position if he takes action prior to the creditors' meeting (see **3.28**).

Landlord's position prior to the creditors' meeting

2.22   A VA is capable of restructuring existing rent liability so that it is reduced or even eliminated completely (*Inland Revenue Commissioners v Adam and Others* [2002] BCC 247). If a landlord is unhappy with the result of the VA he is left in a position of being able to challenge on three grounds:

(1)   the proposals are unfairly prejudicial contrary to IA 1986, s 6;

(2)   the process under which the proposals were passed by the creditors' meeting constitutes a material irregularity in the process contrary to IA 1986, s 6 and IR 1986, r 1.17A(5) (see **1.54**); and

(3)   the VA purported to compromise liabilities owed to the landlord in ways which are not permitted under IA 1986 and therefore do not constitute a VA (see **5.82** and *Prudential Assurance Co Ltd v PRG Powerhouse* [2007] BCC 500)).

2.23   However, the landlord is free to take any action it feels appropriate prior to the creditors' meeting. The only exceptions to this are:

• where there is a small company moratorium in place pursuant to IA 1986, Sch A1 (see **1.48**); or

• where an individual proposing an IVA is covered by a moratorium under an interim order (IA 1986, s 252, see **1.24**); or

• where the company is in administration and the administrator is proposing the VA (IA 1986, s 1(3) and Sch B1, para 43).

2.24   In the absence of a moratorium, the landlord is in a strategic position. The landlord is entitled to a minimum of 14 days' (and a maximum of 28 days') notice of the creditors' meeting. During this period the landlord may be able to present a winding-up petition, although there is little point in this as the petition is unlikely to be heard prior to the creditors' meeting and any existing petition is likely to be stayed on the tenant's application. More usefully the landlord may seek to forfeit the lease or levy distress (CRAR) (see chapter 3). The tenant's reaction to these threats will depend on whether:

• the tenant requires the property going forward for the purposes of its restructured business; or

• there is value in the lease or assignment; or

- there is any short-term need for the property (eg to facilitate a post-CVA asset sale).

2.25 The property may be of no value to the tenant. This may be obvious from the terms of the proposals (the tenant may have proposed that the landlord treat the lease as surrendered; see **5.82**). If the property has value to the tenant, then a landlord will have a short window prior to the creditors' meeting in which to take action and exercise a proprietary remedy. This may place the landlord in a position where he can effectively hold the proposers to ransom or absent the property from the process (ie forfeit the lease where right has arisen – but it is the tenant's right to seek relief from forfeiture; see **4.144**).

Rent arrears and other obligations due prior to VA

2.26 Rent which has become due but has not been paid prior to the creditors' meeting would be expected to be caught as a debt within the CVA, although the position in relation to future rents is not so clear (*Thomas v Ken Thomas Ltd* [2007] BLR 429, CA as per Neuberger LJ):

> 'There is no doubt that the rent, which accrued due but was not paid, before the CVA was proposed in this case would be expected to be caught at least in its capacity as a debt within the CVA. As at present advised it appears to me that the rent falling due after the CVA should by no means necessarily be expected to be caught by the terms of the CVA, even if it is capable of being so caught (as was held at first instance in *Re Cancol Ltd* [1996] 1 All ER 37).'

2.27 Therefore in relation to existing rent arrears the landlord will usually be an unsecured creditor. If the arrangement is approved and not successfully challenged then the landlord is bound to accept the terms of the arrangement (together with any reduction in payment or liability that the terms of the arrangement impose). IA 1986, s 5 provides:

> 'The voluntary arrangement –
>
> (a) takes effect as if made by the company at the creditors' meeting, and
> (b) binds every person who in accordance with the rules –
>   (i)   was entitled to vote at the meeting (whether or not he was present or represented by it), or
>   (ii) would have been so entitled if he had had notice of it,
>   as if he were a party to the voluntary arrangement.'

2.28 Together with all the creditors of the company, landlords are bound by the terms of the CVA even if the landlord has not accepted the terms and irrespective of whether he even voted. Creditors are deemed to have agreed to the contractual nature of the arrangement (*Re Kudos Glass Ltd (in liquidation)* [2001] 1 BCLC 390). The terms of the arrangement stick even if the landlord has not received notice of the proposed creditors' meeting where the CVA has been passed (IA 1986, s 5(2)) (but see **1.47** in relation to a landlord's right to challenge an approved arrangement subject to IA 1986, s 6 on the grounds of material irregularity).

2.29 The landlord may, in fact, receive no dividend at all. There is no absolute requirement that the arrangement will produce certain payments to creditors. This was the position in the case of *Inland Revenue Commissioners v Adam and Partners* [2002] BCC 247 where the Inland Revenue challenged the terms of a CVA on the basis that it provided no return to unsecured creditors.

2.30 The position is the same in relation to all existing liabilities (service charge arrears, damages for dilapidations etc). There is little difference between liquidated and unliquidated claims (in relation to future rents see **2.35** and in relation to the calculation of voting rights see **1.47**).

Future rent – the landlord's position in relation to rent and obligations falling due post-VA meeting

2.31 As part of a rescue or reconstruction of the tenant's business in an insolvency situation the VA proposal may seek to try and bind the landlord to some reduced rent for the future which will make the business conducted in the demised premises more viable. In relation to future (post-VA) rents the position is complex.

2.32 In *Re Cancol Ltd* [1996] 1 All ER 37, Knox J held that a landlord who was entitled to a future payment of rent was a creditor for the purposes of IR 86, r 1.17(1) and (3) and IA 1986, s 5. On this basis a VA can bind the landlord and preclude him from recovering all or a proportion of future rent and other liabilities. This has to balanced with the landlord's right to forfeit (see **4.85**).

2.33 However, the VA must expressly bind future rents. In *Burford Midland Properties Ltd v Marley Extrusions Ltd* [1994] BCC 604, Cooke J held that the express terms on a strict construction must be sufficient to actually release future rent liability. This underlines the difficulties in drafting a properly constituted VA. Any proposed release must be made abundantly clear on a plain reading of the document. Cooke J also made the following useful distinction:

> ' . . . as the authorities stand, I think the following is clear: (1) a future prospective debt cannot include a debt that arises out of a future transaction; (2) that it can and will include a debt that arises out of an existing transaction as a result of which the basic liability is incurred which depends on the reaching of a future date or the happening of a future event to make it payable if it is ever to be payable. Where there is less clarity is whether a future debt includes a liability under a subsisting series of obligations when the future event goes to the whole root of the obligation.'

Cooke J held that if a future rent liability was to be compromised this would only work if the provisions also dealt with future obligations to landlords.

Future rent and service charge obligations are executory because they depend on the landlord continuing to supply the premises and carrying out the landlord's covenants. On this basis it is easier to understand how the compromise of future rents would work best where combined with the release of the landlord's obligations (ie the offer of a surrender in the proposals).

2.34 Perhaps the most comprehensive review of this point comes in Neuberger LJ's judgment in the Court of Appeal decision in *Thomas v Ken Thomas Ltd* [2007] BLR 429:

> ' . . . it appears to me that the rent falling due after the CVA should by no means necessarily be expected to be caught by the terms of the CVA, even if it is capable of being so caught . . . it strikes me that, at least normally, it would seem wrong in principle that a tenant should be able to trade under a CVA for the benefit of its past creditors, at the present and future expense of its landlord. If the tenant is to continue occupying the landlord's property for the purposes of trading under the CVA (and hopefully trading out of the CVA) he should normally, as it currently appears to me, expect to pay the full rent to which the landlord is contractually entitled . . .'

Lord Neuberger thought that any VA that restricted the landlord's entitlement to future rent whilst allowing the tenant to continue to trade from the premises (paying a lower rent) was inherently unreasonable. On this basis any such VA approved by the creditors could be challenged by affected landlords under IA 1986, s 6 (not forgetting that if a poorly advised landlord fails to challenge the decision within 28 days he is likely to be bound by the terms of the VA regardless of the unfairness of the position).

2.35 Lord Neuberger also left open the ability of a VA to compromise future rents by providing that premises be vacated and surrenders offered to landlords. This takes us back to *Re Cancol Ltd* [1996] 1 All ER 37 where Knox J accepted that it was not necessarily unfair for a VA which involved multiple premises occupied by a tenant to differentiate between those where occupation would continue (and the relevant landlords paid future rents in full) and those where vacant possession would be offered (and the relevant landlords had their future rent claims compromised).

2.36 Future rent (once this liability is aggregated for the remaining life of the lease) can make a substantial difference to the quantum of the landlord's claim. The landlord is unlikely to be given a vote based on a calculation of the full rent which may fall due (where the premises are to be vacated). Future liabilities (including where fixed amounts are prescribed/ascertainable from the terms of the lease) are treated like an unascertained debt. This means that the chairman of the creditors' meeting can ascribe a value of as little as £1 to the debt (see *Doorbar v Alltime Securities Ltd* [1995] 1 WLR 456). Peter Gibson LJ giving the leading judgment held that a landlord claiming the total amount which could fall due in terms of future rent was 'wrong in principle'. This is because it was reasonable for the chairman of the creditors' meeting to take account of the likelihood that a landlord faced with empty premises would exercise its right of re-entry and forfeit the lease (a period of one year's future rent was offered to the landlord by the chairman). He also held that this treatment of future rent would not amount to *unfair prejudice.*

2.37 The level of vote usually reflects the dividend that a landlord is to be paid. If the landlord is given entitlement to vote for one or two years' rent, the dividend share will normally flow from this. Therefore if unsecured creditors are to receive a payment of 10% of their debt paid, the landlord's dividend may be calculated as a proportion of a limited period regardless of how long the lease may have to run. *Re Newlands (Seaford) Educational Trust* [2007] BCC 195 dealt with a CVA where a landlord had submitted a claim for 2 years' future rent together with a dilapidations claim for £875,000. Limited evidence was submitted to support either claim (in the form of a brief surveyor's report on the difficulty of obtaining a replacement tenant and a schedule of dilapidations without a valuation of the diminution in value of the landlord's reversion under the Landlord and Tenant Act 1927, s 18). The court held that the chairman was justified in ascribing the minimum value (£1 under IR 1986, r 1.17) as the evidence was still insufficient for the chairman to make a proper appraisal of the two claims. The lesson for landlords is that to succeed in maximising the level of their voting rights, detailed compelling and readily accessible evidence must be adduced in good time before the meeting to have any prospect of persuading the chairman to accept a higher value. Sir Andrew Morritt C said:

> 'The evidence before me and before the chairman is essentially the same. The future rent element of the claim depends on whether the lease is forfeit in the future and remains unlet for a period of two years. I do not see any basis on which either contingency can be given any value. One can only say that they may or may not happen. Likewise in the case of dilapidations the schedule prepared in April 2004 does not quantify individual terms . . . it may well be that the minimum value of the landlord's claim is greater than the sum of £1 attributed to it by r 1.17(3) but I do not see any basis on which the chairman could have put any higher value on it.'

However, any prejudice to the landlord has to be balanced by the fact that the landlord may retain its right to forfeit the lease (although review the comments of Lightman J in *March Estates plc v Gunmark Ltd* [1996] 2 BCLC 1 – see **4.11** and *Thomas v Ken Thomas* [2007] BLR 429).

Where the landlord has additional security over the tenant's property

2.38 Occasionally landlords have taken a charge over the lease. With the benefit of a charge the landlord has additional rights. A VA cannot affect a secured creditor's right to enforce its security (IA 1986, s 248) without their consent. A landlord with security may be able to appoint a fixed charge receiver and take control over the tenant's business (see **17.2**). This practice is becoming more prevalent.

2.39   If the landlord is in the position of being a secured creditor then he will continue to be entitled to enforce the security notwithstanding the existence of the voluntary arrangement. Security includes mortgages, charges, liens or any other security. It does not include creditors who have levied execution where the execution has not been completed (IA 1986, s 248 and therefore may not include CRAR – see **3.22**).

Liabilities where VA is not approved

2.40   If the VA fails to receive the requisite support from the creditors (see chapter 5) then the VA will fail.

2.41   If a moratorium was in place then the moratorium is released at the point that the VA fails to receive the approval of the creditors. At this stage the landlord will be able to exercise its full rights and remedies (including forfeiture, distress or issuing proceedings in relation to rent arrears or other breaches of covenant).

2.42   If the CVA is passed then the landlord has 28 days from the date the VA is approved, or from the date they became aware that the VA had been approved, in which to challenge the CVA pursuant to IA 1986, s 6 on the grounds of material irregularity or unfair prejudice (see **1.54**).

Where the lease has been guaranteed

2.43   The position of guarantors to a lease is dealt with at **5.3**. However, a guarantor/surety of a tenant counts as a contingent creditor of a tenant and the guarantor may be obliged to continue to discharge the liabilities in question (see *Johnson v Davies* [1998] BPIR 607).

LIQUIDATION – RENT AND LIABILITIES

2.44   Liability for rent and other lease obligations is treated in the same way in relation to both voluntary and compulsory liquidation. Liquidation does not immediately interrupt the contractual principle. The covenants and obligations in a lease survive and continue after liquidation commences. The obligations continue unless and until the liquidator exercises his right to disclaim the lease as an onerous contract pursuant to IA 1986, s 178. In relation to disclaimer see chapter 7. Although the lease remains in place this does not mean that the liquidator will be able to meet the company's contractual obligations. A landlord needs to know just how much he is likely to receive. In turn the liquidator needs to understand the rights and remedies of landlords together with the appropriate order of distribution to creditors.

2.45   Lease liabilities are treated differently depending on whether they were incurred before or after the commencement of the liquidation. The position can be divided into the following categories:

(1)   rent and other obligations arising prior to the commencement of liquidation (generally ordinary unsecured debt); and

(2)   rent and other obligations arising after the commencement of liquidation:
      (a)   where they have fallen due (generally ordinary debt);
      (b)   where they are payable as an *expense* of the liquidation (see order of priority at **2.47**);
      (c)   where they have not yet fallen due (generally ordinary debt); and
      (d)   damages following a disclaimer (generally ordinary debt).

2.46   Having realised the company's assets the liquidator's duty is to distribute the assets to the creditors and pay the liquidation expenses. In *Re Leyland Daf Ltd* [2004] 2 AC 298, Lord Hoffman at p 308 described the process as follows:

> 'The winding up of a company is a form of collective execution by all its creditors against all its available assets. The resolution or order for winding up divests the company of the beneficial interest in its assets. They become a fund which the company thereafter holds in trust to discharge its liabilities . . . it is a special kind of trust because neither the creditors nor anyone else have a proprietary beneficial interest in the fund. The creditors have only a right to have the assets administered by the liquidator in accordance with the provisions of the Insolvency Act 1986. But the trust applies only to the company's property. It does not affect the proprietary interests of others.'

2.47   The company's assets will be distributed by the liquidator in the following order of priority:

(1)   Creditors with *fixed charges* will be able to exercise their rights first, with or without the liquidator's involvement. Assets subject to a fixed charge are taken out of the sums available to pay expenses and other creditors (see chapter 6 in relation to sums held by a landlord in a rent deposit). The proprietor of the charge has a proprietary interest. The company has only an equity of redemption.

(2)   Liquidation *expenses* (now higher in the order than following IA 1986, s 176ZA. This is subject to the liquidator's requirement to obtain prior approval from preferential creditors and floating chargeholders for some expenses. (This was introduced in 2008 by way of an amendment and IR 1986, r 4.218A–4.218E.)

(3)   *Preferential debts* (IA 1986, s 175).

(4)   Debts secured by a *floating charge*. The definition of a floating charge now includes all charges created as such even if there has been a subsequent crystallisation and the charge has become fixed (IA 1986, s 251). In *Re Leyland Daf* the House of Lords decided that the assets subject to a floating charge were not available for the payment of expenses. This was reversed by the Companies Act 2006 which introduced

IA 1986, s 176ZA giving expenses priority over floating charge assets (however, the liquidator must make available a proportion of the net property available for the payment of floating chargeholders for the payment of ordinary creditors (ie the *prescribed part*, IA 1986, s 176A).

(5)   *Ordinary debts* (IR 1986, rr 4.180 and 4.181 – the majority of rent arrears will fall into this category).

(6)   *Interest* (IA 1986, s 189(2)).

(7)   *Postponed debts.*

(8)   Surplus to *shareholders* (IA 1986, s 154).

Rent prior to commencement of liquidation

2.48   Landlords can prove for rent up to the date the company went into liquidation (IR 1986, r 4.92(1)). Under this provision a creditor may prove for any amount of a periodic nature.

2.49   Landlords without security (which represent the vast majority) rank as unsecured creditors in relation to rent arrears and other lease claims arising prior to liquidation. The fact that a company is in liquidation does not always interfere with a landlord's right to levy distress (or CRAR) or to forfeit the lease. In voluntary liquidation a landlord has more freedom to exercise proprietary rights (in relation to these rights see **3.51** and **4.109**). A landlord will often consider distress or forfeiture prior to conceding to the prospect of ranking as an unsecured creditor and being left to the vagaries of the liquidation process. The Enterprise Act 2002 improved the position for landlords and all unsecured creditors by introducing a requirement that the liquidator must make available a prescribed part of the company's net property for the satisfaction of unsecured debts. This is now known as the 'prescribed part'. It is calculated on a sliding scale (currently 50% of the first £10,000 and a further 20% from £10,000 up to a maximum prescribed part of £600,000 – see Insolvency Act 1986 (Prescribed Part) Order 2003, SI 2003/2097).

Quantification and procedure of landlord's claim – proof of debt

2.50   In relation to sums falling due up to the commencement of liquidation, the landlord has the right to submit a proof of debt in the liquidation and receive a dividend (if there are sufficient funds available to pay a dividend to unsecured creditors or if there is to be a payment from the prescribed part – see IA 1986, s 176A). This is a right shared with all unsecured creditors and is the way that landlords are able to declare the amounts due to the liquidator.

2.51   The submission of a proof of debt is at the landlord's expense. The landlord may incur costs in resolving any valuation issues which may arise in relation to the level of debt (such as an unliquidated claim for dilapidations). This expense can only be added to the proof if the lease expressly provides for the recovery of such sums.

2.52 In compulsory liquidation a landlord must submit a proof (IR 1986, r 4.73(1)). The form is prescribed by the rules (Form 4.25) (there is a specimen of the form with the various claims a landlord may make at Appendix 9). In voluntary liquidation there is no absolute requirement for creditors to submit a proof, unless the liquidator directs this to be the case (IR 1986, r 4.73(2)).

2.53 Pursuant to IR 1986, r 4.92(1), the landlord is able to prove for the amount of rent due and unpaid *up to the date when the company went into liquidation.* In relation to compulsory liquidation this date is the presentation of the winding-up petition to the court. In relation to voluntary liquidation this date is the date the company passes a resolution to commence the voluntary winding-up procedure (IA 1986, s 86).

2.54 The landlord is able to submit a proof of debt in relation to all rent arrears which have fallen due prior to the date the winding up commenced. Where rents are payable quarterly in advance then a full quarter's rent can be claimed even if the liquidation commenced immediately after the quarter date. Where rent is payable in arrears and liquidation occurs prior to the next payment which has fallen due the landlord can apportion the amount of rent due up to the date of the liquidation (see *Re South Kensington Co-operative Stores* (1881) 17 Ch D 161, and pursuant to IR 1986, r 4.92 and the Apportionment Act 1870).

2.55 The liquidator will send all creditors known to him a copy of a standard form of proof prescribed by the rules and this usually will be sent at the same time as the notification of the first meeting of creditors. However, there is no longer any obligation for a liquidator to provide forms. It is only those creditors who request a proof who are entitled to receive one (Insolvency (Amendment) Rules 2004, SI 2004/584). However, it is good practice for proofs to be automatically sent if there is a reasonable prospect of a dividend being paid (this is now often the case as a consequence of the introduction of the prescribed part for unsecured creditors).

2.56 The landlord's solicitor or agent is able to sign the proof on the landlord's behalf. There is no time-limit for the liquidator to accept or reject a proof. The liquidator may have a number of reasons to reject the proof in whole or part, including:

- the tenant company may have a set-off relation to any breach of the landlord's covenants which the liquidator is entitled to take into account pursuant to IR 1986, r 4.90;

- the landlord may have received sums through a completed distress or a partially completed distress in a voluntary liquidation;

- parts of the claim may be unliquidated and the liquidator may reject the evidence that the landlord provides (eg relating to service charges, sums claimed under an express costs provision in the lease etc);

- the position on whether sums are due on a rent review depends on the status of the review and the express mechanism for the review under the lease; and

- dilapidations – the damages may be reduced by the statutory cap under the Landlord and Tenant Act 1927, s 18 or a defence may be available under the Leasehold Property (Repairs) Act 1938.

The liquidator must provide the landlord with written reasons as to why the proof has been rejected in whole or part. There is no time-limit for the liquidator to make the determination. However, if the proof is rejected then the landlord has 21 days from receiving the liquidator's reasons to make an application to the court to challenge the decision (IR 1986, r 4.83(2)).

Unliquidated claims

2.57   The landlord is also able to submit claims for unliquidated debts such as for a breach of a repairing obligation (ie dilapidations claims). IR 1986, r 12.3 provides:

> '. . . that all claims by creditors are provable as debts . . . whether they are present or future or certain or contingent, ascertained or sounding only in damages.'

2.58   In relation to quantum the liquidator is able to estimate the value of the claim for the purpose of the proof of debt (pursuant to IR 1986, r 4.86). The liquidator also has the right to require the landlord to evidence the proof by way of an affidavit.

2.59   Perhaps the biggest challenge for a liquidator is dealing with a landlord's dilapidations claim. The liquidator should not take a dilapidations claim at face value even where it appears to be detailed and costed. If the lease is still continuing then any damages claim may also be subject to the Leasehold Property (Repairs) Act 1938. The Property Litigation Association Pre action Protocol for Terminal Dilapidations Claims suggests that the landlord serves a valuation of the effect the dilapidations have on the value of the landlord's reversionary interest. The reason for this is that the Landlord and Tenant Act 1927, s 18 limits the landlord's claim to the *diminution* in value of the reversionary interest.

2.60   Landlords could seek to reduce the prospect of a dispute as to the quantum of damages by entering the property and carrying out the repairs at his cost. The landlord will generally only be able to do so if he has expressly reserved the right to enter the demised premises for this purpose (*Jervis v Harris* [1996] 1 All ER 303).

Interest

2.61 Many leases contain an express interest provision allowing the landlord to claim interest on rent arrears. However, even where there is no express contractual provision in the lease, the landlord is still able to claim interest (providing the lease is in writing) pursuant to the Judgment Act 1838, s 17. Interest is recoverable under the Act up to the date of the commencement of the winding-up. Where the lease is not in writing, interest can only be included in a proof where the landlord has demanded the unpaid rent in writing, in which case the sum is recoverable from the date of demand until the commencement of the winding up (see IR 1986, r 4.93). The current interest rate under the Judgment Act 1838 is 8% per annum. Where the assets of the company are sufficient, creditors are also entitled to receive interest on their claims for the period commencing after the company entered liquidation pursuant to IA 1986, s 328(5).

Rent falling due after the commencement of the liquidation

2.62 The liquidation does not prevent the continuing contractual liability for the ongoing rents being incurred unless and until the liquidator disclaims the lease (see chapter 7). Rent accruing after the date of the winding-up poses a bigger problem. The landlord will be concerned that he is paid for the ongoing rents and he may be able to claim these rents as an expense of the liquidation (see **2.64**). If there is a disclaimer then the landlord can submit a proof for damages consequential upon the disclaimer pursuant to IA 1986, s 178(5) (also see *Re Park Air Services plc* [2000] 2 AC 172). However, uncertainty arises if no disclaimer takes place, or in relation to the status of the rent liability which falls due in between the onset of liquidation and a disclaimer.

Rent and other obligations arising which have fallen due after the commencement of liquidation

2.63 Rent which has fallen due after the date of the liquidation is a provable debt. It is included in the wide definition set out in IR 1986, r 12.3. IR 1986, r 13.12 defines debt to include:

> ' . . . any debt or liability to which the company is subject at the date at the date on which it goes into liquidation . . . [and] any which the company may become subject after that date by reason of any obligation before that date.'

In relation to rents which have not yet fallen due and the effect of disclaimer see **2.77** and **2.79**.

Liquidation expenses

2.64 Landlords might be forgiven for believing that there is little prospect of recovering the post-liquidation rents. The possibility of making a recovery may seem bleak. The landlord proving in the liquidation stands in line with all the other unsecured creditors to be paid an abated proportion of the outstanding debt (in accordance with IR 1986, r 4.181). Once a tenant goes into liquidation commercial landlords will often write off the prospect of recovering the continuing rents. Even where there is no sign that the liquidator will disclaim the lease, landlords will sometimes allow leases to continue (without seeking permission to forfeit). This decision is often taken simply to avoid liability for business rates, while informally marketing the premises. However in some circumstances the liquidator will agree to pay post-liquidation rents and other sums as an *expense* of the liquidation. Liquidation expenses have priority over unsecured debts (some categories of expense have priority over the liquidator's own remuneration as to priority see **2.47**).

2.65 Accordingly, the prospect of receiving the payment of ongoing rents as an expense is of utmost importance to landlords.

The liquidation expense principle – the old law

2.66 In *Re Atlantic Computer Systems plc* [1992] Ch 505, Nicholls LJ adopted the doctrine for liquidation expenses which had been established over a long period and predated IA 1986. He reaffirmed the liquidation expenses principle and maintained:

> 'It is just and equitable that the burden of the debt should be borne by those for whose benefit the insolvent estate is being administered the latter principle is not confined to new debt incurred by the liquidator. It applies also to continuing obligations under existing contracts such as leases that the liquidator chooses to continue for the benefit of the winding-up.'

2.67 He held that a liquidator had a degree of discretion to determine what should be payable as an expense. Nicholls LJ was upholding a principle which was established in the nineteenth century. The principle required a liquidator to discharge, as an expense of the liquidation, only those liabilities that have arisen as a result of the liquidator's acts and have been carried out for the benefit of creditors. Prior to IA 1986, mere inactivity by the liquidator in using the property for any purpose was insufficient for a landlord to claim that the continuing rent should be an expense. Nicholls LJ decided that the court had an element of discretion to determine whether any particular claim should be treated as an expense. This doctrine has subsequently dominated the treatment of liquidation expenses and led to a number of practical consequences:

- The liquidator would exercise this discretion against a landlord if the premises are empty or unused for the purposes of the liquidation.

- The discretion would be exercised in the landlord's favour where:
  - the liquidator had expressly retained possession of the property for the purposes of the liquidation (*Re ABC Coupler and Engineering Co Ltd (No 3)* [1970] 1 All ER 650). This may happen where the liquidator has not disclaimed the lease and is seeking to assign the lease for a premium or is using the property to effect a sale of assets;

–   where the liquidator has paid rent to prevent the landlord from forfeiting the lease (*Re Linda Marie Ltd* [1989] BCLC 46);
–   where a notice has been served on the liquidator asking him to elect to disclaim within 28 days pursuant to IA 1986, s 178 and no disclaimer takes place (see **7.16**).

No discretion – the new law

2.68   However, this traditional way of dealing with expenses has in recent years been the subject of vigorous judicial scrutiny (in particular see *Re Toshoku Finance UK plc* [2002] 1 WLR 671 and *Exeter City Council v Bairstow* [2007] BCC 236). As a consequence the system of post-insolvency distribution to creditors in relation to continuing debt (such as continuing lease liabilities) has been left in a position of uncertainty.

2.69   Prior to *Toshoku* insufficient attention had been paid to IR 1986, r 4.218 which deals with the priority of liquidation expenses (ie the priority of one category of expense in relation to the others). However, Lord Hoffmann in *Toshoku* held that if a liability falls within the provisions of the rule it is automatically an expense. The liquidator has no discretion in the matter. Therefore it is not necessary to determine whether 'the liability was incurred as a result of a step taken for the benefit of the insolvent estate' (Hoffmann LJ).

2.70   Toshoku Finance UK plc was in creditors' voluntary liquidation. It had a corporation tax liability arising from interest owed to it on a debt. This debt was Toshoku's only asset. The liquidator was unable to obtain payment either of the principal amount or of interest. Although corporation tax was due to be paid on the interest under tax law, the liquidator reasonably argued that as Toshoku would never see the money, payment of the tax would be unfair. The House of Lords decided that the tax was payable as an expense of the liquidation. It also decided that it did not have any discretion to exclude the liability from being an expense. This applied not only to taxes, but to any liability that could properly be defined as a liquidation expense. In relation, the House of Lords held that Lord Nicholls (in *Re Atlantic Computer Systems plc* [1992] 2 WLR 367) had wrongly decided that the determination as to whether debts should count as expenses is a matter for the courts' discretion. Lord Hoffmann stated (at para 38):

> 'The court will of course interpret r 4.218 to include debts which . . . are deemed to be expenses of the liquidation. Ordinarily this means that debts such as rents under a lease will be treated as coming within paragraph (a) . . . but the application of that principle does not involve an exercise of discretion any more than the application of any other legal principle to the particular facts of the case.'

2.71   With regard to a tenant in liquidation, the question of whether the continuing rent should count as an expense of the liquidation is no longer a matter for the judge's discretion. Instead, it depends upon whether the continuing rents come within a fair interpretation of the items listed in IR 1986, r 4.218. The rule provides two possibilities that can apply to continuing property rent, which could be:

(1) an expense properly chargeable or incurred by the liquidator in preserving, realising or getting in any assets of the company (IR 1986, r 4.218 (1)(a)); or

(2) a necessary disbursement incurred by the liquidator in the course of administration (IR 1986, r 4.218(1)(m)).

2.72 In *Toshoku* the liability (as a statutory liability) arose after the commencement of the liquidation. Lease liabilities are distinguished because they will invariably predate the commencement of the liquidation. Therefore the liability to pay rent exists at the point of liquidation (of a future or contingent nature) and becomes due and payable during the course of the liquidation. Post-*Toshoku* a liquidator has no discretion to determine whether such rents should be payable as an expense because it is a matter of construction only. As a consequence, until a liquidator disclaims the lease, it is a question of construction as to whether ongoing, post-liquidation rent is payable as an expense (as an 'expense properly incurred' or a 'necessary disbursement'). If not then the ongoing rent is provable as an ordinary debt (see **2.78**).

2.73 On the question of construction, liabilities existing at the commencement of the winding-up do not obviously constitute 'an expense properly incurred' as the liability already exists. The liability to pay rent may perhaps falls more easily into the category of 'any necessary disbursement'. To some extent this fundamental question was left hanging by *Toshoku* as the House of Lords was not required to deal with this specific question. Lord Hoffmann gave some limited guidance referring to a number of distress for rent cases and in particular *Re Lundy Granite Co* (1870–71) LR 6 Ch App 462 where distress was allowed to continue where the property was being used for the purposes of the liquidation. On this basis where a landlord would be able to successfully obtain permission to distrain for rent the ongoing rents should be payable as an expense (see **3.13** in relation to distress and CRAR).

2.74 Although this may seem like the old style *liquidation expense principle* the fact that the liquidator is in possession of the property for the benefit of the insolvent estate appears to remain a relevant factor. Inactivity by the liquidator might not be enough. It is also not enough to show that both the landlord and liquidator want to preserve the lease (eg for a potential assignment of the lease favoured by both parties, see *Toshoku*, Lord Hoffmann, at para 27).

2.75 Landlords are therefore left with the following paradox. The House of Lords has on one hand decided that there is no discretion to decide what constitutes an expense whilst on the other hand suggests that in relation to pre-winding-up liabilities that create post-winding-up obligations, such expenses may be payable under a revised liquidation expenses principle. This leaves an unsatisfactory position for landlords.

2.76 In any event until this question is finally determined landlords potentially have an enhanced right to claim ongoing rents as an expense. The answer for liquidators is to decide as quickly as possible whether to disclaim leases. If there is no disclaimer or late disclaimer, the landlord may be able to claim rent as an expense. We will have to wait to see how *Toshoku* will be applied to commercial property (in relation to business rates and administrations see IR 1986, r 2.67 and *Re Trident Fashions plc* [2006] EWCA Civ 203 and **2.101**).

Rent not yet fallen due

2.77 IR 1986, r 4.92 is the only provision that expressly identifies rent as provable and this limits the amount provable to the sums due and unpaid at the commencement of the liquidation.

2.78 However, future debts which haven't fallen due can be proved for pursuant to IR 1986, r 12.3 and r 13.12. At first blush these rules appear to be inconsistent with r 4.92. It appears that where rents have already fallen due at the time of the proof they can be included notwithstanding that they post date the liquidation whilst the landlord cannot include payments which are to fall due in the future. In a number of older cases (which predated the IA 1986) it was held that a landlord could prove for future rents (such as *Re House Property and Investment Co* [1954] Ch 576). However, Lord Hobhouse ruled in *Christopher Moran Holdings Ltd v Bairstow* [1999] 1 All ER, HL, [2000] 2 AC 172 that:

> ' . . . the position under a lease has particular characteristics which it may share with other types of synallagamatic relationship. Whilst the lease is subsisting, the lessor is not entitled to prove for any instalment of rent until the date upon which that payment becomes due. Similarly if the lease is determined, the right to rent is determined . . . the provisions of r 11.3 would not have applied . . .'

This decision appears to be at odds with r 11.13. Where a creditor has proved for future debts (or other claims such as for dilapidations), the payment of which is not due at the date of the dividend, the claim will be discounted according to the formula set out in IR 1986, r 11.13. The reduction is designed to remove the effect of any windfall a creditor may have as a consequence of accelerated receipt. Given Lord Hobhouse's judgment it seems contradictory that the modifications to r 11.3 made by the Insolvency (Amendment) Rules 2005, SI 2005/527, were made in response to the general criticism made by the House of Lords in *Christopher Moran Holdings Ltd v Bairstow* [2000] 2 AC 172. Therefore, under r 11.13, future debt is reduced to take into account accelerated receipt and the formula is:

$$\frac{x}{1.05}$$

Where 'x' is the amount of the admitted proof and 'n' is the period beginning with the beginning of the insolvency and ending whenever the payment would otherwise be due.

Rent following disclaimer

2.79 If the liquidator disclaims the lease then damages are payable under IA 1986, s 178(5) (this is dealt with at **7.69**).

ADMINISTRATION – RENT AND OTHER LIABILITIES

2.80 When a tenant is in administration it remains liable for the rent past, present and future. Administration is designed to achieve one of the three hierarchical objectives set out by IA 1986, Sch B1, para 3(1) (see **1.70**). However, the practical outcome of administration is to give the company breathing space in order to find a solution for its problems. Although the process does not immediately affect a tenant's liability to pay rent and meet other liabilities, the general effect of the administration provisions is to prohibit any action against the company. All liabilities stay in place albeit the court's permission (in the absence of the administrator's agreement) is required to commence or continue an action for the recovery of rent, or for other breaches (see IA 1986, Sch B1, para 43 and **3.55**).

Pre-administration rent arrears and other liabilities

2.81 Rents and other liabilities that accrued prior to the administration are usually an unsecured debt with no priority (assuming the landlord's interest is not secured by a charge over the lease). The administration does not extinguish the liability but from the landlord's perspective administration is a clear indication that the prospect of receiving rents is at best uncertain.

2.82 However, the existence of rent arrears and other breaches may lead to the landlord having the right to press the administrator into making a payment as an expense of the administration (see **2.113**), particularly where the landlord wishes to utilise the premises or extract value from the lease going forward.

Post-administration rents and liabilities

Rent – expense of administration

2.83 Although the administration of a tenant does not prevent the insolvent tenant from incurring liability for continuing rents, it will leave the landlord in a precarious position as to whether the rent will be paid. There is a prospect that the landlord will receive a dividend as an unsecured creditor for the rent arrears up to the date of the administration. Future rent obligations may be met as an *expense* of the administration, but the position there is complex.

2.84 Whether ongoing rents and other lease payments are to be paid as an *expense* is therefore an important question which will often make a substantial difference to a landlord's level of recovery in an administration. It is therefore perhaps surprising that what constitutes an expense remains a complex question with uncertain conclusions notwithstanding a number of recent high-level cases which have narrowed the issues. This is the position for both administrations and liquidations. There are now two regimes for administration expenses:

(1) the provisions dealing with expenses in old-style administrations (ie administrations still governed by the regime which predates or are unaffected by the coming into force of the Enterprise Act 2002) which are principally found in IA 1986, s 19; and

(2) the provisions dealing with new style administrations governed by IA 1986, Sch B1 and IR 1986, r 2.67.

Old-style administration expenses governed by IA 1986, s 19

2.85 IA 1986, s 19 still applies to a limited set of administrations, including building societies, water utility providers, railway companies and public-private partnerships (Enterprise Act 2002, s 249). IA 1986, s 19 set outs what was to happen at the end of an administration when the administrator was to leave office. It creates a statutory charge to secure:

- the administrator's remuneration and any expenses properly incurred by him (IA 1986, s 19(4)); and

- any sums payable in respect of debts or liabilities incurred, while he was an administrator, under contracts entered into by him or a predecessor of his in the carrying out of his or his predecessor's functions (IA 1986, s 19(5)).

2.86 IA 1986, s 19 no longer has any effect for the majority of administrations (having been repealed by the Enterprise Act 2002). However, for those administrations that fall under the old regime, s 19 sets out the basic order of priority between expenses providing that contractual liabilities/debts entered into by the administrator (under s 19(5)) have priority over the administrator's remuneration and other expenses (see *Re Atlantic Computer Systems plc at first instance* [1990] BCLC 729 and *Re a Company* [2000] 1 WLR 502 at 512).

2.87 The purpose of s 19 was to provide a charge over the administration assets to secure the payment of unpaid expenses. It does not prescribe a comprehensive regime for determining what constitutes an administration expense nor when expenses should be paid.

2.88 As explained at **2.66**, in *Re Atlantic Computer Systems plc* [1992] Ch 505, Nicholls LJ reflected on the fact that there was an established doctrine for *liquidation expenses* but not for administration expenses. The underlying basis for an expense was that 'the burden of the debt should be borne by those for whose benefit the insolvent estate is being administered'.

2.89 However, Nicholls LJ did not believe that for administrations this amounted to a definitive principle, holding that an administrator has to balance the interests of creditors and has a degree of discretion to determine what should be payable as an expense. The administrator's discretion was then underlined in a number of cases (such as *Re Paramount Airways Ltd* [1994] BCC 416 at 180, (Dillon LJ), *Re Salmet International Ltd* [2001] BCC 796 at 803 (Blackburn J) and *Exeter City Council v Bairstow* [2007] BCC 236).

2.90 It was also decided that administrators are able to pay expenses as they go along if they have sufficient assets to do so (even though s 19 purports to deal only with the treatment of expenses once the administration has come to an end). In *Re TXU UK Ltd* [2003] 2 BCLC 341 the court referred back to *Re Paramount Airways* at 180 where Dillon LJ said:

> 'Although strictly sums are, under s 19(5), only payable when the administrator vacates office, it is well understood that administrators will, in the ordinary way, pay expenses of the administration . . . as they arise during the continuance of the administration. There is no need to wait until the end, and it would be impossible as a practical matter to do that.'

2.91 It is perhaps surprising that there is no express duty for an administrator to pay expenses as and when they fall due. It is a position that is sometimes exploited by some administrators who would prefer to defer payment to a point when there is a sufficient realisation of assets and receipt of funds into the administration. However, there is an implied duty to make payments of expenses during the course of the administration (e g see *Re Maxwell Fleet and Facilities Management Ltd* [2001] 1 WLR 323 at 329 ('the administrators ought therefore to discharge [contractual claims] as they arise in the course of the administration') and *Re Trident Fashions Ltd* [2006] EWCA Civ 203).

2.92 Reviewing the extent of s 19, Hoffmann L classified the expenses in old administrations in three categories (*Centre Reinsurance International Co v Freakley* [2006] 1 WLR 2863):

(1) remuneration;

(2) expenses/costs; and

(3) liabilities arising under contracts with third parties.

2.93 The essential factor was that such liabilities only counted as an expense if the administrator expressly decided to incur the particular liability, either personally or on behalf of the company. In *Exeter City Council v Bairstow* [2007] BCC 236, David Richards J held (at para 26) that 'unless the administrator had decided to incur the expenditure in question, either by undertaking it personally or by making a contract on behalf of the company, a liability incurred by the company during the administration would not rank for priority under s 19(4) or super-priority under s 19(5)'. This treatment of expenses precludes the automatic payment of periodic payments falling due after the date of the administration arising from a pre-administration contract. Post-administration rent is therefore unlikely to be an expense unless the administrator expressly decides to make payment to avoid forfeiture and preserve the property for the purposes of the administration. In *Centre Reinsurance International Co v Freakley* [2006] Hoffmann L held that a cost for handling claims under a contract of insurance (where the contract predated the administration) should not be paid as an administration expense.

2.94 On this basis under old administrations neither rent nor rates are automatically treated as an expense of the administration.

2.95 In *Exeter City Council v Bairstow* [2007] BCC 236 David Richards J held (at para 27) that, following the principles set down in *Re Atlantic Computer Systems plc* there is 'no automatic presumption that . . . the rent on premises let to the company before the administration but used by the company during, and for the benefit of, the administration should be paid as an expense'. However, the position for new administrations is potentially different and now in line with liquidations (see **2.98**).

2.96 Administrators are then faced with the difficult decision as to when they should decide that it is appropriate to make the decision that certain rent payments should be payable as an expense. However, even where the premises are being used for the purpose of the administration there is no strict doctrine of *administration expenses* which requires the administrator to make this decision and ongoing rents from the company's assets as an expense of the administration in priority to other debts (*Re Atlantic Computer Systems plc* [1992] Ch 505, CA). Notwithstanding the absence of any such strict doctrine a landlord will in many cases be able to procure that the current rent is paid only when the premises are being used.

2.97 The court has a discretion to order the administrator to make such payments even where any such liability is not covered by s 19. Lord Hoffmann stated in *Centre Reinsurance International Co v Freakley* [2006] 1 WLR 2863 (at para 17) that:

> ' . . . the court . . . has a broad discretion to authorise or direct the administrator to make payments or enter into contracts for the purposes of the administration.'

New-style administration expenses governed by IR 1986, r 2.67

2.98 In relation to new administrations (ie most but not all forms of administration commencing after the coming into force of the Enterprise

Act 2002), the position has significantly changed. For new administrations, expenses flow from IA 1986, Sch B1, para 99(3), which provides that when an administrator leaves office:

'The former administrator's remuneration and expenses shall be–

(a) charged on and payable out of property of which he had custody or control immediately before cessation, and
(b) payable in priority to any security to which paragraph 70 applies [assets secured by a floating charge].'

2.99 However, the Insolvency (Amendment) Rules 2003 and 2005 introduced new provisions that deal with administration expenses and, in particular, inserted the new IR 1986, r 2.67. The amendments import into the new administration procedure rules governing the priority of such expenses. They are based upon the long-established rules that govern liquidations (see **2.68** and IR 1986, r 4.218).

2.100 Ostensibly, this provision deals only with the prioritisation of payment of the different categories of expense (not forgetting that all categories have priority over unsecured creditors). However, its effect reaches further than may first be apparent. IR 1986, r 2.67(1) provides that the expenses of the administration are payable in the following order of priority:

'(a) expenses properly incurred by the administrator in performing his functions in the administration of the company;
    . . .
(f) any necessary disbursements by the administrator in the course of administration ...
(g) the remuneration or emoluments of any person who has been employed by the administrator to perform any services for the company ...
(h) the remuneration of the administrator . . .
(j) the amount of any corporation tax on chargeable gains accruing on the realisation of any asset of the company (without regard to whether the realisation [of any asset] is effected by the administrator, a secured creditor, or a receiver or manager appointed to deal with a security).'

2.101 The question which then arose is whether these provisions should be subject to the same discretion as applies to the old-style administrations (still governed by s 19) or whether they should be treated in the same way as IR 1986, r 4.218 for liquidations. This question was scrutinised by Richards J in *Exeter City Council v Bairstow* [2007] BCC 236 in the context of whether non-domestic business rates should be payable as an administration expense. The local rating authority claimed the rates falling due during the period of the administration should be payable as an expense pursuant to IR 1986, r 2.67(1)(a) (ie an expense properly incurred) or under r 2.67(1)(f) (ie a necessary disbursement).

2.102 In 2002, Lord Hoffmann comprehensively reviewed this position in relation to liquidation expenses in his House of Lords judgment in *Re Toshoku*

Finance UK plc [2002] 1 WLR 671 (see **2.68**). However, as IR 1986, r 2.67 was based upon r 4.218, the guidance provided by Lord Hoffmann indirectly applies to administrations. Following the introduction of r 2.67 the principal question becomes whether any particular liability (such as post-administration rent) can properly be construed as an expense. If it can be fitted into one of the categories set out by r 2.67, it will be an expense, whether it is an 'expense properly incurred' or a 'necessary disbursement'. If it is an expense, the administrator will have no choice but to pay it. However, the logical connection between r 2.67 and r 4.218 was not reviewed by the courts until the *'Trident'* case (*Exeter City Council v Bairstow*).

2.103 Prior to *Trident*, administrators treated expenses on the basis that they had a large degree of discretion to determine what amounted to an administration expense and when to pay. In other words little had changed in real terms from the conventions that had developed in connection with old-style administrations. Administrators generally agreed to pay rent and rates only if they actively used or needed the property. However, *Trident* cast doubt on that practice. The case concerned the payment of continuing liability for business rates. In *Trident*, in applying *Toshoku* Richards J held that business rates are always payable as an expense of an administration. This was the case even if the property is of no use to the company in administration and the administrator wants to surrender the lease. He held that the administrator had no discretion. For the purpose of determining whether rates are payable as an expense it didn't matter that the property was not occupied for the purposes of the administration. The administrator did not even have to carry out the balancing act set out by Nicholls LJ in *Re Atlantic Computer Systems* (see **3.56**). In effect, Richards J applied Lord Hoffmann's interpretation of IR 1986, r 4.218 for liquidation expenses to r 2.67 for administration expenses.

2.104 Following *Trident*, administrators were left in the position that they had to pay both occupied and unoccupied rates as an expense. This was a controversial position which caused a shockwave in the insolvency industry. The immediate concern for administrators in relation to rates was alleviated by the Non-Domestic Rating (Unoccupied Property) (England) Regulations 2008, SI 2008/386 which provided companies in administration with an exemption for unoccupied rates.

2.105 Therefore, if rates are payable as an administration expense, why not post–administration rent and other property charges? This difficult question is left open. IR 1986, r 2.67 does not give an administrator discretion. The question is reduced to one only of construction. This uncertainty creates a significant degree of uncertainty for administrators and landlords.

2.106 There is no clear reason why rents and other costs falling due after the date of an administration should not be payable as an expense where other statutory costs (eg rates and other taxes) are payable. The contradiction is further twisted by the acceptance that sometimes rents will be payable as an expense but not always. As the current legislation stands this is not easy to square with the fact that the *Trident/Toshoku* interpretation of r 2.67 is that there is no discretion that can be applied. However the Court of Appeal in *Innovate Logistics Ltd v Sunberry Properties Ltd* [2008] EWCA Civ 1261 reopened the debate when Mummery LJ expressly stated (at para 59) that 'the court has a wide discretion according to the circumstances of the case'. However the case only touched upon the issue of administration expenses and there was no analysis of the *Trident/Toshoku* position.

2.107 Unfortunately, this leaves little guidance as to when ongoing rents are to be paid as an expense. If the continuing rent does count as such, it will be afforded the priority set out above.

Administration expenses – the practical position

2.108 In the absence of an administration expense principle and left with a simple question of construction, administrators are left in a difficult position. This question has to be determined on a frequent basis and the points set out below represent what has been built up as the pragmatic resolution.

The administrator's position

2.109 Administrators will invariably resist the payment of rents as an expense, unless there is perceived to be some need for the company to retain the property. In deciding whether there is a need the administrator is required to have regard to the objectives set out by IA 1986, Sch B1, para 3(1). He must first decide whether the property is necessary to achieve one of the statutory objectives (in the following hierarchical order):

(1)   to rescue the company as a going concern; or

(2)   to achieve a better result for the company's creditors as a whole than would be likely in a liquidation; or

(3)   to realise the property in order to make a distribution to a secured or preferential creditor.

2.110 In practice this decision is made with the following issues in mind:

• short-term value, where the administrator requires the premises for storage of the tenant's assets pending a sale;

• in the sale, the administrator may need to include a promise to use reasonable endeavors to procure an assignment of the lease to a purchaser of the tenant's business;

• if the rent under the lease is significantly below the market rate and there is no pending rent review then there may be a premium value on assignment which the administrator wishes to realise;

- if the lease is of a property in a highly sought after location (eg a top pitch in a primary shopping centre) then there may be a premium value on an assignment.

The landlord's position

2.111 It is perhaps not surprising that administrators refuse to pay ongoing rents as a matter of course. The administrator as an agent of the company does not have a personal liability to pay rent. However, the rent will continue to accrue unabated by the administration. The following points therefore arise:

- Where an administrator wants to retain the property for the purposes of the administration but refuses to pay rent, a commercial landlord is able to insist that rent is payable as an expense pursuant to IR 1986, r 2.67(1)(a) (as an *expense properly incurred*). The concept of expenses properly incurred is sometimes compared to the cost of salvage (see *Powdrill v Watson* [1995] 2 AC 394). The salvage principle suggests that if a contract is adopted for purpose of the more beneficial conduct of the administration then consequential liabilities incurred after adoption are an expense. This principle follows a long line of liquidation cases, including *Re Lundy Granite Co* (1871) LR 6 Ch App 462. Those administrators who use a property for the purposes of the administration have adopted the contract. Accordingly, if the property is being used by the company in administration, the administrator will have no discretion and should pay any ongoing rent as an expense properly incurred.

- Rent may be payable as a necessary disbursement, even if the administrator is not using the property. This is best illustrated where the administrator seeks to obtain a premium value for a lease on assignment or wishes to retain it pending a sale of the business (which may or may not include the company's trading sites). In *Re Linda Marie (in liquidation)* [1989] BCLC 46, Warner J decided that the post-liquidation rent should be payable by the liquidator as a necessary disbursement of the liquidation. The liquidator had not disclaimed the lease. Administrators do not have the power to disclaim. For administrations the introduction of IR 1986, r 2.67 will make it easier for landlords to demand payment of the post-administration rent as a necessary disbursement.

- Where the administrator wants to surrender the property (administrators have no power to disclaim, unlike liquidators), the argument remains that the ongoing rents should be payable as an expense under the category of being a necessary disbursement (as defined by IR 1986, r 2.67(1)(f)). This is because if continuing rents fall into the category of 'necessary disbursements', then the administrator (or the court) may have no discretion but to allow the claim.

2.112 The administrator has a duty to take into account the circumstances of the company's failure and the prospects for its future. The received wisdom is that if the administration is to restructure the company (or part of its business) as a going concern, or if the administrator requires the property for any temporary purpose of the administration, there is a compelling argument that the rents should be paid.

Pay or forfeit

2.113 Landlords will normally ask the administrator to provide an assurance that the rents will be paid as an expense, failing which they may threaten to seek permission from the court to forfeit or to levy distress (shortly CRAR). The court can order the administrator to pay the rent as a condition to counterbalance a refusal to allow forfeiture. This was the position with old-style administrations (*Re Salmet – Spring Valley Properties Ltd v Harris* [2001] BPIR 709). The administrator is then forced to decide whether to pay (as an expense) or to allow the landlord to exercise his rights (in relation to these proprietary rights see **3.56** and the guidelines set out by Nicholls LJ in *Re Atlantic Computer Systems plc* [1992] Ch 505).

2.114 However, landlords are in a stronger position than is sometimes accepted by administrators. IR 1986, r 2.67 will often provide a strong argument that the ongoing rents should be paid. Administrators face an increased risk of failing to pay a proper expense when they are obliged to. Pursuant to IA 1986, Sch B1, para 75 an aggrieved landlord can bring this matter before the court. If the administrator has misapplied monies (perhaps by mistake), he can be ordered to repay, restore or account for the funds (which was the consequence of *Trident* and also see IA 1986, Sch B1, para 75(3)). This exposes the administrator to personal liability in the same way that a director can be liable in misfeasance. Accordingly any failure to take proper account of a landlord's claim may be at the cost of the administrator's own remuneration.

LIQUIDATION/ADMINISTRATION SET-OFF

2.115 The tenant company (in liquidation or administration) may have a cross-claim against the landlord in relation to any rent claim. The cross-claim may arise from a breach of the landlord's express or implied covenants.

2.116 The non-insolvency restrictions in relation to set-off generally do not apply to administrations and liquidations (for the general picture, see *Stein v Blake* [1996] AC 243 at 251, per Hoffman L).

2.117 Mutual credits and set-off in relation to liquidations is dealt with in IR 1986, r 4.90. This allows a liquidator to adjust any distribution to a creditor and set off any sums due to or from the company whether payable now or in the future (IR 1986, r 4.90(4)). This will apply to rents payable both prior to the liquidation and rents incurred or to be incurred after the commencement of the liquidation. A liquidator can apply a set-off even where the lease contains an express provision which requires payment of rents without deduction or set-off.

Most commercial leases have an express covenant requiring the tenant to pay its rents without deduction or set-off. However, if after the date of the liquidation, the landlord assigns the right to recover the rent, then a liquidator will not be able to apply a mutual credit or set-off to a proof submitted by an assignee of the debt owed to the landlord (IR 1986, r 4.90(2)(d); for administrations see IR 1986, r 2.85(2)(e)).

2.118 Liquidation expenses cannot be reduced by the set-off of a cross-claim if it constitutes a debt 'arising out of an obligation incurred at a time when the creditor had notice that . . . a meeting of creditors had been summoned under s 98; or a petition for the winding up of the company was pending' (IR 1986, r 4.90(3)(a)). However, where rents are payable as an expense as the liability generally arises from a pre-liquidation lease the liquidator can still apply a set-off. A landlord could seek to enhance his position by elevating the payment of the rents as an expense pursuant to a fresh obligation. It might be that obtaining an appropriately worded undertaking to this effect may suffice.

2.119 Under the original administration regime, there is no provision corresponding to IR 1986, r 4.90. The principle of *insolvency set-off* was not applicable. IR 1986, r 2.85 was substituted by the Insolvency (Amendment) Rules 2005 with effect from 1 April 2005. IR 1986, r 2.85 (mutual credit and set-off) allows an administrator to adjust any distribution to a creditor and set-off any sums due to or from the company whether payable now or in the future (IR 1986, r 2.85(4)). This provision is broadly the same as IR 1986, r 4.90 for liquidations.

2.120 Administration expenses cannot be reduced by the set-off of a cross-claim if it constitutes a debt 'arising out of an obligation incurred after the company entered into administration'. However, where rents are payable as an expense as the liability generally arises from a pre-administration lease the administrator can still apply a set-off. A landlord could seek to enhance his position by elevating the payment of the rents as an expense pursuant to a fresh obligation. It might be that obtaining an appropriately worded undertaking to this effect may suffice.

2.121 In relation to both administrations and liquidations, where there is a rent deposit no question of set-off arises where a landlord has a contractual right to make deductions from the deposit (see *Re Greenport Ltd* [2004] 1 BCLC 555 and chapter 6 generally in relation to rent deposits).

Chapter 3

DISTRESS FOR RENT AND COMMERCIAL RENT ARREARS RECOVERY

Peter Levaggi (in conjunction with Peter Mooney)

3.1 Landlords have long enjoyed the common law right to levy distress for rent. The law of distress allows landlords to appoint a bailiff (or if the landlord is an individual to proceed without a bailiff) to impound goods on the demised premises to collect all sums reserved as rent (that is in arrears). Perhaps the most important factor is that distress can be levied without obtaining a court order and without any requirement to provide notice to the tenant (although see the changes to be brought in by Tribunals, Courts and Enforcement Act 2007). This popular remedy is available to a landlord whenever rent is in arrears. It is an automatic right arising from the obligation to pay rent. This ancient common law remedy gives the landlord the initial right to seize and impound goods found on the demised premises irrespective of ownership. However, a landlord using this remedy has to comply with a complex and sometimes anachronistic set of rules developed over centuries of case-law and statute. In the 1960s case of *Abingdon Rural DC v O'Gorman* [1968] 2 QB 811, Lord Denning MR described distress as 'an archaic remedy which has largely fallen into disuse'. However, this seemingly provoked a strong resurgence in the use of this powerful direct action remedy so that in recent years the remedy has become very common. This is particularly the case in relation to commercial premises where it has become the landlord's favourite remedy, a fact neatly summed up in *Wharfland Ltd v South London Co-operative Building Co Ltd* [1995] 2 EGLR 21:

> ' . . . at one stage the remedy of distress seemed to be passing out of use but it seems that it has come back into fashion and one can see why. Seizure of modern office equipment involves great disruption and the threat of seizure will often be enough to persuade solvent businesses to pay the sums demanded rather than risk disruption.'

3.2 However, distress also gives a clear advantage to a landlord who suspects that a tenant is about to go into an insolvent arrangement (see **3.28**).

3.3 Distress has been reformed by the Tribunals, Courts and Enforcement Act 2007 (TCEA 2007). This chapter will deal with distress and the new procedure of Commercial Rent Arrears Recovery (CRAR) to be introduced by TCEA 2007. When TCEA 2007 comes into force distress will be abolished and replaced with CRAR under ss 71 and 72 (see **3.10**).

DISTRESS (PRIOR TO CRAR)

3.4 We are in the dying days of distress in its current form. In principle, distress is a simple operation; a landlord who is owed rent is able to take goods from the demised premises and sell them. It is only available where there is a landlord and tenant relationship. From the proceeds he is able to satisfy the arrears of rent together with the prescribed costs of using the remedy (in relation to costs see the Distress for Rent Rules 1988, SI 1988/2050). However, over time the process became complicated. The procedure is primarily regulated by the Law of Distress Amendment Act 1888, the Law of Distress Amendment Act 1908 and the Distress for Rent Rules 1988.

3.5 There are limited circumstances where distress is frozen or prohibited by statute without first obtaining the court's permission (or the permission of the administrator or liquidator). However, in relation to the majority of distress actions, the landlord does not need any court sanction. The court's permission is required only in the following situations:

- under the Rent Act 1977, s 147, no distress can be levied on a dwelling house let on a protected tenancy or subject to a statutory tenancy;

- under the Housing Act 1988, s 19, no distress can be levied on a dwelling house let on an assured tenancy;

- under certain types of insolvency no distress can be levied without the permission of the court – but this does not apply to all insolvencies (this is expanded below, see **3.17**).

3.6 At common law, landlords could levy distress against any goods found on the demised premises. This allowed distress to be taken against goods belonging not only to the debtor (ie the tenant) but also goods belonging to a third party. Under the current regime third party goods can still be taken but subject to a level of statutory protection. Potentially this creates a harsh regime where innocent third parties can have their goods seized even where they had little connection with the debtor/tenant. A series of nineteenth-century statutes gave some third parties rights culminating in the Law of Distress Amendment Act 1908 which softened the effect of this principle. Section 1 of the 1908 Act provides a degree of protection from distress for:

- lodgers (the *lodger* has the burden to prove he satisfies this description, which is to be given its *popular meaning, Thwaites v Wilding* (1883) LR 12 QBD 4, CA, Bowen LJ this follows the earlier protection created by the Lodgers' Goods Protection Act 1871);

- under tenants (but only where the under tenant is liable to pay rent no less frequently than by equal quarterly instalments and providing the rent payable represents *the full annual value of the premises or of such part thereof as is comprised in the under tenancy* (s 1(a)) and the under tenancy must be lawfully granted in compliance with the tenant's obligations in the head tenancy, *Parsons v Hambridge* (1916) 33 TLR 117);

- third parties (without any beneficial interest in the tenancy, s 1(c)).

3.7 The protection afforded by Law of Distress Amendment Act 1908, s 1 is not automatic but creates an after the event remedy (*Rhodes v Allied Dunbar Pension Services Ltd* [1989] 1 All ER 1161). A landlord can levy distress on the goods of any third party if the goods are situated on the demised premises. The third party claiming the protection of the Act must then serve on the landlord or bailiff a statutory declaration (under s 1 of the 1908 Act) of his status and until he does this the remedies created by the Act are not effective. Under tenants and lodgers must also undertake to pay to the superior landlord any rent due to the immediate landlord and any rents which will become due until the arrears under the head lease are paid off. Once the declaration has been served (and rents tendered by an under tenant/lodger) then if the landlord proceeds with the distress it becomes illegal contrary to the Law of Distress Amendment Act 1908, s 2.

3.8 However, the 1908 Act does not protect all third parties. Landlords can with impunity levy distress and seize the goods on the demised premises belonging to (s 4):

- the husband or wife of the tenant;

- a third party who has given permission for the tenant to have the goods in his possession – if the goods are in the reputed ownership of the tenant;

- a business where the tenant has an interest;

- a third party who has stored goods on the premises and has failed to remove them having been given at least one month's notice to do so;

- a company where the tenant is a director or officer of the company;

- a hire purchase company unless a default notice has been served (s 4A).

3.9 Distress cannot be used in relation to certain categories of goods which are exempt:

- as 'absolutely privileged' (such as Crown property (*Secretary of State for War v Wynne* [1905] 2 KB 845), certain essential public trade materials (*Challoner v Robinson* [1908] 1 Ch 49, CA), perishable articles, money, utility fittings for gas, water and electricity and tenant's fixtures); or

- as 'conditionally privileged' (such as farm animals and tools of the trade where there is no other sufficient distress).

THE REFORM OF DISTRESS AND REPLACEMENT WITH COMMERCIAL RENT ARREARS RECOVERY (CRAR)

3.10   When TCEA 2007 comes into force it will abolish the common law right to distain for arrears of rent in its entirety (s 71). Distress will be replaced by CRAR (s 72). This has caused great alarm for commercial landlords who have relied heavily on distress. Distress has been a major tool for the commercial property industry, reducing the amount of rent arrears significantly. The major advantage of the current system is that it was on many occasions quick and effective for landlords and did not require any court procedure. In the consultation to TCEA 2007 the commercial property industry lobbied aggressively to retain distress. Gary Burns (a leading property consultant, BES Properties) stated:

> 'The law of distress may be an archaic remedy. However, it has been used by many commercial landlords as a valuable counterbalance to the growing number of insolvencies. In our experience we, like most landlords, are generally very sensitive to the prospect that some tenants are in a vulnerable position. We only use the remedy in the most appropriate of situations and often as an exercise to start reasonable negotiations. I believe that the proposed changes to the law of distress will force landlords to fall back on insisting on larger rent deposits, more stringent reference requirements and tighter lease terms. This may lead to more tenants failing as a consequence of a significant rise in the amount of security that landlords will be forced to seek. The replacement procedure CRAR represents a serious loss of power for landlords and ultimately this will increase market rents with good tenants across the industry paying extra to compensate for the bad.'

3.11   However, the remedy has long been the subject of criticism. The Law Commission Report published in 1991 (*Landlord and Tenant Distress for Rent*) recommended that distress should be abolished but only when improvements to the court system made the other remedies effective. Distress had also been the subject of judicial criticism. Particularly in the case of *Fuller v Happy Shopper Markets Ltd* [2001] 1 WLR 1681 where Lightman J entertained the possibility of a challenge under the European Convention of Human Rights (ECHR):

> 'The ancient (and perhaps anachronistic) self help remedy of distress involves a serious interference with the right of the tenant under article 8 of the European Convention on Human Rights to respect for his privacy and home under Article 1 of the first protocol to the peaceful enjoyment of his possessions. The Human Rights Implications of Levying Distress must be in the forefront of the mind of the landlord before he takes the step and he must fully satisfy himself that taking this action is in accordance with the law.'

3.12   Landlords lobbied hard to retain distress and in the event secured an alternative. In replacement of distress landlords will be able to use the CRAR procedure in TCEA 2007, Sch 12 which is a reformed version of distress. CRAR retains the essential ingredients of distress in that, generally, the process can be used without obtaining a court order. The position in relation to insolvency remains broadly the same as for distress (although there are some key distinctions dealt with at **3.22** et seq). In fact TCEA 2007, Sch 13, para 85 inserts a new definition for *distress* into IA 86, s 436:

> '"distress" includes use of the procedure in Schedule 12 to the Tribunals, Courts and Enforcement Act 2007, and references to levying distress seizing goods and related expressions shall be construed accordingly.'

CRAR AND INSOLVENCY

3.13 Like distress, CRAR will sometimes be restricted by the insolvency process. However, perhaps the first question which arises is whether there is a prima facie right for a landlord to use the remedy. TCEA 2007 sets out strict preconditions for the exercise of CRAR which are more restrictive than for the current distress process. The preconditions arguably make CRAR significantly less effective than distress. In order to exercise CRAR the landlord must be able to show that the following conditions are met:

- there must be a landlord and tenant relationship. A licence will not suffice; it must be a tenancy whether this is in law or equity. A tenancy at will is expressly included, but a tenancy at sufferance is excluded (TCEA 2007, s 74). The landlord's right to use CRAR in a licence situation cannot be extended by agreement (unlike in relation to distress – see *Re Roundwood Colliery* [1897] 1 Ch 373);

- the lease must be of commercial premises (where not a single part of the premises can be let as a dwelling or actually used as a dwelling – the only exception being where the tenant is residing on the premises in breach of an express prohibition in the lease (TCEA 2007, s 72). As distress is often used for secondary/tertiary properties which are often of mixed use (eg retail unit with upstairs flat), this will materially reduce the number of occasions when CRAR will be used;

- the lease must be evidenced in writing and still in existence although CRAR can still be exercised after the lease has come to an end (TCEA 2007, s 79) provided the following conditions are met:
  - the lease did not end by forfeiture;
  - not more than 6 months has passed since the day the lease ended;
  - the tenant remains in possession of the demised premises;
  - the rent is due from the tenant as at the end of the lease;
  - the landlord exercising CRAR must be the same landlord as at the end of the lease;
  - if the tenant is occupying the demised premises under a new lease this remains a commercial lease;

- also CRAR can be exercised after the contractual term of the lease has come to an end where:

- the tenant is holding over by virtue of the Landlord and Tenant Act 1954, Part II; or
- the tenancy is contracted out of the provisions of the Landlord and Tenant Act 1954 and the tenancy continues at will (*Javad v Aqil* [1991] 1 All ER 243; *Cardiothoracic Institute v Shrewdcrest Ltd* [1986] 3 All ER 633);

- a warning notice must be served (pursuant to TCEA 2007, Sch 12, para 7) and then the prescribed time must expire before CRAR can commence;

- the rent must be due and owing (TCEA 2007, s 77):
  - the amount of rent due must be at least at the level of the minimum amount prescribed by the rules calculated at both the time immediately before the warning notice and then again immediately before CRAR is to be attempted. Distress is often used for relatively small collections. It is more cost effective than the court process. This provision may lead to increased levels of rent deposits for low rent properties; and
  - the landlord must be able to ascertain the rent due and this may lead to the difficult task of calculating the value of any counterclaims which have been raised by the tenant. To use CRAR the landlord must reduce the amount due by any of the following (TCEA 2007, s 77(7)):

  'Deduction, recoupment or set-off that the tenant would be entitled to claim (in law or equity) in an action by the landlord for that rent';

- the landlord may have to seek the court's permission as a result of various insolvency conditions (see **3.22** and **3.66**).

3.14 CRAR is limited to the recovery of outstanding rent (together with interest and VAT) unlike distress which can be used in relation to any sums which were reserved as rent under the terms of the lease. CRAR can therefore not be used in relation to other sums such as rates, services, repairs, maintenance or insurance (TCEA 2007, s 76). Rent is defined as the amount payable for possession and use of the demised premises together with interest and VAT. Where it is not clear how much the *pure rent* is, then the landlord must assess how much of the arrears are reasonably attributable to the possession and use of the premises (TCEA 2007, s 76(3)). Many landlords have commented about the harshness of this new provision. Typically landlords will have actually expended certain sums on services and insurance and will be out of pocket. It seems unnecessary to have a total exclusion given that the landlord is only permitted to use CRAR for ascertained amounts which would take account of any disputes as to the level of service charge.

3.15 The requirement to provide a warning notice is perhaps the most controversial change to be introduced by TCEA 2007 (Sch 12, para 7). Until this notice has been given an *Enforcement Agent* (the new status for bailiffs under TCEA 2007, s 63) will not be able to take control of goods. The regulations to TCEA 2007 will specify the minimum period of notice and the form of the notice. There will be prescribed circumstances that will allow shorter notice periods to be provided (and perhaps limited circumstances where no notice will be required). However, dispensation with the notice provisions will depend upon an application to the court and the regulations (which have yet to be published). The warning notice will take away the current ability that landlords enjoy to levy distress by way of an ambush. The fear is that the warning will give the tenant more opportunity to remove goods from the premises. The problem is offset by the fact that the tenant's goods will be subject to a statutory binding which takes effect as soon as the notice is served (TCEA 2007, Sch 12, para 4).

Unification of distress and execution – the new procedure for taking control of goods

3.16 Together with distress TCEA 2007 will sweep away the current forms of enforcement that involve taking control of debtors' goods. There will be one unified system of enforcement to replace distress, High Court and county court execution. The system is set out in TCEA 2007, Sch 12. Landlords who are able to exercise CRAR (given the preconditions set out above) will then be governed by the same provisions as enforcement agents executing High Court and county court judgments. In some ways this will simplify the position for insolvency officeholders who will now be able to deal with all forms of execution in the same way. Where a landlord has the right to exercise CRAR or a judgment creditor has obtained a writ of control in the High Court or a warrant of control in the county court, the procedure is as follows (in approximately the following sequence):

- The debtor's goods are bound and cannot be assigned or transferred (Sch 12, para 4). The binding takes effect as soon as:
  - the writ or warrant of control is endorsed by the court (Sch 12, para 4(3)); or
  - a landlord gives notice that CRAR will be used.

- An enforcement agent obtains entry to a place where control of a debtor's goods can be taken (Sch 12, para 9) which is:
  - for the execution of court judgments, any place where the debtor usually lives or carries on a trade or business (Sch 12, para 14);
  - for CRAR, the demised premises unless a warrant is obtained to follow goods elsewhere (Sch 12, para 15). TCEA 2007 creates a new remedy which for the first time will give landlords the ability to apply for a warrant for an enforcement agent to enter other specified premises (a bailiff levying distress could only gain entry or levy distress on the demised premises, unless there had been a pound breach); or

  – if goods are located on the highway then they can be taken there. This extends to CRAR and represents a further extension of the landlord's rights (Sch 12, para 9).

- TCEA 2007 creates yet another remedy allowing enforcement agents to use force to gain entry. The use of force was prohibited for distress and execution and so this right is likely to make a significant difference. In relation to CRAR enforcement agents will have to apply to the court for permission to use force. This could be combined with an application to gain entry to a premises other than the demised premises and was introduced to rationalise the complexities of the current system (see *Khazanchi v Faircharm Investments Ltd* [1998] 1 WLR 1603, CA and *Mcleod v Butterwick* [1998] 2 All ER 901, CA). In order to take control of goods the enforcement agent will do one of the following (Sch 12, para 13):
  – secure the goods on the premises where they are found;
  – if the goods are on the highway, secure them on the highway;
  – remove the goods from the premises or the highway and secure them elsewhere;
  – enter into a *controlled goods agreement* with the tenant.

- Walking possession agreements have been replaced by controlled goods agreements (Sch 12, para 13(4)). This will be the most common form of impounding goods as it will be the most cost effective. When a tenant becomes insolvent it is not unusual for an insolvency officeholder to discover that the goods on site are subject to walking possession. Where there is such an agreement the tenant:
  – is permitted to retain possession of the goods;
  – acknowledges that the enforcement agent (currently the bailiff) has taken control of them; and
  – agrees not to remove the goods or dispose of them, nor to permit anyone else to, before the debt is paid.

- We do not yet know how controlled goods agreements will be regulated. There is likely to be a greater degree of formality than for walking possession under the current system where sometimes an oral agreement may suffice (see, eg, *Mcleod v Butterwick* [1996] 1 WLR 995).

- TCEA 2007 will then require the enforcement agent to obtain a valuation of the goods that have been taken under control and the tenant is given an opportunity to obtain an independent valuation. The valuation must take place before the end of the *minimum period* (Sch 12, para 39).

- The goods are held for the *minimum period* (to be prescribed by the rules) prior to an enforcement sale and then the enforcement agent must give notice to the tenant of the sale. The regulations will prescribe the form, contents, notice period, and method of service of the notice (Sch 12, para 40). If no notice is given within 12 months of the date the goods are taken under control (*the permitted period*) then the goods are deemed to be abandoned by the enforcement agent.

THE EFFECT OF INSOLVENCY ON DISTRESS/CRAR – REMEDIES

3.17 When faced with distress/CRAR insolvency officeholders have two strands of protection and remedies. Firstly, there are the remedies which are in any event available to the tenant regardless of the insolvency. Secondly, there are remedies and protection available as a direct consequence of the insolvency.

General remedies available with or without insolvency

3.18 TCEA 2007 creates a new remedy available to tenants (and other debtors) in relation to any breach of the provisions of Sch 12 (including where an enforcement agent is acting under a defective writ or warrant or other instrument which creates an enforcement power). Although a breach or defect does not make the enforcement agent a trespasser, the debtor has the right to call upon the remedies provided by Sch 12, para 66. The tenant/debtor can:

- claim damages as a consequence of any breach or defect of Sch 12;

- require the return of the goods as a consequence of any breach or defect of Sch 12;

- claim damages where the amount outstanding has been paid in full pursuant to Sch 12, para 58 and the enforcement agent takes a further step contrary to para 58(3) – but only where the enforcement agent has had notice that the amount has been paid.

3.19 TCEA 2007, Sch 12, para 66 replaces the remedies available for all forms of defective and excessive distress. However, until TCEA 2007 comes into force, tenants can claim damages where there has been:

- illegal distress, for example, where no rent was due or forced entry was used or privileged goods have been taken or goods sold after a third party has notified the bailiff of its interest (currently a third party serves a statutory declaration under the Law of Distress (Amendment) Act 1908, s 1) or excessive force is used generally (also see *Khazanchi v Faircharm Investments Ltd* [1998] 1 WLR 1603, CA);

- irregular distress where the initial distress was properly constituted but the procedure was not properly followed under Distress for Rent Act 1737, s 19 (to be repealed by TCEA 2007);

- excessive distress where goods are taken which are obviously of a value which far exceeds the amount due to the landlord. In some circumstances items of disproportionate value can be taken where there are other items available to be distrained upon. This is a principle that goes back to the Statute of Marlborough 1267 which provides 'distresses shall be reasonable, and not too great; and he that taketh great and unreasonable distresses, shall be grievously amerced for the excess of such distresses' (at Chapter 4 of the Statute which incidentally will remain in force when TCEA 2007 comes into force).

3.20 The tenant can also apply for an order restraining the right to exercise CRAR or staying the process if it has already commenced (TCEA 2007, s 78). This application could be used by insolvency officeholders where no moratorium is in place under IA 1986.

3.21 Distress/CRAR is also restricted by the insolvency process which creates a number of preconditions, restrictions and remedies which are dealt with in the next section. Each type of insolvency has its own treatment of distress.

Distress/CRAR and insolvency

Receivership and distress/CRAR

3.22 The appointment of a receiver in respect of the tenant's property has little automatic effect on the right to use any enforcement process including distress/CRAR. This is true of the two forms of receivership (ie where receivers are appointed under the terms of a fixed charge or administrative receivers are appointed under the terms of a debenture over the whole of the tenant's assets or substantially the whole of the assets (see **1.62**) – also note administrative receivership is being phased out (see **1.63**)).

3.23 A receiver appointed under the terms of a charge acts as an agent of the tenant to realise assets to discharge the debts owed to the secured creditor. The rights of other creditors largely remain intact. There is no restriction on levying distress for rent and there will be no direct restriction on exercising CRAR. The rights of landlords are unaffected by receivership (see *Re Roundwood Colliery* [1897] 1 Ch 373). However, the introduction of CRAR and the unification of distress with other forms of execution may make a significant difference to this principle (see below).

Receivership and distress contrasted with court execution

3.24 Surprisingly execution creditors have not been in the same position as landlords. Whereas landlords were allowed to levy distress for rent, execution put in place by a judgment creditor was subject to the rights of secured creditors with a fixed charge. The reason for this is that where a floating charge has crystallised over goods, the floating charge becomes a fixed charge and the charge remains intact over the proceeds of any sale of the seized assets. This is set out in Lord Justice Buckley's judgment in *Cretanor Maritime Co Ltd v Irish Marine Management Ltd* [1978] 3 All ER 164:

'The debenture holder is now an equitable assignee of the deposited fund that the [enforcement] gives the owners no present rights against the deposited fund but was made merely with the view to the retention of that fund in England still has to be available in the event of the owners becoming able to levy execution on it, and that, if the owners were here after to attempt to levy execution their rights as execution creditors would have to give way to prior rights in the fund, including the rights of the debenture holder . . .'

3.25 In *Cretanor* a freezing injunction did not prevail against a debenture holder even though the floating charge crystallised after the injunction was granted. This was because the injunction did not actually give the claimant rights against the assets (such rights could be acquired later if he obtained judgment, but until then rights are against the defendant personally). The rights of the debenture holder stemmed from the creation of the debenture.

3.26 Once a charge has crystallised over goods the preference enjoyed by the chargee prevails even where prior to the crystallisation a High Court Enforcement Officer has progressed with the court execution and already bound and seized the goods (*Re Standards Manufacturing Company* [1891] 1 Ch 627, CA; *Re Opera Ltd* [1891] 3 Ch 260, CA; *Re London Pressed Hinge Co Ltd* [1905] 1 Ch 576). This priority which gives debenture holders preferential status over execution creditors has been criticised (see Hare and Milman 'Debenture holders and judgement creditors – problems of priority' [1981] LMCLQ 57 and Calnan 'Priorities between execution creditors and floating chargees' [1982] 10 NZULR 111) and appears to be inconsistent with the landlord's right to levy distress (or CRAR) notwithstanding the appointment of a receiver. This position is not clear where prior to the crystallisation of the charge the enforcement agent has sold the goods, but still retains the proceeds of sale. It is unlikely that in such a case execution creditors will have priority (*Robson v Smith* [1895] 2 Ch 118; *Taunton v Sheriff of Warwickshire* [1895] 2 Ch 319, CA).

Fixed charges, receivership and CRAR

3.27 However, the introduction of CRAR may affect this principle. In relation to receivership and fixed charges generally, CRAR will be treated differently to distress in the following ways:

• Now that the law of distress has been unified with court execution, CRAR may be subject to the same priority given to a fixed chargeholder (*Cretanor Maritime Co Ltd v Irish Marine Management Ltd* [1978] 3 All ER 164). CRAR and court execution will be regulated by the same rules under TCEA 2007, Sch 12.

• A receiver when warned that CRAR may be exercised (following service of a notice pursuant to TCEA 2007, Sch 12, para 7) can apply to the court to set the notice aside under TCEA 2007, s 78. Under this provision the court can be asked to freeze the CRAR process. TCEA 2007 is currently silent as to the grounds that a receiver or other applicant would have to show but this may have similarities to the application that a liquidator in a creditors' voluntary liquidation (CVL) can make in relation to distress under IA 1986, s 112 (see **3.51**).

- Pursuant to TCEA 2007, Sch 12, para 10 an *enforcement agent* may take control of goods 'only if they are goods of the debtor'. This will allow control to be taken of goods where the title is held by the tenants. This includes goods which are co-owned by the tenant with a third party.

- If those goods are subject to a charge (fixed or crystallised) then the debenture holder would be an *equitable assignee* of the goods pursuant to the terms of the charge. This is likely to fall within the definition of 'co-owner' in TCEA 2007, Sch 12, para 3 as 'a person . . . who has an interest in the goods'.

- Where an enforcement agent distributes the proceeds of sale co-owners will be paid first then he must apply the proceeds of sale according to the priority in TCEA 2007, Sch 12, para 50. This provides that the co-owner is paid first in priority (the priority being even ahead of the enforcement agent's costs, see para 50(6)).

At the time of writing, the regulations to TCEA 2007 have not been published and there may be express provision which affects this point (particularly in relation to the definition of *exempt goods* as defined by Sch 12).

Voluntary arrangements and distress/CRAR

3.28　In relation to most company voluntary arrangements (CVAs) prior to the creditors' meeting there is no restriction upon the landlord levying distress (nor will there be in relation to CRAR). With notice of a proposed meeting for a CVA a landlord may decide to act quickly and levy distress in the interregnum period prior to the meeting (a minimum of 14 days notice of the creditors' meeting must be given). Where a tenant company is fearful that its CVA proposals may provoke the landlord into taking the immediate action the directors may instead decide to explore the possibility of administration prior to the CVA (see **1.92**).

3.29　Even where there is no small company moratorium under IA 1986, Sch A1, it may still be possible to obtain an order that no further step be taken in the CRAR process on the basis of the proposed CVA under TCEA 2007, s 78. Until the regulations to TCEA 2007 are published it is not known as to how such applications will operate.

3.30　If the CVA is approved by the creditors then the landlord is bound to accept payments in accordance with the CVA in substitution for his right to recover the rent (see effect of approval at **1.52**). Following the leading judgment of Lord Justice Neuberger in the Court of Appeal case of *Thomas v Ken Thomas Ltd* [2006] EWCA Civ 1504, which dealt with a landlord's right to forfeit following a VA there is no reason why distress should not be caught by the same analysis in this regard (see **4.93**). If rent arrears are caught by the VA then the mere fact that distress/CRAR may be described as a proprietary right should not enable the landlord to levy distress or CRAR as if the rent was still owing. If the VA also reduces the liability for future rent then it is likely that the right to levy distress/CRAR will also be diminished proportionately. A VA (subject to the landlord's right to challenge the decision on the grounds of unfair prejudice under IA 1986, s 6 and see **1.54**) on the basis of Lord Justice Neuberger's judgment is able to compromise past and future claims of the landlord and remove the landlord's proprietary rights to undermine this principle. In effect this may compel a landlord to continue to provide a tenant the use of a property into the future on terms which he would not be commercially prepared to countenance.

3.31 Small companies and individuals are entitled to a moratorium prior to the meeting.

Individual voluntary arrangements – moratorium

3.32 IA 1986, s 252 creates a comprehensive moratorium for the period of the interim order leading up to the creditors' meeting. The interim order has the effect that after it is in force (or until the creditors' meeting):

'(b) No other proceedings and no execution or other legal process, may be commenced or continued and no distress may be levied against the debtor or his property except the leave for the Court.'

3.33 The effect of the interim order is to impose a moratorium on proceedings against the debtor (see *Frost v Unity Trust the Bank* [1998] BPIR 459). Under the current law of distress this doesn't stop a landlord's bailiff seizing goods belonging to a third party (subject to the restrictions of the Law of Distress Amendment Act 1908). However, when TCEA 2007 comes into force the landlord will only be able to use CRAR in relation to the tenant's goods. There will be no exception for third party goods (*Clarke v Coutts* [2002] EWCA Civ 943). However, if distress/CRAR was commenced prior to the date of the moratorium, but not completed, there is a possibility it could be continued. The wording in IA 1986, s 252 should be noted for the absence of any restriction on *continuing* distress (contrast with execution and other legal process which cannot be *continued*). Distress was held not to be a *legal process* in *McMullen & Sons Ltd v Cerrone* [1994] BCC 25. Therefore if the levy (entry, seizure and impounding) was made prior to the interim order the distress should be capable of completion. The wording in s 252 should also be contrasted with the wording of IA 1986, Sch B1, para 43(6) in relation to the moratorium which arises in administration. Paragraph 43 makes it clear that the landlord cannot continue 'legal proceedings, execution or distress'. It must be submitted that this difference is material and has a real effect.

3.34 The position may be different in relation to CRAR which will be governed by the same rules under TCEA 2007 as execution. However, the mere fact that CRAR and execution are governed by the same rules will not automatically make CRAR a legal process (given that unlike an execution creditor a landlord will be able to use CRAR without any court sanction). Also the word *distress* is to include 'the procedure in Schedule 12 to the Tribunals Courts and Enforcement Act 2007, and references to levying distress seizing goods and related expressions shall be construed accordingly' (TCEA 2007, Sch 13, para 85 and IA 1986, s 436). Therefore the point can still be made for CRAR.

Small company – moratorium

3.35 Small companies proposing a CVA have the right to apply for a moratorium (see **4.85**). During the period the moratorium is in force distress/CRAR is restricted:

> ' ... no other proceedings and no execution or other legal process may be commenced or continued, and no distress may be levied, against the company or its property except with leave of the court and subject to such terms as the court may impose.'

This provision is contained in IA 1986, Sch A1, para 12(1)(h). The wording of the provision prohibits execution and legal processes being commenced or continued. However, the prohibition in relation to distress only relates to act of *levying* or commencing the process. Paragraph 12 was introduced by the Insolvency Act 2000. The wording used is the same as the wording used for IA 1986, s 252 in relation to individual voluntary arrangements (IVAs) and interim orders (see **3.32**) which once again must be contrasted with the moratorium that arises in administration which expressly prohibits the *continuation* of distress. On this basis it seems that if a distress or CRAR is commenced prior to the date of the moratorium the landlord would be able to continue it.

Compulsory liquidation and distress/CRAR

3.36 Where a tenant is in compulsory liquidation the right to levy and complete distress/CRAR will depend upon when the process commenced and whether it was:

- commenced and completed prior to winding-up petition;

- commenced prior to winding-up petition but not completed;

- commenced in the period after winding-up petition but before winding-up order;

- commenced after winding-up order.

Where distress/CRAR is commenced and completed prior to the petition

3.37 Where at any time during the 3 months prior to a winding-up petition goods or effects of the tenant company have been distrained upon by a landlord the goods (or the proceeds of sale) are charged with the benefit of the company with the preferential debts to the extent that the company has insufficient assets to pay its preferential debts (IA 1986, s 176(2) save that this will no longer apply to Crown preference (see below and TCEA 2007, s 88). Otherwise there is no bar on distress/CRAR.

Where distress/CRAR is commenced prior to winding-up petition but not completed

3.38 Where a landlord has commenced the process (ie distress/CRAR) and then a winding-up petition is presented, the company or any other creditor may be able to apply to the court under IA 1986, s 126 to stay the process. If no application is made then distress/CRAR can be completed providing this happens prior to the winding-up order.

3.39 However, once a winding-up order is made then where the distress has been commenced prior to the petition the creditor must make an application to continue under s 130(3). The court's usual policy is to allow the distress to continue if it was commenced prior to the date of the petition unless there are specific reasons to make the distress inequitable (such as fraud). In *Venner's Electrical Cooking and Heating Appliances Ltd v Thorpe* [1915] 2 Ch 404, CA, Couzens Hardy MR stated:

> 'No equitable ground has ever been made out for restraining the landlord from levying the distress, unless there have been some circumstances outside the levying such as fraud, or unfair dealing which would entitle the tenant to earn junction.'

3.40 This principle should also apply to CRAR. However, when the procedure for distress becomes unified when TCEA 2007, Sch 12 comes into force the position may be affected by IA 1986, ss 183 and 184. Currently where a creditor has commenced court-based execution and subsequently a winding-up petition is presented against the debtor, then the creditor is not entitled to retain the benefit of the enforcement process. Under IA 1986, s 183:

> 'Where a creditor has issued execution against the goods or land of the company or had attached any debt due to it and the company is subsequently wound up he is not entitled to retain the benefit of the execution or attachment against the liquidator unless he has completed the execution or attachment before the commencement of the winding up.'

3.41 Under IA 1986, s 184, where a company's goods are taken in execution, the enforcement agents may be obliged to deliver the goods and any money seized or received to the liquidator. This applies where before a sale and where a notice is served on the enforcement agent:

- a provisional liquidator has been appointed; or

- a winding-up order has been made; or

- a resolution for voluntary winding up has been passed.

3.42 If an enforcement agent receives a notice under s 184 then the costs of execution are the first charge on the goods or money and the liquidator may sell the goods or a sufficient part of them to settle his costs. Even where the enforcement agent is not aware of the liquidation he is required to retain the proceeds of sale for a period of 14 days. If he receives the notification during the period he is required to pay the sale price to the liquidator (less the costs of enforcement). This will only apply if the judgment debt is more than £500.

3.43 Currently this position applies to execution but not distress. However, following the unification of the two processes (once TCEA 2007 comes into force) then this position may be held to apply to CRAR (although this is thought to be unlikely as CRAR will still be distinguishable from execution as it does not require a prior court judgment; see *Re Modern Jet Support Centre Ltd* [2006] BCC 174 where Warren J held that the ordinary meaning of 'execution' did not include distress and ss 183 and 184 did not apply, even though the distress in question arose under statute).

3.44 In any event distress and CRAR would still be subject to the charge in favour of preferential debts under IA 1986, s 176 although pursuant to TCEA 2007, s 88 'Crown preference for the purposes of execution against goods is abolished' (*Herbert Berry Associates Ltd v IRC* [1978] 1 All ER 161, HL).

Where distress/CRAR commenced in the period after winding-up petition but before winding-up order

3.45 After a winding-up petition has been presented to the court, but before the order is made, any enforcement action which is commenced is void (under IA 1986, s 128). The compulsory liquidation process commences with the petition and s 128 makes void any 'attachment, sequestration, distress or execution put in force against the estate or effects of the company'. If there are goods seized then no interest is acquired. There are exceptions to this principle:

- Distress against a third party with goods on the tenant's demised premises remains possible (*Re Traders' North Staffordshire Carrying Company* (1874-75) LR 19 Eq 60). This right is subject to the protection that some third party creditors have under Law of Distress Amendment Act 1908 (see **3.6**). This exception will not apply to CRAR which can only be exercised against the tenant's goods (TCEA 2007, Sch 12, para 10).

- Where a winding-up petition has been presented against a tenant, a landlord will still be able to serve a notice under the Law of Distress Amendment Act 1908, s 6 requiring a subtenant to pay its rents directly to the landlord. Following service of the notice distress can be levied. Law of Distress Amendment Act 1908, s 6 is to be replaced by TCEA 2007, s 81 which will allow CRAR to be exercised.

- Surprisingly, it may also be possible that distress/CRAR can be commenced by a head landlord against a subtenant even where a petition has been presented against the subtenant itself (following service of a notice under Law of Distress Amendment Act 1908, s 6 or TCEA 2007, s 81). This is because a notice served under s 6 does not make a head landlord a *legal* creditor of the subtenant (*Re Lundy Granite Co, ex p Heaven* (1871) 6 Ch App 462, CA). The head landlord has no right to prove in the liquidation of the subtenant. A s 6 notice operates to transfer to the head landlord the right to receive and provide good receipt for the subrents (see **5.63**). Even an offer by the liquidator of the subtenant to allow the head landlord to prove for the rent does not deprive the landlord of the right to levy distress (*Re Regent United Service Stores Ltd* (1878) LR 8 Ch D 616, CA).

- In *Re Carriage Co-operative Supply Association, ex p Clemmence* (1883) 23 Ch D 154: a company took an underlease of property. Rent was due to the head landlord – the company gave a promissory note for the amount due (the court decided on the evidence that the head landlord had not accepted the company as tenant but agreed to accept the promissory note as collateral security). The rule in previous cases had been that, if the landlord is a stranger to the company, he could distrain after commencement of winding up, but if he had a right to prove for rent in the winding up he could not. Fry J held, where the landlord had a right of proof upon a collateral security, he would also be allowed a right of distress against the goods of a third person (the company, who were strangers to him). This allows a landlord to levy distress against a subtenant.

- Where distress begins prior to the petition (see below).

- In *Re New City Constitutional Club Co, ex p Purssell* (1887) 34 Ch D 646, CA execution was allowed to continue where the goods were the subject of a debenture and there was negative equity (so that the debenture holder was owed more under the charge than the goods charged were worth). The landlord is allowed to distrain where the goods are mortgaged for a debt more than their value, but only where it can be shown that the liquidator has no interest in the assets (*Re South Rhondda Colliery Co (1898) Ltd* [1928] WN 126).

- The right to levy distress/CRAR may be reactivated for arrears falling due between the presentation of a winding-up petition and the winding-up order pursuant to an application for the court's permission under IA 1986, s 130(2). It is probable that an application under s 130(2) could be made to validate a distress/CRAR commenced in between petition and order which would otherwise be rendered void by s 128. These principles predate the IA 1986 (see *Re Coal Consumers' Association* (1876) 4 Ch D 625).

Where distress/CRAR is commenced after winding-up order

3.46   Following the making of a winding-up order IA 1986, s 130(3) provides:

'... no action or proceeding shall be proceeded with or commenced against the company or its property, except by leave of the court and subject to any terms the as the court may impose.'

A comparable provision applies when a provisional liquidator has been appointed under s 130(2).

3.47   In *Re Memco Engineering Ltd* [1986] Ch 86 Davies J held that *distress* was an 'action or proceeding'. This was a surprising decision given that no court process is involved. The decision was later placed in a contradictory light by *McMullen & Sons Ltd v Cerrone* [1993] BCC 25 which decided that in relation to the original IVA interim order moratorium the word 'proceedings' did not include distress (as a consequence the Insolvency Act 2000 amended IA 1985, s 252 to include an express reference to *distress* but see **3.32**). However, the decision in *Re Memco* followed the House of Lords decision in *Herbert Berry Associates Ltd v IRC* [1978] 1 All ER 161, HL and has not been subsequently challenged.

3.48   If there is any residual doubt as to whether IA 1986, s 130(2) would restrict distress then the argument for landlords may be further weakened by the fact that the CRAR process is to be unified with court execution. It may be seen to be inconsistent if s 130 would effectively prevent court-based *taking control of goods* and not CRAR-based *taking control of goods* (both governed by TCEA 2007, Sch 12). However, one important distinction will still remain, CRAR like distress will not be commenced with a court application. Court-based *taking control of goods* is to be commenced by means of a county court warrant of control or a High court writ of control (under TCEA 2007, s 62). The position should also be contrasted with the moratorium which arises in relation to VAs (see IA 1986, s 252 and Sch A1, para 12 and **3.35**).

3.49   A creditor potentially has the right under IA 1986, s 130 to make an application to the court to allow the distress/CRAR to continue. As discussed above if the distress had been commenced prior to the petition such an application has a strong chance of success. However, where the distress has not been commenced the starting point is that commercial landlords and other judgment creditors do not have priority as creditors and rank *pari passu* with other unsecured creditors. In the case of *Re Caribbean Products (YAM) Importers Ltd* [1966] Ch 331, CA it was thought that an application maybe worthwhile where enforcement has been delayed by undue influence or misrepresentation by the debtor (also see *Re Redmon (Builders) Ltd* [1964] 1 All ER 851).

3.50　*Where the liquidator is using the demised premises for the purpose of the liquidation*: Liquidators may decide that the tenant (in liquidation) will retain occupation of the demised premises to facilitate a sale of a business or an asset sale. In one way a landlord is a creditor and supplier. Where the liquidator retains the property, the landlord is in a position of being forced to continue to supply the property. Other creditor suppliers usually have the right to cease supply. It is not so easy for landlords because the right to forfeit is restricted. If the lease is not disclaimed by the liquidator and the property is retained for the benefit of the liquidation then the landlord has an argument that the ongoing rent should be paid as an expense of the liquidation under the IR 1986, r 4.218 (see the discussion about liquidation expenses at **2.64**). If there is a dispute about this then the landlord has the right to ask the court to allow distress/CRAR to be levied (for forfeiture, see **4.112**). The prospects of a successful application would depend on the following factors:

- If rent fell due prior to the date of the winding-up petition then the court would generally not give permission to levy distress/CRAR. To do so, would put the landlord in a better position than ordinary creditors. In a similar way, the court is unlikely to give permission for any creditor to enforce the debts fallen due prior to the date of the winding-up petition.

- An application for permission will only be successful to allow distress/CRAR in relation to unpaid debts which have been incurred during the period of the liquidation (from the date of the petition onwards). If rent arrears (or other liabilities) are incurred during the period of a liquidation, the creditor may have a reasonable argument that permission should be given. This is on the basis that a liquidator should pay rent if he has use of the premises (*Re Linda Marie Ltd* [1989] BCLC 46, *Exeter City Council v Bairstow* [2007] BCC 236 and *Re Toshoku Finance UK plc* [2002] 1 WLR 671).

- As a consequence of this, where the liquidator is making use of the premises (eg before a sale of the business together with the assignment of the lease as a going concern) then often a liquidator will reach agreement with a landlord that the ongoing rents for the period of occupation will be paid as an expense of the liquidation (see **2.76**).

Voluntary liquidation

3.51　If a tenant is in voluntary liquidation there is no automatic restriction upon a landlord's right to levy distress or to take enforcement action. The position will be the same under TCEA 2007 in relation to taking control of goods under Sch 12 and exercising CRAR. If there is a voluntary liquidation, landlords will not require the permission of the court to exercise CRAR.

However, a liquidator may apply to the court and request that the restrictions which apply to enforcement in compulsory liquidation be applied to voluntary liquidation. This application will be made under IA 1986, s 112 (ie an application for a direction).

3.52 However, in the absence of such an application in a voluntary liquidation there is no provision which makes enforcement (whether execution or distress) void if it is commenced after the liquidation started. However, the provisions of IA 1986, ss 183 and 184 do not currently apply to distress and are unlikely to apply to CRAR (see *Re Modern Jet Support Centre Ltd* [2006] BCC 174 and **3.40**). IA 1986, s 176 (distress/CRAR) does apply to a voluntary winding-up.

3.53 The question then arises as to when a liquidator will be able to successfully apply for a stay of a distress.

*   Where the distress is commenced prior to the commencement of the liquidation the liquidator may not be granted a stay. CRAR is to be preceded by a warning notice under TCEA 2007, Sch 12, para 7 which has the effect of binding the tenant's goods under Sch 12, para 4. Arguably, if this binding takes effect prior to the commencement of the winding-up the landlord will be able to resist the stay.

*   Where the distress relates to pre-liquidation rent and is commenced after the liquidation then the liquidator will be in a stronger position. In relation to CRAR the liquidator will be able to combine an application under IA 1986, s 112 with an application under TCEA 2007, s 78 for an order setting aside a CRAR notice under Sch 12, para 7 (also see *Re Margot Bywaters Ltd* [1942] Ch 121).

*   Where the landlord has an argument that the post-liquidation rents should be paid as an expense under IR 1986, r 4.218 (see **2.64**) then if the liquidator fails to give adequate assurance that the rents will be paid he is unlikely to be granted a stay or order restraining distress/CRAR.

It should be noted that a failure to refer to there being a distraint/CRAR in place in the landlord's proof of debt is likely to be treated as an abandonment of such action pursuant to IR 1986, r 4.96 (and see *LCP Retail v Segal* [2006] EWHC 2087(Ch)).

Administration

3.54 When the debtor is a company in administration then all enforcement is subject to a detailed and comprehensive moratorium (IA 1986, Sch B1, paras 42, 43 and 44). The moratorium provisions were redrafted by the Enterprise Act 2002 which came into force in September 2003 to affect all new administrations. All forms of enforcement are bound by the moratorium which does not render the enforcement void but merely prevents the enforcement continuing (or being commenced if it has not yet started) during the currency of the administration period.

Effect of moratorium

3.55 Under IA 1986, Sch B1, para 43 no enforcement action over a debt can be commenced or continued (including distress/CRAR) without:

- the consent of the administrator; or

- the permission of the court.

If enforcement is commenced prior to the administration then there is no reason why the enforcement cannot be reactivated after the administration comes to an end (see below). This might depend on the exit route for administration. If the company enters into a VA then the debt subject to the enforcement may be compromised (see **3.30**).

When will the court's permission be granted?

3.56 In *Re Atlantic Computer Systems plc* [1992] 1 All ER 476, Nicholls LJ giving the lead judgment in the Court of Appeal set out a number of guidelines as to when enforcement in relation to fixed-term contracts (such as for leases of equipment and plant) should be allowed. Nicholls LJ ruled that in deciding whether or not to give permission the court should carry out a balancing act taking into account the following factors:

- the creditor has the initial burden and must make out the case for permission to be given;

- the debtor company's financial position, its ability to pay ongoing rent;

- the administrator's proposals – including whether ongoing debts such as accruing rent will be paid as an expense of the administration;

- the effect on the administration if permission were given (following the introduction of the changes made by the Enterprise Act 2002 this effect should be measured against the administrator's ability to achieve one of the three hierarchical statutory objectives laid down by IA 1986, Sch B1, para 3(1));

- the effect on the debtor and creditor (landlord) if permission were refused;

- the prospect of a successful outcome in the administration if permission is refused;

- the conduct of the parties.

The status of the distress if no application to continue the distress is made

3.57 Landlords will often decide that there is little immediate prospect of a successful application under IA 1986, Sch B1, para 43 to continue with the distress. If no application is made then an interesting and important question arises. A landlord could make it clear that he has not abandoned the distress and insist that it remains intact in the background whilst the administration takes its course. He is not able to continue the distress whilst the para 43 moratorium is in effect, but when the administration comes to an end and the moratorium is terminated, would the distress still be there?

3.58 There is an argument that the distress has preserved the landlord's rights as a quasi form of security (which exists but cannot be continued until the administration comes to an end). In practice this is a low cost argument that is increasingly run by landlords and is sometimes known as the Lazarus principle. However, there is virtually no judicial guidance on this point even though it is a frequently encountered problem which can make a substantial difference to a landlord's position.

3.59 Originally bailiffs had no power of sale and therefore a distress was completed when the goods were impounded. In modern distress there are four stages: entry; seizure; impounding; and sale. Distress is not therefore completed until a sale. The moratorium under IA 1986, Sch B1, para 43 typically affects the distress after impounding (including where a walking possession agreement has been taken). Although the distress cannot be *continued* this does not necessarily mean that impounded goods are released. An insolvency moratorium does not expressly terminate the distress. The distrained assets are not available for distribution or sale by the officeholder (see the two liquidation cases by analogy *Re Modern Jet Support Centre Ltd* [2006] BCC 174 and *Herbert Berry Associates Ltd v IRC* [1978] 1 All ER 161, HL).

3.60 No doubt the argument on this point will have to take into account the following factors:

- If the frozen distress still exists then the administrator might not be able to dispose of the assets which are subject to the distress. An administrator cannot take any action which 'affects the right of a secured creditor of the company to enforce his security' although it is unlikely that impounded goods would fall within this category (IA 1986, Sch B1, para 73). It is unclear whether the administrator could make an application under IA 1986, Sch B1, para 73 to sell the assets as if they were not subject to the distress.

- When CRAR comes into force an application could be made by the administrator to terminate the distress under TCEA 2007, s 78.

- If the administrator proposes an exit through a CVA then the right of the landlord in relation to the security cannot be compromised (IA 1986, s 4(3)) although the underlying debt can be compromised which will affect the amount the proprietary right attaches to in value (see *Thomas v Ken Thomas Ltd* [2006] EWCA Civ 1504). The distress/CRAR may remain intact and the value which is free from security may therefore increase.

- If the administration is followed by a CVL then as the distress was commenced prior to the liquidation the landlord may be successfully able to continue the process (see **3.51**).

Bankruptcy

3.61 Surprisingly, the presentation of the bankruptcy petition does not act as an automatic moratorium on enforcement. In fact IA 1986, s 347(9) preserves the landlord's right to levy distress for rent.

3.62 The right to levy distress remains intact in the face of the following provisions:

- Under IA 1986, s 285:

    '(1) At any time when proceedings on a bankruptcy petition are pending or an individual has been ajudged bankrupt, the Courts may stay any action, execution or other legal process against property or person of the debtor or as the case may be of the bankrupt.

    (2) Any Court in which proceedings are pending against any individual may on proof that a bankruptcy petition has been presented in respect of that individual or that he is an undischarged bankrupt either stay the proceedings or allow them to continue on such terms as it thinks fit.'

- A limited moratorium is created by IA 1986, s 285 once the bankruptcy order is made:

    'After the making of a bankruptcy order no person who is a creditor of the bankrupt in respect of a debt provable in the bankruptcy shall–
    (a)   have any remedy against the property or person of the bankrupt in respect of that debt, or
    (b)   before the discharge of the bankrupt, commence any action or other legal proceedings against the bankrupt except with the leave of the Court and under such terms as the Court may impose.'

3.63 Surprisingly, distress has been held not to be a legal process for the purpose of these provisions (but see *Smith v Braintree District Council* [1990] 2 AC 215, HL). CRAR may be distinguished and be brought within these provisions (or other restrictions) on the following bases:

- CRAR can only be used against the assets of the tenant (under TCEA 2007, s 72) providing the tenant is also the 'debtor' (under TCEA 2007, Sch 12, para 1).

- When the tenant becomes bankrupt the title to his assets (including goods on the demised premises) automatically vests in his trustee in bankruptcy pursuant to IA 1986, s 306. The tenant's lease will also automatically vest in the trustee but the trustee does not become liable for the arrears. The trustee may become the 'tenant' under TCEA 2007, s 72 but is not liable to pay rents which fell due prior to the date of the automatic transfer as he will fail to qualify as the 'debtor' under the definition in TCEA 2007, Sch 12, para 1. CRAR can only be used to take control of goods if they are goods of the 'debtor'.

- It is therefore difficult to see how CRAR can be used without an application for permission under IA 1986, s 285 and even then with difficulty. The unification of the CRAR process with court-based execution under TCEA 2007 is likely to bring it within the definition in IA 1986, s 285 in any event.

- However, the word 'distress' in IA 1986, s 347(9) will be extended by TCEA 2007 to include CRAR and therefore the express reservation will include the right to exercise CRAR (TCEA 2007, Sch 13, para 85 inserts a new definition for *distress* into IA 1986, s 436).

- Contrary to the above if the regulations to TCEA 2007 make it possible to use CRAR then an application could be made for an order freezing the CRAR process under TCEA 2007, s 78.

- If CRAR is treated in an identical way to execution then after a bankruptcy order the enforcement agent will have to account to the trustee in bankruptcy for the proceeds of sale (once costs have been deducted) under IA 1986, s 346. However, the court has the discretion to allow the claimant to retain the benefit of the enforcement (IA 1986, s 346(6)).

Bankruptcy restrictions which apply to both distress and CRAR

3.64 IA 1986, s 347(9) expressly preserves the right to distrain (or use CRAR) against property comprised in the bankrupt's estate notwithstanding that the bankrupt's assets automatically vest in the trustees (but see above in relation to CRAR).

3.65 The right to levy distress (or use CRAR) is restricted by IA 1986, s 347(1). This provides that the landlord's right to distrain (or exercise CRAR) upon the goods and effects of an undischarged bankrupt is limited to a maximum of 6 months' rent accrued due before the commencement of the bankruptcy. If the landlord has distrained after presentation of the bankruptcy petition but before the bankruptcy order and an order is subsequently made any sum recovered in excess of 6 months' rent is to be held for the bankrupt or his estate (IA 1986, s 347(2)). This restriction relates only to the 6-month period ending with the date that the bankruptcy petition that has been presented to the court. Accordingly, if the tenancy continues (and the trustee in bankruptcy effectively retains possession of the premises) then distress can still be levied.

Distress and CRAR v execution

3.66 Under the pre-TCEA 2007 regime, where a debtor's goods are taken in execution by an enforcement agent, they cannot be removed from the premises unless the execution creditor pays the landlord any rent arrears up to a maximum of one year (Landlord and Tenant Act 1709, s 1 and County Courts Act 1984, s 102). IA 1986, s 347(6) limits this right to 6 months where the tenant is bankrupt. These provisions have been abolished by TCEA 2007 and landlords will lose this advantage when CRAR comes into force.

Chapter 4

FORFEITURE (AND POSSESSION)

4.1 This chapter deals with circumstances where the tenant is insolvent and the landlord wishes to recover possession of a property. Insolvency is often a contractual ground for prematurely terminating a tenancy creating a contractual right to forfeit. However, the contractual tenancy can be brought to an end in a number of ways, including surrender, merger, effluxion of time, service of a notice to quit (for periodic tenancies), disclaimer (see chapter 7), frustration, rescission and so on. If the contractual tenancy has been brought to an end the landlord has a prima facie right to recover possession. This right is often restricted by statute and common law, with different regimes applying to different forms of tenancy (the main distinction resting between residential and commercial premises).

4.2 Before deciding to take an active step to repossess the landlord must establish whether the termination of the contractual right to occupy also gives the right to repossess. In addition to the consideration of the relevant insolvency restrictions, the landlord should first establish whether in principle he is able to repossess (the expressions forfeiture/re-entry/repossession are interchangeable in this context).

OVERVIEW

4.3 Landlords requiring possession from an insolvent occupier should carry out the following analysis (in this order):

(1) establish the status of the occupier – tenant or licensee;

(2) establish how to terminate the contractual/common law tenancy;

(3) establish whether the tenant has any statutory right to remain in occupation after the contract has been determined;

(4) establish the steps which must be satisfied under the relevant statute in order to end the statutory tenancy and obtain possession;

(5) establish whether the tenant has any additional statutory rights as a consequence of insolvency;

(6) establish the likelihood (if any) of an application for relief from forfeiture.

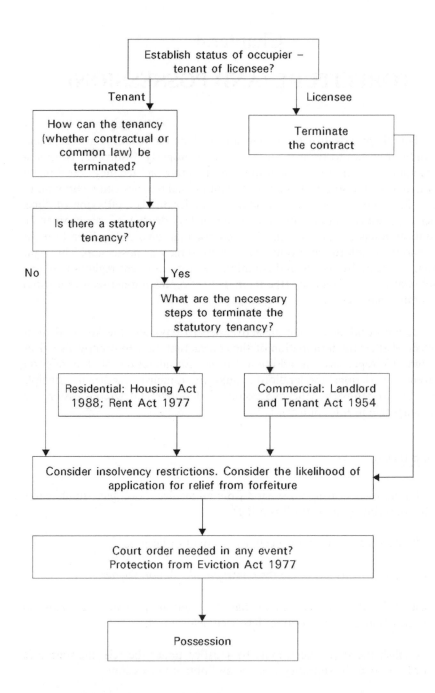

THE STATUS OF THE TENANT

4.4 Where someone other than the freeholder occupies property, the occupier will be one of the following:

- a leaseholder/tenant;

- a licensee;

- a trespasser; or

- a trespasser who has acquired rights over the freehold (or an intermediate landlord's reversion) by way of adverse possession.

4.5 Licensees do not have as much protection as most tenants. There is limited statutory intervention or regulation for a *licence* (however the Protection from Eviction Act 1977 ensures that most residential licensees are, at least, entitled to be warned of their rights and not to be evicted without court process). In contrast, statute intervenes and allows many forms of *tenancy* to continue where the contractual term has come to an end. For this reason landlords are often keen to describe a right of occupation as a *licence*, hoping to avoid the protection afforded to commercial tenants (under the Landlord and Tenant Act 1954) and residential tenants (under the Rent Acts 1977 and the Housing Act 1988), or alternatively ensure that the tenancy that is contracted out of these statutory provisions (if possible).

4.6 In *Street v Mountford* [1985] AC 809 the House of Lords created a framework to determine whether an occupier is a tenant or licensee. The House of Lords decided that if an occupier has *exclusive possession* and if, in addition, the occupier is contractually obliged to pay for the occupation, the result will be a tenancy. If the landlord/property owner can be shown to have intended to grant exclusive possession then it will be a lease as opposed to a licence.

4.7 On this basis, the court will look beyond the label put on an occupation agreement and review its true nature. This was neatly summed up by Lord Templeman in *Street v Mountford* who stated:

> 'The manufacture of the five pronged instrument for manual digging results in a fork even if the manufacturer unfamiliar with the English language insists that he intended to make, and has made, a spade.'

4.8 It does not matter that an occupation agreement is given the title 'licence'. If the intention was to grant exclusive possession for a fixed (or periodic) term on basic terms of payment of rent then the arrangement will be a lease/tenancy (the expression lessee/leaseholder/tenant are in reality interchangeable). However, where the landlord and tenant have taken legal advice and are on equal bargaining terms then the fact that they have agreed a right of occupation should not create a tenancy and should be respected. In these circumstances the parties' agreement to create a licence is likely to prevail (*Scottish Widows plc v Stewart* [2006] EWCA Civ 999). The intention of the House of Lords was to protect unwitting tenants from being deprived of their statutory rights. In *Street v Mountford*, Lord Templeman warned that the courts must be:

'Astute to detect and frustrate sham devices and artificial transactions whose only object is to disguise the grant of a tenancy and to evade the Rent Acts.'

4.9 Ultimately, the licence/tenancy question must depend on the circumstances of each case. However, Lord Templeman made it clear that the circumstances should focus on a true construction of the agreement and not necessarily the intention of the parties.

4.10 There are other exceptions to the principle that where there is exclusive possession then there is a tenancy. These exceptions include where there is a service occupancy (*Norris v Checksfield* [1991] 23 HLR 425, CA), where there is no intention to create legal relations such as a family arrangement (*Heslop v Burns* [1974] 3 All ER 406) and where there is no power to grant a tenancy (*Bruton v London Quadrant Housing Trust* [1997] EG 125 CS, CA).

STATUS OF SUBLICENCE TO OCCUPY GRANTED BY AN ADMINISTRATOR OR LIQUIDATOR

4.11 There are occasions where an administrator or liquidator of an insolvent tenant company will allow a purchaser of the tenant's business to occupy the demised premises pending the resolution of negotiations with the landlord for an assignment of the lease. Such arrangements are common but controversial. Officeholders have sometimes arranged a quick sale for sound commercial reasons (typically known as a 'pre-pack'). Landlords and other creditors are sometimes suspicious of the speed of such arrangements particularly where there is a connection between the insolvent company and the management and ownership of the proposed purchaser (a 'phoenix company'). Proceeding in this way by granting a licence to a phoenix company raises a number of difficulties for officeholders:

- If the occupier is granted possession this is likely to be a breach of the alienation provisions of the lease (unless the landlord's consent is obtained) on the basis that it constitutes *parting with possession* or *sharing possession*. This is this case even where the arrangement is a temporary one.

- If the occupier has exclusive possession this may lead to the grant of a tenancy and the tenancy may have the protection of Part II of the Landlord and Tenant Act 1954.

- An administrator/liquidator should not commit a wilful breach of a negative covenant (such as parting with or sharing possession without consent). In some cases this may amount to misfeasance on the basis that it is a breach of duty under IA 1986, Sch B1, para 75(3)(c). The administrator could be held to be liable to *contribute a sum to the company's property by way of compensation for breach of duty*. A landlord could also make an application under para 74 to challenge the conduct of the administrators. The risks associated with this practice were the subject of *Metro Nominees (Wandsworth) (No 1) v K Rayment* [2008] BCC 40. In this case the landlord applied for permission to bring forfeiture proceedings under para 43. The administrator had allowed a purchaser of a tenant's business to take possession of the demised premises without obtaining the landlord's consent. The landlord's application for permission succeeded and Norris J noted the comments of Neuberger LJ in *Akici v LR Butlin Ltd* [2006] 1 WLR 201, CA:

> 'The court should not be too indulgent to a lessee, especially one who is not honest with his lessors.'

- However, the court will also take into account the full circumstances of an administration even where a pre-packaged sale proceeds by an administrator allowing a purchaser of the insolvent tenant's business into occupation pending the acquisition of licence to assign from the landlord (see **8.25**). The court may permit an administrator to repudiate or breach the terms of the lease, particularly where it does not cause the landlord any additional loss. The court is able to carry out the balancing exercise set out in *Re Atlantic Computer Systems plc* [1992] Ch 505, CA. This was made clear by the Court of Appeal in *Innovate Logistics Ltd v Sunberry Properties Ltd* [2008] EWCA Civ 1261, see also **8.26**.

4.12 In order to limit the potential difficulty the way forward for administrators and liquidators is to take the following precautionary steps:

- If early possession is to be granted to a purchaser then it should be by way of an express licence (following *Scottish Widows plc v Stewart* [2006] EWCA Civ 999) making the terms and circumstance of the licence clear and fully negotiated.

- Without prejudice to this label consideration should be given as to whether the licence should be made terminable as a *tenancy at will* to avoid any argument that security of tenure has been granted (ie to cover both alternatives in one document).

- If it is made clear that the licence has been granted to facilitate the negotiations with the landlord for consent to assign then the occupier is unlikely to acquire security of tenure (see *Javad v Aqil* [1991] 1 All ER 243 and *Cardiothoracic Institute v Shrewdcrest Ltd* [1986] 3 All ER 633).

- If required by the lease the officeholder should obtain the landlord's consent to the *parting with or sharing possession* in accordance with the terms of the lease, even where the risk of inadvertently granting security of tenure has been reduced as a consequence of taking the above steps.

- In any event if the landlord requests confirmation as to the identity of the occupier the officeholder should provide this information (*Metro Nominees (Wandsworth) (No 1) v K Rayment* [2008] BCC 40).

4.13 The distinction between parting with possession and sharing possession was the subject of *Akici v LR Butlin Ltd* [2006] 1 WLR 201; Neuberger LJ held in the Court of Appeal that breaching a covenant not to part with possession (eg granting a subtenancy) is different to a breach of a covenant not to share possession. The former was not capable of remedy whilst sharing possession denoted a licence arrangement which could be undone and the breach remedied. Therefore any steps taken by the landlord had to reflect the reality of the occupation that had been allowed by the administrator (see **4.67** in relation to s 146 notices). Importantly Neuberger LJ made it clear that the tenant/administrator/liquidator must not conceal the fact that possession/occupation had been given up.

TERMINATION OF THE CONTRACTUAL INTEREST AND COMMON LAW RIGHT TO OCCUPY

4.14 Following on from determining the status of the occupier the next question is how to terminate the contractual interest and this will depend on whether the occupation is a licence or a tenancy.

Termination of licence

4.15 If the occupation is a licence then the licensor can bring the agreement to an end in accordance with the terms of the licence (or if the licence is silent on the issue, by giving reasonable notice; see *Hurst v Picture Theatres Ltd* [1915] 1 KB 1 at 481). It used to be thought that if a licensor terminated a licence in breach of contract then the only remedy for the licensee was an action for damages and not reinstatement (if the licence is gratuitous then the licensee would not even be able to claim damages). The licensee had no proprietary interest and no security of tenure. In a number of post-war cases this position has been qualified so as to give the licensee a degree of security. A licensee can apply for an injunction to restrain the licensor from threatening to terminate (where there is no contractual right to do so, eg see the judgment of Lord Denning in *Tanner v Tanner* [1975] 3 All ER 776 at 780 and *Chandler v Kerley* [1978] 2 All ER 942, CA) or by an application for specific performance to restore a dispossessed licensee to possession (see *Verrall v Great Yarmouth Borough Council* [1980] 1 All ER 839 where Lord Denning controversially ordered a newly elected Labour council to honour a licence granted by the previous Conservative administration for the hiring of the Pier Pavilion in Great Yarmouth for a National Front conference).

4.16 Therefore during the term of the licence the licensee is able to enforce the terms of the licence. However, there is no right in common law or statute to continue a licence once it has come to an end under its own terms (against the wishes of the licensor).

Residential licence

4.17 A licence agreement may be for a fixed term or on a periodic basis. Where it is periodic there may be an express provision compelling the licensor to provide a specified notice period to terminate. Where there is a periodic licence to occupy premises as a dwelling then the licensor may have to comply with the Protection from Eviction Act 1977, s 5(1A). If the licence qualifies for protection then the licensor is required to serve a notice to quit containing prescribed information and provide a minimum of 4 weeks' notice. If this provision is breached the notice will be invalid and the licence will continue until the Act is complied with. This provision applies to the circumstances where a bankrupt is permitted to remain living in his home after a bankruptcy order has been made. Where the bankrupt had owned the property the bankruptcy order has the effect of automatically transferring the legal title to the trustee in bankruptcy under IA 1986, s 306 (also see chapter 18).

Termination of tenancy on a contractual basis

4.18 A contractual tenancy comes to an end in one of the following ways:

- when there is a fixed-term tenancy which has expired by effluxion of time and isn't renewed;

- where a periodic tenancy (oral or in writing) is terminated by the service of a notice to quit which expires;

- where the landlord has the right to bring the contractual tenancy to an end prematurely as a consequence of the tenant's breach (forfeiture – see **4.47** et seq);

- where the landlord or tenant have the right to bring the tenancy to an end prematurely by the service of an option to determine ('break notice');

- where the landlord and tenant agree a surrender of the tenancy;

- where a liquidator or trustee in bankruptcy disclaims the lease pursuant to IA 1986, s 178;

- where the lease has been *frustrated* (see *National Carriers Ltd v Panalpina (Northern) Ltd* [1981] AC 675);

- where the tenant prejudices the landlord's title (sometimes called *denial of landlord's title* see *Abidogun v Frolan Health Care Ltd* [2001] L&TR 16); and

- where there is a right to rescind as a consequence of misrepresentation (innocent or fraudulent), mistake or as a breach of condition.

4.19 The question of statutory continuation does not arise unless the contractual/common law tenancy has been brought to an end. Where there is no statutory continuation the termination of the contract will create an immediate right to possession (although where the tenant is insolvent permission may be required to exercise the right – see below).

4.20 Under the Protection from Eviction Act 1977, s 5(1) no notice to quit is valid (where the premises have been *let as a dwelling* on a periodic basis) unless at least 4 weeks' notice is given and the notice contains prescribed information.

4.21 Forfeiture is dealt with at **4.47** et seq.

STATUTORY PROTECTION

4.22 The determination of the common law 'contractual tenancy' may not be sufficient to allow a landlord to have the right to repossess the premises. A substantial number of tenants have statutory protection. The nature of this protection depends on whether it is a residential or commercial or agricultural property.

Which statutory code applies?

4.23 The following questions need to be considered:

(1) *Is the property used for business purposes?*
    If so, then regulated by the Landlord and Tenant act 1954.

(2) *Is the property used for residential purposes?*
    If so:
    (a) *Is there a public sector landlord?*
        If so, then regulated by the Housing Act 1985.
    (b) *Is there a private sector landlord?*
        If so, when was the tenancy granted?
        (i) If granted before 15 January 1989 then regulated by the Rent Act 1977.
        (ii) If granted after that date then regulated by the Housing Act 1988.
        If Housing Act 1988 applies is the tenancy assured or assured shorthold?

(i)   If tenancy granted before 28 February 1997 then s 20 shorthold notice requirements in the original Housing Act 1988 apply.

(ii) If granted after 28 February 1997 then the shorthold regime introduced by the Housing Act 1996 applies.

Business tenancies

4.24 Most business tenancies have statutory protection under Part II of the Landlord and Tenant Act 1954. Protected business tenants generally have the right to apply to the court to have their tenancies renewed and the potential right to recover compensation if their application is refused (on a non-fault ground under s 30(1) see below).

Conditions for protection

4.25 In deciding whether a tenancy is protected by the Act there are important conditions, all of which must be satisfied.

(1)   The tenant must occupy the premises for the purposes of his business (including where an associate company of the tenant is in occupation or the tenancy is held on trust for a beneficiary who occupies for the purpose of the business – see the Landlord and Tenant Act 1954, s 41). The tenant's use of the premises must be permitted under the terms of the tenancy or, if prohibited under the terms of the lease, the default has been waived by the landlord.

(2)   The tenancy must not fall within the specific exclusions of the Landlord and Tenant Act 1954 as follows:
(a)   a tenancy of less than 6 months;
(b)   a mining lease;
(c)   an agricultural holding;
(d)   an employee's right to occupy granted in consequences of and determinable on the end of the employment;
(e)   in licensed premises;
(f)   where the landlord is a government department or local authority and has been given a certificate excluding the tenancy on grounds of public interest (this includes other statutory undertakers);
(g)   a tenancy contracted out of the Landlord and Tenant Act 1954 pursuant to s 38.

(3)   If the premises are used for part-residential and part-business purposes then the property will not be protected by the residential statutes because it would not be a separate dwelling house (therefore the Rent Act 1977 or the Housing Act 1988 will not apply). Accordingly, where there is a flat above a shop let under one tenancy it will be treated as commercial premises and covered by the Landlord and Tenant Act 1954. In relation to mixed use premises, Lord Denning set out four different categories in the case of *Cheryl Investments v Saldanha* [1979] 1 All ER 5:

(a) *Where a businessman who has two premises, an office where he works and a flat.* The office would be a business tenancy (protected by the Landlord and Tenant Act 1954) and the flat would be a residential tenancy (at the time protected by the Rent Act 1977 (now a modern tenancy would be covered by the Housing Act 1988 in these circumstances)).

(b) *Where a business man takes a tenancy in one house with the intention of carrying on his profession in one room (ie operating a clinic).* The tenancy will be a business tenancy pursuant to the Landlord and Tenancy Act 1954.

(c) *Where someone enjoys a residential protected tenancy but subsequently starts to carry out a business activity at home.* In this case he ceases to have a protected residential tenancy; he only has a business tenancy.

(d) *Where someone has a mixed-use premises but decides to give up the business use at home.* He does not get a regulated or assured tenancy of his original home, even though he occupies it now only as his home because it was never let to him as a separate dwelling unless the landlord agrees to the change.

Security of tenure

4.26 Where a business tenancy is protected by the Landlord and Tenant Act 1954 then it continues automatically unless brought to an end by one of the methods allowed by the Act (under ss 24–28). A tenancy that would have come to an end under its contractual terms (eg a fixed term expires by effluxion of time) will continue under the provisions of the Act.

Cesser of business use

4.27 If the tenant ceases occupying the premises for business purposes *prior to the expiry of the fixed term* then the tenancy will come to an end on the term date (this is because a tenant is no longer occupying the premises for business purposes and the protection falls way – see the Landlord and Tenant Act 1954, s 27 and *Esselte AB v Pearl Assurance plc* [1995] 2 EGLR 61). However, if the tenant remains in occupation for business purposes *after the expiry of the fixed term* and then subsequently ceases occupation the tenancy will continue to be protected. Colyer J in *Esselte* stated:

'Once a tenancy has been a business tenancy [regulated by the Landlord and Tenant Act 1954] mere cessation of business user will not prevent the tenancy continuing . . .'

4.28 The automatic statutory continuation of a business tenancy can only be brought to an end in one of the ways allowed by the Landlord and Tenant Act 1954. This includes three common law methods (as exceptions to the Landlord and Tenant Act 1954 – see first three points below) and five statutory methods.

- Forfeiture: the right to bring the tenancy to an end on the basis of the tenant's default is preserved by s 24(2). This does not create a stand alone right to forfeit. The landlord can only forfeit in accordance with the forfeiture provisions in the lease (see **4.51**).

- Notice to quit given by the tenant (not the landlord): where there is no fixed term and the tenancy is periodic, provided that the tenant cannot serve a notice until he has been in occupation for a month (s 24(2)(a)).

- Surrender: provided it is not executed until the tenant has been in occupation for a month (s 24(2)(b)).

- Where the landlord serves a s 25 notice to terminate the tenancy (subject to the tenant's right to make an application for a new business tenancy under s 29).

- Where the tenant has made a request for a new tenancy in accordance with s 26 (once again the tenant retains the right to apply for a new tenancy under s 29).

- Where the tenant serves a notice to terminate the tenancy under s 27 (either before, ie a s 27(1) notice, or after, ie a s 27(2) notice, the fixed term has expired).

- Where the tenant vacates the premises prior to the end of a fixed term where no notice is required (s 27, see **4.27**).

- Where the landlord and tenant agree terms of a new lease under s 28.

Business tenant's right to apply for a new tenancy

4.29 The landlord can terminate the current tenancy by serving a notice pursuant to the Landlord and Tenant Act 1954, s 25. Following the service of the s 25 notice the tenant has the right to apply to the court for a new tenancy. The s 25 notice must give a minimum of 6 months' and a maximum of 12 months' notice and this cannot expire prior to the expiry of the current contractual term. If no application is made then the tenancy expires when the notice expires (unless the period is extended by agreement in writing under s 29B). The tenant can commence the process by serving a s 26 notice. If no notices are served and the tenant remains in occupation then the tenancy continues under s 24 on its existing terms. The landlord can seek to resist this application on one of the statutory grounds set out in the Landlord and Tenant Act 1954, s 30(1). These grounds are:

- partly based on the tenant's poor conduct (ie dilapidations under s 30(1)(a), persistent delay in paying rent under (b) and other substantial breach of covenant under (c));

- partly based on non-fault (eg suitable alternative accommodation under (d), where it is more economical for the landlord to relet a subdivided property as a whole under (e), where the landlord intends to demolish or reconstruct the premises under (f) and where the landlord intends to occupy the property for the purposes of his own business under (g)); and

- for non-fault grounds the tenant is entitled to claim statutory compensation under s 37 which amounts to a sum equivalent to the rateable value of the *holding* or twice the rateable value if the tenant has occupied the holding for a period of 14 years or more (s 31).

4.30 Should the landlord be unable to make out one of statutory grounds of opposition, the tenant will be able to successfully use the procedure in the Landlord and Tenant Act 1954 to obtain a new lease. The terms of the new lease generally follow the terms of the old lease save for rent (which is set at the market rate and in the absence of agreement is valued by the court pursuant to the assumptions and disregards set out in s 34) and term (see *O'May v City of London Real Property Co Ltd* [1982] 1 All ER 660, HL). The new tenancy will commence on an agreed date or if the matter is determined by the court then the old tenancy will determine (and if granted the new tenancy will commence) 3 months after the date that the application is finally disposed of (s 64(1)). This final disposal may be the conclusion of the court case (including any appeal) or it may be brought about by the withdrawal of the tenant's application (in which case the tenant is likely to be liable to pay the landlord's costs pursuant to CPR, r 38.6).

Assignment of statutory business tenancy

4.31 As we have seen, the Landlord and Tenant Act 1954 has the effect of continuing the tenancy after the contractual term would have ended. This is unlike a protected statutory residential tenancy under the Rent Act 1977 where there is no *continuation* as such. The Rent Act 1977 creates a new tenancy when the contractual tenancy comes to an end and this represents a personal right for the tenant to claim a new tenancy and therefore cannot be assigned (although the tenant's spouse can acquire the right to his/her own statutory tenancy when the other dies by way of succession, see **4.34**). A Landlord and Tenant Act 1954 business tenancy doesn't come to an end simply when the contract expires. There is no creation of a new statutory tenancy; instead the old tenancy is continued by the Act (albeit on the same terms and until it is brought to an end in accordance with the Act under s 25 or s 26). This is not a personal right. The continuation of the tenancy remains an interest in land. As a consequence of this the tenant is able assign or sublet the tenancy.

4.32 The assignment can take place at any time prior to the termination of the tenancy. The right to assign can be exercised even where the court proceedings for a new tenancy are progressing – the normal procedure is for the assignee to apply for an order to be joined to the proceedings and be substituted as the tenant claimant (or if the application has been commenced by the landlord under s 29 then as the defendant). This will be the case where an administrator or liquidator seeks to assign as part of a business sale.

Residential tenancies

4.33 There are a number of statutory codes which apply to residential tenancies. The following factors determine which statute regulates the tenancy:

*   whether the tenancy was granted to be used for business or residential (or agricultural) use;

*   the level of rent (tenancies of high rental and low rental are excluded from protection – as defined by the Rent Act 1977 and the Housing Act 1988);

*   the length of fixed term – long residential leases are excluded from Rent Act and Housing Act protection although have limited protection under Part I of the Landlord and Tenant Act 1954;

*   public sector landlords are excluded and covered by the Housing Act 1985, registered social landlords (Housing Associations) are covered by the Housing Act 1985 (for tenancies granted before 15 January 1989) and by the Housing Act 1988 (for tenancies granted after 15 January 1989);

*   the date the tenancy was granted – private sector residential tenancies granted prior to 15 January 1989 are regulated by the Rent Act 1977 and those granted after that date are regulated by the Housing Act 1988 (as amended by the Housing Act 1996).

Rent Act 1977

Qualification

4.34 The number of Rent Act tenancies is slowly dying out as the tenancy must satisfy the following conditions:

*   the tenancy must have been granted before the commencement of the Housing Act 1988 – ie before 15 January 1989;

*   the tenant must reside at the property and use it as a dwelling house. The tenant may reside at the property even after long intervals of absence (*Gofor Investments Ltd v Roberts* (1975) 29 P & CR 366).

4.35 There are a number of exceptions excluding tenancies with certain characteristics including:

*   where the Crown or a local authority is the landlord (ss 13(2) and 14);

- student and holiday lets;

- where board or attendance is provided, the payment of which is included in the rent (s 7(1));

- where the rent is below the prescribed minimum (s 5(1));

- where the rateable value is above the prescribed maximum (s 4(1)); and

- where the landlord is also resident at the property (s 12).

Grounds for possession

4.36 Once the landlord has brought the contractual tenancy to an end the protected tenant is entitled to a statutory tenancy. The landlord can only terminate the statutory tenancy on one of the statutory grounds and a court order granting possession. The grounds are divided into:

- discretionary cases (listed in the Rent Act 1977, Sch 15, Part I) including: rent arrears, breach of obligation in the statutory tenancy, nuisance, waste/neglect, damage to furniture, subletting without consent, former employees with service tenancies, possession required for the landlord's family, charging a subtenant more than the maximum amount for that part;

- mandatory cases (listed in the Rent Act 1977, Sch 15, Part II) including: where the landlord wants to return to the property to live, the property was let with the intention that possession would be given up once the landlord retires, tenancy needed for a minister of religion, certain farmhouses and agricultural employees; and

- a further stand alone discretionary ground arises where there the court is satisfied that *suitable alternative accommodation* is available (Rent Act 1977, s 98).

Housing Act 1988

4.37 The Housing Act 1988 created a revolution when it came into force on 15 January 1989. The Housing Act was designed to redress the balance which was thought to have gone too far in the tenant's favour (ie the regime created by the Rent Acts was thought to be too tenant friendly). It is thought that increased regulation had reduced the amount of private investment in providing new rented houses. The Housing Act 1988 created *assured* tenancies and *assured shorthold* tenancies which reduced the amount of security of tenure that residential tenants enjoyed and allowed landlords to charge a full market rent on rent review or renewal.

4.38 The Housing Act 1996 reduced the amount of security even further by removing the requirement (under the original s 20 of the Housing Act 1988) for landlords to serve a warning notice on prospective tenants prior to the commencement of a tenancy informing the tenant of shorthold nature of the tenancy. The Housing Act 1996 repealed this provision so that all new tenancies covered by the Act become assured *shorthold* tenancies unless the landlord and tenant agree to the contrary. As a consequence of this the vast majority of modern residential tenancies are assured shorthold (AST) where the landlord has comparatively straightforward rights to obtain possession.

Qualification

4.39 The following tenancies are excluded by the Housing Act 1988 (as amended by the Housing Act 1996):

- tenancies entered into before 15 January 1989;

- tenancies of dwelling houses with high rateable values (Housing Act 1988, Sch 1, Part I, para 2 where the rent exceeds £25,000 p a);

- tenancies at a low rent under Housing Act 1988, Sch 1, Part I, para 3 where rent in Greater London is less than £1,000 p a and elsewhere £250 p a;

- business tenancies;

- licensed premises;

- tenancies of agricultural land;

- lettings by recognised educational institutions to students;

- holiday lettings;

- resident landlords (but only where the premises are the only or principle home);

- Crown tenancies; and

- Local Authority tenancies.

4.40 All tenancies regulated by the Housing Act 1988 are assured tenancies. Some are also ASTs. If the tenancy was granted before 28 February 1997 then the tenancy will only be an AST if prior to the commencement of the tenancy the landlord served a notice pursuant to s 20 warning the tenant that the tenancy will be an AST. However, tenancies granted after 28 February 1997 are automatically ASTs unless the landlord and tenant agree to the contrary.

4.41　If an assured tenant ceases to qualify then the assured status is lost.

Grounds for possession

4.42　For all assured tenancies the first step for a landlord is to serve a notice seeking possession (NSP) which must comply with certain requirements.

4.43　Where a tenancy is an AST then the landlord has a significant advantage as he can bring the tenancy to an end after 6 months (unless there is a longer fixed term) by serving a notice under s 21 giving 2 months' notice. If served during the fixed term the notice must be a simple 2 months. If the tenancy is periodic then the notice has to expire on a specified date which must:

- be the last date of a period of the tenancy; and

- not be earlier than the date the tenancy could have been brought to an end by the service of a notice to quit (s 21(4)).

4.44　It is important to specify the correct date as the notice will be invalid if an incorrect date is given (such as the first day of a period instead of the last day – even if more than 2 months is given, see the Court of Appeal decision in *Lower Street Properties Ltd v Jones* (1996) 28 HLR 877, CA).

4.45　An AST landlord can also rely upon the grounds for possession available for all assured tenancies. All forms of assured tenancy are subject to the provisions of the Housing Act 1988, s 7(6).

4.46　These grounds can be used in the first 6 months and at any time in the tenancy. The grounds fall into discretionary and mandatory categories and there are similarities with the Rent Act 1977:

- mandatory grounds (under Housing Act 1988, Sch 2, Part I) include: landlord who is a returning owner-occupier, mortgagee requiring possession, holiday and student lets, accommodation for ministers of religion, landlord wanting to demolish and reconstruct, and serious rent arrears which, depending on the period of the tenancy may be 2 months/8 weeks/1 quarter/3 months (at the time of the NSP and at the time of the hearing);

- discretionary grounds (under Housing Act 1988, Sch 2, Part II) include: suitable alternative accommodation, rent arrears generally, breach of obligation, tenant allowing the property to deteriorate through waste and neglect, nuisance, damage to furniture and employees.

To rely on one of these grounds the landlord must serve a NSP in the prescribed form in accordance with s 8. Although minor deviations may be excused it must contain all the warning information required (*Mountain v Hastings* (1993) 25 HLR 427). The NSP must state the grounds relied upon. In rare cases the court will allow a NSP to be amended (s 8(2)), but generally if a further ground is required the landlord will have to start again. The NSP sets out the notice requirements for each ground and the circumstances where the period can be shortened to 14 days or dispensed with.

FORFEITURE

Forfeiture of statutory protected tenancies

4.47 Statutory protection does not automatically preclude the landlord's right to forfeit a tenancy. If a tenancy has acquired statutory protection under the Rent Act 1977, the Housing Act 1988 or the Landlord and Tenant Act 1954 then this may have an effect on the remedy of forfeiture; depending upon which code protects the tenancy.

4.48 If a tenancy is protected under the Rent Act 1977 the effect of successful forfeiture proceedings will be to convert the contractual tenancy into a statutory tenancy and the landlord will not be entitled to possession unless he can establish the statutory grounds for possession. Forfeiture is still useful to expedite the time when the landlord can rely on the statutory grounds for possession.

4.49 If the tenancy is an assured tenancy under the Housing Act 1988, then the situation is different. Forfeiture is excluded and an assured tenancy can only be brought to an end by relying on the statutory grounds of possession. On this basis where a head lease is being forfeited an assured subtenant has no right to claim relief from forfeiture (see *Artesian Residential Developments Ltd v Beck* [2000] 2 WLR 357, CA).

4.50 The Landlord and Tenant Act 1954 does not restrict the landlord's right to forfeit a business tenancy and obtain possession in any way. Section 24 expressly preserves the right to forfeit. However, a condition in a lease which claims to give the landlord the express right to forfeit in the event that the tenant takes steps under the Act to obtain a new tenancy is void under s 38(1).

When can the landlord forfeit?

Forfeiture clause

4.51 Most leases will have an express forfeiture clause (often called the *proviso for re-entry*) this will provide the landlord with a contractual right to bring the tenancy to an end in circumstances where a tenant is in breach. The forfeiture clause will set out the precise circumstances in which the landlord may re-enter the property and terminate the tenancy. This will be a question of the construction of the proper terms of the clause. Normally a forfeiture clause will allow the landlord to forfeit on the grounds of breach of covenant and the non-payment of rent and also on the grounds of insolvency (in *Cadogan Estates Ltd v McMahon* [2000] 3 WLR 1555, a tenant had a statutory tenancy by virtue of the Rent Act 1977, then went bankrupt. The landlord sought an order for possession on the basis that the original lease had a condition that he could re-enter on the tenant's bankruptcy. Lord Hoffman held that there was 'no reason to distinguish between forfeiture for bankruptcy and forfeiture for breach of covenant').

4.52   The forfeiture clause must make clear the grounds that the landlord can rely on to use the remedy. The grounds will be strictly construed in the tenant's favour. Any ambiguity in the forfeiture clause will be resolved against the landlord (following the principle of *contra proferentum* where any ambiguity is resolved against the party relying upon the clause – see *Creery v Summersell and Flowerdew & Co* [1949] Ch 751). In the case of *Doe d Abdy v Stevens* (1832) 3 B&AD 299 a proviso for re-entry which allowed forfeiture on the basis of 'any *act* contrary to and in breach of covenant' was held not to include a breach of a repairing covenant as this was an *omission* and not an *act.*

4.53   Where there is no express forfeiture clause, then a landlord may have the right to forfeit if he can show the tenant has breached a *condition* of the lease. A lease covenant may be expressly made a *condition* or it may be implied. A covenant will only count as an implied condition if it is fundamental to the contractual relationship between the landlord and tenant (*Rainbow Estates Ltd v Tokenhold Ltd* [1999] Ch 64). Landlords are keen to avoid this problem by insisting upon a detailed express clause:

•   From a landlord's perspective a well-drafted forfeiture clause will allow the landlord to forfeit where the tenant has breached any of the covenants of the lease. Rent is usually treated separately and the tenant is typically allowed a grace period before the right to forfeit arises (often 14 or 21 days after a quarter day).

•   Conventionally the forfeiture clause is expanded to allow the landlord to forfeit if the tenant becomes insolvent (see below).

Insolvency event as a condition allowing forfeiture

4.54   Most modern leases will contain an express condition which allows the landlord to forfeit if the tenant enters into any form of insolvency. It is necessary to have an express provision as there is unlikely to an implied condition (*Hyde v Warden* (1877) 3 Ex D 72). On the particular facts of a case there may be some argument that a condition should be implied (*Chester v Buckingham Travel Ltd* [1981] 1 All ER 386). The automatic vesting in the trustee in bankruptcy does not create an implied condition (see *Re Riggs, ex p Lovell* [1901] 2 KB 16) and is probably not a breach of the alienation provision against assigning.

4.55   Therefore it is important for a modern commercial lease to contain a detailed condition which covers all forms of insolvency (updated to take account of the Enterprise Act 2002 and current legislation). Practitioners may find that older leases have a forfeiture clause which does not contain a condition allowing the landlord to forfeit for all modern forms of insolvency.

4.56 A properly drafted insolvency condition will be valid on the basis that it has a similar effect as a covenant against assignment (see *Roe d Hunter v Galliers* (1787) 2 Term Rep 133).

Standard forfeiture clause

4.57 The following is an example of a standard forfeiture clause:

'Conditions for Re-entry

1 The Landlord may re-enter the Property (or any part of the Property in the name of the whole) at any time after any of the following occurs:

(a) any rent is unpaid [21 days] after becoming payable whether it has been formally demanded or not;

(b) any breach of any condition of, or tenant covenant, in this lease;

(c) where the Tenant or any guarantor is a corporation:

  (i) the taking of any step in connection with any voluntary arrangement or any other compromise or arrangement for the benefit of any creditors of the Tenant or guarantor; or

  (ii) the making of an application for an administration order or the making of an administration order in relation to the Tenant or guarantor; or

  (iii) the giving of any notice of intention to appoint an administrator, or the filing at court of the prescribed documents in connection with the appointment of an administrator, or the appointment of an administrator, in any case in relation to the tenant or the guarantor; or

  (iv) the appointment of a receiver or manager or an administrative receiver in relation to any property or income of the Tenant or guarantor; or

  (v) the commencement of a voluntary winding-up in respect of the Tenant or guarantor, except a winding-up for the purpose of amalgamation or reconstruction of a solvent company in respect of which a statutory declaration of solvency has been filed with the Registrar of Companies; or

  (vi) the making of a petition for a winding-up order or a winding-up order in respect of the Tenant or guarantor; or

  (vii) the striking-off of the Tenant or guarantor from the Register of Companies or the making of an application for the Tenant or the guarantor to be struck-off; or

  (viii) the Tenant or guarantor otherwise ceasing to exist,

(d) where the Tenant or any guarantor is an individual:

  (i) the taking of any step in connection with any voluntary arrangement or any other compromise or arrangement for the benefit of any creditors of the Tenant or guarantor; or

  (ii) the presentation of a petition for a bankruptcy order or the making of a bankruptcy order against the Tenant or guarantor.

2 If the Landlord re-enters the Property (or any part of the Property in the name of the whole) pursuant to this clause, this lease shall immediately end, but without prejudice to any right or remedy of the Landlord in respect of any breach of covenant by the Tenant or any guarantor.'

Waiver

4.58 The effect of a forfeiture clause is to make the lease terminable at the option of the landlord. When faced with a breach of the lease the landlord must decide whether or not to forfeit. He is put to an *election* as to whether to treat the lease as terminated or allow it to continue. The crucial date for this election is when the landlord becomes aware of the breach. As soon as the landlord knows that a breach has occurred he must decide what action to take and make his intentions clear (*London and County (A&D) v Wilfred Sportsman* [1971] Ch 764). He cannot waive until the breach is brought to his attention. Buckley LJ summarised the components of waiver in *Central Estates (Belgravia) v Woolgar (No 2)* [1972] 1 WLR 1048 at 1054:

'If the landlord by word or deed manifests to the tenant by an unequivocal act a concluded decision to elect in a particular manner, he will be bound by such an election. If he chooses to do something such as demanding or receiving rent which can only be done consistently with a certain state of affairs viz the continued existence of the lease he cannot thereafter say that the state of affairs did not then exist.'

4.59 The danger for a landlord is that if he takes any action which is consistent with the continuation of the tenancy then he may be deemed to have waived the breach. The acts of waiver may be committed by an employee or agent of the landlord (see *Metropolitan Properties v Cordery* (1979) 251 EG 567). However, if the landlord has been misled by the tenant to conceal the nature of the breach then the right to forfeit may survive (see *Cornillie v Saha* (1996) 28 HLR 561). The doctrine of waiver is complex. An act of waiver has to be *unequivocal* but may be accidental. This creates an objective test which sometimes creates a minefield for landlords. Waiver may be implied by the landlord's actions even if there was no intention to waive (see *Expert Clothing Service and Sales Ltd v Hillgate House Ltd* [1986] Ch 340 at 360).

Acts of waiver

4.60 The most common allegation of waiver arises where a landlord (with knowledge of the breach) accepts rent from a tenant. The mere demand of rent is also a waiver. In *Segal Securities Ltd v Thoseby* [1963] 1 QB 887 it was decided that even where the landlord intended to reserve his rights using the words *without prejudice* he would still be deemed to have waived the right to forfeit. Even where rent is accepted by mistake or where the landlord's agent (without knowledge of the breach) demands or accepts rent, this will still amount to a waiver.

4.61 Any other act which could be construed to be the landlord's acknowledgment of a continuation of the lease potentially may be a waiver. This will include the service of a Schedule of Dilapidations or notice to carry out repairs (in *Doe d De Rutzen v Lewis* (1836) 5 Ad & El 277) or where the landlord serves a notice to quit (*Marche v Christodoulakis* (1948) 64 TLR 466).

4.62 The levy of distress is an act of waiver, as will be serving a notice that CRAR will be used under the Tribunals Courts and Enforcement Act 2007, Sch 12, para 7. However, levying distress before the right to forfeit arises (eg after a quarter day but before the expiry of a 21-day or 14-day grace period allowed in a forfeiture clause) will not be an act of waiver.

4.63 The effect of waiver depends upon the nature of the breach of covenant. There are two categories of breach *once and for all* breaches and *continuing* breaches.

4.64 If a *once and for all* breach is waived (such as a breach of covenant against parting with possession) then the landlord will lose the right to forfeit. Once and for all breaches include:

- parting with possession, assignment, subletting without consent;

- failure to pay rent or other sums once fallen due; and

- alterations carried out without consent.

4.65 If the breach is a *continuing* breach, such as a failure to repair, the right to forfeit will arise again on the day after the waiver and therefore the right to forfeit is not lost. Continuing breaches include:

- disrepair (although the covenant must be expressed to be a continuing obligation, eg *Farimani v Gates* [1984] 2 EGLR 66, and may include the breach of a notice served on the tenant requiring repairs to be carried out by a certain date);

- breaching the user clause; and

- nuisance.

Restrictions on forfeiture

Warning notice under the Law of Property Act 1925, s 146

4.66 Law of Property Act 1925 (LPA 1925), s 146 provides that the landlord cannot exercise a right to forfeit a lease unless he first serves a notice on the tenant which:

- states the breach complained of;

- if the breach is capable of remedy, requires the lessee to remedy the breach;

- requires the lessee to provide compensation for the breach;

- restricts the landlord from forfeiting the lease until the lessee has had a reasonable time to remedy the breach (if it is capable of remedy) and provide reasonable compensation (s 146 (1)).

4.67   There is an important exception to this principle in that a landlord does not have to serve a s 146 notice prior to forfeiting where the breach relates to non-payment of rent (or the failure to pay sums reserved as rent under the terms of the lease). The objective of s 146 is to require the landlord to formally set out the breach complained of and provide reasonable time for the tenant to remedy. The notice must specify the breach complained of accurately. A notice which specified 'parting with possession' was held not to be sufficient to cover a breach which consisted only of *sharing occupation* (*Akici v LR Butlin* [2006] 1 EGLR 34).

Remediable/irremediable breach

4.68   The distinction between breaches which are remediable and breaches which are irremediable is not entirely consistent and not easy to comprehend in relation to the potential undoing of the breach. In reality, the test is whether the damage caused by the breach is capable of remedy by the tenant being able to comply with the covenant within a reasonable time so that any damage caused to the landlord is resolved. If in doubt the landlord should require the breach to be remedied (*Savva v Hussein* [1996] 2 EGLR 65). The distinction is affected by whether the covenant is negative or positive:

- Where a tenant has breached a positive covenant then arguably the action required to remedy the breach is easier to stipulate. Where a tenant is in breach of a repairing obligation, the tenant can correct the position by putting the premises into good repair (*Expert Clothing Services v Hillgate House Ltd* [1986] Ch 340).

- Where a tenant has breached a negative covenant the position is more complex. If the covenant relates to something which should not be done (eg where there is a breach of the permitted user of the premises under the terms of the lease) and once done is difficult to reverse (or do at a later date) then it is more likely to be irremediable. This may include parting with possession which is a problem encountered sometimes by liquidators and administrators in relation to a pre-packaged ('pre-pack') sale (see **8.18**).

4.69   The case of *Akici v LR Butlin* [2006] 1 EGLR 34 illustrates the difference between *parting with possession* and *sharing occupation*. Both are usually prohibited by the lease covenants (without landlord's consent). However, in

Akici Neuberger LJ ruled that *sharing possession* (such as granting a licence to occupy) was capable of remedy where *parting with possession* (such as granting a subtenancy) was an irremediable breach.

4.70 A breach of a negative covenant will be viewed more severely by the courts; see *Rugby School (Governors) v Tannahill* [1935] 1 KB 87, *Egerton v Esplanade Hotels London Ltd* [1947] 2 All ER 88, *Hoffman v Fineberg* [1949] Ch 245. These cases all involve a breach of covenant not to cause or permit immoral use of the premises and the stigma that would attach to the property once it had been used for prostitution.

Bankruptcy/liquidation exceptions to s 146

4.71 Where a tenant is insolvent, there are often a number of potential breaches of covenant together with unpaid rent which would entitle the landlord to forfeit. Notwithstanding other breaches the landlord is also usually able to forfeit on the ground that the tenant has become insolvent (see above). However, there are exceptions to s 146 when relying on a condition relating to bankruptcy or liquidation.

4.72 Under s 146(9) there are a number of special case leases where there is no requirement to serve a s 146 notice. To fall within this exception the insolvent tenant (bankrupt or in liquidation) must have a lease of:

- agricultural land;

- mines or mineral rights;

- licensed premises;

- a dwelling house (only where the house is let with furniture or other chattels); or

- where the tenant has personal qualifications which help preserve the character or value of the property.

4.73 The burden is on the landlord to demonstrate that a lease does not fall within one of the special cases (*Hockley Engineering v V & P Midlands* [1993] 1 EGLR 76). In *Earl Bathurst v Fine* [1974] 1 WLR 905, Denning LJ held that if the lease fell within one of the exceptions there was no jurisdiction to grant relief from forfeiture.

4.74 Under s 146(10) in relation to the insolvency condition (for bankruptcy and all forms of liquidation) s 146 does not restrict a landlord's right of forfeiture after a period of a year has passed after the commencement of the bankruptcy or liquidation. During the first year the landlord can still forfeit but must comply with s 146 and if appropriate serve a s 146 notice before forfeiting. After the year has passed s 146 does not apply (although the landlord must still ensure the right of forfeiture *remains and hasn't been waived*; see *Civil Service Co-operative Society v McGrigor's Trustee* [1923] 2 Ch 347).

4.75 This also means that the statutory right to claim relief from forfeiture is also lost after a year has passed under s 146(10) (see **4.142**).

Other exceptions to s 146

Dilapidations claims

4.76 In relation to claims arising in relation to a breach of covenant to keep or put the property into repair) a special form of notice is required under the Leasehold Property (Repairs) Act 1938. The modified notice warns the tenant that he has the right to object and serve a counter-notice. If a counter-notice is served then the landlord can only forfeit with the court's permission. The application for permission will depend upon the landlord being able to make out one of the grounds under the Leasehold Property (Repairs) Act 1938, s 1(5) and is usually to be made in the county court. However, where the tenant is in compulsory liquidation or has the benefit of a moratorium under IA 1986 (as a consequence of an administration or a proposed voluntary arrangement) then the application can be combined with an application for permission to take forfeiture proceedings through the relevant court with jurisdiction for the insolvency (Leasehold Property (Repairs) Act 1938, s 6). The grounds under s 1(5) are that unless the breach is immediately remedied:

- dilapidations have/will cause substantial diminution in the value of the reversion;

- the landlord will be in breach of a statutory requirement (including bylaws);

- the dilapidations will affect the interests of the occupier of any other part of the premises; and

- there are special circumstances that would make the continued state of dilapidations unjust and inequitable.

4.77 The purpose of the Leasehold Property (Repairs) Act 1938 is to prevent the landlord from putting undue pressure on the tenant in relation to the dilapidations in circumstances where the level of disrepair is of no real detriment to the value of the landlord's interest. With years left to run on a lease and a tenant who represents a good covenant there is often no particular urgency about repairs. However, the problem becomes more acute if the lease is approaching its termination. The Act does not apply where:

- there are less than 3 years left to run on the lease at the time proceedings are issued (or peaceable re-entry is effected); or

- the landlord serves notice under the lease, carries out the repairs on behalf of the tenant and then claims the cost of the repairs from the tenant (*Jervis v Harris* [1996] Ch 195).

Long residential leases

4.78 Tenants that have a long residential lease at a low rent have the protection of Housing Act 1988, s 81 (as amended by Commonhold and Leasehold Reform Act 2002) which provides that a landlord may not forfeit a lease for non-payment of service charges (including service charges reserved as rent) until the amount of the service charge has been agreed or admitted by the tenant or been determined by the court (or the Leasehold Valuation Tribunal (LVT)). One of the practical consequences of this provision is that mortgagees (who often pay the arrears quickly to avoid the risk of forfeiture when notified that the tenant is in rent or service charge arrears) now wait until the landlord has obtained the court/LVT determination before paying.

Insolvency restrictions

4.79 Where a tenant is insolvent the landlord must also consider whether there are any restrictions in relation to forfeiture arising as a direct consequence of the insolvency. Sometimes the landlord is required to obtain the court's permission before taking any steps to forfeit. However, it should be noted that although an application for permission should be made prior to the forfeiture there may be circumstances where the court will ratify the forfeiture after the event (*Razzaq v Pala* [1997] 1 WLR 1336).

4.80 The requirement to obtain permission depends on the type of insolvency.

Receivership

4.81 No moratorium arises in relation to forfeiture where a receiver is appointed (whether this an administrative receiver or a fixed charge receiver). Therefore the landlord is able to forfeit by issuing proceedings or peaceable re-entry with relative impunity. Of course the landlord must ensure that there are no other restrictions (see this chapter generally) and that he has the right to terminate the contractual tenancy as a result of default or otherwise. In relation to the general position for receivers and the receiver's right to apply for relief from forfeiture see *Transag Haulage Ltd v Leyland DAF Finance plc* [1994] BCC 356.

Individual voluntary arrangements

4.82 Where an interim order is obtained by an insolvent debtor who wants to make a proposal for an individual voluntary arrangement (IVA), then a moratorium arises under IA 1986, s 252 which provides that when the period of the interim order is enforced:

'No Landlord or other person to whom rent is payable may exercise any right of forfeiture by peaceable re-entry in relation to premises let to the debtor in respect of a failure by the debtor to comply with any term or condition of his tenancy of such premises except with the leave of the Court.'

4.83 The wording at IA 1986, s 252(2)(aa) was modified by the Insolvency Act 2000 which in particular made forfeiture by peaceable re-entry unlawful without a court order and reversed the position established in the case of *Re A Debtor (13A-IO-1995)* [1995] 1 WLR 1127 where it was held that s 252 as originally drafted allowed a landlord to take this step (see *Clarke v Coutts & Co (a firm)* [2002] EWCA Civ 943, [2002] BPIR 916).

4.84 In relation to the effect the terms of the IVA have on the landlord's right to forfeit see company voluntary arrangements below.

Company voluntary arrangements

4.85 In relation to company voluntary arrangements (CVAs) a moratorium only arises where the debtor company makes an application for a moratorium and where the company satisfies the requirements under the Companies Act 1985, s 247(3) for being a 'small company' (see **1.48**). The moratorium comes into force when the company files its relevant documents at court in accordance with IA 1986, Sch A1, para 8(1) and lasts until the day of the creditors' meeting (pursuant to para 12(1)(f)). The terms of the moratorium provide:

'No Landlord . . . may exercise any right of forfeiture by peaceable re-entry in relation to premises let to the company in respect of a failure by the company to comply with any term or condition of its tenancy of such premises except with leave of the Court and subject to terms as Court may impose and . . . no other proceedings . . . or other legal process may be commenced or continued . . . except with the leave of the Court and subject to such terms as the Court may impose.'

4.86 Companies which do not fall within this category do not have the advantage of a moratorium leading up to the creditors' meeting. During this period the landlord may forfeit; but see below in relation to the tenant's right to rely on the terms of the approved arrangement and apply for relief. Once the arrangement has been approved the creditors are bound (see **1.52**).

The terms of the arrangement and forfeiture

4.87 An insolvent tenant company may put forward CVA proposals which:

- treat pre-CVA rents as an unsecured claim and propose a payment of a reduced dividend in line with the other unsecured creditors;

- treat post-CVA rents in a similar way by proposing to pay only a reduced amount in relation to future rents to make the occupation of the property more economical for the tenant's business going forward.

4.88 Faced with such proposals the landlord's power to resist is as follows:

- to vote against the proposed CVA, although the success of this opposition will depend on the value of his vote and whether he is able to influence the decision of the creditors' meeting (see **1.49**);

- once the CVA is approved to challenge the decision on the basis of unfair prejudice or material irregularity (IA 1986, s 6 and see **1.54**);

- to forfeit prior to the meeting where no moratorium is in place or after the meeting if the result will leave him with rent arrears.

4.89 Until recently it was thought that a voluntary arrangement could not prejudice a landlord's right to forfeit (*Re Mohammed Naeem (A Bankrupt)* [1990] 1 WLR 48 and *March Estates v Gunmark Ltd* [1996] EGLR 38). This view was based on the effect of IA 1986, s 4(3) which provides that a VA will not 'affect the right of a secured creditor of the company to enforce his security'. In *Re Naeem*, Hoffman J said that a CVA:

' . . . was only intended to bind the creditors in their character of creditors. It did not affect proprietary rights such as those of the landlord to forfeit the lease.' (at para 50C)

4.90 Hoffman J thought that relief from forfeiture should be given upon the tenant paying the lesser amount required by the arrangement:

' . . . it does not appear to me to be unfair prejudice that after such modification the right to forfeit should only stand as security for recovery of the modified debt rather than the original one.' (at para 50 H)

4.91 In *March Estates*, Lightman J thought that Hoffman J 'cannot be correct'. He ruled that although through the VA the landlord may have been deprived of his right to sue for the rent in his capacity as a creditor, he was not deprived of his right to forfeit the lease for the non-payment of rent in his capacity as owner of the proprietary right to forfeit. The landlord could insist that relief from forfeiture be given:

'on condition that all arrears be paid [AND] the voluntary arrangement cannot prejudice the lessor's right to forfeit the lease if the full rent reserved by the lease is not paid.'

4.92 However, we now have the benefit of a fully reasoned Court of Appeal decision on this point which has turned this point on its head. Neuberger LJ reviewed the question comprehensively in the leading judgment in *Thomas v Ken Thomas Ltd* [2006] EWCA Civ 1504, [2007] BPIR 959. He held that a VA is able to bind rent arrears falling due at the date of the creditors' meeting as a debt and also potentially bind future rents falling due after the meeting (so that the tenant is able to propose a rent reduction for the remaining term of the lease but subject to a possible challenge by the landlord under IA 1986, s 6 as unfair prejudice; see **1.54**).

4.93   However, in relation to the right to forfeit Neuberger LJ came to the conclusion that the landlord's right to forfeit (in line with all other creditor remedies) would survive only in relation to the tenant's failure to pay the amount (albeit reduced or *crammed down* by the VA) due under the terms of the proposals. This would be the case even where the VA allows the landlord to recover future rent which may be less than the passing rent under the lease and less than the market rate. Neuberger LJ gave the following reasons for this decision (taking a 'different view from that taken by Hoffman J and Lightman J'):

- '• VAs are "concerned with obligations not remedies . . . there is no warrant for holding that if one right is lost in relation to a particular payment as a result of a CVA another right can remain".
- The landlord's ability to forfeit for a debt under the lease is inconsistent with the idea that the debt has been replaced by a different debt under the VA and with the "rescue culture embodied by the 1986 Act".
- The right to forfeit in relation to the original rent arrears has gone just as much as the right to sue for rent – because the rent is no longer due. It has been "substituted by the sums due under the CVA" and any right to forfeit now survives in relation to the substitution only.
- Landlords should not be treated in the same way as secured creditors and in relation to the right to forfeit are not excluded from the class of creditors to be bound by the VA. The landlord does not have the status of a secured creditor and "there is no statutory warrant for such a hybrid status".'

The implication of Neuberger LJ's judgment is that (subject to a claim for unfair prejudice), a VA may be able to restrict the landlord's right to forfeit for failing to pay future rent in full providing the tenant pays the rent provided by the VA. Although Neuberger LJ postulates that this position may give a landlord strong arguments to challenge the decision on the basis of unfair prejudice as 'it would be wrong in principle that a tenant should be able to trade under a CVA for the benefit of past creditors at the present and future expense of its landlord'.

4.94   However the rights to challenge under IA 1986, s 6 are restrictive (not least because if the landlord fails to submit the challenge to the court within the very tight time-limit of 28 days the right is lost) and the support this now gives to the removal of proprietary rights in a VA should not be underestimated.

Administration

4.95   There is a comprehensive moratorium restraining forfeiture when there is an administration. Following the Enterprise Act 2002 most administrations now take place without a court order. The moratorium kicks in as soon as the appointment of the administrator takes effect (IA 1986, Sch B1, para 43). On a director's appointment (under Sch B1, para 22), where a notice of intention to appoint has been filed, an interim moratorium takes effect on the same terms (under Sch B1, para 44). In addition in the rare cases where an administrator's appointment is sought by court order the interim moratorium will apply.

4.96 Under IA 1986, Sch B1, para 43(4):

'A Landlord may not exercise a right of forfeiture by re-entry in relation to premises let to the company except:

(a)   with the consent of the administrator; or
(b)   with the permission of the Court.

4.97 In addition to this under IA 1986, Sch B1, para 43(6):

'No legal process (including legal proceedings . . .) may be instituted or continued against the company or property of the company except:

(a)   with the consent of the administrator; or
(b)   with the permission of the Court.'

It is still possible to forfeit by way of peaceable re-entry in relation to an administration petition presented before the Insolvency Act 2000 came into force on 2 April 2001 – see *Re Lomax Leisure* [2000] Ch 502 (but the circumstances would be very rare).

When will an administrator give permission to forfeit?

4.98 The moratorium aims to provide the tenant company with a breathing space to enable the administrators to implement proposals to rescue the company as a going concern through continued trading, or, if that is impossible, to sell the company's business and assets. The moratorium does not relieve the company from its obligations under the lease but removes the immediate threat of enforcement action against its assets, which might frustrate the purpose of the administration.

4.99 This might appear like a green light for the administrators, to continue trading from, or occupying, premises without paying rent, while avoiding the risk of forfeiture. This is not necessarily the case:

• An administrator may be prepared to hand back the property to the landlord by way of a surrender. However, there is no power to disclaim the lease.

• An administrator may require the property for the short- or long-term objectives of the administration.

• Refusal to give up possession may provide the landlord with the right to claim ongoing rent as an expense of the administration (eg where the administrator requires the premises for storage of the tenant's assets pending a sale or for the potential assignment of the lease; see **2.98**).

4.100 In practice a landlord will threaten to apply for permission to forfeit where the administrator fails to give adequate comfort/assurance that the ongoing rents will be paid as an expense (see **2.113** 'Pay or Forfeit').

4.101 In relation to when the court should give permission to forfeit, Nicholls LJ set out a number of guidelines in the Court of Appeal case *Re Atlantic Computer Systems plc* [1992] Ch 505:

- A landlord should ordinarily be granted permission to exercise its right of forfeiture unless the premises are required by the tenant company in order to facilitate the administration. However, the burden is on the landlord to make the case for permission.

- If the landlord is refused permission then, the court can, and in many cases should, require the administrators to meet the rent that has fallen due during the administration as a condition of any refusal to grant permission to forfeit.

- The court should give the landlord's proprietary rights great weight but these rights need to be balanced against the legitimate needs of other creditors. An administration should not be conducted for the benefit of unsecured creditors at the expense of creditors with proprietary rights.

- One way of carrying out this balancing act is by measuring the damage that would be caused to a landlord by refusing permission against the damage that would be caused to the unsecured creditors by granting permission. The court should take into account all such relevant factors as the administrator's ability to pay the ongoing rents, the proposals to be put to the creditors in relation to meeting the objectives of the administration, the conduct of the parties and whether adequate conditions can be imposed on the administrator if the landlord is refused consent.

- Administrators can agree to pay such rent as an expense of the administration, and they should offer this in the face of a request to forfeit where the administrator requires the continued use of the premises for the purposes of the administration, which would make the landlord's threatened application to court unnecessary.

4.102 Although the Court of Appeal did not consider the question, it is thought that similar considerations should apply on the question of whether permission should be granted for a landlord to exercise its right of distress over assets in the premises.

4.103 Following the decision in *Re Salmet International Ltd (in administration)* [2001] BCC 796, it seems that the court cannot order administrators to meet the rent accruing during the administration. However, the court can impose a condition that payment be made when refusing to grant the landlord permission to forfeit (or distrain).

4.104 In addition to the *Atlantic* guidelines the behaviour of the parties has become increasingly important in deciding questions of forfeiture and the exercise of the courts discretion. In *Akici v LR Butlin Ltd* [2006] 1 WLR 201 Neuberger LJ said:

> 'In principle it seems to me that where the breach is causing no serious continuing commercial harm to the lessors, the court should not be too strict in assessing whether the remedy has been quick enough. On the other hand the court should not be too indulgent to a lessee, especially one who is not honest with his lessors.'

4.105 In reliance on *Akici* and *Atlantic Computers*, Norris J decided *Metro Nominees (Wandsworth) (No 1) v K Rayment* [2008] BCC 40. This case illustrates the courts' approach to applications for permission. The administrators sold the business and assets of the tenant to a third party purchaser. Under the terms of the sale, the administrators agreed to assign any lease relating to any property from which the tenant had formerly traded (including the property the subject of this case). The administrator agreed to apply for the landlord's licence to assign any relevant lease to the purchaser. On assignment, no further consideration would be payable.

4.106 Without obtaining licence to assign the administrators allowed the purchaser to take occupation of the premises under a tenancy at will which constituted a breach of covenant. Some time after the sale, the administrators wrote to the landlord asking for licence to assign. The administrators did not tell the landlord that they had already parted with possession. The landlord refused consent on the financial strength of the purchaser (which was a 'newco', ie a new shell company and in effect a phoenix company). The landlord also relied upon the rent arrears.

4.107 The administrators refused a request for information about the identity of the occupier and refused permission to forfeit the lease. The administrators advised that they continued to require the premises for the purposes of the administration (without setting out why). Importantly they failed to disclose that the purchaser was already in occupation. However, the administrators promised to pay the post-administration rents in full. With this background two applications were made to the court:

- the landlord applied for permission to forfeit under IA 1986, Sch B1, para 43; and

- the administrators applied for a declaration that they did not need the landlord's consent to underlet or in the alternative that the landlord had unreasonably withheld consent to underlet and that the landlord was not entitled to forfeit the lease.

4.108 Norris J accepted that the administration may have resulted in a better result for creditors as a whole. However, the sale had already taken place. The only unresolved business was the proposed assignment. This would benefit only the purchaser (not the creditors as no further consideration was payable) for the purposes of the application the interests of the purchaser were not a proper consideration. The tenant in administration no longer required the premises. Therefore allowing the landlord to exercise its proprietary rights and forfeit would not impede the objectives of the administration. Accordingly the landlord was given permission to take forfeiture proceedings. In reaching this decision Norris J gave weight to the administrators' failure to inform the landlord that they had already parted with possession in breach of covenant. However the Court of Appeal have reaffirmed that the balancing exercise in *Re Atlantic Computer Systems plc* [1992] Ch 505, CA must still be carried out (*Innovate Logistics Ltd v Sunberry Properties Ltd* [2008] EWCA Civ 1261). One of the most important factors in this analysis will be whether allowing the breach will cause the landlord further loss.

Voluntary liquidation

4.109 Where a tenant is in voluntary liquidation the landlord is initially free to exercise any right to forfeit he may have. However, the liquidator is able to make an application to the court to determine any question arising in the liquidation (IA 1986, s 112). The application can also be made by any contributory (ie a person liable to contribute to the company's assets on the winding up) or creditor.

4.110 The court can then exercise any power which it would have in a compulsory winding up including under IA 1986, s 126 to stay or restrain any action or proceeding. This would include court actions for non-payment of rent or forfeiture. However, it is not readily apparent whether this provision could also be used to restrain peaceable re-entry. In *Herbert Berry Associates Ltd v IRC* [1977] 1 WLR 1437 the House of Lords held that the equivalent provision to IA 1986, s 126 in the Companies Act 1948 would include the power to restrain distress for rent (which was then applied in *Re Memco Engineering Ltd* [1986] Ch 86). Although it is arguable that peaceable re-entry might be treated in the same way there is no direct authority for this proposition.

4.111 If the landlord is restrained from forfeiting he may be able to argue that the post-liquidation rents be paid as an expense of the liquidation under IR 1986, r 4.218 (see **2.64**).

Compulsory liquidation

Between winding-up petition and order

4.112 Compulsory liquidation commences with the presentation of a winding-up petition (IA 1986, s 86). There is no restriction on a landlord exercising the right to forfeit between the presentation of a winding-up petition and the making of the winding-up order. During this window a landlord may forfeit the lease of the premises by way of peaceable re-entry or through court proceedings (although there may be insufficient time to conclude forfeiture proceedings before the winding-up order is made). If the landlord elects to issue forfeiture proceedings, then it is possible for creditors to make an application for a stay of proceedings under IA 1986, s 126. An application can be made at any time after the presentation of the petition and the application may be made by the company itself or any creditor or contributory. The court has a wide discretion to determine such applications. This provision allows the court to make an interim order which will remain intact until the hearing of the application. Section 126 only applies to any action or proceeding and arguably not to peaceable re-entry. In *Herbert Berry Associates Ltd v IRC* [1977] 1 WLR 1437 the House of Lords held that the equivalent provision to s 126 in the Companies Act 1948 would include the power to restrain distress for rent (which was then applied in *Re Memco Engineering Ltd* [1986] Ch 86) and therefore there is an argument that it would also apply to peaceable re-entry.

After winding-up order

4.113 After a winding-up order has been made against the tenant (or the court has appointed a provisional liquidator) then s 130(2) kicks in, which provides that:

> '. . . no action or proceeding shall be proceeded with or commenced against the company or its property except by leave of the Court and subject to such terms as the Court may impose.'

This provision provides for an automatic stay of any existing proceedings and also applies after a provisional liquidator has been appointed.

Prospect of landlord obtaining the court's permission to issue forfeiture proceedings

4.114 The court has a general discretion in relation to such applications. Where there is a significant dispute in relation to the issues (such as a defence on the basis of wrongful forfeiture) then the court will not investigate the merits of the proposed forfeiture claim nor consider evidence and detail (see *Re Bank of Credit and Commerce International SA (No 4)* [1995] BCC 453). However, where the landlord has a strong grounds for forfeiture and the liquidator has no real defence then there is a reasonable prospect of obtaining permission to proceed with forfeiture. In a nineteenth-century case (*General*

Share and Trust Co v Whetley Brick Pottery (1882) 20 Ch D 260, CA) the court ruled that a tenant in liquidation should not be placed in a better position than any other lessee. Also in *Re Lloyd (David) & Co* (1877) 6 Ch D 339, CA James LJ said:

> 'The company ought not, because it has become insolvent or has been minded to wind up its affairs, to be placed in the better position than any other lessee with regard to his lessor.'

4.115 In circumstances where there is no real defence the court may give permission to forfeit and at the same time make a summary possession order (*Re Blue Jeans Sales Ltd* [1979] 1 WLR 362).

4.116 However, in relation to modern liquidations a liquidator is likely to have a greater prospect of resisting a landlord's application. Faced with a landlord's application the court must seek to do 'what is right and fair in all the circumstances' (*New Cap Reinsurance Corp Ltd v HIH Casualty & General Insurance Ltd* [2002] EWCA Civ 300). By way of analogy in *Re Swissair Schweizerische Luftverkehr-Aktiengesellschaft v Edwards* [2003] EWCA Civ 63, a claimant had obtained a freezing order over assets and a sum was paid into court in substitution of the order, the Court of Appeal (overruling Neuberger J giving judgment at first instance) ordered that this did not provide the claimant with *security* and therefore refused permission to continue with the litigation. If a landlord's proprietary right to forfeit is to be seen as a quasi secured right then it will be treated in the same way.

4.117 If the party opposed to the forfeiture is a third party (such as a guarantor or a subtenant) then it is not the liquidator's role to oppose the landlord's application. Instead the third party should apply for relief (*Re Brompton Securities Ltd (in liquidation)* (1988) 4 BCC 189 and *Re National Jazz Centre* [1988] 2 EGLR 57).

4.118 There is an argument that IA 1986, s 130 does not restrict peaceable re-entry as it is not an *action or proceeding* (see above).

Bankruptcy

4.119 Following a bankruptcy order there is no automatic restriction on forfeiture. IA 1986, s 285(3) provides that:

> '. . . no person who is a creditor of the bankrupt in respect of the debt provable in the bankruptcy shall:
>
> (a) have any remedy against the property or person of the bankrupt in respect of that debt; or
> (b) before the discharge of the bankruptcy commence any action or other legal proceedings against the bankrupt except leave of the Court on such terms that the Court may impose.'

4.120 This provision does not prevent a landlord from forfeiting arguably because:

- IA 1986, s 285(3) only relates to the property of the bankrupt and after the making of the order the ownership of the lease has automatically become vested in the trustee in bankruptcy under IA 1986, s 306; and

- forfeiture is not a remedy used *in respect of a debt*, it is a remedy to terminate the lease and recover the landlord's own property (*Ezekiel v Orakpo* [1977] QB 260, CA). However, this is to be contrasted with *Harlow District Council v Hall* [2006] EWCA Civ 156, [2006] BPIR 712 where the Court of Appeal held there was no breach of s 285 in relation to executing a possession order unless the lease had been vested in the trustee in bankruptcy (the lease was a secure tenancy which did not become part of the bankrupts estate).

Section 285 does not prevent the landlord forfeiting by way of peaceable re-entry, although the trustee in bankruptcy can apply for relief (*Razzaq v Pala* [1998] BCC 66).

Relief from forfeiture

4.121 Where the right to forfeiture arises and the landlord has complied with any restrictions (such as serving a s 146 notice or obtaining permission to proceed under IA 1986, Sch B1, para 43) then the tenant may still rescue the lease by making an application for relief from forfeiture. Even though the tenant may be in default of its obligations the court has a very wide discretion to relieve the tenant from the sanction of forfeiture and allow the tenant one final opportunity to remedy the breach and compensate the landlord.

4.122 LPA 1925, s 146(2) creates a statutory right to apply for relief:

> 'Where a lessor is proceeding, by action or otherwise, to enforce a right of re-entry or forfeiture, the lessee may, in the lessor's action, if any, or any action brought by himself, apply to the Court for relief; and the Court may grant or refuse relief, as the Court, having regard to the conduct of the parties . . . and to all the other circumstances, thinks fit; and . . . grant it on such terms, if any, as to costs, expenses, damages, compensation, penalty, or otherwise, including the granting of an injunction to restrain any like breach in the future, as the Court in the circumstances in each case, thinks fit.'

4.123 A tenant may apply for relief as soon as a s 146 notice has been served. Alternatively if the landlord brings forfeiture proceedings then the tenant will normally counterclaim for relief (*Pakwood Transport Ltd v 15 Beauchamp Place Ltd* (1977) 3 P & CR 112). If the landlord forfeits by way of peaceable re-entry (without court proceedings) then an application for the relief can still be made (*Billson v Residential Apartments Ltd* [1992] 1 AC 494).

4.124 An application for relief can be made even where the breach is not capable of remedy.

Who can apply for relief?

4.125 In addition to the tenant, subtenants are also entitled to apply for relief under LPA 1925, s 146(4). In fact subtenants have a broader right than the tenant to make the application because:

- s 146(4) also applies where the breach involves non-payment of rent (the tenant's right to claim relief for non-payment of rent arises only at common law as it is more restricted);

- where a tenant is in bankruptcy the subtenant would be able to make the application, even where an insolvent tenant has lost the right under s 146(9) or (10) (see **4.71**).

4.126 A subtenant may apply for relief in relation to part or the whole of the demised premises (however, he is more likely to get relief of just part where he is occupying a self-contained part of the demise: *Clifford v PRs of Johnson (deceased)* [1979] 2 EGLR 41).

4.127 The objective of relief proceedings is to put the landlord back in the position he should have been in prior to the date of forfeiture. The means by which this is done in relation to subtenants is by way of an order vesting the tenancy on the subtenant on the same terms. However, as this process compels the landlord to enter into a direct relationship with the subtenant it is potentially prejudicial and unfair. Therefore relief should be used sparingly (see *Fivecourts v J R Leisure Developments* [2001] L & TR 5 and also *Ropac v Inntrepreneur* [2001] L & TR 93). Any such new tenancy will be on the same terms and for a term equal to the remaining term under the original lease. However, the court can impose any conditions it thinks fit and has a very wide discretion (see, eg, *Chatham Empire Theatre (1955) Ltd v Ultrans* [1961] 1 WLR 817).

4.128 A mortgagee is also entitled to claim relief under s 146(4) in an identical way as if the mortgagee was a subtenant. A mortgagee can apply for relief under s 146(4) even where the lease has been disclaimed by the trustee in bankruptcy or liquidator of the tenant (*Barclays Bank v Prudential Assurance* [1998] 1 EGLR 44).

4.129 Original tenants and previous assignees do not have the right to claim relief (however, for exceptions, see *Fuller v Judy Properties Ltd* [1992] 1 EGLR 75).

Court's discretion

4.130 Section 146(4) provides the court with a very wide discretion (*Southern Depot Co Ltd v British Railways Board* [1990] 2 EGLR 39). Special rules apply to relief where the breach relates to the non-payment of rent (see below).

4.131 In *Rose v Hyman* [1911] 2 KB 234 Couzens-Hardy MR set out a number of guidelines as follows:

• the tenant must so far as possible remedy the breaches alleged in the notice, and pay reasonable compensation (including costs) for the breaches which cannot be remedied;

• if the breach is of a negative covenant (such as a breach for a user clause) then the tenant must undertake not to breach the covenant in the future;

• if the act complained of has caused dilapidation (or *waste*) then the tenants must undertake to make the repairs good, if it is possible to do so;

• in relation to any other kind of breach where damages, other than nominal, might be recovered in an action, the tenant must undertake not to repeat the breach.

4.132 In addition to this a court will take into account:

• the tenant's conduct and whether the breach was *deliberately committed* (*Billson v Residential Apartments Ltd* [1990] 60 P&CR 392);

• the value of the property and the extent of damage caused by the breach;

• the seriousness of the breach (*Scala House and District Property Co Ltd v Forbes* [1974] QB 575);

• whether the tenant is able to remedy the breach effectively and will be able to comply with the terms of the lease in the future (*Darlington BC v Denmark Chemists* [1993] 1 EGLR 62); and

• whether there is a disproportionate advantage to the landlord if he is allowed to forfeit when contrasted with disadvantage to the tenant in not being granted relief (*Billson v Residential Apartments Ltd* [1992] 2 AC 494).

4.133 Where a breach is not capable of remedy the courts are less likely to grant relief (see **4.68** in relation to irremediable breaches). Therefore the most straightforward relief application will involve a breach which can easily be put right (such as where there is a continuing positive covenant to repair) and which is unlikely to cause the landlord any lasting damage (*Expert Clothing Service v Hillgate House Ltd* [1986] Ch 340).

4.134 Where a breach is not capable of remedy the courts are less likely to grant relief. However, relief can still be given (see the position in relation to insolvency cases at **4.141**).

Relief and non-payment of rent

4.135 Special rules apply if the breach of covenant relates to non-payment of rent. Relief becomes (almost) automatic where the tenant is able to pay the rent arrears and the landlord's costs. The tenant's application is made to the county court (under the County Courts Act 1984, s 138 – there is no jurisdiction under LPA 1925, s 146 which does not apply to rent arrears). Under the Civil Procedure Rules (CPR, rr 35.3 and 55.3) the county court has principal jurisdiction for these applications. Most claims will be brought either as part of an existing forfeiture claim (as a counterclaim) or on the basis of a stand alone application.

4.136 Under the County Courts Act 1984, s 138(2) if a tenant pays into court (or pays the landlord direct) all the rent in arrears and costs 5 clear days before the date of the hearing the possession action will automatically cease and the tenancy will continue.

4.137 After a possession hearing (or at the trial) the tenant can still bring an application under s 138(2) (provided that the court has not ordered possession). Under s 138(3) the court will order that the possession will be suspended for a period of at least 4 weeks providing the tenant with a further opportunity to pay all the arrears and costs (within the period specified). It may also adjourn the proceedings to allow time to investigate the tenant's financial circumstances. In a commercial case the court will take a less sympathetic view unless the tenant can pay the rent arrears and costs within a reasonable time (s 138(4); see also *R v A Circuit Judge* (1976) 33 P&CR 423).

4.138 If the tenant has not already applied for relief an application can be made up to 6 months after the landlord has obtained possession. This is sometimes useful in an insolvency situation where the officeholder has decided to take no action being unaware that the lease has some value. The tenant/officeholder retains the power to make the application even where the landlord has re-let (*Bank of Ireland v South Lodge Developments* [1996] 1 EGLR 91 and *Billson v Residential Apartments Ltd* [1992] 2 AC 494).

4.139 Even where the court has made an order for possession and the landlord has recovered possession the tenant may still make an application to the court for relief at any time within 6 months of the landlord recovering possession (s 138(9A)). The tenant can also apply for relief within 6 months of the landlord taking possession through peaceable re-entry (*Billson v Residential Apartments Ltd* [1992] 2 AC 494).

Terms of relief

4.140 Relief is usually granted on condition that rent arrears and costs are paid by the tenant and other breaches (if part of a s 146 notice) are remedied within the time ordered by the court. However, the court's discretion is wide. It is possible that the relief will be given even where the breach will not be remedied (*Associated British Ports v CH Bailey* [1990] 2 AC 703).

Insolvency and relief

4.141 The mere fact that a tenant is insolvent is not of itself a ground for saying relief should not be granted (*Metro Nominees (Wandsworth) (No 1) v K Rayment* [2008] BCC 40). If an insolvent tenant can show a good arguable case for relief the order should be made (*Re Brompton Securities (No 2)* [1988] 3 All ER 677).

4.142 The right to claim relief may be lost in liquidation and bankruptcy under the exceptions set out under the provisions of LPA 1925, s 146(9) (see **4.72**). If the liquidator or trustee in bankruptcy does not sell the lease within a year and fails to apply for relief within that time the right to claim relief is lost (see LPA 1925, s 146(10) and **4.71** and *Official Custodian for Charities v Parway Estates Developments Ltd* [1985] Ch 151, CA).

4.143 If an application for relief is made within the year but not heard during the time then relief can still be granted (see *Pearson v Gee* [1934] AC 272). However, this provision does not affect an assignee of the tenant's interest, providing the acquisition takes place within the year and then the assignee is entitled to the full protection of s 146. An assignment of the lease must be executed within this time or a non-conditional agreement to assign must be entered into within a year of the commencement of the insolvency (*Re Castle & Sons Ltd* (1906) 94 LT 396).

4.144 In order to obtain relief the insolvent tenant (or its proposed assignee on a sale) must usually pay all rent arrears and the landlord's costs (*Pakwood Transport Ltd v 15 Beauchamp Place Ltd* (1977) 36 P&CR 112, CA). However, this is not always the case where:

- the right to forfeit has been waived or any other defect in the process would invalidate the forfeiture (*Sood v Barker* [1991] 1 EGLR 87);

- the rent arrears have been substituted in a voluntary arrangement for a lesser sum then relief may be granted on payment of the reduced amount (see **4.20** and *Thomas v Ken Thomas Ltd* [2007] BLR 429);

- in exercising its discretion the court decides that the damage to the tenant and its creditors as a whole unreasonably outweighs the potential damage to the landlord in granting relief. Arguably where future rents will be paid the landlord will not sustain any additional damage (over and above the damage it has already sustained by suffering the pre-insolvency arrears). Therefore the refusal to grant relief may be disproportionate (in general see *Billson v Residential Apartments* [1992] 2 AC 494);

- in *Metro Nominees (Wandsworth) (No 1) v K Rayment* [2006] BCC 40 it was made clear that even where permission had been given to bring forfeiture proceedings in an administration (under IA 1986, Sch B1, para 43) it may still be open to the administrators to make an application for relief from forfeiture.

Forfeiture – effect

How does forfeiture take place?

4.145 Forfeiture can be effected in two ways:

(1) by the landlord taking direct action and taking back physical possession of the premises (sometimes called *peaceable re-entry*); or

(2) by the issue and service of possession/forfeiture proceedings.

4.146 Forfeiture represents a final and positive act which manifests the landlord's intention to bring the lease to an end. Once the act has taken place the landlord cannot change its mind, the lease will be terminated. So that where a landlord issued and served forfeiture proceedings and then sought to amend its claim to one only claiming rent arrears the Court of Appeal refused to resurrect the lease underlining that the service of the proceedings was the final act of forfeiture (*GS Fashions v B&Q plc* [1995] 1 EGLR 62).

4.147 Peaceable re-entry is a popular remedy for landlords of commercial premises and is usually achieved by changing the locks of a premises, however there are restrictions which must be observed:

- the various statutory restrictions in relation to residential premises and insolvency (in part) restrain the use of peaceable re-entry without going through the court process(see **4.20**);

- even where the usual statutory restrictions do not apply the Criminal Law Act 1977, s 6 makes the use of the remedy an offence where force is used in order to gain entry if someone is physically present on the premises who is opposed to the entry;

- where the tenant is enfranchising the landlord's interest; and

- where the landlord is relying on a breach of a repairing obligation and the tenant has served a counter notice under the Leasehold Property (Repairs) Act 1938.

4.148 Landlords often face a problem with squatters where an insolvent tenant has left the property vacant. Squatters will often display a sign on the property advertising to any potential bailiffs that they are in occupation and will rely upon their rights under the Criminal Law Act 1977, s 6. Faced with this challenge landlords will have to obtain a possession order even where an administrator or liquidator has given permission to peaceably re-enter.

4.149 Where an administrator has given permission to use peaceable re-entry to terminate the lease but the premises are used partly for residential purposes then the landlord will still need to apply to the court for a possession order to satisfy the Protection from Eviction Act 1977, s 2 (*Patel v Pirabakaram* [2006] 1 WLR 3112).

Effect of forfeiture

4.150 Forfeiture will bring an end to the lease and the following consequences apply:

- the effective date of the forfeiture will crystallise the liabilities of both landlord and tenant. All liabilities (on both sides) accrued due prior to the date of forfeiture remain;

- unliquidated claims (such as for dilapidations) will crystallise at the date of forfeiture;

- all derivative interests (eg under leases, mortgages on the lease or under lease) will be terminated when a lease is forfeited (subject to the right to claim relief):

    '. . . it is a rule of law that if there is a lessee and he has created an under lease, or any other legal interest, if the lease is forfeited, then the under lessee or the person who claims under the lease, loses his estate as well as the lessee himself' (Mellish LJ in *Great Western Railway v Smith* (1876) 2 Ch D 235)

Chapter 5

THIRD PARTY LIABILITY

5.1 When negotiating the terms of a new lease with a tenant, a landlord will often insist that some form of security is provided in order to protect the landlord against the default of the tenant. The tenant's insolvency will invariably impact upon the tenant's ability to perform its obligations under a lease and this chapter will deal with the interaction between a tenant's insolvency and the landlord's ability to pursue third parties for payment of the ongoing rents (and any arrears) and the performance of the tenant's covenants under the lease generally.

5.2 The landlord may be in a position to look to any or all of the following third parties to assist in ensuring that the landlord's rental income is protected:

- surety of the existing tenant;

- original tenant ('old lease'), where the original tenant or a previous assignee remains liable on assignment under a lease which predates 1 January 1996 (when the Landlord and Tenant (Covenants) Act 1995 came into force);

- surety to the original tenant (or to a previous assignee) under an old lease;

- authorised guarantee agreements, where the original tenant or a previous assignee remains liable on assignment pursuant to an authorised guarantee agreement under a lease which post-dates 1 January 2006 (a 'new lease');

- subtenant;

- mortgagee.

It should be noted that a landlord does not have to elect who to pursue in the first instance when a tenant defaults. He may seek payment from one or all of the above parties and may do so in any order (*Norwich Union Life Insurance Society v Low Profile Fashions Ltd* (1991) 64 P&CR 187, CA).

SURETY OF EXISTING TENANT

5.3   Landlords will often require their tenants to provide a suitable third party guarantee upon the granting of the lease. Such guarantees are often provided by the tenant's parent company or by the directors of the tenant company. At **5.82** the ability of a tenant to attempt to release a guarantor's liability through the use of a company voluntary arrangement (CVA) is examined. The landlord will look to the guarantor to pay the rent in the event of the tenant's default, following the tenant's entry into formal insolvency. The tenant's entry into a formal insolvency procedure will not bring a guarantor's liability to an end (indeed this is one of the main reasons why landlords take guarantees). In the cases of administration, liquidation and administrative receivership, the lease continues and is not automatically terminated by virtue of the company entering into that process. Accordingly, there is no reason why the landlord should not pursue the guarantor at any time.

5.4   The surety provisions of most leases contain a combination (or all) of three basic forms:

- *a guarantee covenant*, where the surety covenants that the tenant will perform all of its obligations in the lease. The surety becomes liable in damages as soon as the tenant is in breach of covenant. In *Cerium Investments Ltd v Evans* (1991) 62 P&CR 203 this was described as a 'see to it' obligation. The landlord has the right to claim unliquidated damages, but not as a *debt* (in other words the surety could defend any such claim on the basis that the breach might not have caused the landlord actual loss – the landlord can be put to strict proof of the losses, see *Moschi v Lep Air Services Ltd* [1973] AC 331);

- *an indemnity*, where the surety covenants to pay the rent and perform the lease covenants if the tenant does not. The surety becomes liable to pay the rent or other lease sums as a debt if the tenant defaults;

- *obligation to take a new lease,* if the lease is disclaimed or determined by way of forfeiture then the surety promises to enter a new lease for a term equivalent to the balance of the term left on the lease. This provision was originally designed to ensure the surety was not released by an early termination. However, following *Hindcastle v Barbara Attenborough Associates Ltd* [1996] 1 All ER 737, it was decided that a disclaimer did not release a guarantor and the benefit of this provision has been reduced (it will still force the surety to formally take on a lease which is preferable to most landlords).

5.5   The surety of an existing tenant could arise in one of the following ways:

- where the tenant provided a surety on taking the lease; or

- where the landlord had been entitled under an express alienation covenant in a lease to require the assignee to provide a surety (for a new lease or where it was reasonable for the landlord to require one).

5.6 Guarantees are often drafted so that the guarantor is obliged to discharge the liabilities or covenants in the lease as primary obligor, rather than solely as surety. The effect of this is that the guarantor will not be released even where the liability of the tenant may be released or compromised in some way.

5.7 Having discharged the tenant's liabilities under a lease, a guarantor would usually have the right of indemnity from the tenant for any sums paid out. In cases where the tenant is insolvent, the guarantor is left to make a claim in the administration or liquidation of the company for any loss he has sustained by reason of his having to discharge his guarantee obligations. In *Re P and A Swift Investments v Combined English Stores Group plc* [1989] AC 632, CA, Lord Templeman summed up the position as follows:

> 'A surety for a tenant is a quasi tenant who volunteers to be a substitute or twelfth man for the tenant's team and is subject to the same rules and regulations as the player he replaces.'

5.8 The basis of a surety's liability must be determined by reference to the contractual terms agreed between the parties. For example, a surety will generally be liable for increases in the passing rent following a rent review, unless the terms of the guarantee provide that the surety was to be consulted in relation to any rent review, and if he was not, then the rent review will not be binding upon him and he will remain liable only for the original rent (see *Cressey v Jacobs* (unreported) 14 October 1977).

Release of guarantor

5.9 There are a number of actions that may have the effect of releasing a guarantor from liability and the landlord should always consider the implication his actions could have on the liability of any guarantor.

Forfeiture

5.10 The forfeiture of a lease will bring that lease to an end. A landlord may pursue the guarantor for any arrears or breaches of the lease up to the date the lease is forfeited but not beyond this time. The terms of the guarantee may require the guarantor to take a new lease of the premises in the event that the lease is forfeited, but in the absence of such a clause, the landlord should consider the position carefully before forfeiting the lease where he has a guarantor on the hook. Whilst a landlord has no duty to mitigate his loss whilst the lease is continuing and rent is not being paid, the liabilities under the lease will be brought to an end by an act of forfeiture.

Changes to the terms of the lease

5.11 A landlord may inadvertently release a guarantor from liability where he has agreed variations to the terms of a lease with the tenant, without the guarantor's consent to those variations. Whilst not directly relevant to the question of the insolvency of the tenant, landlords should be aware that they may face an argument by the guarantor that they have been released from their obligations prior to the insolvency of the tenant in the event that the terms of the lease were varied without their being made a party to the modification.

5.12 In *Holme v Brunskill* (1878) 3 QBD 495, CA the Court of Appeal by a majority of 2 to 1 decided that a variation to the lease, no matter how minor had the effect of discharging the surety. Dissenting, Brett LJ stated that in order for a variation to have the effect of discharging a surety, that variation must be a material variation that has the effect of prejudicing the surety. However, the other two judges disagreed and said it was for the surety to decide whether or not the variation was material or not.

5.13 Notwithstanding the common law position that a surety will be released by a variation of the lease, there is no reason why contracts of surety should not include provisions that provide that a guarantor will not be released in the event that the lease is varied. The courts have held such clauses to be valid (see *Selous Street Properties Ltd v Oronel Fabrics Ltd* [1984] 1 EGLR 50). Any such clause must be unambiguous as the wording in the clause will be construed strictly against the landlord (see *West Horndon Industrial Park Ltd v Phoenix Timber Group plc* [1995] 1 EGLR 77); *Howard de Walden Estates Ltd v Pasta Place Ltd* [1995] 1 EGLR 79).

5.14 If the landlord and tenant vary the length of the term of the lease by consent this will operate as a surrender of the lease and a re-grant of a new lease. This would release any guarantor (*Friends' Provident Life Office v British Railways Board* [1995] 2 EGLR 55). In considering whether a guarantor has been released by a variation it is necessary to see whether any of the terms he has guaranteed have been varied without his consent.

Other forms of release

5.15 A landlord has been held to release a guarantor when he agrees to give a tenant further time to pay arrears beyond the time for payment stipulated in the lease itself. This was held to be the case in the matter of *Overend, Gurney and Co Ltd (Liquidators) v Oriental Financial Corporation Ltd (Liquidators)* (1874) LR 7 HL 348, HL. In that case there was no evidence that the landlord giving the tenant further time to pay had prejudiced the surety in any way but it was held that the landlord's failure to enforce in a timely manner and in agreeing with the tenant to wait before being paid, could have led to a further deterioration of the tenant's position. In order for the landlord's surety to be released in this way, there must be an agreement between the landlord and the tenant that the tenant should be granted some form of concession. A landlord will not release a surety in circumstances where he has simply not taken any action to recover the rent.

Death of surety

5.16 Unlike some other guaranteed obligations, the death of a surety of a lease will generally not release the surety from liability (although one should always check whether there are any express provisions in the guarantee itself that deal with this eventuality). In the Court of Appeal decision of *Lloyds' v Harper* (1880) 16 Ch D 290, Lush LJ stated:

> 'The lease was intended to be a guaranteed lease and it is impossible to say that the guarantor could put an end to the guarantee at his pleasure, or that it could put an end by his death contrary to the manifest intention of a party.'

5.17 This case was followed in the more recent decision of *Basch v Stekel* (2000) 81 P&CR D1, where the guarantor had covenanted to perform the tenant's obligations in the event of its default and also to take a lease of the premises for the unexpired residue of the term in the event that any liquidator of the tenant disclaimed the lease. The Court of Appeal held that the guarantor's liability survived the guarantor's death (notwithstanding the fact that he had died 3 years before the landlord approached the executors requiring the guarantor to take a new lease). The Court of Appeal ruled that the executors of a contracting party are bound to perform all the deceased contracts (to the extent that his assets would allow), unless a sufficient intention to the contrary is apparent from the terms of the guarantee itself.

Bankruptcy of the guarantor

5.18 Any liabilities that the landlord guarantor will have when he is made bankrupt break up into two distinct claims which a landlord can make, namely:

- liabilities falling due under a lease up to the date the bankruptcy order is made; and

- liabilities falling due after the bankruptcy order is made.

5.19 The position in relation to the pre-bankruptcy liability is straightforward. The guarantor can prove in the bankruptcy estate of the guarantor in respect of liabilities that have fallen due up to the date of the bankruptcy order (*Re Houlder* [1929] 1 Ch 205).

5.20 The position in relation to the post-bankruptcy liability is not so clear. It has been held that the guarantor's liability to guarantee the continuing obligations under a lease that continues after the guarantor's bankruptcy is not a contingent liability that can be proved for in bankruptcy, and accordingly the guarantee continues regardless of the bankruptcy (*Boyd v Robins* (1859) 5 CB

NS 597). Commentators have noted, however, that this ruling may be inconsistent with that of the House of Lords in *Hardy v Fothergill* (1888) 13 App Cas 351, which concerned the indemnity provided by an assignee to an original tenant, which was held to be a contingent liability which could be proved in the bankruptcy of the assignee and be discharged.

The position of a guarantor on the disclaimer of the lease

5.21 This is discussed in more detail in chapter 7. Following the *Hindcastle v Barbara Attenborough Associates* [1997] AC 70 and *Active Estates v Parness* [2002] 3 EGLR 13, obligations of the guarantor pursuant to a guarantee remain enforceable following the disclaimer of a lease, provided the landlord does not take any steps to take possession of the property. By doing so, the landlord is deemed to have acknowledged that the lease has come to an end in all respects. The service of a notice by a landlord on a guarantor requiring him to take a new lease following disclaimer was held not to be an act of taking possession (see *Basch v Stekel* (2000) 81 P&CR D1).

Other liabilities of the guarantor

5.22 On assignment, the assignee and any new surety is often asked to provide an indemnity for previous assignees and the original tenant. In addition the landlord will in practice (when granting licence to assign) extract from the proposed assignee and its guarantor a direct covenant to pay the rent and observe and perform the covenants on the tenant's part for the whole of the residue of the term. Therefore under an old lease the guarantor often has indemnified the following parties:

- the landlord;

- the original tenant; and

- previous assignees.

5.23 An original tenant under an old lease (any lease granted prior to 1 January 1996) or any assignor who has provided an authorised guarantee agreement under a new lease can pursue the guarantor for an indemnity under a subrogated claim in the event that the guarantor fails to discharge the liability to the landlord and the original tenant or assignor is called upon to do so (see *Becton Dickinson UK Ltd v Zwebner* [1989] QB 208).

Liability to landlord's successors in title

5.24 In the case of *P & A Swift Investments v Combined English Stores Group plc* [1989] AC 632, the House of Lords upheld the long-established common law rule that any benefit which relates to or which 'touches and concerns' land will transfer with the land. Therefore the benefit of a surety obligation would pass with any transfer of the reversion to an assignee of that reversion due to the fact that it is an obligation which relates to the land.

Dissolution of the tenant

5.25 Where the guarantee is a simple guarantee (and does not contain an indemnity or a primary obligation on the part of the guarantor), then the dissolution of the tenant will release the guarantor from liability. This is because in those cases, the entire extent of the guarantor's liability is derived from the tenant's liability itself. One way for a landlord to reinstate the guarantor's liability is to apply to the court for an order restoring the dissolved tenant company to the register in order to bring the guarantor back on the hook. Such an application can be made up to 20 years after the company is dissolved in cases where the dissolution was not preceded by a liquidation and up to 2 years after the date of dissolution in all other cases.

Administration – particular guarantor problems

5.26 Where the current tenant is in administration then the landlord can call upon the tenant's guarantor to continue to discharge liabilities under the lease. However, the administrator has no right to disclaim the lease. Therefore the guarantor has no right to apply for a vesting order. In addition the current guarantor is not able to apply for an overriding lease under the Landlord and Tenant (Covenants) Act 1995, s 19. The guarantor will often face a protracted delay paying the rent whilst deriving no benefit from the property.

5.27 A guarantor who is required to pay rent following the default of the tenant generally has a right to be subrogated to the position of the landlord. This will include, where the tenant company is in administration, a landlord's ability to claim the continuing rents from the administrators as an expense of the administration (administration expenses are dealt with in detail at **2.83**). This was held to be the position in the case of liquidations in the matter of *Re Downer Enterprises Ltd* [1974] 2 All ER 1074. Should a guarantor succeed in achieving payment from the administrators as an expense, this will promote the guarantor's claim from its previous unsecured status. That case concerned an assignor under an old lease who had original tenant liability but the principle can be applied to any guarantor.

ORIGINAL TENANT LIABILITY

5.28 The grant of a lease creates an interest in land and it also creates a binding contractual relationship between the landlord and the tenant. Like any other contract, a lease is subject to the rules relating to privity of contract. Before the Landlord and Tenant (Covenants) Act 1995 ('the Covenants Act') came into force, the original tenant under a lease remained liable for the tenant's obligations for the entire term of the lease, notwithstanding that the original tenant may have assigned his interest in the lease to a third party (who in turn may have assigned that interest again). This continuing liability for breaches of the lease by subsequent assignees was deemed to be too onerous. The perceived prejudice was redressed by the introduction of the Covenants Act. The Act abolished original tenant liability in respect of any commercial lease granted on or after 1 January 1996, save in the case of three limited exceptions, namely:

(1) where the lease was granted pursuant to an option or agreement (including a right of first refusal) entered into before 1 January 1996 (s 1(3)(a), (6), (7)); or

(2) where the tenancy was granted pursuant to a court order made before that date (s 1(3)(b)); or

(3) where the tenancy is an overriding lease granted pursuant to s 19 in relation to a tenancy which is not a new tenancy.

Any tenancy that is not a 'new tenancy' will be an old tenancy and original tenant liability will remain. The treatment of old and new tenancies is discussed below.

OLD TENANCIES

5.29 By virtue of there being privity of contract between the landlord and the original tenant, the original tenant is liable for any breach of the lease during any part of the term (see *Walkers' case* [1587] 3 Co Rep 22a). The liability of the original tenant will even survive the disclaimer of the lease by the current tenant's liquidator (under IA 1986, s 178) or trustee in bankruptcy (under IA 1986, s 315; this is discussed in more detail in chapter 18), or by the Crown (under Companies Act 1985, s 656) (see *Warnford Investments Ltd v Duckworth* [1979] Ch 127 and *Hindcastle Ltd v Barbara Attenborough Associates Ltd* [1997] AC 70).

5.30 When faced with an insolvent tenant, a landlord who has the benefit of an old lease may claim the arrears from the original tenant. However, the original tenant's liability will lapse after 6 months from the date when the sum fell due unless the landlord has served a notice pursuant to s 17 of the Covenants Act informing the original tenant that a *fixed charge* is due. A fixed charge includes any rent, service charge and any other liquidated sum payable in the event of a failure to comply with any lease covenant in accordance with s 17(6). The notice must specify the amount of the charge and any interest thereon (see s 17(2)). The notice is also required where there is an authorised guarantee agreement for a new lease.

The s 17 notice

5.31 The landlord must ensure that the s 17 notice is served in the form prescribed by the Landlord and Tenant (Covenants) Act 1995 (Notices) Regulations 1995, SI 1995/2964. Alternatively, the notice must be in a form that is substantially to the same effect as that prescribed (s 27(4)).

5.32 Service of the notice is governed by s 27(5) of the Covenants Act which incorporates the rules as to service set out in s 23(1) of the Landlord and Tenant Act 1927, namely that the notice may be served either personally or by leaving it at the tenant's last known place of abode in England or Wales or by sending it by recorded delivery to that address (or in the case of a Local Authority or Public Utility) to its principal office. The case of *C A Webber Transport Ltd v Railtrack plc* [2004] 1 WLR 320, CA confirmed that a notice sent by recorded delivery is deemed to be served on the date when it is entrusted to the post. It is no defence for a tenant to seek to prove that he never received the notice and the provision of such evidence will not be a bar to the landlord's right to recover from the original tenant following the ruling in *Commercial Union Life Assurance Co Ltd v Moustafa* [1999] 24 EG 155.

Non-release of original tenant

5.33 Where a lease is determined, either by forfeiture or by surrender the original tenant's liability will be determined as at that date (he will remain liable for any breaches of the terms of the lease that have accrued at the date the lease is determined).

5.34 However, there are a number of circumstances where one might expect an original tenant to be released from liability but in fact the courts have held that such liability is not released. These include the following.

Voluntary arrangement of tenant

5.35 An original tenant will remain liable for the performance of the tenant's covenants in the lease notwithstanding the current tenant has entered into a voluntary arrangement, the effect of which could be to reduce or limit his liability under the terms of the lease. In the case of *RA Securities Ltd v Mercantile Credit Co Ltd* [1995] 3 All ER 581 the defendant was an original tenant under a lease that had first been assigned to one party, and then assigned again to another party. The subsequent assignee entered into a voluntary arrangement pursuant to IA 1986, s 1, the effect of which was to compromise the current tenant's liability for arrears of rent and also to impose a surrender of the lease on the landlord, who upon the acceptance of the CVA was deemed to have accepted the surrender by virtue of the statutory deeming imposed by IA 1986. The court held that the original tenant was not released from his liabilities by virtue of the current tenant's compromise of the liabilities under the lease under its voluntary arrangement. The position relating to sureties and voluntary arrangements is discussed in detail at **5.74**.

Variations to the lease agreed by the landlord and subsequent assignees

5.36 Whilst the variation of a lease will often release a guarantor or surety where the guarantor was not a party to that variation, the position in relation to the liability of the original tenant is different. The original tenant will not generally be released from liability where the lease has been varied, even where such variations lead to more onerous obligations than had originally been agreed by the original parties to the lease.

5.37 In *Friends Provident Life Office v British Railways Board* [1996] 1 All ER 336, the landlord and the original tenant's assignee entered into an extensive deed of variation to vary the existing terms of the original lease. The variation included a provision significantly increasing the rent payable pursuant to the lease. The assignee entered liquidation some 8 years later and the landlord sought to recover the arrears of rent from the original tenant. At first instance, it was held that the changes made to the lease were so fundamental that the affect of the deed of variation was to act as a surrender and re-grant by operation of law, which in turn would release the original tenant from its liability. On appeal though, the Court of Appeal held that there had been no surrender and re-grant. While the variations to the lease were extensive and particularly onerous in relation to the increased rental obligations, they did not seek to amend the term of the lease or the extent of the demised premises, therefore these variations did not take effect as a surrender and re-grant.

5.38 The Court of Appeal further rejected the submission that the substitution of a higher rent in the deed of variation had the effect of releasing the original tenant from its personal covenant for the payment of the original rent. These variations would have released a surety. However, it would have taken a variation that amounted to a surrender and re-grant to release an original tenant (eg if the variation had altered the term of the lease this would have effected a release).

5.39 The Court of Appeal held that the original tenant should not be bound to perform the varied obligations under the lease and would only remain liable for the original rent it had covenanted to pay on the grant of the lease. This position also has statutory authority as the Covenants Act, s 18 achieves a similar result.

5.40 In the *Friends Provident* case and earlier cases, it has consistently been held that the liability of an original lessee is not one of surety or guarantor, rather that the original lessee's liability is based on his personal covenant to perform the obligations under the lease upon its grant.

Liability for reviewed rent

5.41 Although the original tenant will not be liable for increases in rent that are effected by way of a variation to a lease, an original tenant will become liable for increases in rent determined following a rent review pursuant to the provisions of the lease (see *Centrovincial Estates plc v Bulk Storage Ltd* (1983) 46 P &CR 393 and also *Selous Street Properties Ltd v Oronel Fabrics Ltd* (1984) 270 EG 643).

Original tenant liability during continuation tenancy

5.42 An original tenant may remain liable to pay the continuing rent falling due beyond the contractual term during any continuation tenancy under Part II of the Landlord and Tenant Act 1954 but this will depend upon the wording of the lease itself, in accordance with the ruling in *City of London Corporation v Fell; Herbert Duncan Ltd v Cluttons* [1993] QB 589, CA. Conversely, the original tenant will not be liable to pay interim rent in any event, unless the lease expressly provides for this (see *Herbert Duncan*).

NEW LEASES

Leases created on or after 1 January 1996

5.43 The effect of the Covenants Act is to abolish original tenant liability in respect of all leases created on or after 1 January 1996 (save in the limited circumstances above). The tenant will be released upon assignment in respect of any breach of covenant occurring after the assignment (s 5(2)), unless the assignment is an excluded assignment as defined by s 11, meaning that:

- the assignment itself was in breach of covenant and occurred without the landlord's consent; or

- it is an assignment taking effect by operation of law (eg a lease held by a bankrupt will automatically vest in his trustee in bankruptcy pursuant to IA 1986, s 306).

5.44 Where there has been an excluded assignment, the release of the original tenant will not take effect until the incidence of the next non-excluded assignment of the lease (s 11(2)(b)).

5.45 The original tenant will remain liable in respect of any breach of the lease occurring prior to the assignment of the lease (s 24(1)). Where the lease was held by joint tenants and one tenant is released, the release of that one tenant will not discharge the liability of the other joint tenant, who will remain liable (s 13(2)).

5.46 In order to compensate the landlord for losing the ability to pursue the original tenant for breaches of the lease by an assignee, the Covenants Act enables the landlord to retain the original tenant's liability by recasting the tenant as a guarantor of his immediate successor. This is achieved through the execution of an authorised guarantee agreement (AGA).

5.47   An agreement will be an AGA if:

- the lease contains a covenant against assignment without consent (whether absolute or qualified); and

- the landlord has provided such consent subject to a condition that the tenant enters into an AGA (s 16(3)); and

- the agreement is entered into pursuant to that condition.

5.48   To the extent that the AGA purports to require the tenant to guarantee the performance of any party other than his immediate assignee, or seeks to impose liability on the original tenant in relation to any liability arising after the assignee himself has been released by virtue of the Act, the agreement will be void as an AGA (s 25).

5.49   If a subsequent assignee agrees a *relevant variation* with the landlord then the liability under the AGA is limited to the liability that would have accrued if the lease had not been varied (see the Covenants Act, s 18). A *relevant variation* for the purpose of the Covenants Act is one which the landlord had the absolute right to refuse.

INTERMEDIATE ASSIGNEE

Old tenancy

5.50   As there is no privity of contract between the landlord and an intermediate assignee, the assignee is not liable for breaches committed by a subsequent assignee after there has ceased to be privity of estate, after the assignment has taken place (see *Valliant v Dodemede* (1742) 2 Atk 546):

- where rent is payable in advance the assignor will remain liable for the entire rent if it fell due while he was still the tenant, notwithstanding the fact that the rental period straddles the date of the further assignment; but

- where the rent is payable in arrears, the earlier assignee will remain liable to the extent that the rent relates to the period of his ownership under the Apportionment Act 1870 (see *Parry v Robinson-Wyllie Ltd* (1987) 54 P&CR 187 and *Swansea Bank v Thomas* (1879) 4 Ex D 94).

5.51   This general rule is usually modified by the parties reaching an express agreement on the intermediate assignee's liability (see *Estates Gazette Ltd v Benjamin Restaurants Ltd* [1995] 1 All ER 129, CA). Most leases require assignees to enter into a direct covenant with the landlord which renews the effect of the privity of contract making assignees liable for the period until the end of the lease even where the lease has been assigned on yet again.

New tenancy

5.52 The intermediate assignee will be released upon the assignment unless the assignment is an excluded assignment (see above) or his liability is extended by an AGA to make him liable for any breach of covenant by his immediate successor.

5.53 The right to recovery against an intermediate assignee is subject to the restrictions noted above imposed by the Covenants Act, ss 17 and 18.

SURETIES OF ORIGINAL TENANT OR INTERMEDIATE ASSIGNEE

Old tenancy

5.54 A surety will normally be discharged following any modification in the contract which he has guaranteed, unless he is a party to the modification (*Holme v Brunskill* (1878) 3 QBD 495, CA; in relation to sureties see **5.3**).

5.55 Unless there is an express release, the assignment of a lease will not release the surety of the assignor from his liability (*Baynton v Morgan* (1888) 22 QBD 74).

5.56 In *Selous Street Properties Ltd v Oronel Fabrics Ltd* [1984] 1 EGLR 50, Hutchinson J held that even if a lease variation significantly increased rental value for rent review purposes such a variation did not discharge the liability of the original lessees. The position of the original lessee's guarantor was different though and in principle he was entitled to be discharged from liability. This was on the basis of the different rules applicable to a surety as compared with an original lessee (although in *Selous* there was a specific proviso in the guarantee clause which excluded the guarantor's release).

5.57 Where there is an express agreement to the contrary, the provisions of any such agreement will be construed restrictively (see *West Horndon Industrial Park Ltd v Phoenix Timber Group plc* [1995] 1 EGLR 77).

New tenancy

5.58 The common law principles relating to the release of a surety discussed above apply equally to sureties and guarantors under new tenancies. Sureties are protected against successive assignments in the same way as their principals. Accordingly the surety will be simultaneously released when its principal is released (the Covenants Act, s 24(2)).

5.59 Finally, the provisions of the Covenants Act, ss 17 and 18 contain provisions for the benefit of sureties of former tenants which provide the same protections afforded to the principals (see above).

SUBTENANTS

5.60   Where a lease is forfeited, the forfeiture will have the effect of forfeiting any subleases or other inferior interests granted under the lease that has been forfeited (*Official Custodian for Charities v Mackey* [1984] 3 All ER 689). This includes the termination of any charge on the lease.

5.61   However, where the head lease is surrendered or disclaimed by a liquidator or trustee in bankruptcy (or by the Crown), the subtenant's interest will continue and the subtenant holds his interest in land on the same terms and subject to the same rights and liabilities that would have applied had the head lease continued. The sublease will continue for the same term and in any event no longer than the head lease would have if there had been no surrender. Under the Law of Property Act 1925, s 139(1):

> 'Where a reversion expectant on a lease is surrendered or merged, the estate or interest which as against the lessee [the Head landlord's interest] . . . shall be deemed for the purpose of preserving the same incidents and obligations as would have affected the original reversion had there been no surrender or merger thereof.'

5.62   The effect of a disclaimer on a subtenant's right to continue occupying property is discussed in detail at **7.59** and **7.60**.

Law of Distress Amendment Act 1908

5.63   Irrespective of whether the landlord's tenant is the subject of formal insolvency proceedings or not, at any time where the tenant is in arrears of rent under a head lease, a landlord may require any subtenant to pay its sub-rents directly to him by virtue of the Law of Distress Amendment Act 1908 ('the 1908 Act'), s 6. The 1908 Act will be abolished when the Tribunals, Courts and Enforcement Act 2007 (TCEA 2007) comes into force. Until then the following procedure applies (the new procedure is set out below). The landlord claims the sub-rents by serving notice on the subtenant and the following considerations apply:

- There is no prescribed form which the notice must take. However, the notice must state the quantum of arrears and require that all future payments, whether outstanding at the date of the notice or not, are to be made directly to the head landlord until his tenant's arrears are satisfied.

- Section 3 of the 1908 Act provides that the effect of the s 6 notice shall operate so as to transfer to the superior landlord the right to recover, receive and give a discharge for the sub-rent. This assigns the benefit of the rent to the landlord who therefore has an enforceable right against the subtenant. The subtenant also has a defence should its immediate landlord seek to recover the sub-rents from its subtenant.

- Following the ruling in *Jarvis v Hemmings* [1912] 1 Ch 462 the notice may be served by registered post or by another means so as to ensure it reaches the subtenant.

- A s 6 notice can be served when the tenant is in administration, liquidation or any other insolvent arrangement which is an invaluable remedy for a landlord who faces a low (or no) dividend from his tenant's insolvent estate. It is unlikely that a s 6 notice would be restrained by any moratorium (see the decision in *Re Olympia & York Canary Wharf Ltd* [1993] BCLC 453 in relation to contractual notices).

- The Court of Appeal decided in *Rhodes v Allied Dunbar Pension Services Ltd* [1989] 1 All ER 1161 that where a s 6 notice had been served the sub-rents were payable even where the bank had appointed a receiver over the tenant's assets.

Tribunals, Courts and Enforcement Act 2007

5.64 TCEA 2007 abolishes the head landlord's right to serve a s 6 notice on a subtenant and replaces this with the new procedure which is commenced by serving a similar notice under s 81. The form and content for the new notice will be prescribed by regulations (which have not yet been published). However, the notice will state the amount of rent due (s 81(5)) and have the effect of transferring the right to receive this to the head landlord until:

- the notified amount has been paid; or

- the notice is replaced or withdrawn (s 81(4)).

5.65 However, the s 81 process will not be as straightforward as the process under the 1908 Act. The landlord will not be able to serve a notice unless commercial rent arrears recovery (CRAR) could be exercised and perhaps the biggest problem arises from s 81(5), which provides that there will be a delay between the service of a s 81 notice and the date it becomes effective. The period of this delay will be prescribed by the regulations. Where the head tenant becomes insolvent the landlord usually rushes to serve a s 6 notice on subtenants, the delay imposed by the new s 81 procedure will provide insolvency officeholders with an opportunity of collecting sub-rents before the landlord's notice bites.

THE EFFECT OF VOLUNTARY ARRANGEMENTS ON THE LIABILITY OF GUARANTORS AND OTHER SURETIES

5.66 When the owner of commercial premises receives a request from a new or recently formed company with no or little trading history to grant them a lease of commercial premises, the landlord will invariably require the prospective tenant to provide the landlord with some form of security to protect the landlord against the default of his tenant. Such security can take the form of:

- a rent deposit (see chapter 6);

- a bank guarantee; or

- a guarantee from the directors or shareholders of the tenant, or the tenant's parent company.

5.67 The purpose of taking security from an individual guarantor or from a parent company is to ensure that the landlord is able to pursue that third party for any breaches of covenant by the tenant, in the event of the tenant's default.

5.68 The dominant purposes of security are to protect the landlord against the possibility of the tenant's insolvency. What then, is the position where the tenant utilises a formal insolvency regime, such as voluntary arrangement to attempt to effect a release not only of its own liabilities to the landlord but also those of any guarantors or sureties?

5.69 This question was brought into sharp focus by the landmark case of *Prudential Assurance Co Ltd and Others v PRG Powerhouse Ltd and Others* [2007] EWHC 1002 (Ch), [2007] BPIR 839. Prior to dealing with this case, it is helpful to review the earlier authorities that led to the ruling in *Powerhouse*.

5.70 Chapter 1, at **1.24**, contains an overview of the procedure that individuals and companies alike can utilise to propose a voluntary arrangement to their creditors.

Overview of arrangements

Schemes of arrangement

5.71 Prior to the introduction of voluntary arrangements into insolvency law, it was open to companies to put forward statutory schemes of arrangement (under Companies Act 1985, s 425 and Companies Act 2006, Part 26). A scheme of arrangement is a compromise with creditors (or any class of creditors) or members (or any class of members). The scheme is binding if 75% of each class of creditors and members vote in favour. Unlike a voluntary arrangement a scheme of arrangement must be sanctioned by the court. If it obtains the requisite sanction from the creditors, members and court, the scheme will bind all members and creditors regardless of whether they had notice.

5.72 The practical difficulty with schemes of arrangement is dealing with each class of creditors. The question arises as to whether it would be appropriate to include a class of creditors all of which enjoyed guarantees from third parties and as to whether a positive vote from 75% of them would be possible.

5.73 In *Re Equitable Life Assurance Society* [2002] BCC 319, and *Re British Aviation Insurance Co Ltd* [2005] EWHC 1621 (Ch), the court made clear that the make-up of the creditor classes should be determined at an early stage and publicised to the creditors. Each class should include creditors or members that have shared rights (see *Re BTR plc* [1999] 2 BCLC 675). Where the creditors are mostly landlords then they could be constituted into a single class. If some of the landlords have the benefit of guarantees then they could be constituted into a separate class. In *Re Hawk Insurance Company Ltd* [2001] 2 BCLC 480, Chadwick LJ held that each class 'must be confined to those persons whose rights are not so dissimilar as to make it impossible for them to consult together with a view to their common interest'.

Voluntary arrangements

5.74 In contrast the voluntary arrangement (VA) procedure allows a debtor to put forward a proposal to all of his unsecured creditors:

- without dividing them into separate groups and subgroups;

- without the need to seek the court's sanction of any proposal; and

- that if put to and approved by the requisite majority of the debtor's creditors and members as a single class will be binding on all.

5.75 There is therefore an inherent risk with VAs that in certain circumstances, it may be possible for a majority of creditors to vote through proposals that do not prejudice them but do prejudice a minority of the debtor's creditors. This risk of accretion of the minority was raised in the case of *Re Hawk Insurance Co Ltd* [2002] BCC 300. The only safeguard that exists to counterbalance this eventuality is the creditor's ability to challenge the VA (after it has been approved) on grounds that:

- the terms of the VA are unfairly prejudicial to that creditor (or group of creditors); or

- there has been a material irregularity (see IA 1986, s 6 (CVAs) and s 262 (IVAs) and **1.57**).

5.76 The effect of the statutory binding in IA 1986, s 5(2)(b) provides that every creditor will be bound into the CVA as if he were a party to it. This operates in the same way as a scheme of arrangement (*RA Securities Ltd v Mercantile Credit Co Ltd* [1994] BCC 598, *Johnson v Davies* [1997] 1 WLR 1511 and *March Estates plc v Gunmark Ltd* [1996] 2 EGLR 38). The rationale behind this approach is that in a scheme of arrangement, a majority of creditors in a different class to the minority of creditors would not be able to push through proposals to the detriment of the class of minority creditors in a formal scheme of arrangement and so the position under a VA should be no different.

5.77 The Court of Appeal's decision in *Johnson v Davies* [1999] BCC 275 though, and in particular the leading judgment of Chadwick LJ created an element of uncertainty and a new interpretation of the nature of the statutory binding under a VA. The Court of Appeal decided that the effect of the passing of the proposal for a VA was to impose a form of deemed consent by every creditor affected by the VA irrespective of whether they voted in favour of the VA or at all.

5.78 In *Thomas v Ken Thomas Ltd* [2006] EWCA Civ 1504, Neuberger LJ held that the effect of the deemed consent was to replace the debtor's existing liabilities with a statutory compromise to the extent that the original liabilities no longer exist.

Effect on third party liability

5.79 However, this by itself does not have the effect of ruling that a debtor wishing to release a guarantor's liability to one of its creditors could be effected via a CVA.

5.80 In *Johnson*, Chadwick LJ opined on whether a VA could effect a release of a third party guarantor. Notwithstanding the fact that the guarantor was not the subject of a VA itself (or even insolvent) he stated:

'The statutory hypothesis requires [the dissenting creditor] to be treated as if he had consented to the arrangement. The consequence, as it seems to me, is that the legislature must be taken to have intended that both the question whether the debtor is discharged by the arrangement and the question whether co-debtors and sureties are discharged by the arrangement were to be answered by treating the arrangement as consensual; that is to say, by construing its terms as if they were the terms of a consensual agreement between the debtor and all those creditors who, under the statutory hypothesis, must be treated as being consenting parties . . . whether or not to exclude co-debtors and sureties from the operation, under the general law, of the terms of a composition or arrangements between a debtor and his creditors is a matter of policy. There are, plainly, arguments of policy which point towards the exclusion; in particular, that it is in the interest of the debtors and his other creditors that a creditor should not be dissuaded from voting in favour of a voluntary arrangement out of concern that he will lose his rights against co-debtors and sureties. But, equally, there are arguments which point towards allowing the general law to have effect; in particular, that it is in the interest of the debtor that he should be able to propose a scheme under which he will obtain a complete release from his liabilities, including the rights or contribution of co-debtors. It is also in the interests of other creditors bound by the scheme, as it should be frustrated by action by a co-debtor (not so bound) in enforcing rights of contribution . . . the general law is to have effect. It is up to the debtor to propose and for the creditor to accept or reject proposals which either do or do not have the effect of releasing co-debtors or sureties. A creditor who is prejudiced by the decision of the majority to approve proposals which have the effect of releasing a co-debtor against whom he would otherwise have recourse can apply to the court, under section 262 of the 1986 Act, for the approval of the meeting to be revoked . . . it follows that I would reject the submission that, as a matter of principle, no term in a voluntary arrangement can have the effect of releasing a co-debtor or surety. In my view, the effect of a voluntary arrangement has to be determined by ensuring its terms.'

Notwithstanding Chadwick LJ's comments, the Court of Appeal was unanimous in its decision that the terms of the IVA in that case did not have the effect of releasing a co-debtor (decided on the terms of that particular arrangement).

5.81 A contract of guarantee may contain an express provision to deny the guarantor the right to be excluded in a VA. Without this a VA that purports to reduce or extinguish the primary debtor's liability to the creditor could in principle effect a release to the same extent of any guarantor or co-debtor. However, there are a number of significant hurdles to this.

- As noted at **5.9**, it is possible that in certain circumstances, a guarantor may be released by the release of the principal debtor. In *Greene King plc v Stanley* [2002] BPIR 491, the debtor took a loan from the claimant brewery in order to finance the purchase of the lease of a public house. The debtor's parents granted Greene King a charge over their home as security for the loan. The debtor experienced financial difficulties and proposed an IVA. Greene King (who had not been repaid in the IVA) issued possession proceedings against the debtor's parents. The Court of Appeal held that they could see no relevant distinction between the position of a surety and that of a co-debtor. The IVA proposal expressly referred to Greene King having rights of security against the debtor's parents' property. This was held to be sufficient to put the debtor's creditors on notice that Greene King intended to preserve its rights against the debtor's parents going forward.

- There have been a handful of reported cases where VA's have attempted to release the liability of guarantors or co-debtors, where the surety of a co-debtor was of limited financial means and so the value of the guarantor to the creditor was of little or minimal value in any case (see *Natwest v Scher* [1998] BPIR 224 and *Re Primlaks* [1989] BCLC 734.

- Chadwick LJ's obiter comments in *Johnson v Davies* made it clear that a VA that provided for the release of guarantor's or co-debtors would be subject to an unfair prejudice argument that a creditor could make under IA 1986, s 6.

- Neuberger LJ in *Thomas v Ken Thomas Ltd* [2006] EWCA Civ 1504 emphasised the effect the statutory compromise has in substituting the original liabilities. Arguably if this is the case it raises an argument that even if a guarantee is not discharged by the VA it would only attach to the lower substituted statutory compromise sum. Neuberger LJ did not discuss guarantees but also did emphasise the danger of unfair prejudice.

Powerhouse

5.82 In the case of *Prudential Assurance Co Ltd and others v PRG Powerhouse Ltd and others; Luctor Ltd and others v PRG Powerhouse Ltd and others* [2007] 19 EG 164 (CS), in 2006, PRG Powerhouse Ltd was the UK's third largest retailer of consumer electrical items and domestic white goods. With a turnover of approximately £300m per year and more than 100 stores across Great Britain, the business increasingly suffered from growing competition from the supermarkets and online retailers. The Powerhouse business (that had been purchased by a New Zealand private equity plc from the administrative receivers of the previous failed business in 2003) was making losses in the region of £20m per annum and those losses were being subsidised by its parent company.

5.83 The directors of Powerhouse believed that if they could extricate the business from those retail outlets that were loss making and concentrate on a core group of approximately 60 stores, that it would be possible to return the company to break-even or even profitable trading. As one of a range of measures that were implemented, Powerhouse made a proposal for a voluntary arrangement in order to release its liabilities to the creditors of its non-profitable/viable stores (predominantly landlords) in exchange for a dividend whilst continuing to discharge its obligations to the landlords of the stores it wished to retain in full. The unusual facts of the *Powerhouse* case were that the UK company's New Zealand parent had guaranteed its subsidiary's performance under its leases across almost its entire portfolio. In order to secure its parent's support for the restructured business going forward, the terms of the Powerhouse proposal provided that in addition to seeking a release of its obligations to the landlords of those premises that they no longer wished to trade from ('the closed premises'). The key proposals were:

• all creditors would be paid in full in relation to debts which existed at the date of the CVA meeting;

• a number of premises would be closed by the CVA;

• landlords of open premises would be paid in full in relation to future rent liability;

• landlords of premises of closed premises would be paid only a dividend in relation to future rent liability; and

• the obligations of its parent to the closed premises landlords would be released in consideration for the parent agreeing to fund the dividend payment.

The guarantees were perceived to be of value to the landlords and it was against this backdrop that the Powerhouse CVA was challenged.

5.84 The Powerhouse CVA proposal was passed by the requisite majority of the company's unsecured and unconnected creditors in February 2006. Two groups of closed premises landlords (totaling approximately 13 in all) sought to challenge the Powerhouse CVA on some or all of the following three grounds:

(1) the terms of the Powerhouse CVA were unfairly prejudicial to the closed premises landlords with the benefit of guarantees;

(2) there were material irregularities at or in relation to the meeting of the creditors; and

(3) the purported extent of the Powerhouse CVA went beyond the scope of what a CVA is empowered to do for the purposes of IA 1986, s 1 (this application was made by way of Part 8 proceedings for a declaration).

5.85 The court ordered the trial of a number of preliminary issues based on an agreed statement of facts. These issues fell broadly into two categories:

(1) whether the CVA had the effect of releasing the guarantees or indemnities, directly or indirectly; and

(2) if it did, then whether that release was unfairly prejudicial to the closed premises landlords.

Did the CVA release the guarantees?

5.86 The answer to the first issue was that the CVA did release the guarantees although not as a consequence of the dicta of Chadwick LJ in *Johnson v Davies* because the vast majority of the guarantee documents contained provisions expressly precluding the release of the guarantor, Etherton J stated:

> '51. The hypothetical agreement resulting from approval of CVA is not, therefore, one between creditors as to rights and obligations between themselves in a capacity other than as creditors of the company. In relation to the guarantees, PRG's obligations are those to the debtor arising out of a contract made by itself as principal on its own behalf. There is nothing in the IA or IR which makes the CVA binding and enforceable as between PRG and the guaranteed landlords in respect of such obligations.'

5.87 Etherton J decided the guarantees were to be treated as having been released because the CVA contained clauses that successfully created a covenant by the closed premises landlords not to sue the parent company in the event that the CVA was passed. Etherton J ruled that the effect of these clauses, and the statutory nature of the closed premises landlords' deemed consent to be bound by its terms under IA 1986, s 5(2)(b), created a contractual obligation on the part of the closed premises landlords to the company not to pursue the parent under the guarantees they held. It should be noted, that this was a covenant enforceable by Powerhouse, rather than by the guarantor itself. The effect of Etherton J's judgment then was that the guarantees would have to be treated as being released, for only as long as Powerhouse was in a position to enforce the landlords' covenant to Powerhouse not to sue its parent.

Unfair Prejudice

5.88 The court then had to consider whether the terms of the CVA were unfairly prejudicial to the claimant group of closed premises landlords (or any of them).

5.89 Whilst there was no evidence before the court that the guarantor was highly affluent, the court ruled that the guarantees had some value to the landlords and even if the parent did not have sufficient assets to discharge the guarantee obligations going forward for an indefinite period, the value to the landlords of having the guarantees was that it would enhance their negotiating position when dealing with the parent and give them rights in relation to the subsequent insolvency of the parent should that occur. The CVA did not attribute any value to the guarantees and so Etherton J ruled that the terms of the CVA were unfairly prejudicial to the landlords of the closed premises with the benefit of parent company guarantees.

5.90 The decision in *Powerhouse* raises a number of important issues but also leaves a number of questions unanswered. The obiter comments of Chadwick LJ in *Johnson v Davies* have been left intact and so it remains open for a company or an individual who has debts that are secured by a guarantor or co-debtor to propose a VA which may include a release of that guarantor or co-debtor (provided the express terms of the contract or guarantee prohibit the release of the guarantee in this way).

5.91 Further, the CVA mechanism may be used to indirectly effect a quasi-release of a guarantee by creating a covenant not to sue, that will be enforceable by the debtor so long as the debtor remains able to enforce it. In order to avoid a potential challenge on the grounds of unfair prejudice, following the ruling of Etherton J the CVA proposal should ensure that value is attributed to the guarantees held by creditors and those creditors with the benefit of guarantees should be compensated for the loss of their right to pursue the guarantor by way of an enhanced dividend (or their agreement not to do so). The level of such enhancement will depend on the facts of each case. Where, for example, there is evidence that the parent company is insolvent and market conditions for the particular property in question dictate that it will be relatively easy to find a new tenant for the premises, then the value to be attributed to the guarantee may be very low. Conversely, where there is evidence that the parent or other guarantor is highly solvent and has significant liquid assets and where market conditions are such that finding a new tenant for the property (on the same terms and at the same rent the debtor was subject to) would prove extremely difficult in the short term, then the compensation required to justify a release will be much higher.

Practical considerations for landlords

5.92 The following are practical considerations for landlords when drafting leases and guarantees following *Powerhouse*:

• Landlords should consider taking alternative forms of security in addition to a guarantee from a parent entity or an individual. Where landlords are in a strong negotiating position, they may decide to demand that their incoming tenant grant them a debenture containing fixed and floating charges over their entire undertaking. The benefits of taking such security are discussed throughout this book but essentially, having a debenture in place would prevent their rights from being compromised by VA without their consent.

• Landlords should ensure that guarantee documents contain clauses to the effect that the guarantees will not be released by any agreement to release or any other form of release that may occur of the primary debtor's liability to the landlord.

• Upon becoming aware of a proposal for a VA or a meeting to vote upon its terms, landlords should consider, and if necessary take immediate advice on the effect that the VA will have on their relationship with their tenant and any contracted guarantee they hold from a third party. The time-limit for challenging VAs is very tight and the courts have confirmed that they have no discretion to extend those time-limits (see *Bournemouth AFC* [1998] BPIR 183 and *Thomas v Ken Thomas Ltd* [2007] EWCA Civ 1504).

Chapter 6

LEASEHOLD SECURITY – RENT DEPOSITS AND OTHER FORMS OF SECURITY

INTRODUCTION

6.1   Third party guarantees have a number of disadvantages over other forms of security:

- the value of the guarantee depends on the solvency of the guarantor (*Prudential Assurance Co Ltd and others v PRG Powerhouse Ltd and others; Luctor Ltd and others v PRG Powerhouse Ltd* [2008] 3 EGLR 131; *National Westminster Bank plc v Scher* [1998] BPIR 224);

- enforcement of guarantees may require the landlord to take positive action such as instigating legal proceedings involving cost and time; and

- guarantors can be inadvertently released by a variation to the terms of the lease (*Holme v Brunskill* (1878) 3 QBD 495, CA).

6.2   The main alternatives available to landlords to secure the obligations under the lease and protect against the insolvency of the tenant are:

- taking formal security over the tenant's lease or business by way of a fixed charge or a debenture containing floating charges (or both) (see **1.62**); or

- the use of rent deposits.

6.3   Rent deposits take a variety of forms, but essentially all provide for the tenant to make a sum of money available that can be drawn upon by the landlord in the event of the tenant's default (usually an amount equivalent to 6 months' or a year's rent). In the event that the landlord has to have recourse to the rent deposit, then most leases contain a covenant by the tenant to replenish the rent deposit.

6.4   The terms governing the parties' rights and obligations in relation to a rent deposit are often contained in a separate document to the lease, known as a rent deposit deed. However, even where the terms governing the rent deposit are contained in a separate document, it is advisable for landlords to ensure that reference is made to the rent deposit in the lease and that the definition of the lease includes reference to the rent deposit deed, so as to bring the tenant's obligations under the rent deposit within the terms of the lease, thereby providing the landlord with the ability to forfeit the lease in the event that the tenant defaults with any of its covenants under the rent deposit deed.

6.5   A liquidator of a tenant of commercial premises, should consider the terms of the lease and any accompanying rent deposit deed carefully so as to ensure that in the event of disclaimer of the lease by the liquidator, the liquidator does not also disclaim the company's rights (if any) to the return of any balance standing in favour of the tenant in the rent deposit account.

6.6   In cases of tenants' insolvency, there is often a dispute between the landlord and the officeholder of the tenant as to the ownership of any rent deposit. In order to ascertain who owns the rent deposit, it is necessary to have reference to and construe the terms of the lease and any accompanying rent deposit deed.

HOW THE DEPOSIT IS HELD

6.7   The deposit may be held in the following ways:

- *Express terms creating a trust:* In cases where the tenant has deposited funds expressly on trust for the landlord, then the landlord will be able to claim that he is entitled to the monies, subject to any balance (if any) being returned to the tenant upon the expiry of the lease (see *Re Chelsea Cloisters Ltd (in liquidation)* (1980) 41 P & CR 98, CA) regardless of the insolvency.

- *Charge:* Where the deposit is secured by a registered charge in the landlord's favour. Many rent deposit deeds will stipulate that the tenant remains the owner of the rent deposit throughout the term of the lease, subject to his granting a charge to the landlord over the deposit. In such cases, the tenant retains ownership of the deposit but the landlord's status is elevated to that of a secured creditor. A rent deposit that creates a charge in this way should arguably be registered as a charge over the property of the tenant company at Companies House within 21 days of creation (Companies Act 1985, s 396). A failure to register the charge may render the security void at the instance of the liquidator (Companies Act 1985, s 399 and see *Re Greenport Ltd (in liquidation); sub nom Obaray v Gateway (London) Ltd* [2000] EGCS 149). This potentially leaves the landlord with having to prove in the liquidation as an unsecured creditor (however, see *Obaray v Gateway (London) Ltd*).The position should be construed with reference to terms of the rent deposit.

- *Contract:* In *Obaray v Gateway (London) Ltd* [2000] EGCS 149, Williamson J held that in the absence of a charge (or a charge that is void for non-registration), the deposit may still operate as a contractual mechanism for giving effect to the landlord's right to deduct not confined to breaches of the lease, but also to include damages which arise as a result of premature termination by disclaimer on insolvency. On that basis, the terms of the deed are intended to have a contractual effect so that the deposit held by the landlord is to the right to return only the balance after relevant deductions. The tenant is never contractually entitled to more than the balance of the monies in the account (after deductions).

• *Quistclose trust:* In the absence of express terms that establish the nature of the beneficial entitlement to the rent deposit, an alternative argument is that the landlord holds the rent deposit on trust for the tenant for the specific purpose of discharging the tenant's obligations. If the landlord or landlord's agent holds the monies on trust for the tenant in a distinct account then the tenant remains the beneficial owner of those funds (unless and until they are utilised by the landlord). This arrangement is often referred to as a 'quistclose trust', following the House of Lords' decision in the case of *Barclays Bank Ltd v Quistclose Investments Ltd* [1970] AC 567, HL.

6.8   Whilst not mentioned in *Obaray,* Hazel Williamson QC's judgment accords with the decision in the case of *Capital Prime v Worthgate* (see **7.44**), where it was held that whilst a liquidator can disclaim the obligations of the company in liquidation, the disclaimer will not operate so as to terminate the rights of any other party to the contract.

6.9   The decision in *Obaray* has been criticised as it is difficult to square with the notion that unsecured creditors should be treated with parity and a landlord with defective security should not be entitled to enjoy any preferential or priority status above the company's other unsecured creditors. The decision in *Re Greenport* remains good law but it is of course advisable for landlords to register their charges at Companies House (notwithstanding that in *Re Greenport*, the court queried whether a rent deposit deed was a charge that had to be registered at Companies House because the deed did not purport to create a charge over the company's book debts).

6.10   From a landlord's perspective, a rent deposit deed should always deal with the position on a disclaimer of the lease by a liquidator of the tenant, and a clause allowing the landlord to deduct the amount equivalent to the landlord's statutory claim for damages on disclaimer is valid.

6.11   Following Hazel Williamson QC's judgment in *Obaray*, rent deposit agreements are often being drafted as loans to the landlord and the terms of the loan agreement stipulates when (and if) the loan is repayable to the tenant. Such loan agreements will usually contain a provision that the landlord will pay interest on the loan (equivalent to the amount of interest the landlord will receive on the funds in his account). However, such an arrangement may cause concern for the tenant, who may of course require security for the loan to safeguard against the insolvency of the landlord. The insolvency of landlords is discussed further at chapter 9.

6.12 The landlord's ability to draw upon funds held in a rent deposit in the event of its tenant's insolvency will depend on the type of insolvency the tenant is faced with.

ADMINISTRATIVE OR OTHER FORM OF LPA/FIXED CHARGE RECEIVERSHIP

6.13 In the case of receivership, there will be no restriction on the landlord from drawing down on funds held or accessible by the landlord, nor is there any restriction on the landlord issuing proceedings against the tenant in circumstances where the landlord is not able to unilaterally withdraw funds.

Voluntary liquidation

6.14 In the case of a creditors' or voluntary liquidation, there is no restriction on a secured creditor from exercising his rights under that security and so nothing preventing the landlord from drawing down funds from the rent deposit. In circumstances where it is necessary for the landlord to commence proceedings against the company in order to effect a draw down, then the liquidator is able to apply to the court for a direction under IA 1986, s 112 that the stay on proceedings against the company that automatically exists in the cases of compulsory liquidation, should be applicable to the liquidation of the tenant.

Compulsory liquidation

6.15 There is no prohibition on a secured creditor from exercising its security in the case of compulsory liquidation but if, for any reason, it is necessary for the landlord to issue proceedings against the tenant in compulsory liquidation to determine the question arising in relation to the rent deposit, then the court's leave to issue proceedings will be required under IA 1986, s 130(2). The position is similar in relation to bankruptcy (see IA 1986, s 285) and where such leave is required, the court is normally likely to give such leave (see *Lloyd v David Lloyd & Co* (1877) 6 Ch D 339, CA).

Administration

6.16 Where a company is in administration, the moratorium provision of IA 1986, Sch B1, para 43 provides that:

> 'No steps may be taken to enforce security over the Company's property except:
>
> (a) with the consent of the administrator, or

(b)   with the permission of the court.'

6.17   Where the rent deposit provides that the tenant will remain the beneficial owner of the funds subject to a charge in favour of the landlord, then this provision indicates that the administrator's consent should be obtained prior to utilising funds held in a rent deposit account (unless the deposit has been drafted as a collateral security arrangement – see below). Save in cases where the administrator disputes the amount to be deducted by the landlord, there will usually be no reason for the administrator not to provide consent to the landlord to make deductions from the rent deposit.

Voluntary arrangements

6.18   IA 1986 expressly provides that the rights of secured creditors cannot be affected by the terms of a voluntary arrangement (VA) in the absence of their express agreement to the contrary. However, the terms of the VA should be scrutinised carefully to ensure that the landlord's rights to utilise the rent deposits are not directly or indirectly compromised by any term of the VA. For further discussion on the rights of secured creditors in relation to VAs see **1.36**.

Financial collateral arrangements and bank guarantees

6.19   In order to avoid any uncertainty in the case of a tenant's administration, landlords may wish to procure bank guarantees from the tenant's bank, so that rather than be bound by the moratorium in the event of the tenant's entry into administration, the landlord can simply make demands on the bank. Alternatively, landlords can draft rent deposit instruments so that they are secured financial collateral arrangements that fall within the Financial Collateral Arrangements (No 2) Regulations 2003, SI 2003/3226. A financial collateral arrangement is an agreement evidenced in writing, where:

'(a)   The purpose of the agreement or arrangement is to secure the relevant financial obligations owed to the collateral-taker;

(b)   the collateral-provider creates or there arises a security interest in financial collateral to secure those obligations;

(c)   the financial collateral is delivered, transferred, held, registered or otherwise designated so as to be in the possession or under the control of the collateral-taker or a person acting on its behalf; any right of the collateral-provider to substitute equivalent financial collateral or withdraw excess financial collateral shall not prevent the financial collateral being in the possession or under the control of the collateral-taker; and

(d)   the collateral-provider and the collateral-taker are both non-natural persons.'

6.20   Provided the rent deposit instrument satisfies the above criteria, then the advantages of the rent deposit being structured in this way are as follows:

- the agreement will not be void if it is not registered at Companies House in accordance with the Companies Act 1985, ss 395, 396 and 399 (reg 4(4) of the Regulations);

- the moratorium provisions restricting the enforcement of security in the event of a company's administration (IA 1986, Sch B1, para 43(2)) do not apply;

- the administrator's power to deal with charged property in accordance with IA 1986, Sch B1, paras 70 and 71 is removed;

- where a company has the benefit of a small company moratorium in place pursuant to IA 1986, Sch A1, then the restrictions imposed by para 20 and para 12(1)(g) will not apply to any security created arising under a financial collateral arrangement;

- in relation to winding-up proceedings, IA 1986, s 127 (which prohibits the disposition of the company's property between the presentation of a winding-up petition and the date of the winding-up order) will not apply;

- IA 1986, s 245 (avoidance of the certain floating charges) shall not apply to any charge created as a security structural as a financial collateral arrangement.

Chapter 7

DISCLAIMER

7.1 In circumstances where a liquidator (in both solvent and insolvent liquidations) or a trustee in bankruptcy is faced with property that he considers to be *onerous* he has the power under the Insolvency Act 1986 (IA 1986), s 178 (liquidation) or s 315 (bankruptcy) to disclaim that property. Disclaimer is only available in these forms of insolvency. Therefore it is not available in administration, receivership or voluntary arrangements (VAs) (although in relation to VAs a contracting party may be bound by the terms of the VA to treat the contract as if it has been surrendered – see **2.22**). A disclaimer:

> '. . . operates so as to determine, as from the date of the disclaimer, the rights, interests and liabilities of the [company/bankrupt] in or in respect of the disclaimed property.' (IA 1986, ss 178(4), 315(3))

7.2 Historically, liquidators and trustees required the leave of the court to disclaim property (the trustee's power to disclaim first arising in 1869 followed by the introduction of a liquidator's power to disclaim by the Companies Act 1929), but the effect of the provisions of IA 1986 was to enable liquidators and trustees (in most cases) to disclaim without first seeking the court's sanction before doing so.

ONEROUS PROPERTY

7.3 Onerous property is defined by IA 1986, s 178(3) as being any unprofitable contract and any other property of the company which:

• is unsaleable or not readily saleable; or

• is such that it may give rise to a liability to pay money or perform any other onerous act.

'Unsaleable or not readily saleable'

7.4 Whereas it will usually be possible for a liquidator or trustee to assign or surrender a lease for a premium value where the rent reserved under the lease is below the current market rack rate, the position will be very different where rents have fallen. The liquidator or trustee can use the disclaimer procedure in such instances to assist them in winding up the affairs of the insolvent estate.

The landlord will be compensated by being able to submit a claim for compensation (discussed below) arising from and following the disclaimer (IA 1986, s 178(6)).

Property giving rise to a liability

7.5 A lease will not automatically determine upon the incidence of liquidation or bankruptcy. The rents and other obligations under the lease will continue to fall due.

7.6 A trustee in bankruptcy may become personally liable for the performance of these covenants, and whilst a liquidator will not, he may have to discharge ongoing rents as an expense of the liquidation (that will rank in priority to his own fees). The issue of liquidation expenses is discussed at **2.64**. A lease therefore, can almost always be construed as being onerous property (see *Eyre v Hall* (1986) 18 HLR 509).

7.7 In *Re Hans Place* [1993] BCLC 768 the court held that it had no general jurisdiction to interfere with a liquidator's decision to disclaim any of the company's property unless the liquidator had acted in bad faith or in the event of 'perversity by the liquidator' (as per Evans-Lombe QC, as he was, sitting as a deputy judge of the High Court) which would justify a challenge under IA 1986, s 168(5) (under which, any person aggrieved by the acts of a liquidator may apply to the court for relief).

7.8 Therefore the term 'onerous property' is widely construed. For example, a waste management licence has been held to constitute such property (*Celtic Extraction Ltd v Bluestone Chemicals Ltd and The Environment Agency* [2001] Ch 475 overruling the decision of Neuberger J in *Re Mineral Resources Ltd* [1999] BCC 422 who had ruled that a liquidator may not disclaim where to do so would constitute a breach of environmental legislation).

7.9 For a detailed discussion of how the courts will determine whether property is onerous see the dicta of Chesterman J in *Transmetro Corporation Ltd v Real Investments Pty Ltd* (1999) 17 ACLA 1,314 at 1,320 and that of Chadwick LJ in *Re SSSL Realisations (2002) Ltd* [2006] EWCA Civ 7.

7.10 It is also possible to disclaim freehold property. The process is called 'escheat' which is dealt with in chapter 11.

DISCLAIMER IN LIQUIDATION (IA 1986, S 178)

7.11 The effect of a liquidator's disclaimer is to bring the company's obligations and interest in respect of the disclaimed property to an end, but so far as possible does not affect the rights or liabilities of any third party who may have an interest in or an obligation under that property (IA 1986, s 178(4)).

7.12 In liquidation, the most common form of property that is disclaimed is the company's interest in its lease(s) of commercial premises. Whilst a liquidator will generally not become personally liable for the rent and other obligations under a lease held by a company on his appointment, such payments may be or may become payable as an expense of the liquidation in accordance with the Insolvency Rules 1986 (IR 1986), r 4.218 in priority to the liquidator's own fees (discussed at **2.64** above).

Procedure in liquidation

7.13 The liquidator does not require the court's permission to disclaim and the property is disclaimed by filing the appropriate notice (Form 4.53) at court. The procedure for preparing and filing the Notice of Disclaimer is contained at IR 1986, rr 4.187–4.194.

7.14 Where a liquidator wishes to disclaim the company's interest in a lease, he must comply with the provisions contained in IA 1986, s 179, which provide that the disclaimer will not take effect until a copy of the sealed Notice of Disclaimer has been served (so far as the liquidator is aware of their addresses) on every person claiming under the company as underlessee or mortgagee and either:

- no application is made for a vesting order (discussed below pursuant to IA 1986, s 181 within 14 days); or

- where such an application is made, the court directs that the disclaimer shall take effect.

7.15 A liquidator can require any person who it appears to him may have an interest in the disclaimed property to declare within 14 days whether he does have an interest in that property. In the event that that party fails to comply with the liquidator's request, the liquidator is entitled to assume that there is no such interest (IR 1986, r 4.192).

Notice to elect (IA 1986, s 178(5))

7.16 Where the liquidation continues and particularly where the liquidator is not making use of the leasehold premises nor paying the ongoing rents as an expense of the liquidation, the landlord may wish to force the liquidator's hand to decide what he intends to do with the lease. Under IA 1986, s 178(5) any party interested in the property may apply to the liquidator requiring him to make a decision as to whether or not he will disclaim the property or not. The liquidator then has a period of 28 days (or such longer period as the court may allow) in which to elect whether or not to file a Notice of Disclaimer.

7.17 An application by a liquidator to extend the 28-day period should usually be made prior to the expiry of that 28-day period, save in exceptional circumstances (see *Re Jones, ex p Lovering* (1874) 9 Ch App 586).

7.18 Where a liquidator fails (or chooses not) to disclaim after receiving a notice to elect the position is unclear. The liquidator is not personally liable (*Graham v Edge* (1888) 20 QBD 683). However, it is arguable that the liquidator has adopted the lease for the benefit of the liquidation and where this is the case the rent should be treated as an expense of the liquidation under IR 1986, r 4.218(1)(m), which will rank in priority to the liquidator's own remuneration. As the landlord cannot submit a proof for future rent (ie post-liquidation rent that has not yet fallen due, see **2.62**), it is perhaps equitable that a liquidator's failure to disclaim after receiving notice to elect should result in a deemed acceptance that the future rent be treated as an expense.

7.19 The notice to elect is a useful tool for a landlord who has a tenant in liquidation, where the landlord wants to take the property back. For landlords, disclaimer often has the following advantages:

- it avoids the need to make an application (in compulsory liquidation cases) for leave to forfeit the lease;

- it enables the landlord to make an enhanced claim in the liquidation than he would have if he simply forfeited the lease or agreed a surrender with the liquidator;

- unlike an act of forfeiture, it will prevent the tenant in liquidation (acting by its liquidator) from making an application for relief from forfeiture in order to enforce breaches of landlord's covenants;

- the service of a notice to elect helps the landlord gain control over the process and achieve clarity at an earlier point in the process.

DISCLAIMER AND THIRD PARTIES

7.20 IA 1986, s 178(4) provides that whilst releasing the company from its rights and obligations, a disclaimer:

> ' . . . does not, except so far is necessary for the purpose of releasing the company from any liability, affect the rights or liabilities of any other person.'

7.21 In respect of leasehold property third parties such as guarantors and former tenants may be affected by the disclaimer of a commercial lease.

Guarantors and former tenants

7.22 A landlord will often seek the comfort of a personal guarantee from a third party company or individual when granting a lease to a company of questionable or uncertain covenant strength. Original tenants under old leases (see chapter 5) may also retain liability as will any assignee who has provided an authorised guarantee agreement in respect of a post-1 January 1996 lease (see chapter 5).

7.23 The terms of any such guarantee may expressly deal with the position as to the guarantor's liability in the event that the lease is disclaimed by a liquidator. Indeed, guarantees often contain a covenant by the guarantor to take a new lease of the premises for the residue of the unexpired term of the disclaimed lease in the event that the lease is disclaimed (see below). In the absence of such an express covenant though, what is the position of the guarantor when a lease is disclaimed?

7.24 In the 1901 Court of Appeal Decision of *Stacey v Hill* [1901] 1 KB 660 the landlord had granted a lease of shop premises. The landlord was concerned as to his tenant's ability to pay the rent and so took a guarantee from the defendant. Approximately one year after granting the lease, the tenant was adjudged bankrupt and a trustee was appointed over his estate. The trustee in bankruptcy disclaimed the lease. The defendant paid the rent up until the date of disclaimer pursuant to his obligations but denied any further liability. In a departure from the previous authority of the House of Lords in *Hill v East & West India Dock Co* (1884) 9 App Cas 448, the Court of Appeal ruled that the lease had ended by virtue of the disclaimer and accordingly that the defendant's guarantor obligations were released from the date of disclaimer.

7.25 The ruling in *Stacey v Hill* was followed in a number of first instance decisions for more than 95 years, before being overruled by the House of Lords in the case of *Hindcastle v Barbara Attenborough Associates* [1997] AC 70. *Hindcastle* concerned a lease of commercial premises that had been assigned on a number of occasions from 1983. In 1992 the current tenant of the premises (the third assignee) was placed into voluntary liquidation. The liquidator disclaimed the tenant's interest in the lease and the landlord sued the original tenant, the original tenant's assignee and his guarantor for the performance of the continuing obligations under the lease. The House of Lords unanimously reversed the Court of Appeal's decision in *Stacey v Hill*. The leading speech was given by Lord Nicholls who made the following comments in relation to the position of third parties:

> 'Disclaimer will, inevitably have an adverse impact on others: those with whom the contracts were made, and those who have rights and liabilities in respect of the property. The rights and obligations of these other persons are to be affected as little as possible. They are to be affected only to the extent necessary to achieve the primary object: the release of the company from all liability. Those who are prejudiced by the loss of their rights are entitled to prove in the winding up of the company as though they were creditors.'

7.26 He then went on to consider what effect the disclaimer had on the existence of the lease:

'If the problem is approached in this way, the best answer seems to be that the statute takes effect as a deeming provision so far as other persons' preserved rights and obligations are concerned. A deeming provision is a common place statutory technique. The statute provides that a disclaimer operates to determine the interest of the tenant in the disclaimed property but not so as to affect the rights or liabilities of any other person. Thus when the lease is disclaimed it is determined and the reversion accelerated but the rights and liabilities of others, such as guarantors and original tenants, are to remain *as though* the lease had continued and not been determined. In this way the determination of the lease is not permitted to affect the rights or liabilities of other persons. Statute has so provided.'

7.27 Lord Nicholls then considered the difficulty this places the guarantor in. In the event that the guarantor does not wish to seek the grant of a vesting order (see below), then the guarantor can remain liable for ongoing rental obligations in circumstances where no party is occupying the property and the lease has come to an end as between the landlord and the tenant. Lord Nicholls was live to this issue though and stated that in the event that the landlord enters upon the property and retakes possession:

'. . . he will thereby end all future claims against the original tenant and any guarantor, not just claims in respect of the shortfall between the lease rent and the current rental value of the property.'

7.28 Re-entry by the landlord then, will constitute a quasi act of forfeiture, thus determining (as at the date of re-entry) all parties' obligations in relation to the disclaimed lease.

7.29 It should be noted that there are situations where a landlord can enter onto demised premises, where such entry will not constitute the unequivocal 'forfeiture' of the disclaimed lease. Not all of these cases have been concerned with disclaimer but it is likely that the same issues will apply in relation to whether or not a landlord of a disclaimed lease has treated the lease as being at an end in all respects, including the liability of any surety. Relevant examples include:

- an attempt by the landlord to relet the property may not constitute such an act (*Oastler v Henderson* (1877) 2 QBD 575);

- the landlord's entry onto the premises in order to secure the premises against intruders has also been held not to constitute an act of surrender by the Landlord (*Relvok Properties v Dixon* (1972) 25 P&CR 1);

- the service of a notice by the landlord on the guarantor exercising his contractual right to require the guarantor to take a new lease following disclaimer is not to be construed as an acceptance by the landlord that the disclaimed lease is at an end in all respects (see below and see *Basch v Stekel*); and

- in *Scottish Widows plc v Tripipatkul* [2004] EWHC 1874 the court rejected an argument by a surety that a landlord had retaken possession by putting the property on the open market and describing it as being 'vacant' in the sales particulars.

7.30 A landlord should always exercise significant caution though when considering what to do with the disclaimed property when there are third parties who remain liable following disclaimer.

7.31 Finally, it should be noted that a landlord is under no obligation to take possession in order to mitigate his loss, as was confirmed in *Bhogal v Cheema* [1998] 2 EGLR 50. In *Cromwell Developments Ltd v Godfrey* [1998] 2 EGLR 62 the landlord had not taken any steps to take possession of the property for 10 years following disclaimer. The court held that the original tenant's liability to pay the rent under the disclaimed lease continued throughout the entire period.

Obligation to take new lease

7.32 Prior to *Hindcastle* the drafting of leases developed to take account of the possibility that guarantors would be released on disclaimer (on the traditional basis put forward in *Stacey v Hill* [1901] 1 KB 660). Therefore modern leases usually contained a provision requiring a guarantor to take a new lease in the event that the lease was disclaimed. Following *Hindcastle* the inclusion of a *new lease* provision is less of an imperative. However, landlords continue to require this on the basis that they prefer the lease to be vested in the guarantor. The obligation will be enforceable unless the disclaimer is by the Crown (following the lease vesting in the Crown bona vacantia) rather than by a liquidator (*Re Yarmarine (IW) Ltd* [1992] BCLC 276). Crown disclaimer is discussed below.

7.33 In the case of *Re a Company (No 792 of 1992), ex p Tredegar Enterprises Ltd* [1992] 2 EGLR 39, the court held that the effect of the landlord serving notice on the surety or guarantor to take a new lease was to create an equitable lease immediately under which the surety is liable to pay the rent.

7.34 Finally, the service of such notice does not release the guarantor from his obligations under the disclaimed lease until such time as the new lease is in place (*Basch v Stekel* [2001] L&TR 1).

7.35 When considering its discretion to make a vesting order under IA 1986, s 181 (see below), the court will balance the effect of the vesting order against the landlord's contractual ability to require the guarantor to take a new lease (see below – *Re AE Realisations (1985) Ltd* [1987] 3 All ER 83).

SUBTENANTS

7.36 *Hindcastle* was not concerned with the position faced by a subtenant following a disclaimer of a lease by a liquidator. However, Lord Nicholls noted the position that a subtenant faces as follows:

'In order to free the tenant from liability, it is necessary to extinguish the landlord's rights against the tenant and also the sub-tenant's rights against the tenant. The tenant's interest in the property is determined, but not so as to affect the interest of the sub-tenant. Determination of the tenant's interest in the property is not necessary to free the sub-tenant from liability. Hence the sub-tenant's interest continues. No deeming is necessary to produce this result. Here the deeming relates to the term on which the sub-tenant's proprietary interest continues. His interest continues unaffected by the determination of the tenant's interest. Accordingly the sub-tenant holds his estate on the same terms, and subject to the same rights and obligations, as would be applicable if the tenant's interest had continued. If he pays the rent and performs the tenant covenants in the disclaimed lease, the landlord cannot eject him. If he does not, the landlord can distrain upon his goods for the rent reserved by the disclaimed lease or bring forfeiture proceedings. In practice, matters are likely to be brought to a head by one of the parties making an application for a vesting order.'

7.37 Provided the subtenant complies with the tenant's obligations to the landlord under the terms of the disclaimed lease, then the sublease will continue. Provided the subtenant complies with the terms of the disclaimed lease, then he cannot be evicted by the landlord (however, where the subtenant fails to comply with the terms of the disclaimed lease the landlord will be able to enforce the terms of the disclaimed lease against the subtenant).

7.38 In *Re AE Realisations* [1987] 3 All ER 83, Vinelott J summarised the position facing subtenants as follows:

'The position under [the earlier statute] as interpreted in *Re Levy, ex p Walton*, (1881) 17 Ch D 746, was simply this: as between the lessor and the bankrupt lessee, the disclaimer operated as a surrender. As between the lessor and the underlessee, the lease was to be treated as still in existence, the underlessee was entitled to remain in possession during the term of the underlease. However, the lessor retained his rights in rem – that is his rights to distrain for rent due under the lease and to forfeit for non-payment of rent or for breach of covenant. If the right to forfeit for non-payment of rent became exercisable then, subject to the statutory power of the court to relieve against forfeiture, the underlease and the underlessee's right to continue in possession fell with it.'

7.39 In circumstances where the rent passing under the disclaimed lease exceeds the rent payable under the sublease, the subtenant may submit a claim in the liquidation for the balance (see *Re Levy, ex p Walton* (1881) 17 Ch D 746, CA).

Subtenancies of part

7.40 The position is further complicated where various subleases have been granted out of the disclaimed leasehold interest. Following the judgment of Lord Nicholls in *Hindcastle*, provided the subtenant complies with the terms of the disclaimed lease, he will be entitled to remain in the premises. In practice though, this may not be feasible where, for example, the disclaimed lease was of a 10-storey office block and each floor of the building has been separately sublet to 10 different subtenants. In such cases, the undertenant must decide whether to accept a potentially higher level of liability to reflect the liabilities under the disclaimed head lease or alternatively apply for a vesting order of the whole or part of the building under IA 1986, s 182 (discussed below).

7.41 Where the landlord takes possession of the property following the subtenant's failure to comply with the terms of the head lease, the subtenant may still apply for relief from forfeiture (see *Griffin v Hill* [1987] 1 EGLR 81 and *Barclays Bank v Prudential Assurance* [1998] 1 EGLR 44).

MORTGAGEES

7.42 The position of a mortgagee is similar to that of a subtenant. Provided the mortgagee discharges the obligations under the disclaimed lease, the mortgagee will retain its rights in the property.

7.43 In relation to the position regarding the net proceeds of sale following the discharge of sums owed to the mortgagee(s) see *Lee v Lee* [1998] 2 BCLC 219.

PARTIES WHO HAVE ACQUIRED RIGHTS UNDER OTHER CONTRACTS

7.44 The disclaimer operates so as to determine the company's liability from the date of disclaimer. However, it will not have the effect of terminating the rights that may have been acquired by any party with whom the company had contracted with prior to the company's entry into liquidation. For example, where the company had, prior to liquidation, entered into a contract for the sale of one of its properties, the liquidator cannot disclaim that contract for the sale of land, without also disclaiming the property itself.

7.45 The purchaser retains the right to enforce the terms of contract against the company in liquidation and may be entitled to an order for specific performance in this regard (see *Capital Prime Properties plc v Worthgate Ltd and Another* [2000] 1 BCLC 647).

7.46 In *Scottish Widows plc v Tripipatkul* [2003] EWHC 1874 (Ch), [2003] BPIR 1413 the court described the status of the lease after disclaimer but before a vesting order as:

> ' . . . to be regarded as continuing in a notional sense, "like the Cheshire Cat's grin", despite the termination of the lease.'

7.47 Where the landlord had sold its interest this would include a 'notional reversion' of the disclaimed lease. The *Scottish Widows* case exemplifies the contradictions this position creates, particularly where the time-limit for making an application for a vesting order is missed (see below).

DEPOSITS AND RETENTIONS

7.48 Where the landlord has the benefit of a rent deposit or other retention then the disclaimer will not defeat the trust objectives underlying the deposit arrangement (see chapter 6). In *Environmental Agency v Hillridge Ltd* [2003] EWHC 3023 a company disclaimed a lease of a waste management site but this did not affect the trust fund that the company had set aside to cover the waste problems.

VESTING ORDERS

7.49 The effect of disclaimer on third parties is mitigated by the ability to apply for a vesting order. IA 1986 incorporates a mechanism allowing any person:

- who claims an interest in the disclaimed property; or

- any person who is under a liability in respect of the disclaimed property (not being a liability discharged by the disclaimer),

to apply to the court for an order vesting the disclaimed property in that person (IA 1986, s 181). The court has a wide discretion to make such an order 'on such terms as it thinks fit'. However, the court will only make an order where it is just to do so 'for the purpose of compensating the person subject to the liability in respect of the disclaimer'. Once made, the effect of a vesting order will take place without any conveyance, assignment or transfer. A grant of a vesting order is in reality a trade off between the release of the third party's liability with the replacement of a newly *vested* liability; supplemented by the third party gaining an interest in possession. Once the vesting order has been made the third party can either attempt to assign the lease or use the demised premises pursuant to the terms of the lease.

Time-limits

7.50 An application for a vesting order must be made within 3 months of the applicant becoming aware of the disclaimer or of his receiving notice of it, whichever is the earlier (IR 1986, r 4.194(2)). The legislation is confusing in this regard because IA 1986, s 179(1)(a) appears to indicate that an application for a vesting order in respect of leasehold premises should be made within 14 days of the date the notice of the disclaimer was served. However, this provision only deals with the date the disclaimer is deemed to take effect and does not preclude a party from applying for a vesting order during the 3-month period outlined above. Under IR 1986, r 4.3, the court has the power to extend this time-limit on such terms as it thinks fit.

7.51 Under IA 1986, s 182(1) the court's power is limited to vest the disclaimed property (of a leasehold nature) in a person:

'(a) subject to the same liabilities and obligations as the company was subject to under the lease at the commencement of the winding up, or
(b) if the court thinks fit, subject to the same liabilities and obligations as that person would be subject to if the lease had been assigned to him at the commencement of the winding up.'

7.52 Under IA 1986, s 182(2) the court may make an order in relation to part only of the property comprised under a lease (e g in relation to a subtenancy of part).

7.53 A review of the parties who may wish to apply for a vesting order is considered below.

Guarantors and other third party sureties

7.54 Parties who retain liability following disclaimer will often wish to apply for a vesting order to obtain a degree of control over the disclaimed property (and thereby limiting their continuing liability so far as possible). The effect of the vesting order would be to enable them to assign the disclaimed lease or underlet the demised premises to a lessee of their choice (subject to satisfying the alienation restrictions (if any) imposed by the lease).

7.55 In *Re AE Realisations (1985) Ltd* [1987] 3 All ER 83 the court declined to make a vesting order because the terms of the guarantee expressly provided that in the event that the lease was disclaimed, the guarantor would take a new lease pursuant to that agreement. The court held that nothing would be achieved by granting a vesting order because the guarantor's desire for a new lease could be dealt with under the contractual provisions of the guarantee (see above).

7.56 The courts have further ruled that where a guarantor's obligations have been discharged by the disclaimer (or by a subsequent act of the landlord), then the guarantor has no standing to make an application for an order vesting the disclaimed lease in him (see *Re No 1 London Ltd* [1991] BCC 118 and *Re Yarmarine (IW) Ltd* [1992] BCLC 276).

The landlord

7.57   Where there is a head lease and a sublease of premises and the liquidator disclaims the head lease, whilst the landlord is a party claiming an interest in the sublease (IA 1986, s 181(2)(a)), he does not immediately satisfy the second condition for eligibility for a vesting order because so long as the subtenant complies with the covenants under the head lease, the landlord is not entitled to possession of the property (IA 1986, s 181(3)(a)).

7.58   This was the position of the parties in *Re ITM Corporation Ltd; Sterling Estates Ltd v Pickard UK Ltd and Others* [1998] BPIR 402. As noted above, the subtenant is entitled to remain in possession of the property, so long as:

*   he complies with the terms of the head lease; or

*   until he refuses to accept a vesting order *(Re Cock, ex p Shilson* (1887) 20 QBD 343); or

*   fails to apply for vesting order within the requisite time-limit.

It is not until one of the three situations above arises that the landlord may become entitled to possession of the disclaimed property.

Subtenants with an underlease of the whole of the property demised by the disclaimed lease

7.59   A landlord cannot seek a vesting order where it remains open to a subtenant to apply for an order vesting the disclaimed lease in him. Subtenants, together with mortgagees have the right of first refusal of the disclaimed lease, followed by guarantors and other sureties. In the event that none of these parties seek the court's relief pursuant to IA 1986, s 181, then the landlord will become so entitled. This hierarchy of competing claims was summarised by Vinelott J in *Re AE Realisations* [1987] 3 All ER 83 as follows:

> ' . . . it is, I think, clear what is contemplated by [IA 1986, ss 181 (liquidation) and 320 (bankruptcy)] is that an application for a vesting order may be made, first, by a person claiming under the bankrupt as underlessee or mortgagee (and, if more than one, in the order of priority of their respective interests inter se); secondly, if none is willing to take a vesting order by any person "liable either personally or in a representative character, and either alone or jointly with the bankrupt to perform the lessee's covenants"; and thirdly, by "any person claiming [an] interest in [the lease] or under any liability not discharged by it".'

Subtenants with an underlease of part only of the property demised by the disclaimed lease

7.60 IA 1986, ss 182(2) and 321(2) enable the court to make a vesting order in relation to part only of the premises demised under the disclaimed lease, such as where a subtenant of part is in occupation of part of the premises. The effect of the vesting order will only render the applicant liable to discharge the liabilities and other covenants contained in the disclaimed lease to the extent that they affect or concern that part of the premises which the subtenant occupies.

7.61 There are a number of obvious shortcomings and ambiguities arising from this provision that will be left for the court to deal with on a case-by-case basis:

- the section provides no mechanism for apportioning rents and service charges as between different parts of the property (although the rent payable under the sublease may be a good starting point subject to market conditions);

- it is unclear whether a subtenant who has been granted an underlease that has been contracted out of the provisions of the Landlord and Tenant Act 1954 (LTA 1954), Part II (because the head lease specified that any such underlettings should be outside the scope of this protection) would be entitled to a vesting order that would include the tenant's status of being protected by LTA 1954, Part II;

- no guidance is given as to who will be responsible for the maintenance of the common parts of the property (or any of them).

Purchasers of leases

7.62 For the relevant authorities on whether a party who has contracted to purchase a lease has sufficient standing to apply for a vesting order see the seemingly conflicting decisions in *Lloyds Bank SF Nominees Ltd v Alladin* [1996] 1 BCLC 720 and *Test Valley BC v Minilec Engineering Ltd* [2005] 2 EGLR 113 (where equitable assignees were held to have sufficient interest in the disclaimed property to apply for a vesting order).

7.63 However, the court held that the purchaser of the landlord's interest could take advantage of the 'notional reversion' which was therefore capable of being assigned, with the benefit of the guarantor's covenant, as if the lease had not been disclaimed (*Scottish Widows plc v Tripipatkul* [2003] EWHC 1874 (Ch)).

Original tenants and previous assignees

7.64 Original tenants and previous assignees may remain liable following a disclaimer. This largely depends on whether the lease is an *old lease* or a *new lease* under the Landlord and Tenant (Covenants) Act 1995 ('the Covenants Act'; see **5.28**). Original tenants and previous assignees as former owners of the lease may have been released by the Covenants Act. If they have not been released then the landlord must serve a notice under s 17 of the Act within 6 months of a fixed charge falling due.

7.65 A former tenant that remains liable in this way has the right to apply for a vesting order. However, this must be made within 3 months (see above) even though the landlord has 6 months in which to serve a s 17 notice. However, if the former tenant misses the opportunity to apply for a vesting order and subsequently receives a s 17 notice he has the right to apply for an overriding lease under the Covenants Act, s 19. Although there is no decided case on this point, it is inconceivable that a former tenant in this position would not be able to avail himself of the s 19 right. The existence of the 'Cheshire cat' lease arguably is sufficient for this purpose (see *Scottish Widows plc v Tripipatkul* [2003] EWHC 1874 (Ch)).

The effect of the vesting order

7.66 The right of a subtenant or mortgagee to apply to the court for relief from the forfeiture of the tenant's lease is usually subject to a condition upon such relief being granted that the subtenant or mortgagee discharge any rent arrears, and further remedies any other breaches of covenant by the tenant. In disclaimer cases, the court is likely to take the same approach when granting a vesting order (see *Re Walker, ex p Mills* (1895) 64 LJQB 783), in order to give effect to IA 1986, s 182(1), which provides that the terms of the vesting order must make the applicant:

'(a) subject to the same liabilities and obligations as the company was subject to under the lease at the commencement of the winding up, or

(b) if the court thinks fit, subject to the same liabilities and obligations as that person would be subject to if the lease had been assigned to him at the commencement of the winding up.'

7.67 Earlier authorities (including *Re Walker* above) suggest that the court will favour the approach under subsection (a) over subsection (b) (which would potentially subject the applicant to less onerous obligations) unless the circumstances of the case are exceptional. This should provide a degree of comfort to landlords, who should not be prejudiced by the terms of any vesting order.

7.68 In *Lee v Lee* [1998] 2 BCLC 219, the court made a vesting order in favour of a mortgagee on terms that directed the mortgagee how to deal with the net proceeds of sale following the redemption of the two registered mortgages. The mortgagees agreed the terms of the order and no argument was heard on the issue although it may be questionable as to whether the court had the power to dictate how the mortgagee was to apply the balance of the sale proceeds.

THE LANDLORD'S CLAIM FOLLOWING DISCLAIMER

7.69   IA 1986, s 178(6) provides as follows:

> 'Any person sustaining loss or damage in consequence of the operation of a disclaimer under this section is deemed a creditor of the company to the extent of the loss or damage and accordingly may prove for the loss or damage in the winding up.'

7.70   Following the disclaimer by a liquidator of a leasehold interest, a landlord will usually submit a proof of debt for the residue of the rents falling due under the unexpired term of the lease, together with a claim in respect of any arrears of rent and dilapidations.

7.71   The appropriate determination of the landlord's claim in the liquidation following a disclaimer was set down by the House of Lords in the case of *Re Park Air Services plc* [2000] 2 AC 172; [1999] BCC 135. The Lords held that whilst the landlord was not entitled to submit a claim for all future rents falling due under the lease, the landlord had a right to compensation (under s 178(6)) that was to be calculated on the same basis as if he was claiming damages for breach of contract. Accordingly, the landlord's claim will be calculated by reference to the future rents that would fall due until the point at which the landlord could reasonably be expected to relet the premises, with a discount for accelerated receipt. The landlord could also claim interest on the debt pursuant to IA 1986, s 189. This position should be contrasted with the landlord's claim in the liquidation following the forfeiture of the lease, where there is no ability to submit a claim for such compensation.

7.72   In *Park Air*, the different approaches taken by the landlord and the liquidator in valuing the landlord's claim were of great significance because the liquidation was a solvent liquidation and so the amount to be determined as the correct amount of compensation would be the amount the landlord actually received in the liquidation. The landlord's claim did not include a discount for accelerated receipt, whereas the liquidator argued that the landlord's claim should be discounted to take account of the fact that the landlord would receive his compensation immediately (the difference between the two figures being approximately £1.5m).

7.73   The House of Lords rejected the Court of Appeal's approach that the landlord's claim could be treated as a future debt because of the nature of a lease. Lord Millett stated:

> '[The landlord] would have had to wait until the rent fell due and then prove quarter by quarter. This is because rent is not a simple debt. It is the consideration

for the right to remain in possession. The tenant's liability to pay future rent is not debitum in praesenti solvendum in futuro. Its existence depends upon the future event. Rent in respect of a future rental period may never become payable at all. Rent payable in the future under a subsisting lease can not be treated as a series of future debts making up a pure income stream.'

Accordingly, Lord Millet held that IR 1986, r 11.13 (which deals with debts payable at a future time) was of no application in that case.

7.74 The 8.5% rate of discount the Lords applied for accelerated receipt was taken to be the yield on gilt-edged securities for an equivalent term. Finally, in relation to interest, the House of Lords held that because the landlord's claim was a claim for damages payable at the date of disclaimer, then interest should accrue on the entirety of the debt from the date of disclaimer under IA 1986, s 189.

OTHER CLAIMS FOLLOWING DISCLAIMER

7.75 Guarantors, mortgagees and subtenants may all sustain loss or damage in consequence of a disclaimer and are therefore deemed to be creditors of the insolvent debtor for the purposes of IA 1986, s 178(6) and may submit a proof of debt in respect of such losses.

Bona vacantia and Crown disclaimer

7.76 Where a company that still has assets is dissolved, those assets will vest in the Crown bona vacantia (Companies Act 1985, s 654 and Companies Act 2006, s 1012).

7.77 If a company is dissolved and its assets included a lease, then the Crown may disclaim that lease, provided such disclaimer is made:

- within 3 months of the date that the vesting of the lease came to the attention of the Crown representative; or

- within 3 months, or such further period as the court may allow, if an application is made by a person interested in the property requiring the Crown representative to decide whether or not to disclaim.

(Companies Act 1985, s 656 and Companies Act 2006, s 1013)

7.78 Where the Crown serves a notice of disclaimer, the effect is that the property is deemed never to have been vested in the Crown and the provisions of IA 1986 relating to disclaimer will apply as if the liquidator had disclaimed the lease immediately before the dissolution of the company (Companies Act 1985, s 657 and Companies Act 2006, s 1014).

DISCLAIMER AND BANKRUPTCY (IA 1986, S 315)

7.79 The provisions dealing with disclaimer in liquidations are almost mirrored in respect of disclaimers in bankruptcy at IA 1986, ss 315–321. The case-law that applies to one regime will invariably be directly applicable to the other.

7.80 The procedures for a disclaimer by a trustee in bankruptcy and associated applications are contained in IR 1986, rr 6.178–6.186.

Distinguishing characteristics of disclaimer in bankruptcy cases

7.81 Whereas the assets of a company do not vest in the liquidator upon his appointment the position is different in respect of a bankruptcy. By virtue of the fact that the bankrupt's property vests in his trustee in bankruptcy upon his appointment (IA 1986, s 306) the trustee will become liable on the covenants under any lease unless and until he disclaims (*Re Solomon, ex p Dressler* (1878) 9 Ch D 252, CA). Disclaimer is therefore an invaluable tool for the trustee because it enables the trustee to divest and discharge himself from any personal liability under the lease.

7.82 Under IA 1986, s 316(2) a trustee who fails to disclaim within the required 28-day period following the service of a notice to elect under s 316(1) is 'deemed to have adopted any contract' he has failed to disclaim (s 316(2)).

7.83 The position in liquidation is different. In *Re ABC Coupler and Engineering C Ltd (No 3)* [1970] 1 All ER 650 at 669 the Official Receiver failed to disclaim its interest in a lease following the service of a notice to elect by the landlord. The landlord claimed that the Official Receiver should be treated as having adopted the lease including the rents falling due after the commencement of the liquidation, and also the dilapidations. The court rejected the landlord's argument. It ordered that the post-commencement rents be paid as an expense because the liquidator had retained the premises for the benefit of the liquidation (see **2.62**), but refused to rule that the lease had been adopted by the official receiver.

Effect of trustee's disclaimer

7.84 A trustee's disclaimer operates so as to backdate the taking effect of the disclaimer to the date the trustee was appointed (IA 1986, s 315(3)(b)). It has been held that because of this, it is not possible to compel a trustee who has disclaimed a lease to pay rent as an expense of the bankruptcy for the period between the date of his appointment and the date the trustee exercises his right to disclaim (*Titterton v Cooper* (1882) 9 QBD 473, CA, *Re Sandwell, ex p Zerfass* (1885) 14 QBD 960; *Metropolis Estates Co Ltd v Wilde* [1940] 2 KB 536, CA).

Where permission of court is required

7.85 IA 1986, s 315 generally operates so as to enable the trustee to disclaim without the court's permission. However, there are a number of instances where the trustee must seek the court's prior consent to disclaiming property comprised in the bankruptcy estate (IA 1986, s 315(4)):

- property that has been claimed by the trustee as after-acquired property under IA 1986, s 307; or

- personal property of the bankrupt that exceeds the reasonable replacement value of any such property (IA 1986, s 308).

7.86 An application can be made without notice (IR 1986, r 6.182(1)) and for the purposes of IR 1986, r 6.182(2) must be accompanied by a report:

- giving such particulars of the property proposed to be disclaimed as enable it to be easily identified;

- setting out the reasons why, the property having been claimed for the estate, the court's lease to disclaim is now applied for; and

- specifying the persons (if any) who have been informed of the trustee's intention to make the application.

Chapter 8

INSOLVENCY SALE OF TENANCY –
ASSIGNMENTS, VALUATIONS AND
'PRE-PACKS'

ASSIGNMENTS

8.1 One of the key reasons that an administrator or liquidator will want to retain the demised premises and resist forfeiture is to sell an assignment of the lease (for other reasons see chapter 2).

8.2 The officeholder can seek to sell the lease (ie by way of an assignment):

- where the contractual term of the lease is still continuing;

- for commercial leases where the contractual term has ended but the tenancy is continuing under the Landlord and Tenant Act 1954 (see **4.22**) – note that residential statutory tenancies often cannot be assigned;

- at any time prior to the termination of the contractual/statutory tenancy. The right to assign can be exercised even where the court proceedings for a new tenancy under the Landlord and Tenant Act 1954 are progressing – the normal procedure is for the assignee to apply for an order to be joined to the proceedings and be substituted as the tenant claimant.

8.3 The right to assign is always subject to the express alienation provisions in the lease (where there is no restriction the tenant is free to assign). There are two types of covenant against assigning, subletting or parting with possession:

- *absolute*: where assignment etc is prohibited in any circumstance; and

- *qualified*: where assignment etc is allowed but only with the consent of the landlord (in which case there is a term implied by the Landlord and Tenant Act 1927, s 19 that consent will not be unreasonably refused).

8.4 When faced with a tenant's application for licence to assign or sublet (where there is a qualified covenant), the landlord is under a duty to come to a decision about whether or not to consent *within a reasonable time* under the Landlord and Tenant Act 1988. He may decide to consent or refuse consent (if it is reasonable to do so) or impose reasonable conditions on any consent given.

8.5 The test for reasonableness was set out in *International Drilling Fluids Ltd v Louisville Investments (Uxbridge) Ltd* [1986] 1 EGLR 39, where Balcombe LJ held that an act must be regarded as reasonable or unreasonable in reference to the circumstances under which it is committed:

> '• The purpose of a covenant against assignment without the consent of the landlord, such consent not to be unreasonably withheld, is to protect the lessor from having his premises used or occupied in an undesirable way, or by an undesirable tenant or assignee . . .
>
> • As a corollary to the first proposition, a landlord is not entitled to refuse his consent to an assignment on grounds which have nothing whatever to do with the relationship of landlord and tenant . . .
>
> • The onus of proving that consent has been unreasonably withheld is on the tenant . . .
>
> • It is not necessary for the landlord to prove that the conclusions which led him to consent were justified, if they were conclusions which might be reached by a reasonable man in the circumstances . . .
>
> • It may be reasonable for the landlord to refuse his consent to an assignment on the ground of the purpose for which the proposed assignee intends to use the premises, even though that purpose is not forbidden by the lease . . .
>
> • . . . while a landlord need usually consider only his own relevant interests, there may be cases where there is such a disproportion between the benefit to the landlord and the detriment to the tenant if the landlord withholds his consent to an assignment, that it is unreasonable for the landlord to refuse consent . . .'

Insolvent tenant's application for licence: can the landlord be compelled to accept an unsuitable assignee simply because it might be in the best interests of creditors?

8.6 In *International Drilling Fluids*, Balcombe LJ accepted that the landlord has to look primarily at his own interests. Accordingly, when an application is made by an administrator/liquidator to assign, a factor might be the effect that a refusal may have on the creditors as a whole (if substantial), but only where there is an insubstantial risk to the landlord. It would be unreasonable to allow a tenant to assign for the benefit of its past creditors at the expense of the landlord who would otherwise be compelled to take an unsuitable assignee and be exposed to future risk (by analogy see *Thomas v Ken Thomas Ltd* [2006] EWCA 1504, [2001] BPIR 959).

8.7 In *Pakwood Transport Ltd v 15 Beauchamp Place Ltd* [1978] 36 P&CR 112, Orr LJ held that a landlord faced with a tenant in liquidation should consider an application for licence to assign even where the landlord intends to bring forfeiture proceedings on the ground of the liquidation.

> 'In my judgment, whatever justification there might have been for deferring a decision, there can be none for declining outright even to reconsider the application.'

However, a landlord is entitled to receive full and accurate information as to the potential purchaser/assignee (*Metro Nominees (Wandsworth)(No 1) v K Rayment* [2008] BCC 40).

8.8   In *Geland Manufacturing Co Ltd v Levy Estates Co Ltd* (1962) 181 EG 209 a tenant in liquidation was refused relief from forfeiture, even though the rent arrears had been tendered. The liquidator wanted to assign the lease to a shell company. *Geland* is authority for the seemingly self-evident proposition that the insolvency of the tenant does not alter the right of a landlord to reject an unsuitable assignee, if it is reasonable to do so under the express provisions of the alienation clause in the lease (as moderated by the Landlord and Tenant Act 1927, s 19).

VALUATIONS

8.9   Landlords are often faced with an administrator/liquidator/receiver seeking licence to assign either as part of a sale of the insolvent tenant's business (or part of the business) or a sale of the lease only. In the sale of the tenant's business where the lease is a constituent part then there is often an imperative for the transaction to take place quickly. This creates certain practical difficulties in that:

- licence to assign may be required quickly – the tenant may already have parted with possession and the sale may have taken place without a licence in place;

- there are dangers in proceeding with a sale on the basis of the parties seeking licence to assign after the contract has been signed (see *Metro Nominees (Wandsworth)(No 1) v K Rayment* [2008] BCC 40);

- a quick sale reduces the possibility of ensuring that a full market premium is obtained on a sale/assignment of the lease.

8.10   The general objective of any insolvency procedure is to protect the position of creditors. This involves maximising the financial return from the assets of the company. In *Re, British American Racing (Holdings) Ltd* [2004] EWHC 2947 (Ch), the court emphasised that an officeholder should take all reasonable steps to ensure that potential purchasers were aware of the assets which were being sold so that the available market could be tested. The officeholder will typically instruct a valuation to be carried out in accordance with the *RICS Appraisal and Valuation Standards Manual* ('the Red Book'). At one time the Red Book recognised the concept of a 'forced sale' (or an *estimated restricted resale price*) as a formal basis of valuation. This is no longer the case; the Red Book puts forward one principal basis of valuation which is *market value* which is defined as:

' . . . the estimated amount for which a property or asset should exchange on the date of valuation between a willing buyer and a willing seller in an arms length transaction after property marketing wherein the parties had each acted knowledgably, prudently and without compulsion.'

8.11 This does not mean that a valuer should not take into account special circumstances which may reduce the available marketing period. Officeholders will often request the valuation on two bases:

(1)   the normal market value; and

(2)   the market value subject to a *special assumption* namely a restricted marketing period (ie where there is insufficient time to fully market the premises).

8.12 However, according to the definition of market value within the Red Book there is an implicit assumption that an adequate period of marketing has been carried out. If a sale proceeds without a full opportunity to market the property then there is a significant danger that market value will not be realised.

8.13 In any event an administrator owes a duty to the company to take reasonable care to obtain the best price in the circumstances as he reasonably perceives them to allow including a duty to take reasonable care in choosing the time at which to sell the property (see *Kyrris v Oldham, Royle v Oldham* [2003] EWCA Civ 1506, [2004] BPIR 165 and *Re Charnley Davies (No 2)* [1990] BCLC 760).

Can the lease be sold without prior court or creditor or landlord approval?

8.14 *Liquidators* may call meetings of creditors and contributories for the purpose of consultation but a liquidator is not bound to accept a direction given by the meeting except in limited circumstances (*Re Medisco Equipment Ltd* [1983] BCLC 305).

8.15 IA 1986, Sch 4, Part III provides liquidators with the:

'Power to sell any of the company's property by public auction or private contract with power to transfer the whole of it to any person or to sell the same in parcels.' (para 6)

Pursuant to IA 1986, ss 165(3) and 167(1)(b), this power can be exercised *with or without sanction* of the court or creditors of the company.

8.16 *Administrators* have an obligation to submit to the creditors a statement setting out the proposals for achieving the purpose of the administration (IA 1986, Sch B1, para 49(1)) and then call a creditors' meeting to discuss the proposals. The proposals should contain details of how it is envisaged that the property and assets of the company will be disposed of.

8.17 Under IA 1986, Sch B1, para 59 'the administrator of the company may do anything necessary or expedient for the management of the affairs, business and property of the company'. In *Transbus International Ltd* [2004] EWHC 932 (Ch) the court considered the effect of para 59 in conjunction with the administrator's obligation under para 68 to manage the affairs and business and property of the company in accordance with the *proposals approved* by the creditors. Relying upon the pre-Enterprise Act 2002 decision in *Re T&D Industries plc* [2000] 1 WLR 646, the court confirmed the ability of administrators to sell the business and assets of the company without prior creditor approval. Although administrators were obliged to place their proposals (including proposals for selling assets) before creditors as soon as reasonably possible, the court recognised that there are cases where administrators will be called upon to make *urgent and important decisions* which did not allow time to hold a creditors' meeting. In any event the administrator (or other office holder) has to comply with the lease and if necessary obtain licence to assign from the landlord (see **8.6** and **8.25**).

8.18 However, there should not be an assumption that there is always a restricted timescale for sale unless there is a genuine need to reflect such issues as an application by the landlord for permission to forfeit together with accruing rental liabilities (which may be payable as an expense of the insolvency; see chapter 2). In fact there is an implicit assumption that the property has been adequately marketed (see above in relation to the Red Book and valuations). From 1 January 2009 administrators will be compelled to provide full information of the valuation process if the sale proceeds without first being proposed in a creditors' meeting (see **8.27**).

'PRE-PACKS'

8.19 An officeholder (whether receiver, liquidator or administrator) may wish to quickly sell the business and assets of the tenant, perhaps to a special purchaser who may have been identified prior to the officeholder's appointment. There is often a compelling case for such a sale on the basis that the sale of the business and assets of the company may realise more if sold as a going concern than would be realised if the business was broken up and sold in its constituent parts (the lease being one of those parts). The nature of this arrangement is sometimes known as a pre-pack (also known as 'flipping' the business). Officeholders argue that the speed of the pre-pack process helps to minimise the loss of customer confidence which may ebb away if the business faces a protracted sale process. In addition, employees of the company usually prefer stability and early knowledge that the company will survive. A speedy process also reduces the risk of damage in relationships with credit insurers and suppliers.

8.20   The Association of Business Recovery Professionals enthusiastically endorses pre-packs if the conditions are appropriate as the 'best way of extracting value from a dire situation' (R3 – the Association of Business Recovery Professionals, *Briefing on Pre-packs* which also illustrated the sharp rise in the number of pre-packs after the Enterprise Act 2002 with a 'boom' in numbers from May 2003 onwards).

8.21   In *Re T&D Industries plc* [2000] 1 WLR 646 Neuberger J noted that the professional skill and experience required to effect a quick sale to obtain the best value of the business as a going concern was considerable. He recognised that an administrator makes 'important and urgent decisions in a responsible and demanding role'. The administrator was in the best position to decide whether it was appropriate to proceed in this way. *T&D Industries* is often cited as authority that pre-packs are acceptable.

8.22   However, the creditors often disapprove of pre-packs for the following reasons:

- the speed of the sale process appears to contradict the usual Red Book marketing valuation guidance. There is a serious risk that the sale will take place at an undervalue given that a pre-pack is unlikely to provide sufficient time to properly test the market value of the property;

- for administrations, pre-packs appear to sit outside the regulatory framework as the entire sale process is concluded long before any proposals are served on the creditors and inevitably rendering the statutory creditors' meeting ineffective; and

- the process appears to be open to abuse by a small minority of unscrupulous officeholders. On a sale back to former management of the failed company there is a sense that the insolvency has been whitewashed with nothing left for the creditors to consider or decide. Landlords are particularly unhappy when they receive an application for licence to assign from a connected phoenix business rising from the flames of the insolvent tenant free of the baggage of pre-existing debt and liability.

8.23   In *Re T&D Industries plc* [2000] 1 BCLC 471 Neuberger J advised administrators to bear in mind the sense of disenfranchisement creditors may feel. Neuberger J held that administrators had power to sell the assets of the company prior to obtaining creditors' approval but that this should be undertaken with caution. The decision in *T&D Industries* does not remove the administrator's responsibility to put proposals before the creditors as soon as possible. The administrator has a duty to consult and should consider whether an urgent meeting of creditors could be held on short notice to discuss any specific proposal. *Transbus International Ltd* [2004] EWHC 932 (Ch) followed the decision in *T&D Industries* in relation to the new administrations governed by the new procedure brought in by the Enterprise Act 2002 (IA 1986, Sch B1).

8.24 In *British American Racing (Holdings) Ltd* [2004] EWHC 2947 (Ch) the court held that the administrators are bound to take steps to ensure that potential purchasers are aware of the assets, business and property of the company on the market so that any potential purchaser's existing bid could be tested against the market. This does not stop the officeholder relying upon marketing which occurred prior to appointment. Where a pre-pack can be supported with evidence, then the opposition of a majority creditor is not sufficient ground to refuse an administration order (in *DKLL Solicitors v HMRC* [2007] BCC 908 Simmonds J stated in a contested pre-pack case: 'in applications of this nature the court places great reliance on the expertise and experience of impartial insolvency practitioners, even though it is ultimately for the court to decide if the threshold conditions are satisfied').

Landlord's remedies in relation to a pre-pack

8.25 A landlord has the following remedies in relation to a pre-pack:

- A landlord has the right to receive full information about proposed assignees (often the purchaser in a pre-pack) and details of the current occupation of the premises (*Metro Nominees (Wandsworth) (No 1) v K Rayment* [2008] BCC 40 and see **4.11**).

- If the premises have been retained for purposes of the administration (for the proposed sale) then the landlord can seek payment of arrears and if terms cannot be agreed then apply for permission to forfeit (under IA 1986, Sch B1, para 43 and see chapter 4).

- A landlord should consider whether the administrator might be liable under the *unfair harm/misfeasance provisions* in IA 1986, Sch B1, paras 74 and 75.

8.26 Pre-packs often include a component where the office holder allows the purchaser into occupation pending the acquisition of licence to assign from the landlord (see **4.11** and **8.7**). However, the mere fact that an administrator has repudiated or breached the terms of the lease does not displace the discretion of the court when undertaking the balancing exercise promulgated by Lord Nicholls in *Re Atlantic Computer Systems plc* [1992] Ch 505, CA. This was made clear by the Court of Appeal in *Innovate Logistics Ltd v Sunberry Properties Ltd* [2008] EWCA Civ 1261. One of the most important factors in this analysis will be whether allowing the breach will cause the landlord further loss. Stanley Burnton LJ noted that Sunberry (the landlord) had no readily available alternative tenant/assignee and had little to lose by the payments being offered from the occupier for a temporary period. He summed up the position as follows:

'When considering whether to grant or refuse leave[to forfeit] the court has regard to the consequences of the administration and of the order sought for the persons affected by them: in other words, it follows the guidance given in Atlantic Computers ... it follows that [where the landlord] had benefited from the making of the administration order, together with the agreement entered by the administrators with [the purchaser] for the occupation of the property at the same rate as the rent payable under the lease, as against what it would have received if the company had gone into liquidation ... the result was obviously in favour of refusing permission.' (para 67)

8.27 With effect from 1 January 2009 the insolvency regulatory bodies have jointly agreed the introduction of Statement of Insolvency Practice 16 (SIP 16) which acknowledges that, where the circumstances warrant it, an administrator has the power to sell assets without the prior approval of the creditors or the permission of the court. However, administrators are warned of their liability under IA 1986, Sch B1, paras 74 and 75. SIP 16 sets out the information which should be disclosed to creditors in all cases of a pre-packaged sale. The creditors will be entitled to full details of the sale and valuation process and to receive this with the first notification to creditors and given the opportunity to make representations at the initial creditors meeting 'as soon as possible after his appointment' (SIP 16, para 11). In addition to this the Joint Insolvency Committee have produced a proposed addition to the Insolvency Code of Ethics to supplement SIP 16 and this is likely to be endorsed by all the regulatory bodies (already having been endorsed by the Insolvency Practitioners Association in November 2008, *Transparency and Confidentiality; a Guidance Note*).

Part 2

FREEHOLDER/LANDLORD INSOLVENCY

Chapter 9

LANDLORD'S COVENANTS AND INSOLVENCY

9.1 This chapter deals with the effect that the insolvency of a landlord has on rights and liabilities arising under lease covenants. Landlord covenants often include:

• the maintenance of the structure of a premises (subject to the tenant paying a service charge) unless the tenant has a full repairing lease of the whole of the premises; and

• in residential lease, to enforce tenant covenants against all other tenants in the estate equally.

9.2 Where a landlord is in breach of covenant the measure of damages is generally the difference between the value of the lease with the covenant performed and its value with the covenant breached (*Barnes v City of London Real Property Co* [1918] 2 Ch 18). However, this is the starting point in the analysis as the diminution in value is not always a fair assessment (see *Wallace v Manchester City Council* [1998] 3 EGLR 38; *Shine v English Churches Housing Group* [2004] EWCA Civ 434 and *Earle v Charalambous* [2006] EWCA Civ 1090). The purpose of a damages claim against the landlord is to put the tenant in the same position (as far as money can achieve) as if the landlord had observed his obligations.

9.3 If the landlord breaches the covenant of quiet enjoyment then the measure of damages may include the expense of removal (if the tenant is forced to vacate the premises) and the sum that a willing tenant would have paid for the tenancy less the amount the actual tenant would have had to pay in rent (*Lawson v Hartley Brown* (1995) 71 P&CR 242, CA).

9.4 Where the breach occurred prior to the commencement of formal insolvency and the landlord is in liquidation or administration or bankruptcy the damages claim will rank as an ordinary unsecured debt.

TENANT'S PROOF IN LANDLORD'S LIQUIDATION

9.5   The tenant's right to submit a proof for unliquidated damages such as for a breach of a landlord's repairing obligation is contained in the Insolvency Rules 1986 (IR 1986), r 12.3 which provides:

> ' . . . that all claims by creditors are provable as debts . . . whether they are present or future or certain or contingent, ascertained or sounding only in damages.'

9.6   In relation to quantum the liquidator is able to estimate the value of the claim for the purpose of the proof of debt (pursuant to IR 1986, r 4.86). The liquidator also has the right to require the tenant to evidence the proof by way of an affidavit. It might be difficult to assess a tenant's unliquidated damages claim. The liquidator should not take a dilapidations claim at face value, which is not connected to the cost of repairs. The tenant must demonstrate the losses the lack of repair has caused to its business and amenity.

9.7   The liquidation does not prevent the continuing contractual liability for ongoing liabilities that continue pursuant to the landlord's covenants unless and until the liquidator sells the company's interest (or disclaims the freehold (see chapter 11). Where the liquidator does not quickly sell or disclaim, the continuing damages pose a bigger problem (ie where the breach continues and the damages accrue after the date of the winding up). The tenant may have an argument that ongoing losses flowing from the continuing breach should be paid as an expense of the liquidation. If there is a disclaimer then the tenant can submit a proof for damages consequential upon the disclaimer pursuant to the Insolvency Act 1986 (IA 1986), s 178(5).

9.8   A claim for damages which occurs after the date of the liquidation is a provable debt. It is included in the wide definition set out in IR 1986, r 13.12 which defines debt to include;

> ' . . . any debt or liability to which the company is subject at the date on which it goes into liquidation . . . [and] any which the company may become subject after that date by reason of any obligation before that date.'

9.9   The tenant proving in the liquidation stands in line with all the other unsecured creditors to be paid an abated proportion of the outstanding claim (in accordance with IR 1986, r 4.181). Accordingly the prospect of receiving the payment of damages as an expense is important to any creditor. The liquidator is likely to realise value from a sale of a freehold and therefore a tenant may argue that the continuing damages should be paid as an expense because:

> 'It is just and equitable that the burden of the debt should be borne by those for whose benefit the insolvent estate is being administered the latter principle is not confined to new debt incurred by the liquidator.' (*Re Atlantic Computer Systems plc* [1992] Ch 505, per Nicholls LJ)

9.10 In *Re Toshoku Finance UK plc* [2002] 1 WLR 671 and *Exeter City Council v Bairstow* [2007] BCC 236 the House of Lords decided that the determination of what should count as an expense of the liquidation is no longer a matter for the judge's discretion. Instead, it depends upon whether debts and liabilities come within a fair interpretation of the items listed in IR 1986, r 4.218 (for a more detailed review of liquidation expenses see chapter 2). A post-liquidation damages claim may fall within the definition of either:

- an expense properly chargeable or incurred by the liquidator in preserving realising the value of the freehold as an asset of the company (IR 1986, r 4.218(1)(a)); or

- a necessary disbursement incurred by the liquidator in the course of administration (IR 1986, r 4.218(1)(m)).

Whether or not a tenant can claim post-liquidation losses as an expense, the tenant should be able to prove for such losses pursuant to IR 1986, rr 12.3 and 13.12.

TENANT'S PROOF IN ADMINISTRATION

9.11 When a landlord is in administration it remains liable in relation to damages claims. Liabilities that accrued prior to the administration are usually an unsecured debt (with no priority). The administration does not extinguish the liability. The tenant may have the right to press the administrator into making a payment as an expense of the administration particularly where the administrator wishes to sell the property.

9.12 Future obligations may be met as an *expense* of the administration (see **2.80** in relation to administration expenses). In relation to new administrations IR 1986, r 2.67 governs the priority of expenses. A tenant's claim for damages for a post-administration breach may be an expense:

- under r 2.67(1)(a) as an expense properly incurred by the administrator in performing his functions in the administration of the company; or

- under r 2.67(1)(f) as a necessary disbursement incurred by the administrator in the course of administration.

VOLUNTARY ARRANGEMENTS

9.13 Where a landlord enters a voluntary arrangement (individual voluntary arrangement (IVA) or company voluntary arrangement (CVA); see **2.16**) and is liable in damages to a tenant then any such liability which has accrued due but has not been settled prior to the creditors' meeting would be expected to be caught within the VA. The position in relation to future liabilities is not so clear. A VA is capable of compromising ongoing breaches but if the landlord and other creditors benefit at the future expense of the tenant (who has to continue to suffer an ongoing breach) this is likely to be inherently unfair (see the judgment of Neuberger LJ in *Thomas v Ken Thomas Ltd* [2007] BLR 429, CA which concerned a tenant entering a VA) and be subject to a challenge on the basis of *unfair prejudice* (under IA 1986, s 6).

RECEIVERSHIP

9.14 The tenant retains its right to bring a claim for damages suffered before and after the appointment of a fixed charge or administrative receiver (see **2.3**).

BANKRUPTCY

9.15 Liabilities on bankruptcy are dealt with in chapter 18. The case is perhaps clearer in bankruptcy where the bankrupt landlord's estate (benefit and burden) is transferred automatically to the trustee in bankruptcy pursuant to IA 1986, s 306.

SET-OFF

9.16 Where the lease is still continuing the tenant can often achieve full or partial reimbursement against the insolvent landlord (in liquidation or administration) by withholding rents and service charges and exercising a set-off in relation to any cross-claim which may arise from the breach of the landlord's express or implied covenants. For tenants this will often be more successful than any other remedy.

9.17 Mutual credits and set-off in relation to liquidations is dealt with in IR 1986, r 4.90. This allows a liquidator to adjust any distribution to a creditor and set off any sums due to or from the company whether payable now or in the future (IR 1986, r 4.90(4)). This will apply to liabilities arising prior to the liquidation and incurred after the commencement of the liquidation. A liquidator should apply a set-off even where the lease contains an express provision which requires payment of rents without deduction or set-off. For administrations, IR 1986, r 2.85 (mutual credit and set-off) allows an administrator to adjust any distribution to a creditor and set off any sums due to or from the company whether payable now or in the future (IR 1986, r 2.85(4) and see **2.115**).

INJUNCTIVE RELIEF

9.18 The tenant may consider applying for injunctive relief to either restrain the landlord from continuing to breach a negative covenant or to specifically perform a positive covenant. The grant of an injunction is discretionary. The court will consider the degree of injury being suffered by the tenant and if urgent will grant an interim injunction (*American Cyanamid Co v Ethicon Ltd* [1975] 1 All ER 504, HL). If damages are an adequate remedy then an injunction may be refused although damages are unlikely to be adequate where a landlord has failed to undertake necessary repairs (*Jeune v Queens Cross Properties Ltd* [1973] 3 All ER 97).

Insolvency restrictions

9.19 A tenant with the right to apply for injunctive relief against an insolvent landlord may be prevented from taking action without the officeholder's permission or the court's permission (see enforceability of freehold covenants below at chapter 10).

Chapter 10

FREEHOLD COVENANTS AND INSOLVENCY

10.1 Where two parties enter into a covenant in relation to freehold land it is binding between the original covenanting parties. However, the rules are more complex where the property is no longer owned by one of the original parties to the covenant. An insolvent freeholder may be entitled to the benefit of a covenant or be subject to the burden. The enforceability of such covenants becomes a pressing concern for insolvency practitioners as it will inevitably have a material effect on the value of the property (positive or negative). Covenants can be negative (where the covenantor has promised not do some act) or positive (where the covenantor has promised to carry out some act such as make payments or repairs).

THE BURDEN IN COMMON LAW

10.2 The general rule is that the burden of a covenant affecting land does not run with the land at common law. This results from the principle of privity of contract; a person may not sue (or be made liable) on a contract unless he is a party to it. In relation to positive covenants, this common law principle still prevails. Therefore, the general rule is that positive covenants are not enforceable by an action for damages (or specific performance) against an assignee of a covenantor.

10.3 To avoid this rule, landowners have developed a number of ways to attempt to create positive covenants which are enforceable against an assignee and these include:

- abandoning the freehold model and adopting a lease structure as positive covenants can be enforced in a landlord and tenant relationship;

- imposing an obligation on a covenantee to obtain a fresh covenant from an assignee before the transfer is registered (and registering a restriction under the Land Registration Act 1925, s 58 and the Land Registration Act 2002, s 40);

- in some cases a positive covenant can be enforced where a number of covenantors wish to take advantage of a service or facility (eg a road or drain) and the obligation imposed by way of burden is matched by a mutual benefit in being able to use the service or facility (*Halsall v Brizell* [1957] 1 All ER 371);

- where long leases are turned into freeholds under the various enfranchisement regimes (such as the Leasehold Reform Act 1967) the newly acquired freehold can be made subject to a burden in respect of the upkeep or regulation of a property for the benefit of the surrounding buildings or locality.

THE BURDEN IN EQUITY – RESTRICTIVE COVENANTS

10.4 The burden of a negative/restrictive covenant can be enforced against an assignee because an equitable doctrine has been created to allow this to happen. In the landmark case of *Tulk v Moxhay* (1848) 2 Ph 744 it was held in relation to a restrictive covenant that a purchaser of land, with notice of a restrictive covenant affecting it, would be restrained from using the land in a way inconsistent with that covenant.

10.5 Under *Tulk v Moxhay*, restrictive covenants are enforceable by way of an injunction restraining the improper use of the land and/or the court has power to grant damages (perhaps in lieu of an injunction). Following *Tulk v Moxhay* a restrictive covenant is enforceable not only against the original covenantor but against successors in title (see *Baxter v Four Oaks Properties Ltd* [1965] 1 All ER 906). This is subject to the following exceptions:

- as the right to enforce against an assignee is an equitable remedy, it is not possible to enforce against *a bona fide purchaser of a legal estate for value without notice of the covenant*;

- at the time the covenant is created there must be an intent that the burden of the covenant should run with the land which should be clear from the nature of the covenant or by virtue of the Law of Property Act 1925, s 79 which provides that a restrictive covenant shall, unless a contrary intention is expressed, be deemed to be 'made by the covenantor on behalf of himself his successors in title and the persons deriving title under him or them, and, subject as aforesaid, shall have effect as if such successors and other persons were expressed' (see *Tophams Ltd v Earl of Seffton* [1966] 1 All ER 1039); and

- there must be land which is benefited by the covenant and the claimant must show that he has an interest in that land (see, eg, *Wrotham Park Estates Co Ltd v Parkside Homes Ltd* [1974] 2 All ER 321).

10.6 Although the doctrine applies to restrictive covenants and not positive covenants, it is sometimes far from clear as to how this distinction works in practice. It is possible to enforce a covenant which is negative in substance, even though positive in form (in fact this was the position in question in *Tulk v Moxhay*). Some covenants may be partly negative and partly positive. In *Shepherd Homes Ltd v Sandam (No 2)* [1971] 2 All ER 1267, Megarry LJ reflected that 'there can not be any doctrine of contagious proximity whereby the presence of the positive inhibits the enforcement of the neighbouring negative'. In other words it will usually be possible to enforce the negative element of a mixed covenant.

THE BENEFIT

10.7 The benefit of the covenant runs with land in common law (whether the covenant is positive or negative) subject to the following points:

- the covenant must *touch and concern the land*, ie it must be annexed to the land. The covenantee must be able to show that he has land which is capable of benefiting from enforcing the covenant. Where the covenantee's land is subsequently divided the benefit may attach to each part or just one part and this depends upon the construction of the covenant (*Drake v Gray* [1936] 1 All ER 363);

- annexation removes the need for assignment but the words must be clear such as:

    'With intent that the covenants ... might enure for the benefit of the vendors ... their heirs and assigns and others claiming under them to already of their lands adjoining or near to the said premises' (*Rogers v Hosegood* [1900] 2 Ch 388);

- an express assignment of the benefit is not usually necessary. If the benefit of the covenant is annexed to the land then it will be passed on to a purchaser under the Law of Property Act 1925, s 78. Where a covenantee is bankrupt the benefit will be automatically assigned to his trustee in bankruptcy as a consequence of IA 1986, s 306 (*Federated Homes Ltd v Mill Lodge Properties Ltd* [1980] 1 All ER 371). If the benefit of the covenant is not annexed to the land then an express assignment is necessary (such as where the a reversion is sold without the benefit of a covenant of guarantee, see *Re Distributors and Warehousing Ltd (in Liquidation)* [1986] BCLC 129);

- the land to be benefited must be identified by the document creating the covenant;

- there must be an intention that the benefit would run with the land from the outset (*Smith & Snipes Hall Farm Ltd v River Douglas Catchment Board* [1949] 2 All ER 179);

- equitable owners are able to enforce the benefit of a covenant in the same way as legal owners and in turn a restrictive covenant can be enforced against an equitable covenantee (*Test Valley BC v Minilec Engineering Ltd (in liquidation)* [2005] 2 EGLR 113); and

- the necessity to show either express annexation or express assignment of the benefit of the restricted covenant is avoided in relation to a *scheme of development*. This is where there is an estate of properties within a defined area where the purchasers mutually covenant on the basis of mutual enforcement. In *Brunner v Greenslade* [1970] 3 All ER 833, Megarry J recognised 'the major theoretical difficulties based on the law of covenant seem to me to disappear when instead there is an equity created by circumstances which is independent of contractual obligation'.

INSOLVENCY RESTRICTIONS AND ENFORCEMENT OF FREEHOLD COVENANTS

10.8 Liquidators, administrators and receivers are able to enforce the benefit of a covenant, expressly assign, or sell with an implied assignment (IA 1986, Sch 1, para 5 and Sch 4, para 4).

10.9 However, it may be difficult for a party with the benefit of a covenant to enforce a burden against an insolvent covenantor particularly in the short term.

10.10 The position varies in accordance with each form of insolvency:

- there are no restrictions where the covenantor is in receivership (see **2.3**);

- no action can be taken by a covenantee against a covenantor in administration without obtaining the permission of the administrator or the court (under IA 1986, Sch B1, para 43; see **1.88**);

- in voluntary liquidation there are no automatic restrictions but the liquidator could apply for an order restraining any proceedings brought (under IA 1986, s 112; see **1.111**);

- in compulsory liquidation the court's permission is required to commence or continue proceedings (under IA 1986, s 130(2); see **1.113**). The court will seek to do *what is right and fair in all the circumstances* and may impose terms on any such application;

- voluntary arrangements for small companies (IA 1986, Sch A1) and individuals (interim orders under IA 1986, s 252) have moratoriums which would require a covenantee obtaining the permission of the court before taking action;

- in bankruptcy the restrictions arise in relation to remedies against the bankrupt but not against the trustee under:
  - IA 1986, s 286 which provide that the courts may stay any action, execution or other legal process against property or person of the debtor (between petition and order) or as the case may be of the bankrupt;
  - IA 1986, s 285 once the bankruptcy order is made:

    ' . . . no person who is a creditor of the bankrupt in the respect of a debt provable in the bankruptcy shall-

    (a) Have any remedy against the property or person of the bankrupt in respect of that debt; or

    (b) Before the discharge of the bankruptcy commence any action or other legal proceedings against the bankrupt except with the leave of the Court and under such terms as the Court may impose.'

    However, there is no direct restriction against taking action against the trustee in relation to a cause of action which arose after the bankrupt estate has vested in him and which cannot be the subject of a proof of debt. The trustee does not become personally liable for pre-bankruptcy damages but he becomes liable for continuing contracts unless they are disclaimed (see **7.79** and *Re Solomon, ex p Dressler* (1878) 9 Ch D 252). The trustee will become personally liable for lease obligations if he elects to take the continuing benefit of the property for the purpose of the bankruptcy;
  - IA 1986, s 345 may be used by against a trustee by a covenantor who seeks to discharge his obligations. The court has a broad discretion to grant discharge and impose conditions on the order.

10.11 The presence of an insolvency restriction does not mean that an insolvency officeholder has power to wilfully commission the breach of a covenant. There is no mandate to ignore the burden created by the covenant. The court is likely to give permission to a covenantee to enforce a freehold covenant against the trustee as it is unlikely that to do so will put any creditor in an unfair or prejudicial position. If a creditor does not gain an unfair advantage over other creditors in the same class, then enforcement will be permitted (*Re Oaks Pitts Colliery Co* (1882) but see *Innovate Logistics Ltd v Sunberry Properties Ltd* [2008] EWCA Civ 1261).

10.12 Insolvency should not deny a creditor the benefit of its proprietary rights and the court will allow the enforcement of a restrictive covenant unless there is a compelling case not to (*Re David Lloyd & Co* (1877) 6 Ch D 339). Permission is likely to be granted so as to make a company comply with its obligations and restrain harm which would otherwise be committed to others (*Wyley v Exhall Coal Mining Co Ltd* (1864) 33 Beav 538). Permission may be given for an action of specific performance where the covenantee has rights only in equity (*Re Coregrange Ltd* [1984] BCLC 453).

Chapter 11

DISCLAIMER OF FREEHOLD – ESCHEAT

11.1 In rare situations, a freehold estate can be disclaimed and where this happens, the property reverts through the residual feudal system that underpins the law of property in England and Wales. Freehold ownership is sometimes mistakenly regarded as absolute. In reality it is just an interest in land, which is superior to leasehold interests but inferior to the hierarchical interests of the feudal lord of the estate. Today this means the Crown as the supreme feudal lord or one of the Royal Duchies. When the freehold is disclaimed, it is removed under the doctrine of escheat. In the past, a freehold interest could be extinguished for a variety of reasons, such as where the owner was convicted of a felony. Now the process of escheat is as a consequence of disclaimer following an insolvency. Although this may seem arcane, 300–500 freehold estates escheat to the Crown every year.

11.2 Therefore escheat occurs where a liquidator of a company disclaims a freehold owned by that company (perhaps because the charges secured on it are greater than its value) or where a trustee in bankruptcy disclaims on the same basis. When a freehold is disclaimed:

- the freehold no longer exists and the interest in possession of the land reverts back (escheated) to the Crown or one of the Royal Duchies;

- the title is removed from the register because the estate no longer exists;

- the property becomes part of the allodial lands of the Crown (although see the treatment of inferior interests below);

- the Land Registration Rules 2003, SI 2003/1417, r 173 provides that the registrar may make a note of the fact of determination of the freehold estate in the register; and

- the land will remain subject to any charges or other encumbrances created by the former freehold owner or his predecessors.

11.3 The liquidator's right to disclaim a freehold interest as onerous property arises under the Insolvency Act 1986 (IA 1986), s 178. A trustee in bankruptcy has the right to disclaim under IA 1986, s 315. Once the freehold has been disclaimed and the land becomes escheated it creates significant problems for the Crown in relation to the treatment of inferior interests. Although it is sometimes said escheated land becomes part of the allodial land (in other words unencumbered) of the Crown estate, as a consequence of IA 1986, s 178(4)(b) the disclaimer does not 'affect the rights or liabilities of any other person'.

11.4 Therefore inferior interests such as rentcharges, underleases and mortgages are not directly affected by the determination of a disclaimed estate (see chapter 7).

11.5 It is relatively common for a trustee in bankruptcy to disclaim where freehold property (such as the common parts of a block of flats) would ordinarily pass to the trustee to be realised but has no real value and would otherwise be a burden to the estate.

11.6 However the process of escheat can be reversed where any person with an inferior interest makes an application for a vesting order under IA 1986, s 181.

11.7 Although escheated property is owned by the Crown, it is not part of the Crown Estate unless the Crown (through the Commissioners) completes the escheat, by taking steps to exert rights as owner.

11.8 One consequence of the Land Registration Act 1925 was that only estates in land (freehold or leasehold) could be registered. Land held directly by the Crown, known as property in the 'Royal Demesne' is not held under any feudal tenure and there is therefore no estate to register. This has had the consequence that freeholds that escheated to the Crown ceased to be registrable creating a slow leak of property out of registration. Hundreds of freehold titles each year were being vacated from the register. The Land Registration Rules 2003, r 173 now allows an escheated title to be noted on the register.

11.9 It was held in the case of *Scmlla Properties Ltd v Gesso Properties (BVI) Ltd* [1995] BCC 793 that upon a freehold estate in land escheating to the Crown:

- on an escheat brought about by disclaimer the Crown became the owner of the land freed from the previous freehold interest; however

- an escheat did not terminate a subordinate interest. Inferior interests such as tenancies and charges held under it do not determine but the Crown does not become liable under any mortgage or lease liability unless it decides to assume this liability by taking a positive act; and

- at the date of disclaimer the tenants had no right to be preserved by s 178(4). The right which they claimed to enforce arose as a result of the disposal of the freeholds by their mortgagee subsequent to the disclaimer.

11.10 However, there is no clear case guidance as to what happens where the Crown does not accept liability. In *Hackney LBC v Crown Estates*

Commissioner [1996] BPIR 428 the claimant was given a vesting order of the freehold (free of encumbrances) in priority to a mortgagee and the Crown as it had a liability to the derelict property and the others had taken a passive stance (for disclaimer generally and the right to prove for damages following a disclaimer under IA 1986, s 178(5) see chapter 7).

Chapter 12

DEVELOPER/CONSTRUCTION INSOLVENCY

12.1 There are various possible contractual structures where a developer owns freehold land (or has possession of land subject to a lease). The developer may also be the main employer in relation to a building contract. He may have entered into a main contract with a number of associated subcontracts or he may have acted as both employer and main contractor and have entered into smaller contracts directly. Should the landowner/employer become insolvent in the middle of a development project, this can create a complex domino effect in relation to the various construction contracts with contractors and subcontractors.

12.2 Where the landowner/employer becomes insolvent in the middle of building works, a way has to be found to have the works completed. This task may be taken on by:

- an insolvency practitioner acting as an administrator (see **1.83**);

- a liquidator (see **1.9**);

- an administrative receiver (where it is still possible to appoint one; see **1.62**);

- an LPA receiver appointed under the terms of a fixed charge (see **17.1**); or

- a purchaser of the development.

12.3 The completion of the works will either be undertaken by an insolvency officeholder, receiver or by a purchaser. As the project is carried out by contractors and subcontractors, prospective purchasers of the land (together with any receiver or officeholder) will want to carry out a detailed analysis of:

- the works completed;

- the works to be completed;

- the sums owed to contractors and subcontractors;

- the solvency of any contractors;

- the allocation of work which needs to be completed by each contractor;

- whether plant and machinery is on site and the difficulties in replacing this;

- whether certain specialist contractors would be difficult to replace;

- who owns all relevant intellectual property rights in the design plans and drawings for the build;

- all retention of title claims;

- whether the insolvency or related events have terminated any of the construction contracts; and

- the termination provisions in the various contracts to assess whether the works are capable of reaching practical completion under the existing contractual structure.

TERMINATION

12.4 Contractors (or subcontractors) may seek to terminate their contractual obligations when they hear of an employer/landowner's insolvency. The most common complaint will be the landowner/employer's failure to pay contractual sums which have fallen due (or a related ground such as a failure to appoint a certifier or make an interim payment). However, to rely upon insolvency or non-payment the contractor must establish that he has a contractual right to rely upon this as a ground for termination.

No express termination clause

12.5 In the absence of an express right to terminate, contractors are required to demonstrate that there has been a fundamental/repudiatory breach which goes to the root of the contract. A breach of an express or implied condition of contract amounts to a repudiatory breach which if accepted will bring the contract to an end. In relation to a failure to pay, it must be shown that time for payment has been made of the essence (see *Decro-Wall v Practitioners in Marketing* [1971] 1 WLR 361 and *Dalkia Utilities v Celtech International* [2006] 1 Lloyd's Rep 599). The right to terminate for non-payment will always turn upon the particular facts (see, eg, *Mirimskaya v George Evans* [2007] EWHC 2073 (TCC) where the Technology and Construction Court (TCC) resolved a complex contract termination where no binding agreements were in place).

12.6 Where termination occurs following the acceptance of a repudiatory breach, the unperformed future obligations of the contract are released save for the provisions relating to termination and consequential damages (*Photo Productions v Securicor* [1980] AC 827). The contractor will be able to prove in a liquidation or administration for the value of the works completed prior to the termination (*Explora Group v Hesco* [2005] EWCA Civ 646).

12.7 An insolvency officeholder or a purchaser may decide to try to terminate the construction contracts. It is sometimes possible to do this if the contractors have refused to carry on with the works. This is most clear where there has been an abandonment of the works (see *CFW Architects v Cowlin Construction* [2006] EWHC 6 (TCC)). However, if there has been a delay whilst the parties work out their prospective positions following an insolvency this is more difficult (*Shawton Engineering v DGP International* [2006] BLR 1).

Express termination clause

12.8 Properly drawn construction contracts will have an express termination provision. Where the landowner/employer becomes insolvent the contractor will often be able to rely on two express grounds to terminate:

(1)   default by employer (usually failure to pay); or

(2)   the employer's insolvency.

12.9 The terms of such clauses are strictly construed and to be able to terminate the clause must adequately cover the event relied upon. The various standard form construction contracts have a comprehensive list of insolvency events which allow either party to terminate on the insolvency of the other. There is usually a contractual definition of insolvency such as the example in clause 8.1 of the JCT Design and Build Contract 2005 which contains an express provision allowing either party to terminate where the other:

• enters into an arrangement, compromise or composition in satisfaction of his debts (excluding a scheme of arrangement as a solvent company for the purposes of amalgamation or reconstruction);

• without a declaration of solvency, passes a resolution or makes a determination that he be wound up;

• has a winding-up order or bankruptcy order made against him;

• has appointed to him an administrator or administrative receiver; or

• is the subject of any analogous arrangement, event or proceedings in any other jurisdiction.

If the contractor or employer becomes *insolvent* in accordance with this definition then he has the right to serve a notice of termination (providing the contract contains equivalent provisions to JCT 2005) and such termination shall take effect on receipt of the relevant notice.

12.10　Whether or not a termination notice is served the employer has to immediately inform the contractor in writing if he makes any proposal, gives notice of any meeting or becomes the subject of any proceedings or appointment relating to any of the matters referred to in clause 8.1. As from the date the employer becomes insolvent, the contractor's obligations to carry out and complete the works shall be suspended. If the express contractual terms do not expressly cover administration then this will not count as an insolvency event unless the clause is drafted so widely that it is deemed to be covered by the generality of the expressions used (see *Merrill Lynch v Winterthur* [2007] EWHC 893 (Comm)). Therefore a clause which is limited to the presenting of a petition and/or the making of an administration order, but is silent on the non-court-based procedure to appoint an administrator (under the Enterprise Act 2002) is unlikely to be sufficient to cover the new style of administrations.

12.11　Similar principles of construction apply to the interpretation of termination clauses in construction contracts as to the interpretation of forfeiture clauses in leases (see chapter 4 on provisos for re-entry/forfeiture clauses).

Waiver

12.12　If the contractor wishes to rely on the right to terminate the contract (eg on the grounds of an express insolvency event or on the basis of non-payment) then he must take care that he doesn't waive the right to accept the repudiatory breach (see **4.58** in relation to waiver and forfeiture clauses in leases). In *Ellis Tylin v Co-Operative Retail Services* [1999] BLR 205 the right to terminate had not been waived where a conditional notice of termination had been served and a further breach committed. If the contractor waives the right to terminate then he must wait for a further breach before the right to terminate arises again.

Termination and moratoria

12.13　The moratorium which arises in relation to some voluntary arrangements (see **1.47** and IA 1986, s 252 and Sch A1) and the moratorium which applies to administrations (under IA 1986, Sch B1 and see **1.88**), do not prevent a contractor with proper grounds treating a repudiatory breach as a termination of the contract. However, it is possible to extend the effect of a moratorium contractually to prevent a termination in certain circumstances (see *Martyn Rose v AKG Group* [2003] 2 BCLC 102).

Effect of termination on subcontracts

12.14　Where the contract is terminated the subcontracts are usually drafted so that the contractor is able to terminate them at the same time. However, if there are no express provisions for the simultaneous termination of subcontracts the position is more complex. In *Iezzi Constructions v Currumbin* [1994] BCL 408, the employer went into liquidation; the contractor terminated the main contract and in breach of the provisions of the subcontracts attempted to terminate them. The contractor was held liable to pay damages which had accrued at the time of the termination. In practice a well drawn contractual structure will ensure that the subcontracts consistently reflect the termination provisions of the main contract.

12.15 Where the landowner/employer is a company in liquidation or a bankrupt individual the construction contract can be disclaimed as an onerous contract (IA 1986, ss 178 and 315 and see chapter 7). However, the disclaimer of the main contract does not automatically discharge the liabilities of the subcontracts.

LIABILITIES, POST-INSOLVENCY

12.16 Under clause 8.5.3 of JCT 2005 if the landowner/employer becomes insolvent (in accordance with the definition in clause 8.1, see above) then the ongoing contractual obligations are frozen until one of the parties serves notice. This allows the contractor a period to negotiate a continuation on terms or to end the contract and claim losses.

12.17 A contractor will be reluctant to continue to work for an insolvent landowner/employer in circumstances where payment is uncertain and will usually threaten to terminate whilst attempting to negotiate terms with the insolvency practitioner. The contractor may be faced with arrears for works which have already been completed and future costs and sums which will fall due as the work continues. In relation to the arrears these can be proved for in a liquidation or an administration as an unsecured debt (by analogy see chapter 2 in relation to the treatment of rent arrears in leases). Future payments which may fall due will depend upon whether the works are completed or the contract is terminated and the contractor claims damages under the contract. Such future claims are also provable under the terms of IR 1986, r 13.12. The contractor is able to submit claims for unliquidated debts under IR 1986 and r 12.3 provides:

> '. . . that all claims by creditors are provable as debts . . . whether they are present or future or certain or contingent, ascertained or sounding only in damages.'

12.18 In relation to quantum the liquidator is able to estimate the value of the claim for the purpose of the proof of debt (pursuant to IR 1986, r 4.86). The liquidator also has the right to require the contractor to evidence the proof by way of an affidavit.

12.19 Contract sums which have fallen due after the date of the liquidation are provable debts. They are included in the wide definition set out in IR 1986, r 12.3. IR 1986, r 13.12 defines debt to include:

' . . . any debt or liability to which the company is subject at the date on which it goes into liquidation . . . [and] any which the company may become subject after that date by reason of any obligation before that date.'

12.20   IR 1986, r 11.3 applies to future contract sums and reduces the amount to take into account accelerated receipt.

12.21   A contractor may be able to persuade an administrator or a liquidator to pay future payments as an expense (under IR 1986, r 4.218 or r 2.67). If a liquidator/administrator is able to confirm that future payments will be made as an expense then this provides the contractor with some comfort that he will be paid (see **2.80** in relation to rents).

12.22   If a liquidator disclaims the contract then the contractor is left with an unsecured damages claim in the liquidation (IA 1986, s 178(5)).

COMPLETION OF THE WORKS

12.23   Following the formal insolvency of a landowner/employer a practical problem arises for officeholders where on termination the contractor remains in possession of the site. The contractor has no automatic right to remain on site or to continue with the works. Contractors have been known to apply for specific performance to continue the contract. However, where a company is in administration an application for permission would have to be made under IA 1986, Sch B1, para 43 (see **1.88**) and if the company is in liquidation the contract could be disclaimed. Contractors are not able to exercise a lien over the land or plant and equipment which they do not own.

12.24   Mortgagees often retain the contractual right to step in and replace the landowner/employer's position in the contract where there is a threat that the contractor is about to terminate the contract. In relation to LPA receivers this right is one which arises from either the inherent right of the receiver to act as the mortgagor's agent or from the express terms of the charge (see chapter 17).

12.25   A debentureholder with step-in rights retains the right to appoint an administrative receiver (being one of the exemptions to the Enterprise Act 2002 prohibition on new appointments) under IA 1986, Sch 2A, para 6.

Chapter 13

INSOLVENCY SALE OF FREEHOLD

13.1 When an officeholder (in this chapter to include an administrator, receiver or liquidator) sells a property, the sale documentation will reflect the nature of the appointment and the date on which it took effect. If more than one officeholder has been appointed, they should all be named in the contract and it should reflect whether the liquidators have been appointed to act jointly, or jointly and severally. The contract will set out the basis of the sale including the officeholder's capacity to discharge mortgages and other encumbrances:

ADMINISTRATION

13.2 In the case of administrations the following considerations should be applied when preparing the sale contract:

- The contract will recite the nature of the administrator's appointment, which will be either by the court under the Insolvency Act 1986 (IA 1986), Sch B1, para 10 or by the company or its directors under para 22, or by the holder of a qualifying legal charge under para 14. The acts of an administrator will be valid notwithstanding any defect in the appointment process (IA 1986, s 232), although this will not be the case where there was no power to appoint in the first place.

- The company (in administration) will be the vendor. The administrator acts as agent of the company (IA 1986, Sch B1, para 69). He has the power to sell under the statutory powers vested in him under IA 1986, Sch 1, para 2 *by public auction or private contract*. There is no express power to divide the property into parcels and sell each part separately (contrast with liquidations below) although the significance of this discrepancy has never been tested.

- Administrators are able to sell property which is subject to a floating charge as if the property were not subject to the security. This power additionally arises if the charge 'as created' was floating 'on its creation' but has subsequently become fixed as a result of crystallisation (IA 1986, s 15 and in relation to most new administrations under IA 1986, Sch B1, para 70).

- An administrator can sell property subject to a fixed charge although he can only do so as if the property were not subject to the security with the court's permission (under IA 1986, Sch B1, para 71). The administrator must be able to demonstrate that the disposal of the property 'would be likely to promote the purpose of administration in respect of the company' (IA 1986, Sch B1, para 71(2)(b)). The net proceeds of the sale must be used to pay the chargeholder and if there is a shortfall in relation to open market value then the order may be conditional on the administrator paying the difference as an expense of the administration.

• If the court's permission is obtained the contract should set out details of the court application, and the order made, and that the administrator has satisfied IR 1986, r 2.51 requiring the administrator to give notice of the order to the holder of the fixed charge (failure to give notice is an offence). This application can also be combined with an urgent application for the court to determine any questions of validity of the charge so that a sale can proceed with certainty (see *Arthur D Little Ltd (in administration) v Ableco Finance LLC* [2002] EWHC 701 (Ch)).

LIQUIDATIONS

13.3   Where the sale is by a liquidator the sale contract should be drafted with the following considerations in mind:

• The contract will recite the nature of the liquidator's appointment, ie whether as a result of a winding-up order or as a resolution of the company. The powers of the directors of the company cease when the liquidator is appointed. Accordingly the contract would normally state whether the liquidation is compulsory or voluntary. The acts of a liquidator will be valid notwithstanding any defect in the appointment process (IA 1986, s 232), although this will not be the case where there was no power to appoint in the first place.

• Usually the company will be the vendor as the property of the company does not automatically vest in the liquidator, although the liquidator can apply to the court for vesting of company property in the liquidator (under IA 1986, s 145). Therefore normally the liquidator acts as the agent of the company and has the power to sell under IA 1986, Sch 4, para 6 *by public auction or private contract with power to transfer the whole of it to any person or to sell the same in parcels.* If the liquidator sells in his own capacity as a direct party to the sale then the contract should record the details of the vesting order.

• The liquidator should declare whether any challenge to the proposed sale has been made by a creditor or contributory under IA 1986, s 167(3). Where a challenge is made, the court is unlikely to interfere with a sale unless the liquidator is acting in a way in which *no reasonable liquidator would act* or unless he is acting fraudulently (see *Leon v York-O-Matic Ltd* [1966] 3 All ER 277 and *Re Greenhaven Motors Ltd (in liquidation)* [1999] 1 BCLC 635).

- The vendor might be a receiver. A fixed charge receiver can, after a liquidation, sell the company's property. This will not be a contravention of IA 1986, s 127. Where a debenture/floating charge provides a receiver with a full power of attorney on appointment then the receiver retains the power to execute sale documentation (see *Sowman v David Samuel Trust Ltd* [1978] 1 All ER 616).

- The liquidator and members of the liquidation creditors' committee are prohibited from purchasing the company's property without a validation order under IR 1986, r 4.149 which should be recited in the contract.

RECEIVERSHIP

13.4   The following factors will apply to the contract for a sale by a receiver:

- The contract should recite the instrument empowering the receiver's appointment and the date the appointment was accepted. However, the acts of an administrative receiver will be valid notwithstanding any defect in the appointment process (IA 1986, s 232), although this will not be the case where there was no power to appoint in the first place. A purchaser for value and acting in good faith does not have to inquire whether the receiver is acting within his powers (IA 1986, s 42(3)).

- An administrative receiver acts as the agent of the company and has the power to sell under the terms of the charge or pursuant to IA 1986, Sch 1, para 2 (the same provision for administrators). The agency will continue until the company goes into liquidation (IA 1986, s 44). However, if the instrument appointing the receiver makes him an attorney he may still be able to sell (see above and *Sowman v David Samuel Trust Ltd* [1978] 1 All ER 616).

- Fixed charge receivers and/or mortgagees are able to exercise the power of sale expressly created by the charge or as a power *incident* to the mortgagee's estate under the Law of Property Act 1925, s 101 and regulated by s 103.

- An administrative receiver is able to sell property free of the charge which was the security under which he was appointed. In relation to any other charge the administrative receiver can apply to the court for an order to sell free of that charge. The chargeholder may have the right to sell and overreach subsequent mortgages (Law of Property Act 1925, s 104; see chapter 16). The court will allow a sale if it is satisfied that the sale would *promote a more advantageous realisation of the company's assets than would otherwise be effected* (under IA 1986, s 43). If the court makes an order it will be a condition that the net proceeds of sale will be applied to discharge the sums owed on the security. If the net proceeds realised are less than would be realised in an open market sale then the receiver will be ordered to pay the appropriate sum to the chargeholder to make up the deficiency. The contract should record any relevant orders which have been made.

REPRESENTATIONS, LIABILITIES AND WARRANTIES OF TITLE

13.5   In a sale contract where the insolvent company is the vendor, liquidators and administrators have no automatic liability. Officeholders can become personally liable if they enter into personal covenants or in limited circumstances if they put forward misleading and incorrect representations. However, receivers are personally liable on any contract they enter into on behalf of the company unless the contract expressly excludes liability (IA 1986, s 37). In practice all officeholders will seek to expressly exclude liability. In practice the contract will include an express statement that the officeholder is acting in a representative capacity as agent for the seller and will not incur any personal liability. This will be the case for all formal insolvency sales even where there is no presumption that the officeholder is acting in his personal capacity such as in liquidation (see *Stead Hazel & Co v Cooper* [1933] 1 KB 840).

13.6   Ideally the officeholder will want to sell the property with vacant possession. However, the officeholder will only have limited knowledge of the property. If the officeholder is unable to guarantee that vacant possession will be given on completion then the sale contract should expressly reflect this to avoid uncertainty. Although the Standard Commercial Property Conditions (SCPC) (2nd edn) make no reference to the property being sold with vacant possession, the special conditions (on some printed forms of sale contract) do include an express special condition that the property will sold with vacant possession on completion.

13.7   Where vacant possession is not guaranteed a buyer should establish whether:

• anyone is in occupation; and

• any formal leases or licences to occupy exist.

13.8   In any event the officeholder will seek to make the sale subject to any leases, tenancies or licences to occupy which may affect the property.

13.9   The contract will usually provide that no covenants for title will be given because it is unlikely that the officeholder will have sufficient knowledge of the property to give any title guarantee.

13.10 Officeholders will usually seek an express indemnity and release in the contract. For this reason they will also be a party to the transaction and will execute the transfer in their own right (not as vendor but to take the benefit under seal of the indemnity and release). The officeholder will want the contract to represent the entire agreement so as to exclude liability for any pre-contractual statements or representations. Once again as the officeholder is likely to have limited knowledge of the property, he will not be in a position to give comprehensive replies to pre-contract enquiries.

13.11 The purchaser must assess the risk associated with entering into a contract in circumstances where he is contractually excluded from relying on any statement, representation, warranty, collateral agreement or other assurance (whether made negligently or innocently) made by the officeholder (save that it usual to retain a liability for fraud).

13.12 The transfer can be executed by the officeholder (acting as agent for the seller).

Part 3

MORTGAGEES AND RECEIVERS

Chapter 14

OVERVIEW OF MORTGAGES AND THE POSITION OF THE MORTGAGOR

14.1 A mortgage is created where a party (the mortgagor) grants a charge over his property to act as security for the repayment of a loan (or other obligation) made by another party (the mortgagee). The Law of Property Act 1925 (LPA 1925), s 205(1)(xvi) defines the term 'mortgage' as 'any charge or lien on property for securing money or monies worth'.

14.2 In the event that the loan is not repaid in accordance with the terms of the agreement between the mortgagor and the mortgagee, then the mortgagee will have a number of remedies against the mortgagor that will comprise the following:

• suing under the mortgagor's covenant to repay the loan;

• entry into possession by the mortgagor;

• sale of the mortgaged property;

• the appointment of a receiver; or

• foreclosure.

These remedies are available to both mortgagees with the benefit of a legal mortgage and those who have been granted equitable mortgages. Mortgage remedies are regulated by LPA 1925. As a consequence receivers appointed under a mortgage are colloquially known as *LPA receivers*.

LEGAL MORTGAGES

14.3 LPA 1925, s 87 provides that for a mortgage to be a legal mortgage, the charge must be created by deed and expressed to be made by way of legal mortgage. The charge must be registered at the Land Registry. Failure to register would render the charge enforceable only in equity.

EQUITABLE MORTGAGES

14.4   In the event that the charge is not made by deed or is not registered, then a secured obligation to make a payment is likely to constitute an equitable mortgage instead. The following documents are all forms of equitable mortgage:

- a contract to create a legal mortgage (including where the parties have intended to create a legal mortgage but there is a defect in registration on the basis that equity treats as done which ought to be done);

- an 'informal' mortgage by the deposit of the deeds to the charged property being deposited by the mortgagor with the mortgagee (provided there is also a document evidencing the mortgage signed 'by or on behalf of each party' (Law of Property (Miscellaneous Provisions) Act 1989));

- an equitable charge (where there is no express agreement to create a legal mortgage but a promise to charge land with the payment of a debt (see *Swiss Bank Corporation v Lloyds Bank Ltd* [1982] AC 584)); and

- a mortgage of an equitable interest (created by assigning a beneficial interest with a proviso for reassignment when the mortgage is redeemed).

THE POSITION OF THE MORTGAGOR

14.5   The law has developed in this area to provide mortgagors with a degree of protection against the (usually) dominant position of the mortgagee (who will often be in a position of strength when the terms of the charge are being negotiated).

14.6   The mortgagor:

- retains the right of redemption (*equity of redemption*);

- may have the benefit of collateral terms in the mortgage;

- must not be the subject of an extortionate credit bargain; and

- must not be subjected to any duress when deciding whether or not to grant the security to the mortgagee.

The right of redemption

14.7   The mortgagor has the right to repay the mortgagee and, in turn, to have the property released from the security upon discharge of the secured debt.

14.8   The right to redeem must not be excluded from the charge, although the courts have held that it may be justified to postpone the right to redeem (see *Deverges v Sanderman Clark & Co* [1902] 1 Ch 579).

THE TERMS OF THE MORTGAGE

14.9   A mortgage deed will usually provide the mortgagee with additional powers to those contained in LPA 1925 (see below). In line with the parties' freedom to contract as they wish, there is no prohibition or restriction to the inclusion of additional or supplemental powers and protections provided that:

- the terms are not unfair or unconscionable (see *Cityland and Property (Holdings) Ltd v Dabrah* [1968] Ch 166 and *Multiservice Book Binding Ltd v Marden* [1979] Ch 84);

- the terms do not unfairly restrict the right of redemption (see *Biggs v Hoddinott* [1898] 2 Ch 307; *Noakes & Co Ltd v Rice* [1902] AC 24; *Bradley v Carritt* [1903] AC 253; *Kregliner v New Pategoloa Meat and Cold Storage Co Ltd* [1914] AC 25);

- the mortgage does not impose terms that seek to restrain the mortgagor's trade (see *Esso Petroleum Co Ltd v Harpers Garage (Stourport) Ltd* [1968] AC 269 and *Alec Lobb (Garages) Ltd v Total Oil Great Britain Ltd* [1985] 1 WLR 173); and

- the terms do not constitute an extortionate credit bargain for the purposes of the Consumer Credit Act 2006, ss 19-22 or an extortionate credit transaction pursuant to IA 1986, s 343.

Undue influence

14.10   In *Barclays Bank v O'Brien* [1994] 1 AC 180 the House of Lords concluded that where persons:

- who are in a non-commercial relationship (such as a marriage);

- who own property jointly; and

- where one of the co-owners wishes to grant a lender a charge (or second charge) over the property,

then the lender should consider whether it is appropriate to take steps to ensure that the other co-owner takes independent legal advice and understands the nature of the charge, together with the implications of it being granted. The absence of independent advice left open the possibility that the other co-owner could challenge the mortgage on the basis of misrepresentation and/or undue influence.

14.11   The mortgagee's duty in this regard was extended and clarified in the *Etridge* case (*Royal Bank of Scotland v Etridge (No 2)* [1998] 4 All ER 705, CA). The House of Lords set the following guidelines to reduce the risk of undue influence. The mortgagee should:

- ensure both parties receive advice from a solicitor of their choosing;

- write directly to each of the parties separately;

- obtain written confirmation from the solicitor that full advice has been given.

The solicitor advising can act for both co-owning parties provided there is no conflict, either actual or potential.

14.12   In *First National Bank plc v Achampong and Others* [2003] EWCA Civ 487 and *Charter v Mortgage Agency Service* [2003] EWCA Civ 490 the courts have penalised lenders for not providing the co-owner with the full facts and background to the loan and proposed security.

14.13   In relation to banks' duties when explaining contractual obligations to prospective mortgagors generally see *Morgan and Another v Lloyds Bank plc* (1998) LTL 3/3/98, [1998] Lloyd's Bank Rep 73.

Chapter 15

INTERACTION BETWEEN THE RIGHTS OF MORTGAGEES AND FORMAL INSOLVENCY REGIMES

15.1 The mortgagee's remedies are governed by LPA 1925 and the terms of the mortgage itself. They are not dependent on the insolvency (or otherwise) of the mortgagor (although the insolvency of the mortgagor may be a triggering event enabling the mortgagee to exercise its powers). However, the two will often go hand in hand and so mortgagees should take care before exercising their powers where they are aware that the mortgagor is subject to formal insolvency proceedings.

BANKRUPTCY

15.2 Where an individual mortgagor is adjudged bankrupt, a mortgagee will usually be able to enforce its security without restrictions. IA 1986, s 385(4) provides that restrictions on unsecured creditors taking action against the property of the debtor at any time after a bankruptcy petition has been presented do not apply to secured creditors. For these purposes 'security' includes a mortgage, charge, lien or other security (IA 1986, s 383(2)).

VOLUNTARY ARRANGEMENTS (COMPANY AND INDIVIDUAL)

15.3 Under IA 1986, s 4(3) (company voluntary arrangements (CVAs)) and s 258 (individual voluntary arrangements (IVAs)) a meeting of the debtor's creditors may not approve any proposal or modification to the debtor's proposal for a voluntary arrangement which 'affects the right of a secured creditor of [the debtor] to enforce his security, except with the concurrence of the creditor concerned'.

15.4 The position under IA 1986 in the case of both CVAs and IVAs, is that the rights of secured creditors will not be affected by the voluntary arrangement unless they expressly agree to be so bound (see *Khan v Permayer* (2000) LTL 22/6/2000 CA).

15.5   A secured creditor who submits a claim in a voluntary arrangement for his unsecured shortfall (or more), may subsequently seek to exercise his rights under the security to recover the full amount of the entire debt that was outstanding. The courts have consistently held that by proving in the voluntary arrangement for any unsecured shortfall, the creditor does not relinquish his right to enforce the security (eg *Whitehead and Another v Household Mortgage Corporation plc* [2002] EWCA Civ 1657). Where the secured creditor does enforce his security he is entitled to recover the entire secured debt. The only amount of credit to be given to the debtor while doing so is the actual amount the creditor received by way of dividend, rather than the amount of the value of the creditor's unsecured claim in the voluntary arrangement. This comes down to the distinction between the mortgagor's covenant to repay the mortgage debt (which may be compromised in circumstances where the secured creditor votes in relation to any unsecured shortfall) and the mortgagee's right to possession of the property in order to realise that security to discharge the mortgage debt (or any part of it).

15.6   In *Whitehead and Another v Household Mortgage Corporation plc* [2002] EWCA Civ 1657, the debtor was indebted to the mortgagee in the sum of £90,492. The debtor made a proposal for an IVA and the mortgagee valued its security at £65,000, leaving a shortfall of around £25,000. The mortgagee submitted a revised claim in the IVA and received and accepted a dividend from the debtor in respect of this shortfall (in the sum of £1,874, being £5.05 in the £). The mortgagee subsequently sold the property for an amount in excess of the entire mortgaged debt. The question that arose on an application by the debtor was whether the mortgagee was entitled to retain the monies that represented the unsecured shortfall that it had proved for in the IVA, or whether the mortgagee's claim to these monies had been compromised by the IVA, leaving the mortgagee with the ability to only retain those monies that related to the value of its security at the time the IVA was approved. In dismissing the debtor's appeal, the Court of Appeal unanimously decided that the mortgagee was not to be treated as having elected to abandon its security for any part of the mortgage debt by proving in the voluntary arrangement nor as having agreed that it would not rely on its security for so much of the mortgage debt as exceeded £65,000 (or any other figure).

15.7   Chadwick LJ distinguished the case from the court's decision in *Khan v Permayer* (2000) LTL 22/6/2000, CA because there was nothing in the terms of the debtor's proposal indicating that the mortgagee intended to abandon its security, and so whilst the mortgagee was precluded from suing the debtor on his covenant to repay the unsecured element of the mortgaged sum, the mortgagee was not taken to have abandoned its security in relation to this amount and was entitled to exercise all its rights in doing so (save that credit had to be given to the debtor for the actual amount received by way of dividend). The court came to the same conclusion in the case of *Khan and Another v Mortgage Express* [2000] LTL 26/1/2002 (unreported elsewhere).

15.8 In the circumstances, individual debtors and nominees tasked with advising debtors (and often their partners) on the prospects of their IVAs and the implications of them should ensure that the debtor is fully aware that a dividend payment made to a mortgagee will not (usually) result in a reduction of the mortgage debt for the purposes of valuing and realising the mortgaged debt in the future.

ADMINISTRATION

The effect of the moratorium

15.9 IA 1986, Sch B1, para 43 (and para 44 in respect of the interim moratorium) provides that a creditor's right to take action in relation to his debt is severely restricted in the absence of either the administrator's consent or the leave of the court.

15.10 IA 1986, Sch B1, para 43(2) provides in relation to security that:

'No step may be taken to enforce security over the company's property except–

(a)   with the consent of the administrator; or
(b)   with the permission of the court.'

15.11 Whilst there is a restriction on enforcing the security, the administration of the mortgagor will not affect the validity of the security. In the event that the administrator unreasonably refuses to provide consent to the mortgagee enforcing its security, then the mortgagee is likely to seek a costs order against the administrator on any application to the court for leave to enforce his security.

Sale of mortgaged property by the administrator

15.12 Where an administrator (as part of a sale of the mortgagor's business for example) wishes to sell property subject to a fixed charge then the court has the power to enable the administrator to sell that property as if it were not subject to the security (see IA 1986, Sch B1, para 71(1)).

15.13 The administrator may need to invoke this provision where the mortgagee is not willing to consent to a sale of the mortgaged property (and refuses to provide the appropriate release upon completion) because the sale will not result in the complete repayment of the secured indebtedness. The mortgagee may prefer to allow the security to remain in place in order to take advantage of property value increases in a rising market in the future. It is at this point that the interests of the mortgagee and these of the mortgagor's other creditors may come into conflict. On an application pursuant to para 71, the administrator may sell the mortgaged property if the court is satisfied that the sale will promote the purpose of the administration.

15.14   Any such order will provide that the net proceeds of sale should be paid to the secured creditor, together with an additional amount (up to the market value of the property), in the event that the administrator proposes to sell the property at below the current market value of the property (para 71(3)). In relation to insolvency sales generally see chapter 8.

LIQUIDATION

Creditors' voluntary liquidation

15.15   Where a mortgagor is in creditors' voluntary liquidation, a mortgagee may enforce its security without restriction. The only caveat is that, if the liquidator considers that doing so would be prejudicial to the company's creditors or his ability to achieve the purpose of the liquidation, the liquidator may apply to the court for a direction under IA 1986, s 112 that the liquidation should be treated as if it were a compulsory winding up by the court.

15.16   An LPA receiver can still be appointed notwithstanding there being a liquidator in office (see *Re Henry Pound Sons & Hutchinson* (1889) 42 Ch D 402 and *Re Potter Oils Ltd (No 2)* [1986] 1 WLR 201).

Compulsory liquidation

15.17   IA 1986, s 130(2) provides that when a winding-up order is made (or a provisional liquidator appointed):

> 'No action or proceeding shall be preceded with or commenced against the company or its property, except by leave of the court and subject to such terms as the court may impose.'

15.18   The enforcement of a mortgage by the mortgagee against the mortgagor may constitute an action against the property of the company and so the court's leave will be required before proceeding to enforce the mortgagee's security.

Chapter 16

MORTGAGEES' REMEDIES

16.1 A mortgagee has five core rights under its mortgage as follows:

(1) suing under the covenant to repay;

(2) entry into possession;

(3) sale;

(4) appointment of a receiver; and

(5) foreclosure.

SUING UNDER THE COVENANT TO REPAY

16.2 In addition to the mortgage security, the mortgage deed will create ordinary contractual obligations on the parties, and in the event of default of any of those obligations, the mortgagee will have a right to sue the mortgagor for breach of contract. This might be an action in relation to a failure to repay the mortgage instalments as they fall due, or the breach of any other obligation.

16.3 The limitation period for suing under a breach of covenant is discussed below.

ENTRY INTO POSSESSION

16.4 The mortgagee under a legal charge is generally entitled to take possession of the property immediately upon the mortgage deed being executed (LPA 1925, s 95(4); see *Four-Maids Ltd v Dudley Marshall (Properties) Ltd* [1957] Ch 317).

16.5 This rather draconian rule has been tempered by statute and also the inclusion of contractual terms in mortgage deeds to prevent mortgagees from abusing their powers and to safeguard the interests of the mortgagor. However, there are some restrictions to this rule as set out below.

The right to possession – the restrictions

16.6 In order to provide the mortgagor with a degree of security and comfort, most modern mortgage deeds will provide that the mortgagee will not take possession of the property until there is a default under the terms of the mortgage by the mortgagor.

16.7 In the absence of consent by the mortgagee, the court has no inherent power to delay delivery of possession to the mortgagee, save to provide an adjournment in cases relating to property occupied as a dwelling house by the mortgagor for a short period of time in order to give the mortgagor an opportunity to discharge the mortgage in full or to satisfy the mortgagee in some other way (*Birmingham Citizens Permanent Building Society v Caunt* [1962] Ch 883).

Statutory restrictions on the right to possession in respect of residential property

16.8 Invariably, a mortgagee will issue proceedings for possession prior to taking possession of a property, particularly where the property is occupied. It is an offence to use or threaten the use of violence to obtain entry onto premises where someone is present on those premises (Criminal Law Act 1977, s 6). Further, the usual reason for a mortgagee entering possession is to enable him to effect an unencumbered sale of the mortgagor's title with vacant possession and so consideration must also be given to the mortgagor's rights (if any) under the Protection from Eviction Act 1977.

Vacant property

16.9 The statutory restrictions that apply to residential property that is occupied by the mortgagor do not apply to properties that are vacant. In addition to being able to take possession immediately upon the mortgage being granted, the mortgagee is entitled to take possession without any prior notice or demand being given to the mortgagor, and without the need for a court order. This position was confirmed in *Ropaigealach v Barclays Bank plc* [2000] 1 QB 263, where the claimant bank demanded repayment of all monies due and owing under the mortgage. The mortgagee was not living at the property and the property was vacant. The bank proceeded to sell the property at auction without first obtaining a court order. The Court of Appeal held that the bank had the right to take possession under common law without first obtaining a court order.

Administration of Justice Acts

16.10 There can be serious consequences of evicting a person and his or her family from their home. In order to provide a degree of protection to defaulting mortgagors in appropriate circumstances, the Administration of Justice

Act 1970 (AJA 1970), s 36 was enacted. AJA 1970, s 36 applies to mortgages over land consisting of or including a dwelling house and provides that where:

> ' . . . the mortgagor is likely to be able within a reasonable period of time to pay any sums due under the mortgage . . . the Court (a) may adjourn the proceedings; or (b) on giving judgment, or making an order, for delivery of possession of the mortgaged property, or at any time before the execution of such judgment or order, may (i) stay or suspend execution of the judgment or order; or (ii) postpone the date for delivery of possession, for such a period or periods as the Court thinks reasonable.'

16.11 Administration of Justice Act 1973 (AJA 1973), s 8 clarified the uncertainty in the drafting of AJA 1970, s 36 as to what was meant by 'any sums due'. It is the arrears on the account and not the full balance of the loan that is to be repaid within a reasonable period. AJA 1973, s 8(2) further clarifies how the court should exercise its discretion under s 36. It states that the court should only exercise its power to adjourn or suspend possession where the mortgagor is likely to be able both to clear the arrears within a reasonable time and also maintain the current monthly instalments during that period.

Exceptions to AJA 1970 and AJA 1973

16.12 There are types of mortgage that do not enjoy the protections afforded by AJA 1973, s 8 and AJA 1970, s 36 namely mortgages repayable on demand and mortgages regulated by the Consumer Credit Act 1974 (CCA 1974) or Consumer Credit Act 2006.

Mortgages repayable on demand

16.13 AJA 1973, s 8 applies to instalment mortgages (most household mortgages) because the repayment of the balance is deferred and is gradually discharged by payment of instalments. Repayable on demand mortgages (or all monies charges) contain no provision for early repayment and therefore s 8 has no application because under these mortgages the monies are not repayable at all until a written demand has been made. In order for the court to adjourn or suspend possession, the mortgagor must show that they are able to repay the full balance outstanding on the mortgage within a reasonable period of time (*Habib Bank v Tailor* [1982] 3 All ER 561).

16.14 Mortgages that are repayable on demand tend only to be used where the loan covers more than just a loan to purchase land, such as security for a business loan and an overdraft.

Mortgages regulated by Consumer Credit Act 1974 and Consumer Credit Act 2006

16.15 Where a mortgage is regulated by either of the Consumer Credit Acts, neither AJA 1970, s 36 nor AJA 1973, s 8 apply. Such mortgages are usually those lending up to £25,000. Some consumer credit agreements are exempt from being regulated and in such cases s 36 and s 8 will apply. These exemptions include house purchase and improvement loans secured by mortgage and granted by a bank or building society.

Reasonable period for repayment

16.16 If a defaulting mortgagor (who is able to seek the court's relief under s 36 and s 8) can demonstrate to a court that he can discharge the arrears within a reasonable time and can maintain monthly instalments in the meantime, the court may adjourn or stay possession. In determining a reasonable period under AJA 1970, s 36 and AJA 1973, s 8, the court is usually referred to *Cheltenham and Gloucester Building Society v Norgan* [1996] 1 All ER 449. In *Norgan*, the court ruled that it could take into account the whole of the residue of the unexpired term of the original mortgage as a starting point for considering relief. Accordingly, if the court is satisfied that the mortgagor would be able to discharge the remaining payments under the mortgage in full by the expiry of the mortgage term, then relief can be granted. The wide discretion of the court and the limited guidance on this point means that what is considered a 'reasonable period' can vary widely between judges.

Costs of an application for a possession order

16.17 The court's discretion as to costs should usually be exercised so as to reflect contractual rights. In most cases, the mortgagee's costs will be added to the security (see *Gomba Holdings (UK) Ltd v Minories Finance Ltd (No 2)* [1992] 3 WLR 723). The court will often remain silent on the question of costs where the mortgagee deed provides the mortgagee with the ability to add his costs of enforcement to the mortgage debt (see also **16.36** below).

The status of the mortgagee in possession

16.18 A mortgagee who takes possession does not act as trustee for the mortgagor. A mortgagee does not have to act in the best interests of the mortgagor as there is no fiduciary relationship. While he has certain duties, such as to act in good faith and with reasonable care (particularly when seeking to sell the property), he does not have to exercise his rights as mortgagee for the benefit of the mortgagor and is under no duty to exercise those rights, even though by doing so he may improve the mortgagor's position (see *Palk v Mortgage Services Funding plc* [1993] Ch 330 and *China and Southsea Bank Ltd v Tan* [1990] 1 AC 536).

16.19 Further, a mortgagee is under no duty to explain the risks and implications of entering into the mortgage deed to the mortgagor (see *Barclays Bank v Khana* [1992] 1 WLR 623; [1993] 1 FLR 343, CA), although note the position above in relation to third party occupiers and co-owners following the *Etridge* case (see **14.11**).

16.20 Whilst he is not a trustee, the mortgagee is subject to the following restraints:

- he must act in good faith (see *Tomlin v Luce* (1890) 43 Ch D 191 and see *Cuckmere Brick Co Ltd v Mutual Finance Ltd* [1971] Ch 949). In the Privy Council decision in *Downsview Nominees Ltd v First City Corp Ltd* [1993] AC 295 the court found that there had been a breach of the mortgagee's duty to act in good faith and to act in the best interests of subsequent mortgagees. In *Downsview*, a receiver appointed by a debenture holder refused to accept payment of the entirety of the mortgagor's indebtedness to his appointor from the holder of a subsequent debenture that ranked behind the appointor bank. The case also highlights the distinction between the negligence of the mortgagee (or his receiver) and a breach of duty;

- the mortgagee must act with reasonable care (see *Standard Chartered Bank Ltd v Walker* [1982] 1 WLR 1410 and *American Express International Banking Corporation v Hurley*;

- the duty to exercise reasonable care is particularly apparent with regard to taking reasonable care to achieve the best price on a sale of the mortgaged property (see *Cuckmere Brick Co Ltd v Mutual Finance Ltd* [1971] Ch 949). In *Cuckmere*, Salmon LJ described the mortgagee's powers and duties as follows:

  > 'It is well settled that a mortgagee is not a trustee of the power of sale for the mortgagor. Once the power has accrued, the mortgagee is entitled to exercise it for his own purposes whenever he chooses to do so. It matters not that the moment may be unpropitious and that by waiting a higher price could be obtained. He has the right to realise his security by turning it into money when he likes. Nor, in my view, is there anything to prevent a mortgagee from accepting the best price he can get at an auction, even though the auction is badly attended and the bidding exceptionally low. Providing none of those adverse factors is due to any fault of the mortgagee, he can do as he likes. If the mortgagee's interests, as he sees them, conflict with those of the mortgagor, the mortgagee can give preference to his own interests, which of course he could not do were he a Trustee of the power of sale for the mortgagor';

- the mortgagee owes a duty to the mortgagor to act fairly (see *Palk v Mortgage Services Funding plc* [1993] Ch 330);

- finally, there are a number of equitable rules that apply to a mortgagee which establish and regulate the mortgagor's right of redemption. The mortgagee's interest in the property is limited to his security and so whilst the mortgagor's right of redemption remains intact, the mortgagee is barred from personally profiting out of the mortgage property in any way not envisaged or expressly referred to by the terms of the mortgage.

16.21 Provided the mortgagee exercises his rights with reference to the duties listed above, then the mortgagee is afforded a number of rights in relation to the mortgaged property. The mortgagee has the right to receive rents and profits so long as the mortgagor remains in possession of the property. Further, where the mortgagee goes into possession of the property he is entitled to the rents and profits in respect of any tenancies that were created prior to the date of the mortgage deed, together with any rents in relation to any leases granted after the date the mortgage deed was created, provided the contractual terms of the mortgage deed provide for this.

16.22 Where a lease was created after the date the mortgage was created and there is no express provision contained in the mortgage deed allowing the mortgagor to take the benefit of future rents, the mortgagee will not be entitled to collect these rents as there is no contractual or common law right to do so. In such cases though, the mortgagee can serve notice on the tenant requiring the tenant to demand payment of the rents and the tenant should start paying the rent thereafter to the mortgagee and not to the mortgagor as puisne profits (see *Rusden v Pope* (1868) LR 3 Exch 269 at 275).

Rights of the mortgagee

16.23 LPA 1925, s 101(3) provides that in addition to the power afforded to a mortgagee pursuant to the Act, it is also open for the parties to agree that the terms of the mortgage deed will provide the mortgagee with supplementary powers:

> 'The provisions of this Act relating to the foregoing powers, comprised either in this section, or in any other section regulating the exercise of those powers, may be varied or extended by the mortgage deed, and, as so varied or extended, shall, as far as may be, operate in the like manner and with all the like incidents, effects, and consequences, as if such variations or extensions were contained in this Act.'

Right to enforce leasehold covenants

16.24 In relation to tenancies created prior to 1 January 1996, LPA 1925, s 141 provided a mortgagee with the ability to enforce leasehold covenants contained in any lease (including any rights of re-entry). It was even possible for a mortgagee of the reversion of any interest to re-enter the demised premises in respect of breaches committed prior to the creation of the mortgage (unless they had been waived or released) (LPA 1925, s 141(3)).

16.25 In relation to tenancies created after 1 January 1996 the position has changed. The Landlord and Tenant (Covenants) Act 1995, s 15 provides that the mortgagee in possession of a leasehold interest may enforce any covenant of the lessor (unless the covenant is stated to be personal to a particular individual or is unenforceable for want of registration – s 15(5)). Prior to 1

January 1996, as mortgagees did not enjoy privity of estate with the lessor, they had no right to enforce or procure the performance of any of the lessor's covenants.

Mortgagee's right to carry on business

16.26 A mortgagee in possession has a common law right to manage the mortgaged property and where the mortgaged property comprises business premises, the mortgagee has the right to carry on the business for a reasonable time where he intends to sell the mortgaged property and the business thereon as a going concern. The mortgagee is entitled to use the mortgagor's name for this purpose (see *Cook v Thomas* (1876) 24 WR 427). The terms of the mortgage deed are likely to extend the scope of the mortgagee's powers and those of any receiver the mortgagee chooses to appoint (see below).

16.27 In taking possession of the mortgaged property for the purposes of running the mortgagor's business, it is not the case that the employment of any employees of the mortgagor will automatically be determined and the mortgagee should have reference to the Transfer of Undertakings (Protection of Employment) Regulations 2006, SI 2006/246 and employment law generally.

Agricultural land

16.28 Where the mortgaged property comprises agricultural land, the mortgagee is entitled to all crops growing on that land to the exclusion of the mortgagor (see *Bagnall v Villar* (1879) 12 Ch D 812). However, if the crops have been cut or removed prior to the mortgagee taking possession, then those crops will constitute chattel assets of the mortgagor and will therefore not fall within the scope of the mortgagee's security (*Re Phillips, ex p National Mercantile Bank* (1880) 16 Ch D 104).

Mortgagee's right to grant and surrender leases

16.29 LPA 1925, s 99 makes provision for the creation of tenancies by a mortgagor in possession and by a mortgagee who has subsequently gone into possession, provided the terms of the mortgage contract do not exclude this right. However, even if this right is excluded by the mortgage deed, it will not prevent a mortgagor in possession from granting a lease to a third party that will remain effective between himself and his new lessee (see *Dudley and District Benefit Building Society v Emerson* [1949] Ch 707) and (*Rust v Goodale* [1957] Ch 33).

16.30 The ability to grant leases under s 99 is supplemented by LPA 1925, s 100, which enables the mortgagor or mortgagee to accept surrenders of leases in order to enable another lease to be granted. A surrender may be accepted by a mortgagee in possession or by his receiver (if he is still acting), or by the mortgagor, if he is in possession (s 100(1)).

16.31 A lease granted by the mortgagor prior to the mortgage being executed is generally binding on the mortgagee. The tenancy may be protected for the purposes of the Land Registration Act 2002 if the lease satisfies the provisions of s 29 of that Act. This provision affords leases created and registered before the registration of a mortgage priority in circumstances where, amongst other things:

- the leasehold estate was granted for a term not exceeding 7 years; and

- it is not a grant of a lease out of an unregistered legal estate pursuant to a right to buy or where the grant of a lease out of that interest leads to a secured tenant no longer being a secured tenant (see *Skipton Building Society v Clayton* (1993) 66 P&CR 223 and *Woolwich Building Society v Dickman* [1996] 3 All ER 204).

16.32 In *Barclays Bank v Zaroovabli* [1997] Ch 321, the High Court confirmed that a lease created after the mortgage was executed but prior to its registration will be binding on the mortgagee. Where the mortgagee is bound in this way, for the purposes of the Protection from Eviction Act 1977, the mortgagee will be the 'owner' of the leaseholder's reversionary interests.

16.33 A mortgagee will not generally be bound by an unauthorised lease granted after the creation of the mortgage unless:

- the mortgagor is granted an express power to grant leases under the terms of the mortgage without consent;

- LPA 1925, s 99 has not been excluded by the terms of the mortgage deed (see above);

- the mortgagee consents to the lease being granted; or

- the mortgagee acts in a way that is consistent with the granting of the lease, for example by treating the tenant as his own. As stated above, the grant of an unauthorised tenancy by the mortgagor will remain binding between the mortgagor and his tenant. In *Mann v Nijjer* (1998) 32 HLR 223, the mortgagee bank had accepted rent from the mortgagor's assured tenant after the mortgagee had fallen into arrears with her mortgage. The mortgagee's tenant was entitled to a declaration that the bank's taking of possession and removing his possessions was unlawful and was successful in claiming damages under the Housing Act 1988, ss 27 and 28 against the bank for unlawful eviction.

THE MORTGAGEE'S POWER OF SALE AND OTHER REMEDIES

16.34 The mortgagee's statutory powers and remedies that arise upon the mortgagor's default (or when the mortgage monies become due) are contained in LPA 1925, ss 101–110. Essentially, they provide the mortgagee with two remedies namely, to exercise a power of sale or to appoint a receiver (often known as an 'LPA receiver'). The rights and status of such receivers is considered in chapter 17.

16.35 When considering a mortgagee's power of sale and the ability to appoint a receiver, it should be noted that the requisite provisions of LPA 1925 are often varied, extended and sometimes excluded altogether in favour of alternative contractual provisions contained in the mortgage deed itself (which will usually give any mortgagee wider powers in the event of the mortgagor's default than he is afforded by LPA 1925). Such variations are expressly permitted by LPA 1925, s 101(3).

16.36 The Pre-Action Protocol for possession claims based on mortgage or home purchase plan arrears in respect of residential property came into effect on 19 November 2008. The protocol obliges the lender to provide information relating to debt management prior to issuing possession proceedings and to consider reasonable proposals from the borrower. There are likely to be adverse costs consequences for lenders who fail to comply with the protocol without reasonable excuse.

The statutory power of sale (LPA 1925, s 101)

16.37 Where a number of mortgages have been registered against the title to a property and there is insufficient equity in the property to ensure that the entirety of the mortgage debt is redeemed, a mortgagor has no power to compel the mortgagees to consent to a sale proceeding. However, where the sale is by a mortgagee, the mortgagee can sell free from all mortgages registered against the title to the property over which he has priority. This is provided by LPA 1925, s 104:

'(1) A mortgagee exercising the power of sale conferred by this Act shall have power, by deed, to convey the property sold, for such estate and interest therein as he is by this Act authorised to sell or convey or may be the subject of the mortgage, freed from all estates, interests, and rights to which the mortgage has priority, but subject to all estates, interests, and rights which have priority to the mortgage.'

16.38 The statutory power of sale under LPA 1925, s 101 is introduced into every mortgage that is made by deed. LPA 1925, s 205(1)(xvi) defines the term 'mortgage' as 'any charge or lien on property for securing money or monies worth'. LPA 1925, s 101(1) provides as follows:

'A mortgagee, where the mortgage is made by deed, shall, by virtue of this Act, have the following powers, to the like extent as if they had been in terms conferred by the mortgage deed, but not further (namely):

(i)   a power, when the mortgage money has become due, to sell, or to concur with any other person in selling, the mortgaged property, or any part thereof, either subject to prior charges or not, and either together or in lots by public auction or by private contract, subject to such conditions respecting title or evidence of title, or other matter, as the mortgagee thinks fit, with power to vary any contract for sale, and to buy in at an auction, or to rescind any contract for sale, and to re-sell, without being answerable for any loss occasioned thereby . . .'

16.39   The scope and extent of the mortgagee's discretion when exercising a power of sale has been shaped and codified in a substantial body of case-law that is discussed below.

16.40   For a recent unsuccessful attempt by a mortgagor of residential premises to argue that LPA 1925, s 101 is inconsistent with the provisions of the ECHR see *Horsham Properties Group v Clark and Another* [2008] EWHC 2327 (Ch).

When the power of sale arises

16.41   The mortgagee's power of sale will arise on the triggering of three events. All three of the following circumstances must be present before the power of sale will arise:

(1)   the mortgage is made by deed and the mortgage money has become due (LPA 1925, s 101(1)); and

(2)   the mortgagor is in default of his obligations under the mortgage deed; and

(3)   there is nothing in the mortgage deed itself that would preclude the power of sale being exercised – for example, the mortgagee providing the mortgagor with a grace period prior to taking any enforcement action.

When the three elements above are satisfied, the mortgagee's power of sale will arise.

16.42   There is a distinction between the power of sale arising under LPA 1925, s 101 and that power of sale being exercisable. A mortgagee may not (in the absence of a provision in a mortgage deed to the contrary) proceed to sell the mortgaged property until the provisions of LPA 1925, s 103 have been complied with. LPA 1925, s 103 stipulates that the statutory power of sale may not be exercised until at least one of three conditions has been satisfied, namely:

(1)   the mortgagee has served a notice on the mortgagor requiring payment of the mortgage money and the mortgagor has failed to pay any or all of that mortgage money for 3 months after the service of such notice (s 103(1)); or

(2)   an amount of interest under the mortgage is in arrears and remains unpaid for the period of 2 months after becoming due; or

(3)   there has been a breach of a provision contained in the mortgage deed by the mortgagor or the mortgagor is in default of any of its obligations under a provision contained in LPA 1925.

16.43   The notice referred to in (1) above must be in writing and it must be served in accordance with the provisions of LPA 1925, s 196 (unless a contrary intention appears in the mortgage deed itself). Under s 196 the notice will be deemed served if:

- it is left at the mortgagor's last known place of abode or business or is affixed to or left for the mortgagor on the property comprised in the mortgage (s 196(3)); or

- the notice is served by placing the notice through the letterbox of the mortgaged premises (even if those premises are vacant at the time of service);

- it is sent by registered post addressed to the mortgagor (or any other person to be served in accordance with the mortgage deed) and if that letter is not returned by the post office as undelivered, service will be deemed to have been made at the time at which the registered letter would, in the ordinary course of post have been delivered; and

- provided the requirements of s 196 are satisfied, the service of the notice will be valid even if it is never received by the mortgagor (see, eg, *R v Westminster Unions Assessment Committee, ex p Woodward and Sons* [1917] 1 KB 832).

Exercise of the power of sale

16.44   The mortgagee is not a trustee for the mortgagor but the mortgagee does owe the mortgagor three key duties when exercising his power of sale:

(1)   to act in good faith;

(2)   to take reasonable care to obtain the true market value of the mortgaged property; and

(3)   to ensure that the sale is genuine.

Duty to act in good faith

16.45 Historically, the courts have been slow to impose any duty upon the mortgagee to act in any way, other than in *good faith*. In *Cuckmere Brick Co Ltd and Another v Mutual Finance Ltd* [1971] 2 All ER 633 the duty to act in good faith was noted as being 'honestly and without reckless disregard for the mortgagor's interest'.

16.46 The courts would generally not set transactions aside unless there was evidence of fraud. A sale at a significant undervalue was held in a number of cases not to be evidence of mal fides on behalf of the mortgagee. In *Adams v Scott* (1859) 7 WR 213 a mortgagee sold a property that was worth £20,000 for just £12,000. The court rejected the notion that just because the property was sold at an undervalue the mortgagee had acted in bad faith in effecting that sale.

16.47 Where there is evidence of fraud, the court may grant an injunction to restrain the completion of a proposed sale by a mortgagee or could set aside a completed sale. In *Kennedy v De Trafford* [1897] AC 180, HL the purchaser had already purchased the property from the mortgagee for value and without notice of the fraud that the mortgagee had perpetrated. It was held that the mortgagor would have an action in damages against the fraudulent mortgagee.

Duty to obtain best price

16.48 The courts have increasingly questioned whether a mortgagee did or should owe its mortgagor more comprehensive duties in relation to the sale of mortgaged premises. The mortgagor, of course, has a direct interest in the amount the mortgagee is able to realise for the property because the level of the sale price will determine the amount of any shortfall the mortgagee will suffer (which the mortgagor will remain liable for under his covenant to repay), or alternatively, the level that the mortgagor can expect to receive back after the redemption of the mortgage, or the amount to be paid to any subsequent chargeholders.

16.49 Earlier cases in the Privy Council had extended the mortgagee's duty beyond simply a duty to act in good faith and the duty was extended to ensure that 'the borrower may receive credit for the fair value of the property sold' (see *McHugh v Union Bank of Canada* [1913] AC 299 at 311, PC). It wasn't until the Court of Appeal's decision in the case of *Cuckmere Brick Co Ltd v Mutual Finance Ltd* [1971] Ch 949 that the English courts equated the duty to take reasonable care to obtain a fair or proper price for the property with a duty to obtain the true market value of the mortgaged property. The *Cuckmere* case remains the leading authority on this point.

16.50 In *Cuckmere* the claimant mortgagor had borrowed the sum of £50,000 secured against a piece of land that the mortgagor wished to develop into flats. The mortgagor acquired planning permission for the development but for various reasons subsequently changed the planning consent to develop the land to build houses instead. Prior to the land being developed the mortgagee demanded repayment of the sums secured under the mortgage. The mortgagee was aware that a valuer had placed a value on the land of £75,000 but still proceeded to sell the land at auction for £44,000. The auction particulars failed to mention the existence of planning permission for the development of 100 flats. The Court of Appeal undertook a detailed review of the earlier authorities and concluded that the mortgagee must 'take reasonable care to obtain the true market value of the mortgaged property' (as per Lord Salmon at 966).

Contracting out of mortgagees' duties

16.51 It has been suggested that a mortgagee may, under the terms of the mortgage deed seek to limit his liability for failing to comply with his duties under the *Cuckmere* principle (see *Bishop v Bonham* [1988] 1 WLR 742 at 752, per Slade LJ). However, it should be noted that building societies are prohibited from excluding this type of liability pursuant to the Building Societies Act 1997.

16.52 In *Bishop v Bonham* it was held that even where the mortgagee had a right to exercise its power of sale in its absolute discretion, the mortgagee was under a duty to exercise that discretion properly and was consequently under a duty to exercise reasonable care in order to obtain a proper price.

Mortgagees' duties post-*Cuckmere*

16.53 There is a substantial body of case-law that has flowed following the *Cuckmere* case. These cases have predominantly arisen where the mortgagor is dissatisfied with the way in which the mortgagee has exercised his discretion when exercising the power of sale. The following examples are areas where the court has considered the extent of the mortgagee's duty in a variety of circumstances.

No duty to enhance the value of the mortgaged property

16.54 Whilst it is in the mortgagor's interest that the mortgaged property is sold at the highest possible value, the courts have consistently held that a mortgagee is under no duty to take positive action to enhance the value of the mortgaged property, even if such action would almost certainly lead to an increase in the value of the mortgaged property.

16.55 The leading case on this point is the 2003 Court of Appeal decision in *Silven Properties and Another v Royal Bank of Scotland plc and Others* [2003] EWCA Civ 1409. In *Silven* the mortgagee bank had appointed receivers to exercise the mortgagee's power of sale. Prior to the receivers' appointment, the mortgagor had been pursuing a number of planning applications, that if successful would have enhanced the value of the properties by virtue of the ability to sell the properties with the benefit of the planning consents.

16.56 Upon their appointment, the receivers decided not to pursue the planning applications, but proceeded to sell the properties without the benefit of any planning consents. The mortgagor argued that the receivers were under a duty to delay the sales of the mortgaged properties for the purpose of pursuing the planning applications and in order to protect and maximise the mortgagee's position, they should have let the vacant property whilst the planning application was progressing.

16.57 At first instance, the court rejected the mortgagor's arguments on the ground that, as a matter of law, the receivers had no duty to delay the sale for the purposes asserted by the mortgagor and they were entitled to sell the properties without delay in their current condition. The Court of Appeal agreed and dismissed the appeal. In doing so, Lightman J made a number of observations relating to the duties of mortgagees (and subsequently those of receivers – see chapter 17). Lightman J stated as follows:

> '•   A mortgagee has no duty at any time to exercise his powers as mortgagee to sell, to take possession or to appoint a Receiver . . . he is entitled to remain totally passive.
> •   A mortgagee is not a Trustee of the power of sale for the mortgagor . . . a mortgagee is at all times free to consult his own interests alone as to whether and when to exercise his power of sale.
> •   The mortgagee is entitled to sell the mortgaged property as it is. He is under no obligation to improve it or to increase its value.
> •   The mortgagee is free to investigate whether and how he can 'unlock'; the potential for an increase in value of the property mortgaged (eg by application for planning permission for the grant of a lease) . . . By commencing on this path, the mortgagee does not, in any way preclude himself from calling a halt at will.
> •   If the mortgagor requires protection in any of these respects, whether by imposing further duties on the mortgagee or limitations on his rights and powers, he must insist upon them when the bargain is made and upon the inclusion of protective provisions in the mortgage.
> •   When and if the mortgagee does exercise the power of sale, he comes under a duty in equity (and not taught) to the mortgagor (and all others interested in the equity of redemption) to take reasonable precautions to obtain "the fair" or "the true market" value of, or the "proper price" for, the mortgaged property at the date of the sale, and not . . . the date of the decision to sell . . .
> •   . . . there can, accordingly, be no duty on the part of a mortgagee, as suggested by the Claimants, to postpone exercising the power of sale until after the further pursuit (let alone the outcome) of an application for planning permission or the grant of a lease of the mortgaged property . . .'

16.58 Lightman J also ruled that the dicta of Lord Denning MR in *Standard Chartered Bank Ltd v Walker* [1982] 1 WLR 1410 could not stand with later authorities which had stated 'quite categorically that the mortgagee is under no such duty of care to the mortgagor in respect of the timing of the sale'. In *Standard Chartered Bank*, Lord Denning had accepted that there was authority for the proposition that a mortgagee who had decided to sell a property at what could be described as the 'wrong time of year' for the sale of such a property could be liable to account to the mortgagor for his failure to wait until market conditions improved. This proposition was robustly dismissed by Lightman J in *Silven*.

16.59 The mortgagee's duty then, is to sell at the best market price that can be achieved at the date of the sale of the property. It is not the date on which the mortgagee decides to sell that is relevant, nor a later date in the future where it may be possible to obtain a higher price.

Mortgagee's liability for failure to market the property correctly

16.60 In *Cuckmere Brick Co Ltd v Mutual Finance Ltd* [1971] Ch 949 the court ruled that if, in exercising his power of sale a mortgagee advertised a property for sale and failed to mention that the property had the benefit of planning permission for the erection of 100 flats, then the mortgagee would become accountable to the mortgagor for his failure to market the property correctly and would have to account to the mortgagor for the balance between the price the property would have obtained, had it been exposed to the market with the benefit of planning permission and the price it actually achieved.

16.61 In *Roger Michael and Others v D Henry Miller* [2004] EWCA Civ 282, CA the mortgagee had sold the mortgaged property for the sum of £1.625m, after a last minute reduction in the purchase price of £25,000. The mortgagor claimed that the mortgagee had breached its duty to take reasonable care to obtain the best price possible. The judge at first instance concluded that the actual value of the property at the date of sale was £1.75m pounds. However, he further concluded that an acceptable range of valuations stood at between £1.6m to £1.9m. The court held that the mortgagee's valuer had not acted negligently but the mortgagee had breached its duty as mortgagees when they agreed to a reduced purchase price immediately prior to completion of the sale. The court also ruled that the mortgagee should have cultivated the lavender plants that had been growing on the property and marketed them separately since they appeared to be of some commercial value. The trial judge agreed with the mortgagor and found against the mortgagee. On appeal, the Court of Appeal held that the trial judge was entitled to rely upon a range of values and as a matter of principle, there was no reason why a judge should not look at a bracket of potential prices when determining whether or not the mortgagee had acted reasonably. The mortgagee had also appealed on the issue concerning the lavender because it had not been pleaded in the mortgagor's original case. The Court of Appeal set aside the judge's finding of liability on this issue and ordered that further particulars of this issue should be forthcoming.

16.62 Where a mortgagee fails to expose the subject property to the open market (be it by auction, through advertisement or otherwise), then the courts will be quick to punish a mortgagee where it is demonstrated that a better price could have been achieved if the property had been exposed for a reasonable period on the open market. In *Bishop v Blake* [2006] EWHC 831 (Ch) the court cited the *Silven* and *Cuckmere* cases with authority for the proposition that the mortgagee ought to properly expose the mortgaged property to the market. In *Bishop*, the mortgagee was selling a public house. Sir Francis Ferris stated:

> 'The inn was never marketed in any realistic sense. The advertisement in "the Publican" was pathetic. It was inserted at the last minute, it failed to include elementary contact details and the contract with Gillie's Inns was entered into before even the most alert reader of that publication had a realistic opportunity to respond. This episode has, to me, the appearance of a last minute realisation by Mr Albion of the need to market the inn in some way, resulting in an attempt to provide himself and his client with a fig leaf to hide the fact that no marketing of any kind had been undertaken.'

The learned judge went on to state:

> 'Without proper exposure to the market one simply does not know whether or not rival purchasers would have been forthcoming or, if they were, what might have been the outcome of a competitive bidding situation.'

Is there an obligation to sell a portfolio of properties individually?

16.63 The courts have consistently held that provided he does so in good faith, there is no reason why a mortgagee cannot sell a number of properties as a single portfolio, even where it is quite possible that those properties could realise a higher sale value if they were each sold individually on the open market.

16.64 This issue was dealt with in the comprehensive judgment of Patten J in the 2008 decision in *Bell v Long and Others* [2008] EWHC 1273 (Ch). In *Bell*, the first and second defendants were the administrative receivers appointed by the mortgagee bank of the mortgagor company. The bank had the benefit of mortgages over four freehold properties in the ownership of the company. The receivers' valuer had valued the four properties in a best case scenario at £955,000. This was against the mortgagor's indebtedness to the bank in the sum of £645,339.21. Conversely, the mortgagor had received valuation advice that the four properties were worth £1.241m. In either event, the mortgagor was clearly interested in the price at which the four properties were sold because there would either be a return to the mortgagor following the sale, or it may have been that the receivers would only have needed to sell three of the four properties in order to discharge the mortgagor's liability to the bank.

16.65 The receivers received various offers for three of the properties but rather than accept these offers, accepted an offer on all four properties for the sum of £775,000. Patten J applied the principles in *Silven* and found in favour of the receivers, on the basis that whilst there were offers on the table for three of the four properties and in principle, the fourth property was worth in the region of £325,000, there was no offer in existence in relation to the fourth property and so the receivers were entitled to sell when they did at the price at which they did. Patten J held that the receivers' duties did not require them to face the uncertainty of waiting for a longer period and their right to choose the time of the sale would override this in any event. He stated that 'the reality is that at the time of contract no better offer had been received despite the four properties remaining on the market until that time'. The position may have been very different if there had been an offer on the fourth property and the receivers had still concluded a sale to the purchaser of the portfolio as a whole.

Time-limit for challenging the mortgagee's conduct of sale

16.66 The limitation periods within which a mortgagee must exercise his remedies under LPA 1925, s 101 and the mortgage deed are set out below. However, the question of a mortgagor's ability to challenge a mortgagee's conduct of the sale of the mortgaged property (eg upon an allegation that the mortgagee sold at an undervalue) is subject to different considerations. These were considered in the case of *Raja v Lloyds TSB Bank plc* [2001] EWCA Civ 210. The (former) mortgagor of the bank wished to challenge the bank's conduct of the sale of the mortgaged property more than 6 years after the mortgagee had sold the property. The mortgagor contended that the mortgagee's duties to the mortgagor to act in good faith and to obtain the true market value for the property were duties that stemmed from or should be implied into the terms of the mortgage deed itself. In these circumstances, the mortgagor argued that his cause of action against the mortgagee would be an action based upon a specialty, to which the Limitation Act 1980, s 8 applied. The effect of this would be that the limitation period for such actions would be 12 years. The Court of Appeal dismissed the claim, confirming that a mortgagee's duties arise in equity and/or at common law, and as such, are subject to a 6-year limitation period in accordance with Limitation Act 1980, s 2. The Court of Appeal also noted that it was irrelevant whether the mortgagee's duty was based in equity or under common law but in neither event could an action by a mortgagor for a breach of a mortgagee's duty ever constitute an action based on a specialty (unless the mortgage deed expressly provided otherwise).

SALE TO MORTGAGEE

16.67 A mortgagee cannot sell to himself even though the price he is prepared to pay is the full market value of the property he is selling (see *Martison v Clowes* (1882) 21 Ch D 857). Whilst there is not necessarily a conflict in the mortgagee wearing two hats as mortgagee and purchaser, the fact is that a person cannot make a contract with himself and so such a sale is deemed to be a contractual impossibility.

16.68 Whilst a mortgagee will need to take care in ensuring that the sale is a genuine sale to a third party, the courts have held that in the absence of any bad faith on the part of the mortgagee, it is possible for a mortgagee to sell to a company in which, the mortgagee is either a shareholder or even a director (see *TSE Kwong Lam v Wong Chit Sen* [1983] 1 WLR 1349). In *Farrar v Farrars Ltd* (1888) 40 Ch D 395 at 409, Lindley LJ stated:

> 'A sale by a person to a corporation of which he is a member is not, either in form or in substance, a sale by a person to himself. To hold that it is, would be to ignore the principle which lies at the route of the legal idea of a corporate body, and that idea is that the corporate body is distinct from the persons composing it. A sale by a member of a corporation to the corporation itself is in every sense a sale valid in equity as well as at law. It should be noted though that where a mortgagee has a substantial interest in the company acquiring the mortgaged property, the burden would be on the mortgagee and the purchaser to demonstrate that the sale was in good faith and for value.'

16.69 The effect of this ruling is to reverse the burden of proof onto the mortgagee to demonstrate that the sale to a party in whom he has an interest was not otherwise than in good faith. For examples of cases where the court was not satisfied that the link between the mortgagee and the purchaser gave rise to a breach of the mortgagee's duty to act in good faith see *Tse Kwong Lam v Wong Chit Sen and Hodson v Deans* [1903] 2 Ch 647.

The proceeds of sale

16.70 Following sale, the mortgagee becomes trustee of the proceeds of sale for himself, the mortgagor and any other interested parties (such as prior or subsequent chargeholders). LPA 1925, s 105 provides that the sale proceeds are to be applied in the following order of priority:

- the discharge of any prior ranking mortgages (where the sale is expressed to be 'free from encumbrance');

- in the payment of all costs, charges or expenses properly incurred by the mortgagee, incidental to the sale and any attempted sale;

- in discharging the mortgage debt; and

- the balance (if any) is to be paid to any subsequent chargeholders, and if there are none, to the mortgagor.

16.71 Most mortgage deeds will provide that the mortgagor may not grant further mortgages on the property without the consent of the first mortgagee. A mortgagee of a prior ranking legal charge will often require any subsequent chargeholders to enter an express deed of priority to ensure that they are given conduct (or at least the opportunity) to take conduct of any sale and to ensure that the totality of sums secured by the second (or subsequent) mortgage is deferred behind the sums secured by the first ranking mortgagee.

Chapter 17

RECEIVERS

17.1 A receiver may be appointed in four main ways:

(1) under Law of Property Act 1925 (LPA 1925), s 101 by a mortgagee (often referred to as an 'LPA receiver');

(2) pursuant to an express right to do so contained in a mortgage or other charge document (often referred to as a 'fixed charge receiver' or 'LPA receiver');

(3) by the holder of a debenture containing a floating charge that was created prior to 15 September 2003 (and after this date in relation to companies that fall within the excepted cases contained at IA 1986, ss 72B–72G; and

(4) by the court.

LPA RECEIVERS

17.2 When the mortgagee's power of sale arises, a mortgagee has a right to appoint a receiver pursuant to LPA 1925, s 101, provided:

- the mortgage has been made by deed;

- the loan secured by that mortgage has become due; and

- there is nothing stated in the mortgage deed that would preclude the mortgagee from appointing a receiver at that specific time.

17.3 The powers of an LPA receiver are contained in LPA 1925, s 109. A receiver appointed purely under this provision only has the power to receive any income from the mortgaged property. An LPA receiver does not have a power to sell the property (see *Marshall v Cottingham* [1981] 3 All ER 8).

17.4 An LPA receiver may have a power to sell the mortgaged property in three situations:

(1) where the receiver is granted an express power of sale in a mortgage deed;

(2)   where the power of sale is exercised under LPA 1925, s 101(1)(i), namely where the mortgage money has become due and the receiver is exercising the mortgagee's power of sale (although see the position below in relation to the recovery of the receiver's costs in this situation);

(3)   Where an application has been made to the court and the court has granted the receiver a power of sale (as was the case in *Re Henry Pound, Son and Hutchins Ltd* (1889) 42 Ch D 402).

17.5   The majority of modern mortgage deeds expressly grant a receiver appointed by the mortgagee a wide range of powers including the power of sale and often the ability of the receiver to manage the mortgagor's business.

17.6   The provisions of IA 1986, ss 28–41 apply in relation to LPA receivers. IA 1986, s 30 prohibits a company from being appointed as a receiver. Unlike the position in relation to administrative receivers (who must be licensed insolvency practitioners), an LPA receiver is not required to have any specific qualifications in order to qualify for the role. LPA receivers may be estate agents, surveyors, accountants, insolvency practitioners or any other appropriate professional. The only restriction is that the receiver must not act as a receiver while he is an undischarged bankrupt or is subject to a bankruptcy restrictions order (see IA 1986, s 31(1)).

17.7   The receiver's appointment will take effect by the mortgagee appointing the receiver in writing and the receiver accepting that appointment (IA 1986, s 33).

17.8   Where there is an invalid appointment of a receiver, the court can compel the mortgagee or chargeholder to indemnify the receiver against any liability which arises as a result of the invalid appointment (IA 1986, s 34).

FIXED CHARGE RECEIVERS

17.9   In addition to the statutory powers conferred on receivers by LPA 1925, the express terms of the mortgage deed will often provide the receiver with wide-ranging powers to deal with the mortgaged property. Fixed charge receivers are subject to the provisions of IA 1986 referred to above. They will usually have far wider powers than a receiver who derives his powers from LPA 1925, s 109 alone. For example, it is common for mortgage deeds to provide the mortgagor or his receiver with an irrevocable power of attorney with regard to the execution of deeds and the sale of the mortgaged property.

The agency and duties of the receiver

17.10   While a receiver is appointed to preserve and realise the mortgagee's security, LPA 1925, s 109(2) provides that the receiver acts as agent of the mortgagor. This position is often reinforced expressly in the terms of the mortgage deed. Notwithstanding this though, the receiver's duties are predominantly owed to the mortgagee, by whom he is instructed to maximise recoveries under the charge for the benefit of the mortgagee.

17.11 In *Silven Properties and Another v Royal Bank of Scotland plc and Others* [2003] EWCA Civ 1409, Lightman J held that (in the absence of any agreement to the contrary) in the exercise of a power of sale, a receiver owed the same equitable duties to the mortgagor and others interested in the equity of redemption as those owed by the mortgagee (see above). He held that both parties were duty bound to take care to obtain the best price reasonably obtainable (in accordance with the cases of *Cuckmere, Downsview and Yorkshire Bank plc v Hall* [1999] 1 WLR 1713). He also noted that whilst receivers and mortgagees share the same common duties to the mortgagor, a receiver, once appointed cannot remain passive in the same way that a mortgagee perhaps can.

17.12 Lightman J noted that in the absence of a provision to the contrary in the mortgage 'the receiver must be active in the protection and preservation of the charged property over which he is appointed' (eg by triggering a rent review in due time where the receiver is appointed over a lease as per the ruling in *Knight v Lawrence* [1991] BCC 411).

17.13 While the court noted that a receiver has certain duties to act promptly, the court declined to go as far as to say that a receiver had a duty to postpone a sale until after certain steps have been taken (eg the progression and conclusion of an application for planning consent in relation to the mortgaged premises) (see above).

Position of third parties dealing with a receiver

17.14 LPA 1925, s 109(4) provides that any person dealing with an LPA receiver shall not be concerned to enquire whether that receiver has the authority to act.

Remuneration of the receiver

17.15 The receiver's remuneration is governed by LPA 1925, s 109(6) and/or under the terms of the charge itself. Under s 109(6) an LPA receiver is entitled to deduct from monies received by him an amount in respect of his remuneration, and in satisfaction of all costs, charges and expenses incurred by him in acting as a receiver. He is also entitled to a commission at a rate not exceeding 5% on the gross amount of all money received, such rate being specified upon his appointment. In the event that no rate has been specified, then the rate will be 5% unless the court orders otherwise.

Termination of receivership

17.16   The mortgagee may remove the receiver in writing. He may also replace the receiver, again in writing. A mortgagee with a prior ranking charge may appoint its own receiver to displace a receiver appointed by a subsequent mortgagee (see LPA 1925, s 109(5)).

Duties of receivers when managing the mortgagor's business

17.17   Where a receiver is appointed to sell the mortgaged property, then his duties to the mortgagor are clear. He must act with good faith (see *Cuckmere* case) and seek to take reasonable steps to obtain the true market value for the property at the time of sale. Where the receivership requires the receiver to trade the mortgagor's business for a period with a view to preserving the mortgagor's business in order to achieve the maximum sale price for that business, the receiver must undertake a relevant due diligence exercise with a view to taking reasonable steps in order to try and carry on the business profitably. Any failure to do so, could result in a claim by the mortgagor that the receivers had breached their duties to the mortgagor. This was the complaint levelled against the receivers by a mortgagor of agricultural land in *Medforth v Blake and Others* [1999] EGCS 81, CA. The court at first instance held that the receivers owed the claimant a duty of care when continuing the mortgagor's farm business and the standard of care was that of a reasonably competent receiver. The Court of Appeal agreed with the judge at first instance and held that where the receivers had fallen below that standard, they would be liable to account to the mortgagor accordingly.

Costs awards against receivers and third parties

17.18   As the receiver acts as agent of the mortgagor, it is the company and not the receiver that is generally liable for costs in the event that litigation proceedings against the company in receivership are successful or claims brought by the company in receivership (and continued by the receiver) are unsuccessful.

17.19   The perceived unfairness of this position is that where receivers pursue court proceedings unsuccessfully, they are entitled to be indemnified for their own costs from the mortgagor's assets but the costs of the successful defendant of those proceedings will only rank as an unsecured creditor in the receivership.

17.20   This position was considered by the Court of Appeal in *Dolphin Quays Developments Ltd v Mills and Others* [2008] EWCA Civ 385. The mortgagee bank had appointed receivers over the mortgaged property. At the instigation of the receivers, the mortgagor company issued proceedings for specific performance against a third party to complete the purchase of a long lease of one of the units that comprised part of the mortgaged property. Those proceedings were unsuccessful and the alleged purchaser was able to argue that the agreement for lease was unenforceable.

17.21 The successful defendant was entitled to an order for costs against the mortgagor company but such an award of costs would almost certainly have been worthless on the basis of the mortgagor's insolvency, such award ranking equally alongside the mortgagor's other unsecured debts. The defendant applied for a third party costs order against the receivers personally. It had been the receivers' decision to issue proceedings and the defendant considered that it was the receivers who had put them to the expense of having to defend those proceedings. At first instance, the judge held that there were no exceptional circumstances that would justify the making of a third party costs order against the receivers. He further held that by the terms of the charge and LPA 1925, s 109(2) the receivers acted merely as agents of the mortgagor company. He recognised the hardship caused to the defendant but observed that the whole issue could have been avoided had the defendant sought security for costs against the mortgagor company at an early stage. The defendant appealed.

17.22 In dismissing the appeal, the Court of Appeal applied the ruling in the case of *Aiden Shipping Co Ltd v Interbulk* [1986] AC 965 and held that the correct test was whether there were 'exceptional circumstances' that were outside the ordinary run of cases that would justify a third party costs order to be made against the receivers personally. Their Lordships agreed with the judge at first instance that the defendant's remedy in this cases would have been to apply for an order for security for costs, whereupon the proceedings would have been dismissed had the claimant failed to provide whatever security had been ordered (in accordance with the ruling in *Metalloy Supplies Ltd v MA (UK) Ltd* [1997] 1 WLR 1613). The Court of Appeal was clear that neither the respondent receivers nor the bank who appointed them could properly be described as the 'real party' to the proceedings and so the appellant's claim failed.

Cases where the receiver acts as agent of the mortgagee

17.23 The *Dolphin Quays* case should be contrasted with the position where a mortgagee appoints a receiver to 'do his bidding' where there is no express right or ability of the receiver to exercise the rights of the mortgagee and to recover his costs in doing so. This will be so where the mortgage deed does not provide the receiver with any (or only limited) powers in relation to the sale of the property and dealings with other issues relating to the mortgaged property and the mortgagor. In *Vedalease Ltd v Averti Developments Ltd and Another* [2007] 2 EGLR 125 Marshall J held that a mortgagee was not entitled to add the costs of its receiver and its receiver's legal costs to the security because neither LPA 1925 (ss 101 and 109) nor the terms of the mortgage deed itself permitted the mortgagee to do so. The court held that the only costs that could be added to the security were the proper and reasonable costs incurred by the mortgagee (and not the receivers) in appointing the receivers. However, the receivers were entitled to the indemnity for their costs provided by LPA 1925, s 109(6) to the extent that they were acting within the scope of their powers.

Application of receipts by the receiver

17.24　LPA 1925, s 109(a) requires an LPA receiver to apply monies he receives in the following order of priority:

'(i)　　in discharge of all rents, taxes, rates and outgoings whatever affecting the mortgaged property; and

(ii)　　in keeping down all annual sums or other payments, and the interest on all principal sums, having priority to the mortgage in right whereof he is Receiver; and

(iii)　　in payment of his commission, and of the premiums on fire, life or other insurance, if any, properly payable under the mortgage deed or under this act, and the cost of executing necessary or proper repairs directed in writing by the mortgagee; and

(iv)　　in payment of the interest accruing due in respect of any principal money due under the mortgage; and

(v)　　in or towards discharge of the principal monies so directed in writing by the mortgagee;

(vi)　　and shall pay the residue, if any, of the money received by him to the person who, but for possession of the receiver, would have been entitled to receive the income of which he is appointed receiver, or is otherwise entitled to the mortgaged property.'

ADMINISTRATIVE RECEIVERS

17.25　Whereas an LPA receiver or a fixed charge receiver is appointed to manage or sell the property comprised under the mortgagee's fixed charge, an administrative receiver is a receiver or manager of the whole (or substantially the whole) of a company's property and will be appointed by the holder(s) of a debenture or debentures that together provide the debentureholder with floating charge(s) over the whole or substantially the whole of the company's property (IA 1986, s 29(2)). Under IA 1986, s 388, an administrative receiver must be a licensed insolvency practitioner.

17.26　The administrative receiver is appointed by first serving a demand on the company for the amounts outstanding under the debenture. The demand should give the directors of the debtor company 'reasonable time' to make the repayment. However, it should be noted that what constitutes a reasonable time will depend on the circumstances. For example, it has been held that a demand that was made at 10.45 am followed by the appointment of an administrative receiver at 2.15 pm was sufficient notice (see *Cripps (Pharmaceuticals) Ltd v Wickenden* [1973] 2 All ER 606). Where it is apparent that the debtor simply cannot pay, this notice period could be even shorter (as was the case in *Shepherd and Cooper v TSB* [1996] 2 All ER 654).

17.27　Once the demand has been served, the debentureholder must make the appointment in writing (IA 1986, s 33). The appointment must then be accepted by the receiver before the end of the next business day (s 33). Following this acceptance, the receiver must confirm his acceptance in writing within 7 days (IR 1986, r 3.1(2)). Finally, notice of the appointment must be given by the debentureholder to the Registrar of Companies within 7 days of the appointment (Companies Act 1985, s 405(1)).

17.28 The administrative receiver is subject to the same duties as an LPA or fixed charge receiver (outlined above). However, an administrative receiver has additional statutory powers to the other two types of receiver and these are contained at IA 1986, ss 42–49 and Sch 1. These include the power to:

- sell the property of the company;

- bring or defend any action or other legal proceedings in the name and on behalf of the company;

- carry on the business of the company;

- grant or accept a surrender of a lease or tenancy.

17.29 Unlike a liquidator of a company, an administrative receiver has no power to disclaim a contract. Further, under IA 1986, s 44(1), an administrative receiver is personally liable on any contract he enters into when carrying out his functions (although there is no prohibition on him seeking to expressly exclude his liability under the terms of the contract and he will invariably do so). The position is the same in relation to LPA receivers and fixed charge receivers under IA 1986, s 37. The receiver is entitled to be indemnified out of the assets of the company (to the extent that they are sufficient) but it is common for receivers to seek to exclude personal liability on any contracts they enter.

Liability (if any) to mortgagor of third parties instructed by receiver

17.30 It should be noted that it is unlikely that any third party professional instructed by the administrative (or other) receiver will owe any duty of care directly to the mortgagor (confirmed in *Raja v Austin Gray (a Firm)* [2002] EWCA Civ 1965, [2003] BPIR 725). The contrary will only be true where the three-fold test for such liability set down in *Bank of Credit and Commerce International (Overseas) Ltd and Others v Price Waterhouse and Others* [1998] PNLR 564 is made out, namely where:

- there is forseeability of harm to the mortgagor; and

- there is proximity between the mortgagor and the third party; and

- where it is fair, just and reasonable to conclude that a duty is owed to the mortgagor.

The abolition of administrative receivership

17.31 Administrative receiverships are instigated for the benefit of the debentureholder. Parliament decided that administrative receiverships (which tend to be considerably destructive as far as the continuation of the company's business goes) (see **1.62**) did not accord with the Government's desire for the UK to embrace a 'rescue culture' in its insolvency regime and so the amendments to IA 1986 brought in by the Enterprise Act 2002 prohibit the appointment of an administrative receiver in relation to any debenture that was created after 15 September 2003 (save in a number of limited circumstances including where the debtor is an insurance undertaking). The result of this change has been twofold. First, the number of administrations has rocketed but as administration is designed to be a collective regime for the benefit of all of the company's creditors, so too have the appointment of fixed charge and LPA receivers.

FORECLOSURE

17.32 Under LPA 1925, ss 88(2), 89(2) a mortgagee has the right to apply to the court for an order transferring the mortgagor's title in the mortgaged property to the mortgagee, thereby destroying the mortgagor's equitable right to redeem the mortgage.

17.33 While a mortgagee has the statutory power of sale and the right to appoint a receiver to collect rents on a property, there may still be advantages for the mortgagee of applying for foreclosure, particularly if the mortgagee has some interest in retaining the mortgaged property for himself. An attempt to exercise a power of sale will not affect the mortgagee's right of foreclosure (LPA 1925, s 106(2)).

17.34 We have seen at **16.65** that a mortgagee exercising a power of sale should not sell to himself and an order foreclosure would circumvent this problem.

17.35 The modern drafting of mortgage deeds conferring comprehensive express powers on the mortgagee to exercise his rights out of court has made the use of the remedy of foreclosure considerably rare.

17.36 Foreclosure is only available where the mortgagor is in default of the mortgage terms and repayment has become due at law. The court retains a discretion as to whether or not to grant an order for foreclosure, and perhaps because it is seen as being a somewhat draconian measure, the courts have not set down a clear set of rules as to when an order will be made, leaving each case to be determined on its own facts (see *Lloyds & Scottish Trust Ltd v Britten* (1982) 44 P&CR 249).

LIMITATION PERIODS APPLICABLE TO THE ENFORCEMENT OF MORTGAGES

17.37 The question of the limitation periods applicable to the enforcement of mortgages has come before the Court of Appeal and House of Lords on a number of occasions. The limitation period for enforcing mortgages and their constituent parts has not always been clear and variations in the drafting of mortgage deeds has further led to confusion in this area. Set out below are the various remedies available to a mortgagee and the relevant limitation period that applies to each one.

Limitation period for actions to recover land

17.38 The Limitation Act 1980, s 15 provides as follows:

'(1) No action shall be brought by any person to recover any land after the expiration of 12 years from the date on which the right of action accrued to him or, if it is first accrued to some person through whom he claims, to that person . . .

. . .

(6) . . . Part 1 of Schedule 1 to this Act contains provisions for determining the date of accrual of rights of action to recover land in the cases there mentioned.'

17.39 Generally, time will start running from the date the mortgagee becomes entitled to possession of the property. In the absence of any terms to the contrary, a mortgagee has a right to possession from the date the mortgage is created (*Four-Maids Ltd v Dudley Marshall (Properties) Ltd* [1957] Ch 317 at 320). Alternatively, where the mortgage deed provides that the mortgagee will not become entitled to possession of the property until there is a default by the mortgagor, then time for claiming possession will not run until there has been a default under the mortgage (*Wilkinson v Hall* (1837) 3 Bing NC 508).

17.40 This is the basic position. However, where, after the mortgagee's cause of action has arisen (namely the date he becomes entitled to possession), the mortgagor makes a payment of an instalment under the mortgage or acknowledges the mortgagee's rights under the mortgage, then limitation will restart from the date of that payment or acknowledgement (Limitation Act 1980, s 29). Any acknowledgment must be in writing and signed by the person making it (Limitation Act 1980, s 30). For an analysis of the requirements of such acknowledgments see *Surrendra Oversea Ltd v Sri Lanka (The Apj Akash)* [1977] 1 WLR 565 QBD (Comm).

17.41 Failure by a mortgagee to realise his interest in the mortgaged property within the requisite 12-year period from the date the cause of action arises will result in the mortgagee's security being extinguished.

Limitation period for actions to recover mortgage monies where the mortgagee faces a shortfall

17.42 A mortgagee's most effective remedy for securing the repayment of the mortgage debt is often to take possession of the property and sell it. However, particularly in a falling market, a mortgagee will often face a shortfall following the sale of the mortgaged property. In the Court of Appeal decision in *Bristol and West plc v Bartlett and Another* [2002] EWCA Civ 1181 three cases were joined for appeal, all containing a similar set of facts. In each case the mortgagee bank had taken possession of the mortgaged premises and sold the property. In each case, the bank suffered a shortfall in the sale proceeds against the value of the mortgage debt. The banks waited more than 6 years but less than 12 years from the date of sale before issuing proceedings against the (former) mortgagors to recover the shortfall under the covenant to pay under the terms of the mortgage deed.

17.43 The Court of Appeal had to consider whether the banks were statute barred from bringing these further actions and were asked to rule on the appropriate limitation period for such actions. The mortgagors argued that the effect of the sale was to discharge their liability arising under their covenant to pay contained in their mortgage deeds, leaving only an implied obligation to pay under a simple contract, for which a 6-year limitation period applied (Limitation Act 1980, s 5). Accordingly they argued that the banks were out of time. The Court of Appeal robustly dismissed the (former) mortgagors' submission that the effect of a sale was to discharge the mortgagor's covenant to pay under the terms of the mortgage deed. The Court of Appeal held that the appropriate limitation period was that provided for by the Limitation Act 1980, s 20 (rather than s 8 that deals with actions brought on a specialty). Section 20 provides as follows:

'(1) No action shall be brought to recover –

(a) any principal sum of money secured by a mortgage or other charge on property (whether real or personal); or
(b) proceeds of the sale of land;

after the expiration of 12 years from the date on which the right to receive the money accrued.'

17.44 The Court of Appeal held then that a mortgagee has 12 years from the date the cause of action accrued (usually the date of default by the mortgagor unless s 29 applies at a later date (see above)).

17.45 The *Bartlett* decision was cited with approval and followed by the House of Lords in *West Bromwich Building Society v Wilkinson* [2005] UKHL 44.

17.46 In the case of *Scottish Equitable plc v Thompson and Pearson* [2003] EWCA Civ 211, the Court of Appeal applied the ruling in the *Bartlett* case to a situation where mortgaged premises had been sold by the holder of a first legal mortgage registered against the title to the property and the holder of the second registered legal charge faced a shortfall following sale.

17.47 The mortgagor argued that following the second mortgagee's security being discharged following sale, the second mortgagee's only claim would be for breach of contract under a simple claim under the Limitation Act 1980, s 5, where a 6-year limitation period will apply. Following *Bartlett*, the Court of Appeal found in favour of the second mortgagee in that the mortgaged debt had been secured at the time the second mortgagee's cause of action arose and accordingly s 20 applied and not s 5, giving the second mortgagee 12 years from the date of the accrual of the cause of action to issue proceedings against the mortgagor for the shortfall he faced.

Claims for interest

17.48 Whereas a mortgagee will have 12 years from the date the cause of action arose to seek possession of the mortgaged property or to sue for the repayment of the principal loan amount (or the shortfall following sale), the position in relation to interest is different. Limitation Act 1980, s 20(5) provides that a mortgagee shall have 6 years from the date on which the interest became due to recover damages in respect of such arrears. For this reason, when faced with a defaulting mortgagor, the mortgagee will usually apply any payments received by the mortgagor in satisfaction of any arrears of interest before applying the balance against the principal debt.

Part 4

PROPERTY ASSETS AND PERSONAL INSOLVENCY

Chapter 18

PERSONAL INSOLVENCY

INTRODUCTION

18.1   An insolvent individual may be adjudged bankrupt in three ways. First, a creditor with an undisputed debt of more than £750 may present a petition to the court for the individual's bankruptcy following the service of a statutory demand for payment and such demand having not been complied with within the statutory period of 21 days (and the individual not having made an application to set the statutory demand aside within an 18-day period). Secondly, where an individual wishes to take steps to make himself bankrupt, he may attend court and petition for his own bankruptcy. Thirdly, the supervisor of an individual's individual voluntary arrangement (IVA) may present a bankruptcy petition against the individual in circumstances where the individual has failed to adhere to the terms of the IVA. Irrespective of the route into bankruptcy the effect of a bankruptcy order being made in any of those three scenarios is the same.

THE EFFECT OF BANKRUPTCY

18.2   Upon a bankruptcy order being made the Official Receiver will take control of conduct of the bankruptcy in the first instance. In circumstances where prior to his bankruptcy, the individual had assets capable of realisation or where it is possible that the individual entered into certain transactions prior to the incidence of his bankruptcy that require further investigation, then the Secretary of State or the individual's creditors are likely to appoint a licensed insolvency practitioner to act as the individual's trustee in bankruptcy.

18.3   The bankrupt's estate vests in the trustee in bankruptcy upon his appointment pursuant to the Insolvency Act 1986 (IA 1986), s 306 automatically, without the need for any formal conveyance, transfer or assignment.

18.4   The extent of the bankrupt's estate is contained in IA 1986, s 283 and comprises all property belonging to or vested in the bankrupt at the commencement of the bankruptcy (namely the date the bankruptcy order is made), and any other property that is deemed to vest in the trustee in bankruptcy by virtue of the provisions of IA 1986 that apply to bankruptcies. An example of this would be property coming into the hands of the bankrupt whilst he was bankrupt. This so-called 'after-acquired' property is not vested in the bankrupt at the commencement of the bankruptcy but will fall into the bankruptcy estate in accordance with IA 1986, s 307:

> 'The bankrupt's estate will comprise any interest the bankrupt had in any real property at the date of the commencement of the bankruptcy. This will include a right of pre-emption to purchase a property.'(see *Geoffrey John Dear v Reginald Graham Reeves* [2001] EWCA Civ 277).

18.5   In many bankruptcies, the bankrupt's former interest in a property will be the largest asset in the bankruptcy capable of realisation for the benefit of the bankrupt's creditors.

18.6   For many bankrupts, the only significant asset they have is their interest in the home they share with a partner and their family and so the realisation by the trustee of the bankrupt's former interest in the family home is often a highly emotive and contested issue and there is a substantial body of case-law dealing with issues arising on the realisation of the trustee's interest in such property.

THE MATRIMONIAL HOME

Official Receiver's and trustees' inquiries

18.7   When considering the extent and value of the bankrupt's former interest in a property, the trustee will obtain as much information as possible prior to taking any enforcement action. The bankrupt will usually be the first source of information and the trustee will invariably instruct an agent to provide a drive-by valuation of the property at the very least.

18.8   Within 21 days beginning with the date the bankruptcy order is made, the bankrupt must submit a statement of his affairs to the Official Receiver in Form 6.33 (IA 1986, s 288(1)). In this document, the bankrupt will have to provide details of all of his assets and known liabilities and failure by the bankrupt to comply with his obligations under s 288 without reasonable excuse constitutes a contempt of court (s 288(4)). The bankrupt has a duty to deliver both his estate and control of any books and possessions relating to his estate or affairs (IA 1986, s 291) and subsequently has various duties to co-operate with his trustee in bankruptcy (see IA 1986, s 333 and *Morris v Murjani* [1996] BPIR 458 for a review of these duties). The Official Receiver and trustee (and certain third parties) have additional powers to compel the bankrupt to attend before the court to provide information at either a public (IA 1986, s 290) or private (IA 1986, s 366) examination of the bankrupt.

The bankrupt's interest

18.9   In determining the nature of the trustee's interest in the property (the bankrupt's share having vested in him upon his appointment pursuant to IA 1986, s 306) the trustee will first look at how the title to any such property has been registered at HM Land Registry. Official Copy Entries will show who the legal interest in the property is vested. However, as property held by the bankrupt on trust for another person does not vest in the trustee in bankruptcy (IA 1986, s 293(3)(a)) the position is often not as straightforward as that stated at the Land Registry and it is necessary to consider whether any third parties may have rights in the property.

18.10 In order to ascertain whether any third parties may have rights in the property, the trustee should make inquiries of any other persons living at the property, in order to establish whether or not they might claim to have an interest in the property.

The quantification of the bankrupt's beneficial interest in the property

18.11 The legal title to a property may be registered in the sole name of the bankrupt or may be registered in joint names (the most common occurrence being joint registration with a spouse or a cohabiting partner). There is a substantial body of case-law that has developed in respect of how a party's interest in a given property should be determined. These cases have developed (and sometimes confused) the concepts of resulting and constructive trusts. The long line of cases in this area including *Gissing v Gissing* [1971] AC 886; *Pettitt v Pettitt* [1970] AC 777; and *Lloyds Bank v Rossett* [1991] 1 AC 107 have all shaped the way in which the courts have approached the quantification of beneficial interests in a property. In *Gissing* Lord Diplock summarised the position (as it was then) as follows:

> 'A resulting, implied or constructive trust – and it is unnecessary for the present purposes to distinguish between these classes of trust – is created by a transaction between the Trustee and the Cestui que Trust in connection with the acquisition by the Trustee of a legal interest in land, whenever the Trustee has so conducted himself it will be inequitable to allow him to deny to the Cestui que Trust a beneficial interest in the land acquired and he will be held so to have conducted himself if by his words or conduct he has induced the Cestui que Trust to act to his own detriment in the reasonable belief that by so acting he was acquiring a beneficial interest in the land.'

18.12 In *Oxley v Hiscock* [2004] 3 WLR 715 the Court of Appeal developed a line of authority that moved away from the historical analysis of how the parties' interests in a property should be ascertained, and concluded that less emphasis should be placed on the extent of an individual's direct financial contributions towards the purchase or improvement of a property and held that there was a need to look at the entire course of dealings between the parties since the purchase of the property. Such conduct would include payments of the mortgage, payments of household bills, childcare responsibilities, as well as looking at any agreement or conversations the parties had as to how they considered the property to be held.

18.13 In 2007, the issue came before the House of Lords in the case of *Stack v Dowden* [2007] 2 AC 432. In *Stack* a property had been purchased by Mr Stack and Miss Dowden and registered in their joint names. Following the couple's separation, it fell to be determined how the parties held the beneficial interests in the property. The House of Lords concluded that where the property was registered in joint names, the onus was on the party seeking to argue that the beneficial interests in the property did not mirror the entry on the register at the Land Registry as to legal title to prove that the parties' interests were not equal.

18.14 The parties' contributions to the mortgage over the years had been approximately the same and both parties had undertaken childcare responsibilities in relation to their four children. However, Miss Dowden had paid a higher proportion of the deposit on the purchase of the property and for this reason sought to assert that she had a larger interest in the property than Mr Stack, notwithstanding the fact that the legal title to the property was registered in the joint names of the parties at the Land Registry. The parties had made no express declaration of trust that the interests were to be anything other than 50/50 (had they done so then this would have been conclusive). Baroness Hale gave the leading speech in the case concluding that Miss Dowden had provided sufficient evidence to warrant a departure from the presumption that the parties' interests were held equally. Baroness Hale also sought to clarify the complex web of prior decisions by confirming the application of the following principles:

- where there is sole legal ownership it is to be assumed that there is sole beneficial ownership;

- where there is joint legal ownership it is assumed that there is joint beneficial ownership;

- the burden of proof is on the party seeking to demonstrate that the beneficial ownership is different from the legal ownership;

- where a party seeks to argue such a position it is necessary for the court to consider more factors than financial contributions in order to ascertain the parties' true intentions.

18.15 Baroness Hale gave support to the judgment of Chadwick LJ in the case of *Oxley v Hiscock* in her agreement that it is necessary to look at the parties' entire course of dealings in relation to a property, rather than focus solely on their financial contributions towards the property.

18.16 Lord Neuberger gave the (only) dissenting speech in *Stack*. He was of the view that such an analysis was a step too far and that the court imputing an intention on the parties would 'not only be wrong in principle' but would also rail against the House of Lords' decisions in earlier cases. He considered that the case should have been determined by applying the doctrine of resulting trusts to the situation (by giving the parties credit for the direct financial contributions they had made to the purchase of the property). In the event, he came to the same conclusion as to the appropriate split between the parties' interests but highlighted his concerns over the danger (as he saw it) of the court guessing what the parties must have intended to be their understanding in relation to the property by having reference to extraneous factors not linked to the financing of the purchase of the property.

18.17 The *Stack* case is of critical importance in relation to bankruptcy cases because the trustee will always be faced with having to ascertain what the bankrupt's share of the property was at the time the bankruptcy order was made.

18.18 In a speech given to the Property Litigation Association Conference in March 2008, Lord Neuberger expended his concerns about the guidance given in *Stack v Dowden*. He feared that the logical conclusion of Baroness Hale's speech would extend to most forms of familial relationship and even where the parties were both in occupation.

18.19 The case of *Laskar v Laskar* [2008] EWCA Civ 347 related to investment property not purchased as a place for a cohabiting couple to live, giving the lead judgment in the Court of Appeal, Neuberger LJ ruled that where the property in question is purchased as an investment, rather than as a home for a cohabiting couple it will often not be appropriate to apply the *Stack* principles when determining the extent of the parties' beneficial interests. He preferred the resulting trust analysis in such cases. He further concluded (overturning the trial judge's decision) that a party's liability under a mortgage should be treated as a direct contribution to the purchase price. In *Laskar*, this had the effect of raising the appellant's share from the 4.28% awarded by the trial judge to 33%.

ENFORCEMENT OF THE TRUSTEE'S INTEREST

18.20 In times of falling and stagnant house prices, trustees in bankruptcy were in many cases extremely slow to realise their interest in properties. At the time of bankruptcy orders being made in the early 1990s, for example, many bankrupts were faced with negative equity and so trustees in bankruptcy and the Official Receiver were content to leave the matter in abeyance until such times as house price inflation meant that their interest in a property was significant and capable of providing a return to the bankrupt's creditors. As the bankrupt's interest in the property had vested in the trustee in bankruptcy, there was no issue as to limitation and there was no statutory provision stipulating how long the trustee had in which to realise his interest in a property.

18.21 This position was considered by many (including some courts, see the obiter comments of Lawrence Collins J in *Byford v Butler* [2003] EWHC

1267 (Ch), [2003] BPIR 1089) to be highly unsatisfactory. As part of the sweeping reforms brought in by the Enterprise Act 2002, Parliament sought to redress this imbalance by giving the trustee just 3 years to deal with the bankrupt's former interest in the bankrupt's home.

18.22 This provision only applies to the bankrupt's home and is defined as being 'an interest in a dwelling house which at the date of the bankruptcy was the sole or principal residence of either the bankrupt, the bankrupt's spouse or civil partner, or a former spouse or former civil partner of the bankrupt'.

18.23 Any interest that the bankrupt has in any other property (such as a holiday home for example) will not be subject to this 3-year rule and will remain vested in the trustee indefinitely.

18.24 The Enterprise Act 2002, s 264 inserted a new s 283A into IA 1986. It provides that should the trustee in bankruptcy fail to realise his interest in the bankrupt's home within 3 years from the date of the bankruptcy order, that interest in the property shall cease to be comprised in the bankrupt's estate and shall vest back in the bankrupt (without the need for any conveyance, assignment or transfer).

18.25 In order to 'realise' the trustee's interest he must, within the 3-year period have done one of the following:

(a) realised the interest in the property; or

(b) applied for an order for sale in respect of the property; or

(c) applied for an order for possession of the property; or

(d) applied for an order under IA 1986, s 313 in respect of that interest (see **18.29**); or

(e) the parties must have reached an agreement in relation to the purchase of the trustee's interest by the bankrupt or by a third party.

18.26 In *Lewis v Metropolitan Property Realisations Ltd* [2008] EWCH 2760 (Ch) the court decided that the trustee had 'realised' his interest in the bankrupt's former home within the meaning of IA 1986, s 283A(3)(a) by transferring it to a creditor for £1 plus deferred consideration (that would be payable to the trustee on any subsequent sale of the property or of the creditor's interest). This strategy may provide useful for trustees who do not have sufficient funds in the estate to commence possession proceedings against the bankrupt (and his family where appropriate). However, Prondman J expressed concern about the precedent the case might set and she distinguished between a mere finding that the trustee had power to effect such a sale and an order to the effect that it was proper to do so in a particular case. The judge gave leave to appeal the decision, and it is understood that at the time of writing, the appeal is being pursued.

18.27 In respect of bankruptcy orders made before 1 April 2004, the trustee had 3 years from that date in which to take one of the above steps in respect of his interest in the property. However, note that IA 1986, s 283A and the transitional provisions have no application to bankruptcy orders made prior to the coming into force of IA 1986 (29 December 1986 – see *Pannell v The Official Receiver* [2008] BPIR 629).

18.28 Where the trustee's application for one of the orders above is dismissed or where the trustee fails to make an application within the 3-year period, then the interest in the property will revest in the bankrupt unless the court orders otherwise. IA 1986, s 283A(6) gives the court the power to substitute the period of 3 years with a longer period in circumstances where the court thinks it appropriate to do so. There is currently no reported case-law detailing the circumstances in which the court may be minded to grant such relief. The transitional provisions relating to s 283A are contained in the Enterprise Act 2002, s 261(7)–(10).

Applications for an order for possession and sale

18.29 Where the trustee is unable to realise his interest in the property by reaching an agreement with the bankrupt, his family or a third party for the purchase of his interest, then it will either be necessary for the trustee to apply to the court for an order for possession and sale or to apply to the court for a charge over the bankrupt's share of the property under IA 1986, s 313.

Charges under IA 1986, s 313

18.30 If he cannot realise the bankrupt's interest in a dwelling house which is occupied by the bankrupt or his spouse or former spouse or by his civil partner or former civil partner, or if its realisation will not produce significant benefit, the trustee may apply to the court for a charge to be imposed on that interest. The interest in the property will then revert to the bankrupt, subject to the charge (IA 1986, s 313(3)). The charge will remain until redeemed, notwithstanding the bankrupt's discharge in the meantime. The charge shares many of the same characteristics of a charging order made under the Charging Orders Act 1979 (IA 1986, s 313(4)).

18.31 The amount secured under the charging order will be the value of the bankrupt's interest in the property at the date of the order, together with continuing interest from the date of the charging order at the prescribed rate (IA 1986, s 313(2)(a)). This provision (brought in by the Enterprise Act 2002 by way of amendment) ensures that the bankrupt will take the benefit of inflationary rises (if any) in the value of the property (above the rate of interest accruing under the charge).

18.32   In the first instance decision of Lindsay LJ in *Gotham v Doodes* [2005] EWHC 2576 (Ch), [2006] 1 WLR 729, the court held that the trustee had 12 years from the date the charging order is made to exercise his rights to enforce the charge, before he will become statute barred from doing so. However, this decision was overturned by the Court of Appeal, [2006] EWCA Civ 1080, [2006] BPIR 1178, who ruled that the correct interpretation of the Limitation Act 1980, s 20 was that the 12-year time-limit would not start running until the court had made an order permitting the sale of the property (and not from the date the charge was created). This decision will provide significant peace of mind to trustees in bankruptcy.

Orders for possession and sale

18.33   Where there is no reason to delay in obtaining possession of the property for the purposes of realising the trustee's interest, then the trustee will issue proceedings for an order for possession and sale. If necessary (namely where the parties cannot agree), the application may also contain a request for a declaration as to how the beneficial interests in the property are held under the Trusts of Land and Appointment of Trustees Act 1996 (TLATA 1996), s 14. TLATA 1996, s 25(1) and Sch 3, para 23 inserted s 335A into IA 1986 and provides that where a trustee in bankruptcy makes an application under TLATA 1996, s 14 it is to be made to the court that has jurisdiction for the bankruptcy (it should be noted that not all county courts have bankruptcy jurisdiction). Similarly, any application by the trustee to obtain possession of a property where the bankrupt and/or the bankrupt's spouse have registered matrimonial homes rights pursuant to Part IV of the Family Law Act 1996 must also be made in the court having jurisdiction for the bankruptcy of the bankrupt (see IA 1986, ss 336 and 337).

18.34   Prior to issuing proceedings against the bankrupt for an order for possession and sale and a declaration as to beneficial interests (if necessary) the trustee in bankruptcy should notify the bankrupt and other interested parties that there is an interest in a property that has vested in the bankrupt's estate and consists of an interest in a dwelling house which at the time of the bankruptcy was the sole or principal residence of the bankrupt or his spouse, former spouse, civil partner or former civil partner. This notification should be made in Form 6.83 (as described in the Insolvency Rules 1986 (IR 1986), r 6.237), and this should be issued as soon as reasonably practicable, but in any event no later than 14 days before the expiry of the 3-year period (see *Dear IP*, September 2007 – Issue No 33). While it is good practice for the trustee to serve this notice on the relevant parties, a failure to do so will not affect his ability to seek an order in respect of his interest in the property.

18.35   Where the parties are unable to agree on how the trustee's interest should be realised and provided the trustee's interest is not less than the de minimis amount of £1,000 (this is the de minimis prescribed by IA 1986, s 313A) then it will be necessary for the trustee to apply to the court for an order to either realise or secure his interest in the property.

18.36 In practice, trustees in bankruptcy will wait for a period of at least one year before making an application for an order for possession and sale (unless there is a risk that the property will decrease in value or where no proposals have been forthcoming for the purchase of the trustee's interest). The reason for this is that under IA 1986, s 335A the court will assume that unless the circumstances of the case are exceptional, that after the period of one year from the date of the bankruptcy order the interests of the bankrupt's creditors are paramount. There is a significant body of case-law on the question on what will amount to exceptional circumstances that would give rise to the postponement of an order for sale being granted immediately (following the one-year period) and the threshold is very high. In the case of *Barca v Mears* [2004] EWHC 217 (ch). Mr Nicholas Strauss QC (sitting as a deputy judge of the High Court) upheld the decision of Deputy Registrar Agnello in holding that merely because an order for possession may disrupt the bankrupt's son's education (he had special educational needs) that was not sufficient reason to give rise to exceptional circumstances that would warrant the suspension of an order for possession. The judge followed the decision in *Re Citro* [1990] 3 WLR 880. In that case, Nourse LJ, whilst recognising that there was no distinction to be made between cases where a property is being enjoyed as a matrimonial home and where it is not, he summarised the position relating to exceptional circumstances as follows:

> 'What then are exceptional circumstances? As the cases show, it is not uncommon for a wife with young children to be faced with eviction in circumstances where the realisation of her beneficial interest will not produce enough by a comparable home in the same neighbourhood, or indeed elsewhere and, if she has to move elsewhere, there may be problems over schooling and so forth. Such circumstances, while in gendering a natural sympathy in all who hear of them, can not be described as exceptional. They are the melancholy consequences of debt and in providence with which every civilised society has been familiar.'

18.37 There have been cases where the Court has held that the circumstances of the case have been exceptional; see, for example, the cases of *Claughton v Charalambous* [1998] BPIR 558 and *Re Bremner* [1999] BPIR 185. Each case will clearly depend on its own facts but the table below gives an indication as to the approach taken by the courts in a number of cases in determining whether or not circumstances are deemed to be exceptional.

Case name	Circumstances	Held to be exceptional for purposes of IA 1986, s 335A?
Re Holliday [1980] 3 All ER 385	Disruption of children's education and trustee's interest was sufficient to pay off all creditors in full.	Pre-dates IA 1986, s 335A. Court allowed a 4-year adjournment. Almost certainly no longer good law.
Re Citro [1991] Ch 142	Homelessness and disruption to education.	No (see above).
Judd v Brown [1998] 2 FLR 360	Wife undergoing chemotherapy following sudden and serious attack of cancer. Trustee sought possession after conclusion of next round of treatment (8 months).	The circumstances were exceptional. The trustee's application was dismissed on the basis that there was no certainty that W's position would be resolved following treatment.
Re Bremner [1999] 1 FLR 912	74-year-old wife caring for 79-year-old bankrupt husband in poor health.	The needs of the sick husband were not relevant for the purposes of s 335A but the needs of the wife were (namely the need to care for her husband). Sale suspended until 3 months after husband's death.
Re Raval [1998] 2 FLR 718	Wife suffering from paranoid schizophrenia. Evidence that eviction could cause a lapse. Wife sought a 5-year adjournment.	Court ordered 6-month adjournment (extended to 12 months on appeal) on basis that local authority could rehome during this time and it would provide wife with sufficient time to come to terms with move.
Claughton v Charalambous [1999] 1 FLR 740	Wife suffering from renal failure and chronic osteoarthritis. Costs of trustee would consume all equity.	Sale postponed indefinitely. Appeal dismissed.

Re Bailey [1977] 1 WLR 278 at 284	Child of bankrupt was disabled. Substantial modifications had been made to home to accommodate his needs.	Pre IA 1986 – judge satisfied that such circumstances may be exceptional.
1. *Trustee of the estate of Eric Bowe* [1998] 2 FLR 439 2. *Re: Ng (a Bankrupt)* [1998] 2 FLR 386 3. *Trustee in Bankruptcy of Syed Bukhari v Bukhari and Another* [1999] BPIR 157	Sale proceeds would only cover trustee's fees with no return to creditors.	Circumstances not exceptional. Trustees entitled to proceed with sale.
Martin Sklan v White [2006] EWHC 3313 (Ch)	Illness of mother during children's minority.	Illness of mother justified a postponement of sale during the children's minority.

HUMAN RIGHTS AND IA 1986, S 335A

18.38   The appellant's appeal in the case of *Barca v Mears* was partly based on an argument that the Deputy Registrar in the court below had failed to take account of the bankrupt's and his son's right to family life, home and privacy pursuant to Art 8 of the European Convention for the Protection of Human Rights and Fundamental Freedoms (ECHR) (adopted by the Human Rights Act 1998, s 6).

18.39   Article 8 of the ECHR states, amongst other things:

'Everyone has the right to have respect for his private and family life, his home and his correspondence.

There shall be no interference by a public authority with the exercise of this right except such as is in accordance with the law and is necessary in a democratic society in the interests of National Security, public safety or the economic well-being of the country, for the prevention of disorder or crime, for the protection of health or morals, or for protection of the rights and freedoms of the others.'

18.40   The court rejected this argument holding that:

(a)   the right to 'respect' for private and family life and the home is not absolute and that there was a need for there to be a fair balance between the interests of the community and the interests of the individual;

(b)   there had to be an assessment of 'whether the interference complained of corresponded to a pressing social need, whether it was proportionate to the legitimate aim pursued, [and] whether the reasons given by the National Authorities to justify it are relevant and sufficient': *Sunday Times v UK* (1979) 2 EHRR 245 at 277–278;

(c)   the proportionality test is satisfied if:
   (i)   the legislative objective is sufficiently important to justify the limitation on the fundamental right;
   (ii)   the measures designed to meet the legislative objective are rationally connected with it; and
   (iii) the means used to impair the right of freedom are no more than is necessary to accomplish the legitimate objective.

18.41   The court did question whether the narrow approach as to what may be deemed to be 'exceptional circumstances' adopted in *Re Citro* was consistent with the ECHR, and also suggested that there may be a need for a shift in the emphasis in the interpretation of the statute in order to achieve compatibility with the ECHR.

18.42   However, in *Barca* the court was satisfied that an order for possession should have been made.

18.43   The issue arose again in the 2006 decision in the case of *Donohoe v Ingram (Trustee in Bankruptcy of Kirkup)* [2006] 2 FLR 1084. The appellant owned a property jointly with the bankrupt and lived there with her four children. The trustee applied for and obtained an order for possession and sale. The appellant applied to have the order set aside and substituted with an order that the sale be postponed until 2017 (when her youngest child would attain the age of 16) on the basis that Art 8 of the ECHR required the court to interpret IA 1986, s 335A with a greater degree of consideration towards her and her children. In dismissing the appeal, the court held that the exercise of the court's discretion under s 335A was a value judgment that the appellate court would rarely interfere with, and further that even if Art 8 required a wider interpretation of 'exceptional circumstances' there were no such circumstances in this case.

18.44   The apparent dichotomy between the strict approach taken in *Re Citro* and the potential for softening in order to ensure compliance with the ECHR is in need of clarification, although for the time being, the courts have universally approved the ruling in *Re Citro* (save perhaps in *Martin Sklan v White*).

IMPROVING A PARTY'S SHARE AND EQUITABLE ACCOUNTING

18.45   In addition to considering the position under *Stack v Dowden*, a non-bankrupt spouse or partner may seek to assert that either they have an interest in a solely owned property or a greater interest in a jointly owned property for a number of reasons. These include the following (which can similarly be used by a trustee in bankruptcy).

Improvements to the property

18.46 A party may contend that they should be awarded a larger share of the property than they may otherwise be entitled to, on the basis that they have either funded or carried out significant improvements to the property that have added value to it. In relation to married couples, statute provides that a party may enjoy an enhanced share of the beneficial interest by virtue of having made a substantial contribution in money or monies worth to the improvement of any property (Matrimonial Proceedings and Property Act 1970, s 37). In the absence of agreement between the parties, the share of that enhanced interest will be determined by the court.

18.47 In addition to the statutory regime set out above, and distinct from the question of the ascertainment of beneficial interests, the court is able to give credit to a party who has spent money or time improving the property, when undertaking the equitable accounting exercise that often follows the determination of the beneficial interest in the property. In the case of *Re Pavlou* [1993] 3 All ER 955, the court determined that a party was entitled to claim either 50% of the value of the improvements or 50% of the increase in the value of the property that could be attributed to those improvements, whichever was the lower. Accordingly, in the event that the improvements do not add significant value to the property (notwithstanding they may have cost a significant amount of money), the party will be unable to claim more than 50% of the resultant increase in value.

Equitable accounting

18.48 Once the court has determined the parties' respective beneficial interests in a property the court is then often invited to consider whether or not one party has contributed more than the other party towards the value of the property (see *Re Gorman (A Bankrupt)* [1990] 1 All ER 717, [1990] 1 WLR 616; *Re Pavlou* [1993] 3 All ER 955, [1993] 1 WLR 1046). The equitable accounting (often know as 'marshalling' in the family courts) by the court does not alter the size of the beneficial interests of the parties but is designed to compensate a party who has paid more than his proportionate share towards the upkeep and maintenance of the property. For example, where there is a beneficial joint tenancy, then the court is likely to determine that the parties' contributions towards the upkeep of the property should have been equal and may give one party recompense in the event that they have paid more than 50% towards the value of the property.

18.49 Following the House of Lords' decision in *Stack v Dowden* (see above) it is possible that the application of equitable accounting may become less important, as courts become increasingly willing to determine beneficial interests based on the parties' entire course of dealings, rather than those that relate solely to the purchase of the property.

Mortgage payments and occupational rent

Mortgage contributions by the non-bankrupt spouse/partner

18.50 A non-bankrupt spouse or partner will often seek to claim the benefit of payments they have made towards the mortgage since the date of the bankruptcy order. Since the bankrupt's share in the property vested in the trustee in bankruptcy as at the date of the bankruptcy order the non-bankrupt party is unable to argue that the size of their beneficial interest has increased since the making of a bankruptcy order by virtue of them having made mortgage payments. However, the non-bankrupt party can claim the benefit of 50% (in beneficial joint tenancy cases) of capital contributions he or she has made to the mortgage that have led to a reduction in the outstanding balance on a mortgage.

18.51 In relation to payments of mortgage interest though, the position is different. Trustees in bankruptcy have successfully argued that until such time as they are granted possession of the property, they are deprived of the use of the share of the property that has vested in them, while the non-bankrupt party (and often the bankrupt too) have had the benefit of living in the whole property to the exclusion of the trustee. In such circumstances, the trustee will often argue that the non-bankrupt party should be liable to account to the trustee for their occupation of the whole of the property to the exclusion of the trustee. This is often referred to as an 'occupational rent'.

18.52 Trustees will use the occupational rent argument in order to offset the claim of a non-bankrupt party in equitable accounting that they should be compensated for payments of mortgage interest they have made. In *Re Gorman* [1990] 1 WLR 616 the court determined that for the sake of convenience it could be agreed that the mortgage interest was equal to the occupation rent and so the two could be set off against each other, although there is nothing preventing a party from arguing that the two sums are not equal. In *Gorman*, the question of the court's jurisdiction to order the non-bankrupt (former) spouse to account to the trustee for an occupation rent was not opposed by the wife and so this question was not fully explored by the court (although as Blackburne J stated in *Re Peter Francis Barcham* [2008] EWHC 1505 (Ch), [2008] BPIR 857 'it was a concession which the court did not question').

18.53 In the case of *Byford v Butler* [2003] EWHC 1267 (Ch), [2003] BPIR 1089, [2004] 1 P&CR 159, the court held that an occupational rent could be payable in circumstances where there had been no ouster by the non-bankrupt party and the bankrupt continued to live with the non-bankrupt party at the property. Lawrence Collins J stated:

'What the court is endeavouring to do is broad justice or equity as between co-owners. As Millett J said in *Re Pavlou (A Bankrupt)* [1993] 1 WLR 1046, the fact that there has been no ouster or forcible exclusion is not conclusive. The trustee cannot reside in the property nor can he derive any financial enjoyment from the property while the bankrupt's spouse resides in it, and the bankrupt spouse's creditors derive no benefit from it until he exercises his remedies. I do not consider that the policy expressed in the new section 283A of the Insolvency Act 1986 is of any assistance . . . It is true that the trustee could have realised his remedies earlier, but Mrs Byford benefited to a considerable degree by his inaction, while Mr Byford enjoyed the use of the property with Mrs Byford, without any benefit to his creditors.'

18.54 *Byford* was followed by Blackburne J in *Re Peter Francis Barcham*, which contains a useful history of the case-law in this area and an analysis of the distinction between occupational rent payable pursuant to TLATA 1996, s 13(6) and what Blackburne J referred to as the 'equitable compensation' that a trustee in bankruptcy claimed. TLATA 1996, s 13(6) provides that where an application is made to the court under TLATA 1996, s 14 or a determination of beneficial interests, it is open to a party who has the right to occupy the property, but has been excluded from it or has had his or her use of the property restricted to apply for an order requiring the co-owner(s) to '(a) make payments by way of compensation to the beneficiary whose entitlement has been excluded or restricted, or (b) forgo any payment or other benefit to which he would otherwise be entitled under the trust so as to benefit that beneficiary'.

18.55 Blackburne J agreed with the previous line of authorities that TLATA 1996, s 13(6) has no application in cases involving trustees in bankruptcy because while the non-bankrupt co-owner of the property is living in the property to the exclusion of the trustee in bankruptcy, the trustee has no right to occupy the property and so s 13 cannot apply, thereby precluding the trustee from claiming compensation under this provision.

18.56 Notwithstanding this position, Blackburne J went on to conclude that the court had the equitable jurisdiction to compensate the trustee and this was unaffected by the fact that the trustee was not able to claim under TLATA 1996.

Mortgage contributions by the bankrupt

18.57 Prior to realising his interest in the property, the trustee may be content to allow the bankrupt to continue living at the property, provided that he continues to pay the mortgage and other outgoings. IA 1986, s 338 confirms that in making such payments, the bankrupt will not acquire any interest in the property.

18.58 However, where the bankrupt has made payments towards the mortgage and of any other nature that lead to a benefit to the bankrupt's creditors then the bankrupt will be able to claim benefit for these payments when the court undertakes its equitable accounting exercise (see below) (see also *Holtham v Kelmanson* [2006] EWHC 2588).

Equity of exoneration

18.59 In the 1985 case of *Re Pittortou* [1985] 1 WLR 58 at 61, Scott J approved the statement of principle contained in Halsbury's Laws as follows:

> 'If the property of a married woman is mortgaged or charged in order to raise money for the payment of her husband's debts, or otherwise for his benefit, it is presumed, in the absence of evidence showing an intention to the contrary, that she meant to charge her property merely by way of surety, and is entitled to be indemnified by the husband, and to throw the debt primarily on his estate to the exoneration of her own.' (*Bankruptcy & Individual Insolvency* (Vol 3(2) 2002 re-issue) at para 649)

18.60 A good example of how the equity of exoneration works in practice is where a husband and wife have a jointly owned home. The husband is the director of a company and wishes to inject further funds into the business and chooses to do so by taking a loan secured by way of a second mortgage on the matrimonial home. The wife agrees to a further charge being placed on the title to the property but she receives no immediate tangible benefit from the funds advanced on the remortgage. In these circumstances, she is taken to have only agreed to indemnify her husband for his non-performance under the second mortgage and so the equity of exoneration applies in her favour to ensure that the husband's share of the equity is exhausted before any part of the equity belonging to the wife. The principle depends upon the parties' intentions and in the absence of an express agreement between the parties, it can be inferred from the parties' conduct that they intended that the wife would stand in the position of surety only for the husband, rather than agreeing to be jointly liable for the debt. In *Paget v Paget* [1898] 1 Ch 470, it was held that no intention that the equity of exoneration should apply needed to be expressed; it was to be ascertained from all the relevant circumstances of that particular case. Lindley MR stated:

> 'To say that in all such cases there is a presumption in favour of the wife, and that it is for the husband to rebut it, is, in our opinion, to go too far and to use language calculated to mislead. The circumstances of each case must all be weighed in order to see what inference ought to be drawn; and until an inference in favour of the wife arises there is no presumption for the husband to rebut. If this is forgotten error may creep in.'

18.61 The equity of exoneration has been held not to apply in the following cases:

* where there is evidence that the wife intended to make a gift to the husband (*Clinton v Hooper* (1791) 3 Bro CC 201);

- where the money was being borrowed for the wife's benefit such as to service general household and family living expenses (*Hudson v Carmichael* (1854) Kay 613; *Gray v Dowman* (1858) 27 LJ Ch 702; *Re Pittortou* [1985] 1 All ER 285);

- where the wife benefited from the money in another way. For example, if the money was used by the husband to maintain an extravagant style of living for him and his wife (*Paget v Paget* [1898] 1 Ch 470);

- where the money was raised in part to discharge the wife's debts (*Lewis v Nangle* (1752) 1 Cox Eq Cas 240).

18.62 In *Re Pittortou* the bankrupt's husband ran a restaurant business quite separate from his wife. The matrimonial home was in joint names and the parties executed a second charge in favour of a bank to secure the husband's loan that was utilised broadly for the following three purposes:

(a) the debts of the restaurant business;

(b) debts incurred by the husband to the family he left behind when he went and set up his separate home with the wife in this case; and

(c) payments made for the joint benefit of the household, such as living expenses and mortgage instalments.

The court held that items (a) and (b) should be borne by the bankrupt's share of the home, whilst the payments made in relation to category (c) were made for the joint benefit of the parties and so should be borne by the parties' estates in equal shares.

18.63 In the current economic climate where personal guarantees to banks are commonplace by directors, those advising non-bankrupt spouses/partners should be live to the fact that the equity of exoneration could apply in their client's favour when faced with an order for possession and sale.

Bankruptcy and commercial leases

18.64 An individual with a commercial lease that is afforded the protection of Part II of the Landlord and Tenant Act 1954 will vest in a trustee in bankruptcy pursuant to IA 1986, s 306 and will form part of the bankruptcy estate (IA 1986, s 283). The lease will vest in the trustee subject to the covenants contained in the lease (see *Re Solomon ex p Dressler* (1878) 9 Ch D 252, CA and *Wilson v Wallani* (1880) 5 Ex D 155) and the landlord's right to receive rents.

18.65 The landlord may levy distress in the usual way (see **3.61**). The landlord may also forfeit the lease for any breach of covenant including the tenant's bankruptcy. A clause for forfeiture on the bankruptcy of the tenant is lawful, as was indirectly confirmed in *Money Markets International Stock Brokers v London Stock Exchange* [2001] 4 All ER 223.

18.66 This is subject to the trustee's right to apply to the court for relief from forfeiture pursuant to the Law of Property Act 1925, s 146 and whilst bankruptcy is not a breach capable of remedy by a tenant, the court is likely to grant relief from forfeiture if the trustee agrees to pay any rent arrears and is prepared to pay the rent going forward (see **4.121**). The trustee's decision in this regard will clearly be dependent upon the extent of the assets comprised in the bankruptcy estate and the capital value (if any) of the lease itself. Where the lease is of no or little commercial value (in a falling market for example), then the trustee in bankruptcy has the power to disclaim the lease pursuant to IA 1986, s 315 and this is discussed in more detail in **7.79** below.

Residential tenancies

18.67 IA 1986, s 283(3)(a) (introduced by the Housing Act 1988, s 117(1)) provides that the following leasehold interests will not form part of the bankrupt's estate:

- an assured tenancy or an assured agricultural occupancy within the meaning of Part 1 of the Housing Act 1988 or the Rent Act 1977, s 127(5); or

- a protected tenancy, within the meaning of the Rent Act 1977, in respect of which, by virtue of any provision of Part IX of that Act, no premium can lawfully be required as a condition of assignment; or

- a tenancy of a dwelling house by virtue of which the Bankrupt is within the meaning of the Rent (Agriculture) Act 1976, a protected occupier of the dwelling house, and the terms of which inhibit an assignment as mentioned in the Rent Act 1977, s 127(5); or

- a secure tenancy, within the meaning of Part IV of the Housing Act 1985, which is not capable of being assigned, except in the cases mentioned in s 91(3) of that Act.

18.68 These exclusions though, are subject to the trustee's right under IA 1986, s 308A to claim any such tenancy for the benefit of the bankrupt's estate by serving the bankrupt with notice of his intention to do so. Upon the service of such a notice the interest in that tenancy will vest in the trustee and will be backdated as if it had vested at the commencement of the bankruptcy, save as against a purchaser in good faith, for value and without notice of the bankruptcy, to whom the trustee will remain bound. The trustee has 42 days beginning with the day on which the lease in question first came to the knowledge of the trustee (IA 1986, s 309) in order to serve such a notice.

AFTER-ACQUIRED PROPERTY (IA 1986, SECTION 307)

18.69 Bankruptcy lasts for a period of one year in most cases. Where a bankrupt acquires or is given any property between the date the bankruptcy order is made and the date he is discharged from bankruptcy, the trustee may claim any such property for the benefit of the bankruptcy estate. Under IA 1986, s 333(2), the bankrupt has a duty to notify his trustee within 21 days of his becoming aware of the relevant facts (IR 1986, r 6.200(1)). In the event that the bankrupt fails to do this without reasonable excuse, he will be guilty of a contempt of court and liable to be punished accordingly (s 333(4)).

18.70 Upon becoming aware of any after-acquired property, the trustee in bankruptcy then has 42 days with which to claim the property for the benefit of the estate (IA 1986, s 309(1)(a)). During this time, the bankrupt may not dispose of the property without the trustee's written consent (IR 1986, r 6.200(2)). In the context of real property, one of the most common forms of after-acquired property is where the bankrupt is left an interest in a property under a will and the testator dies during the period of the bankruptcy (or a person dies intestate and the bankrupt inherits the property as next of kin).

18.71 In circumstances where a person is or is likely to be adjudged bankrupt, family members and relatives may wish to review and amend their wills to ensure that their property will not go to the bankrupt's trustee in the event of their death during the bankruptcy. There is nothing unlawful about changing one's will in this way. A person of sound mind is entitled to deal with their property as they wish and the beneficiary under a will does not become absolutely entitled to property under a will until the death of the testator. Until that time, a person can change their will at their absolute discretion. Where the bankrupt is one of a number of beneficiaries in a properly constituted discretionary trust, the trustee will have no power to compel the trustees to exercise their discretion in favour of the bankruptcy estate (e g see the judgment of Rattee J in *Re Trusts of the Scientific Investment Pension Plan sub nom Clark and Another v Hicks* [1998] 3 All ER 154 in relation to pension provisions that created discretionary trusts in the event of the member's bankruptcy).

CONTRACTS FOR THE SALE OF LAND

18.72 Where the bankrupt entered into a contract for the sale of an interest in land prior to the presentation of the bankruptcy petition and the sale has not been completed at the time the bankruptcy order is made, then the bankrupt's title to the interest in that property will vest in his trustee, but subject to the interest of the purchaser that was created on the exchange of contracts prior to the presentation of the petition (IA 1986, s 283(5)). The trustee will become bound by the obligation to complete the transfer to the purchaser (see *Re Pooley, ex p Rabbidge* (1878) 8 Ch D 367 at 370, CA and *Re Scheibler, ex p Holthausen* (1874) 9 Ch App 722).

18.73 Where the bankrupt enters the contract after the petition has been presented, then it is likely to be void unless the purchaser enters the contract in good faith, for value and without notice of the bankruptcy petition (IA 1986, s 284(4)(a)), unless the court has validated the transaction either prior to the contract being entered or after the event.

18.74 For the trustee's ability (or otherwise) to disclaim a bankrupt's obligations under a contract for the sale of land see **7.79**.

SECURED CREDITORS

18.75 The rights of mortgagees and other secured creditors are discussed in chapter 16.

Chapter 19

ANCILLARY RELIEF AND BANKRUPTCY

19.1 There has always been an uneasy tension between the family courts and the insolvency courts in cases where there have been overlaps between matrimonial and insolvency proceedings.

PROPERTY ADJUSTMENT ORDERS

19.2 One of the reliefs available to the court in divorce proceedings is to make a property adjustment order. The effect of such an order is to transfer an interest in land from one spouse to the other.

19.3 Once the bankruptcy order is made the Family Court has no power to make a property adjustment order because of the vesting that takes place pursuant to IA 1986, s 306.

19.4 Where the bankruptcy order is made after the property adjustment order but before the transfer of the legal title has been effected, the case-law has developed in favour of the non-bankrupt spouse provided there has been no collusion by the parties and the order was not a device with which to avoid the bankrupt's creditors.

19.5 In the case of *Re Higham (a bankrupt)* [1997] BPIR 389 a consent order had been made under the Matrimonial Causes Act 1973, s 24(1)(c). The order provided that the husband should transfer his interest in the formal matrimonial home to the wife within 3 months of the order. The husband was made bankrupt during the intervening 3-month period. The court held that the order did not effect an immediate transfer of the beneficial interest in the property and held that her husband's interest in the property vested in the trustee in bankruptcy. This case was a direct authority that an order under s 24(1)(a) will not operate to transfer the beneficial interest in a property without further steps being taken. However, in *Harper v O'Reilly and Another* [1997] 2 FLR 816, Michael Hart QC (sitting as a deputy judge in the High Court) held that the *Higham* case had no effect on orders made under the Matrimonial Causes Act 1973, s 24(1)(c) or (d). In relation to those provisions, the learned judge held that the wife would receive the beneficial interest in the property upon the order being made. This decision was subsequently upheld by the Court of Appeal in the decision of *Mountney v Treharne* [2002] 2 FLR 930, CA, where it was held that a property adjustment order made in favour of the wife effected an immediate transfer of the beneficial interest in the property on the decree absolute, even though no deed of transfer had been executed. The Court of Appeal held that equity should treat as done that which ought to have been done.

Insolvency Act 1986, s 284

19.6   In *Treharne* and *Sands v Forrester* [2003] EWHC 2784 (Ch), [2008] BPIR 338 a property adjustment order was made between the presentation of the bankruptcy petition and the making of the bankruptcy order.

19.7   IA 1986, s 284 stipulates that dispositions by the bankrupt of any of his property during this period are void unless the disposition was made for value, in good faith and without notice that a bankruptcy petition had been presented (s 284(4)), or is or was subsequently ratified by the court (s 284(1)).

19.8   The question arose as to whether when complying with the order of the court, it was the husband who was effecting the disposition of his interest in the property or whether it was the court. The court was obliged to find that it was the husband who made the disposition and accordingly, the transfer of property whilst being a transfer directed by the court, was a disposition by the bankrupt for the purposes of IA 1986, s 284 and therefore a disposition that was void without ratification from the court.

19.9   The *Mountney* and *Forrester* decisions provided much needed clarity in relation to when property adjustment orders would be effective. However, neither case ruled on the question of whether or not the making of a property adjustment order within the appropriate time period would or might constitute a transaction at an undervalue or preference for the purposes of IA 1986, s 339 or 340. In both *Mountney* and *Forrester*, the court did refer to s 39 of the Matrimonial Causes Act 1973 which provides as follows:

> 'The fact that a settlement or transfer of property had to be made in order to comply with a Property Adjustment Order shall not prevent that settlement or transfer from being a transaction in respect of which an Order may be made under Section 339 or 340 of the Insolvency Act 1986 (Transactions at an Undervalue and Preferences).'

However the question of whether a wife (in most cases) provided consideration when the court made a property adjustment order was not ruled upon in either case.

Transactions at an undervalue and *Hill and Bangham v Haines*

19.10   Another area where insolvency law has been at odds with matrimonial law has been in relation to the question of what consideration (if any) a spouse gives to the other spouse in return for ancillary relief granted by the court in divorce proceedings. The question of consideration is key in insolvency proceedings because where a party who is subsequently adjudged bankrupt disposes of any property in the 5 years prior to his bankruptcy for either no consideration or for less consideration than that property was actually worth, then such a transaction is liable to be set aside as a transaction at an undervalue pursuant to IA 1986, s 339.

19.11 In early 2007 insolvency law and family law collided in the case of *Hill and Bangham v Haines* [2007] EWHC 1231 (Ch). Following contested divorce proceedings, the court made an order that the husband was to transfer his interest in the matrimonial home within 14 days of the date of the order or 7 days of the date of the decree absolute, whichever was the later. The decree absolute was granted on 21 February 2005 and so, following the ruling in *Mountney*, the transfer became effective on 28 February 2005. On 31 March 2006 a bankruptcy order was made against Mr Haines on his own petition. The execution of the transfer of the property into Mrs Haines' sole name took place after the bankruptcy order had been made but it was accepted by all parties that the transfer of the beneficial interest had taken place prior to the making of the bankruptcy order. Mr Haines' joint trustees in bankruptcy applied for a declaration that the transfer of the beneficial interest in the property constituted a transaction at an undervalue pursuant to IA 1986, s 339. The district judge in the Birmingham County Court dismissed the trustees' application and the trustees appealed the decision to the High Court, that appeal being heard from HH Judge Pelling QC sitting as a Deputy High Court judge at the Chancery Division. Judge Pelling reversed the county court's decision and ruled that the transfer pursuant to the property adjustment order did constitute a transaction at an undervalue and should be set aside in favour of the appellant trustees in order to enable them to realise Mr Haines' former interest in the property for the benefit of his creditors. The decision was based on a number of previous authorities that when read together, were taken by Judge Pelling QC to provide that:

> 'A wife (in most cases) does not have a cause of action in ancillary relief proceedings and accordingly has no right or entitlement to any award. The only right she has is to apply to the Court to ask the Court to exercise their discretion in order to grant her relief. Because she has no right to relief, the wife cannot be giving anything up or providing any consideration for accepting ancillary relief order and so provides no consideration in this regard.'

19.12 Mrs Haines relied on the cases of *Re Abbott* [1983] Ch 45, which had established the proposition that ancillary relief claims under the Matrimonial Causes Act 1973, ss 23–25 were capable of amounting to consideration. The ruling in this case was followed in *Re Kumar* [1993] 1 WLR 224, where it was held that *Re Abbott* was not relevant to the present case because it had concerned the predecessor to IA 1986, s 339, namely s 42(1) of the Bankruptcy Act 1941 and the language used in the two statutes was substantially different. The judge further referred to the case of *Xydias v Xydias* [1999] 2 All ER 386, where the Court of Appeal ruled that an agreement reached in ancillary relief proceedings was not capable of taking effect as an enforceable contract because the court always had a discretion as to whether or not to approve the agreement in the form of an order.

19.13   The court's ruling in *G v G (Financial Provision: Equal Division)* [2002] 2 FLR 1143 had determined that consideration did not pass on a transfer of shares pursuant to a matrimonial order and further in the case of *McMinn v McMinn* [2003] 2 FLR 823, it was decided that an ancillary relief claim was not a cause of action.

19.14   Taking the cases into consideration, Pelling J considered that by virtue of the fact that the wife had no cause of action and secondly that a compromise agreement did not give rise to a binding contract, then an applicant for ancillary relief could not give consideration for agreeing to compromise her claim and he considered that the position was no different in relation to fully contested ancillary relief proceedings.

19.15   The scope and effect of this ruling sent shockwaves through both family and insolvency practitioners. Trustees in bankruptcy reviewed all of their cases where the bankrupt had been involved in divorce proceedings in the 5 years preceding the bankruptcy to ascertain whether or not a similar claim could be brought against the bankrupt's former spouse.

The Appeal

19.16   The effect of the High Court's ruling in this matter was short lived. In November 2007, the Court of Appeal overturned the judgment of the Deputy High Court judge. The Court of Appeal judges were unanimous. Sir Andrew Morritt (the Chancellor), who gave the lead judgment, provided that a wife did give consideration for the purposes of IA 1986, s 339(3)(a). He stated:

> 'I do not suggest that the reference to "an entitlement" indicates any sort of propriety right before the relevant court order is made. But, whatever the position may have been in earlier days, it is, in my view, self-evident that the ability of one spouse to apply to the Court for one or more of the orders referred to in Section 23 to 24d (of the Matrimonial Causes Act 1973) is a right conferred and recognised by the law. Further, it has value in that his exercise may, and commonly does, lead to Court Orders entitling one spouse to property or money from or at the expense of the other. That money and property is, prima facie, the measure of the value of the right.'

19.17   In relation to IA 1986, s 339(3)(c), the Chancellor held that the value of the applicant's statutory right to apply for ancillary relief was not less than the consideration she received upon the making of an ancillary relief order. He stated:

> 'That this is the true interpretation of Section 339(c) appears to me to be confirmed by the terms of Section 39 of the Matrimonial Causes Act 1973. I cannot accept that Parliament intended that what must be one of the commonest orders made by Courts exercising their matrimonial jurisdiction, namely that the husband do transfer his beneficial interest in the matrimonial home to the wife,

should be capable of automatic nullification at the suit of the Trustee in Bankruptcy of the husband against whom a Bankruptcy Order was subsequently made on his own Petition.'

19.18 The effect of the Court of Appeal's ruling in *Hill and Bangham*, whilst providing family practitioners with certainty and reassurance, did leave the door open for unscrupulous couples to engineer ancillary relief claims and settlements with a view to taking advantage of the ruling. This was recognised by Rix LJ in the Court of Appeal who stated (at para 82):

'A collusive agreement by a divorcing husband and wife to prefer the wife and children over creditors and of thus dishonestly to transfer to her more than his estate can truly bare, if the debts were properly taken into account, and thus more than her ancillary relief claim could really and knowingly be worth, is no doubt susceptible to Section 339 Relief despite the existence of a Court Order in her favour (see the decision in *Kumar*).'

19.19 It should be noted that even where a court finds that there has been a transaction at an undervalue, it retains a discretion as to whether or not to grant the trustee in bankruptcy relief (see *Singla (Trustee in Bankruptcy of Brown) v Brown and Another* [2007] EWHC 405 (Ch)).

Part 5

PROPERTY TAXATION AND INSOLVENCY

Chapter 20

TAX

Tarl Lall

INTRODUCTION

20.1 Property transactions entered into by an insolvency practitioner during the course of liquidation, administration or bankruptcy will often involve tax issues which must be given due consideration. The main taxes that are likely to be in issue would be:

- corporation or capital gains tax (CGT) on gains that may arise on the disposal of property;

- value added tax (VAT); and

- Stamp Duty Land Tax (SDLT).

20.2 The UK tax rules do not contain a separate code for the various insolvency and rescue situations. How the tax rules affect an insolvency practitioner depends on whether or not the context involves:

- a liquidation;

- an administrator;

- Law of Property Act 1925 receivership; or

- an individual's bankruptcy.

This chapter will outline the rules applicable in each situation, although it is outside the scope to consider them in any detail.

20.3 Although a liquidator/administrator may have personal liability to tax in certain circumstances, a general rule that applies in such situations is that tax remains the primary liability of the company which is the subject of the insolvency situation. In the case of individuals in bankruptcy, their assets vest in the trustee in bankruptcy, who is responsible for discharging the tax liability of the bankrupt in the course of administrating the bankrupt individual's estate.

20.4 The insolvency practitioner may have to pay tax to Her Majesty's Revenue and Customs (HMRC) on behalf of the company or individual. One prospective advantage of the insolvency practitioner effectively stepping into the shoes of the company or the individual concerned is that reliefs, in particular losses, that may be available to the company or individual could be available for set-off against the gains realised by the insolvency practitioner. The reliefs available and practical points that need to be watched will also be outlined in this chapter.

20.5 Given the lack of a distinct tax code that applies in insolvency situations, the position can be complex. The insolvency practitioner should seek to take expert advice at the earliest opportunity, especially where swift action is required in a rescue situation.

AN OVERVIEW OF TAXES

20.6 This section outlines some key features of various taxes that an insolvency practitioner may encounter.

Corporation tax

20.7 UK-resident companies pay corporation tax on their income and capital gains (Income and Corporation Taxes Act 1988 (ICTA 1988), s 6). Normally they do not pay income tax on their own profits or gains, although they may be required to withhold income tax on certain payments or pay income tax and national insurance contributions (NICs) under PAYE.

20.8 Companies pay corporation tax by reference to profits arising in an accounting period. The appointment of an administrator or liquidator brings the existing accounting period of a company to an end (ICTA 1988, s 12). The difference between an administration and liquidation is that:

- in the case of an administration, the new accounting period starting on the appointment of the administrator (ICTA 1988, s 12(7ZA)) comes to an end on the normal accounting reference date of the company and then continues in the normal way so that the accounting period is not changed;

- in the case of a liquidation, the accounting period commencing on the appointment of the liquidator ends on each anniversary of the beginning of the liquidation so the accounting period of the company is changed (ICTA 1988, s12(7)).

20.9 The significance of an accounting period ending is that certain reliefs, in particular trading losses, may not be accessible to the liquidator or administrator. In outline, the position on accessibility to losses is as follows:

- trading losses can be set-off against the trading profits or capital gains of the same accounting period (ICTA 1988, s 393A(1)(a); the key words being 'of whatever description' just before subsection (a)). However, if a liquidator or administrator realises a post-appointment capital gain, the officeholder will not be able to set off trading losses of the company accrued to the date of the appointment;

- trading losses can be carried back one year and set-off against the previous year's trading profits (ICTA 1988, s 393A(1)(b));

- unused trading losses can be carried forward indefinitely and set-off against trading profits arising from the same trade (ICTA 1988, s 393). A key point to watch is that steps taken to rescue and revive a business could lead to a change in its nature which would prevent the use of carried forward losses;

- capital losses can be set off against other capital gains arising in the same accounting period (Taxation of Chargeable Gains Act 1992 (TCGA 1992), s 8(a)) or if they cannot be so utilised, they can be carried forward indefinitely and set off against capital gains arising in later accounting periods (TCGA 1992, s 8(b)). Capital losses cannot be carried back.

20.10 Where a company is resident abroad, it is not liable to corporation tax on any profits arising from UK activity, unless it has a permanent establishment (ie a base) in the UK (ICTA 1988, s 11(1)). Where an administrator is appointed in respect of an overseas company, provided there is no UK permanent establishment and one is not created by the administrator, an overseas company is liable to income tax on any profits arising from UK activity rather than corporation tax. The issue would not normally arise in the case of liquidations if an overseas liquidator is appointed in respect of the overseas company.

20.11 The activities of a UK administrator could give rise to a UK permanent establishment where the company in question continues to trade through the administrator. Such an outcome can be avoided where the administrator can demonstrate that is an agent of independent status acting in the ordinary course of business (Finance Act 2003 (FA 2003), s 148(3)), although it may be necessary to examine the activities of the administrator in some detail.

Income tax

20.12 As mentioned above companies do not pay income tax on their profits or gains. However, an overseas company, which does not have any UK presence, but has UK source profits, is liable to income tax on those profits rather than corporation tax (ICTA 1988, s 6(1)). The tax is only payable at the basic rate as the higher rate of income tax only applies to individuals (Income Tax Act 2007 (ITA 2007), s 11).

20.13 Income tax is likely to be of more interest to a trustee in bankruptcy appointed in respect of an individual. It is outside the scope of this chapter to consider income tax in any detail. However:

- income tax may be due on any investment income such as interest, dividends or royalties;

- if the individual was involved in any partnership or membership of a limited liability partnership, income tax may be due on any share of trading profits; and

- the trustee in bankruptcy would takeover any open appeal or outstanding claims for relief relating to the years falling in the period of bankruptcy.

Capital gains tax

20.14 A trustee in bankruptcy in respect of an individual who was in partnership or a member of an Limited Liability Partnership (LLP) may, on a disposal of an asset which was leased to a trading business in which the individual was a participator, be able to use entrepreneurs' relief introduced with effect from 6 April 2008 (TCGA 1992, Chapter 3 of Part V). Entrepreneurs' relief (ER) allows £1m of lifetime gains to have the benefit of an effective rate of CGT of 10%. In order to utilise ER the relief must be claimed (TCGA 1992, s 169M). Normally a taxpayer can decide whether or not to use the relief for a gain on a particular disposal. A taxpayer can decide to preserve the relief for future disposals, especially where other reliefs are available to shelter gains arising on a given disposal.

20.15 A trustee in bankruptcy is treated as a nominee of the insolvent individual (TCGA 1992, s 66(1)). Any capital gains arising on the disposal of assets by the trustee in bankruptcy could be subject to CGT, which is the liability of the trustee in bankruptcy (TCGA 1992, s 66(1)). The property held by the trustee in bankruptcy is not settled property (TCGA 1992, s 66(4)) so it is considered that the basic rules on ER would apply rather the rules for trust business assets. A trustee in bankruptcy may be faced with an interesting decision as to whether or not to claim the ER or allow the relief to remain intact for the bankrupt in respect to any future gains. Certain other reliefs, in particular capital losses, reduce the chargeable gains and therefore will be utilised first. A failure to claim ER relief would mean that HMRC's interest as a creditor would be greater as the gain would be taxed at a flat rate of 18%. Claiming the ER and utilising the effective rate of 10% would reduce the level of HMRC's claims. It remains to be tested whether a trustee in bankruptcy would be obliged to claim the relief and reduce the level of HMRC's claim as a creditor.

20.16 An administrator appointed in respect of a non-resident company again needs to take care over whether the appointment creates a UK permanent establishment. Non-resident companies are generally not liable for any corporation tax on capital gains arising in the UK unless the company has a permanent establishment in the UK and the asset in question was held or used for the purpose of the permanent establishment (TCGA 1992, s 10B). Once again, if the insolvency practitioner's appointment creates a permanent establishment gains may come within the UK tax amount where they otherwise would not have been.

Value added tax

20.17 Any person, whether a company or individual who make supplies of goods or services in the course or furtherance of a business with turnover over a prescribed registration limit is required to be registered for VAT. Where a person is not required to be registered for VAT they can apply for voluntary registration. The taxable person effectively acts as tax collector for the government and collects VAT due on taxable supplies made by them.

20.18 All supplies are taxable unless they are exempt (Value Added Tax Act 1994 (VATA 1994), s 4(2)). Supplies are exempt if they fall within certain specified categories. Taxable supplies attract VAT at three different rates, namely the standard rate applies to all supplies and is currently 17.5%. Certain categories of supplies such as the sale of newly built houses are zero-rated. Specific supplies, such as the supplies of energy saving materials, attract VAT at 5%. VAT incurred by a taxable person on his inputs is called input tax. Input tax can be recovered to the extent that the inputs are used for making taxable supplies.

20.19 Insolvency as a general rule does not bring a VAT registration to an end unless the business in question ceases which leads to deregistration. An administrator or liquidator steps into the shoes of the taxable person and must deal with VAT compliance as an effective representative of the taxable person. An administrator or liquidator is obliged to notify HMRC within 21 days of the appointment (Value Added Tax Regulations 1995, SI 1995/2518 (VAT Regs 1995), reg 9). An LPA receiver (discussed in chapter 17) does not step into the shoes of the taxable person in respect of general VAT compliance obligations but still needs to consider and deal with VAT in relation to specific supplies, as to which see **20.30**.

Stamp Duty Land Tax

20.20 SDLT is a tax on land transactions (FA 2003, s 42(1)). Unlike stamp duty (the predecessor to SDLT), SDLT is not a voluntary tax. SDLT is payable by a buyer (FA 2003, s 85). A liquidator, administrator or trustee in bankruptcy would normally be a seller of assets rather than a buyer, therefore SDLT would not as such be a concern to the insolvency practitioner. However, where the SDLT cost to a buyer is high, it may affect the marketability of the property that the insolvency practitioner may wish to dispose of. SDLT could therefore become an issue for the insolvency practitioner. Where circumstances permit, the insolvency practitioner may wish to offer a structure that enables a buyer to mitigate or eliminate the upfront SDLT cost, in which case the insolvency practitioner would need to consider SDLT.

20.21 Insolvency practitioners in relation to group companies also need to be aware of a trap that may involve an SDLT cost. Where an intra-group transfer of property in the previous 3 years has had the benefit of SDLT group relief under FA 2003, Sch 7, there is a clawback of relief where the transferee company leaves the group within 3 years whilst still owning the property in question (FA 2003, Sch 7, para 3). The SDLT is recoverable from the transferee company as the former buyer of the property; but if the tax remains unpaid for 6 months, HMRC have rights of recovery against the former seller company, other group members and certain directors (FA 2003, Sch 7, para 5). When a company goes into liquidation, it loses beneficial ownership of all of its assets. The same does not apply in the case of a receivership (*English Sewing Cotton v IRC* [1947] 1 All ER 679). Where a parent company goes into liquidation, it would lose beneficial ownership of the shares of its subsidiaries. If there has been a previous intra-group transfer of assets from the parent company to a subsidiary, the liquidation can trigger a clawback of relief resulting in a SDLT cost to the subsidiary. The clawback would not arise where the transferee subsidiary is the company that goes into liquidation. There may be similar traps for other group reliefs, in particular for group relief of trading losses.

Other taxes

20.22 The following is a list of other taxes that an insolvency practitioner may have to deal with:

- PAYE and NICs: if the insolvency practitioner takes over employees of a company or an unincorporated business;

- withholding taxes: the principal withholding tax a liquidator may encounter is that yearly interest payable by a company generally and in particular to a person resident abroad may be subject to a deduction of tax at the basic rate, being 20% for the tax year 2008/09 (ITA 2007, s 874). Interest is not, however, subject to withholding tax where it is paid on an advance from a bank within the UK corporation tax net (ITA 2007, s 879);

- withholding tax on any royalty payments for the use of a patent or certain other types of intellectual property which are made to persons living abroad. In the case of royalties for patents, withholding tax applies whether or not the recipient is in the UK or abroad, in the case of payments made abroad, subject to the terms of any applicable double tax treaty;

- tax on rents collected on behalf of a non-resident landlord is the liability of the person receiving or entitled to receive the rents (Income Tax (Trading and Other Income) Act 2005, s 271) unless the non-resident landlord holds a certificate issued by HMRC which allows him to receive the rents gross. The non-resident landlord can apply for gross payments under the Taxation of Income from Land (Non-residents) Regulations 1995, SI 1995/2902;

- administrators may encounter income tax, PAYE and NICs on a business sale, for example on a pre-pack, that involves shares being issued to managers. Shares issued to employees and directors at an undervalue triggers an income tax liability at the point of acquisition under a principle established in the case of *Weight v Salmon* ((1935) 19 TC 174). The income tax may have to be accounted for under PAYE. If PAYE applies, a NIC liability would also be triggered. The share issue may also involve income tax and NIC costs on a future sale, especially if restrictions are applied to the shares (whether in the articles of association or a shareholders or investment agreement). The risks can be mitigated or eliminated by the managers acquiring their shares in the company that would acquire the business on a pre-pack before any agreement for the business acquisition is entered into, which in an urgent rescue situation, may be hours before the business sale agreement is entered into. The managers and the company should also consider making elections under the Income Tax (Earnings and Pensions) Act 2003, s 431 which may involve some income tax cost at the point of acquisition, but if the arrangements are structured properly, can prevent income tax charges arising on a future sale. A s 431 election must be made within 14 days after the acquisition of the shares and is irrevocable. This issue involves a degree of complexity;

- administrators and liquidators may also have to deal with share options or other share incentive rights granted to the employees of the company in question. In a vast majority of cases, the exercise price of the options will be below the market value of the company's shares (assuming that can be readily ascertained). The rules of any applicable scheme must be checked because in most cases they provide that a notice to shareholders for the voluntary winding up of a company will trigger the employees' rights to exercise their options. It would normally be necessary to ascertain the employees' rights in an insolvency situation and in particular when the options in question lapse. In a rescue situation, suitable alternative incentives can be put in place at the appropriate time.

LIABILITY FOR TAX

Liquidators and administrators

20.23 As mentioned, the appointment of a liquidator or administrator for a company brings to an end the company's accounting period and a new one commences. This helps distinguish between pre- and post-appointment tax liabilities.

20.24   As a general rule HMRC is an unsecured creditor in respect of all pre-appointment liabilities. The preferential status HMRC used to enjoy under the Insolvency Act 1986 (IA 1986), Sch 6, paras 1–5C in respect of certain taxes was abolished under the Enterprise Act 2002, s 251(1)(a).

20.25   Liabilities arising in the course of liquidation are payable as expenses of the liquidation. In the case of corporation tax on income profits, the authority for that proposition is the case of *Re Toshoku Finance UK plc (in liquidation)* [2002] STC 368 in which the House of Lords held that the corporation tax on profits arising on a winding up, was a necessary expense payable by the liquidator under the Insolvency Rules 1986 (IR 1986), r 4.218(3)(m). In the case of capital gains, corporation tax on chargeable gains is specifically treated as an expense of administration under r 4.218(3)(p).

20.26   Although the liquidator or administrator is the proper officer under the Taxes Management Act 1970, s 108 and accordingly responsible for filing tax returns, the proper officer is not responsible for paying the company's tax except in the case of a company which was incorporated outside the UK.

Value added tax

20.27   An administrator, who acts as an agent of the company, broadly steps into the shoes of the company for VAT purposes. If the business is continued with a view to its rescue and revival, the administrator is responsible for ensuring that the company complies with its VAT obligations. The company remains liable for the VAT.

20.28   A liquidator is not strictly an agent of the company but does effectively step into the shoes of the company for VAT purposes and is responsible for VAT compliance in respect of continuing supplies. Once again the company remains liable for the VAT.

20.29   HMRC, however, have a power to treat a liquidator or administrator as the taxable person from the date on which the liquidation or administration starts (VATA 1994, s 46(4) and (5) and VAT Regs 1995, reg 9)). Where HMRC exercise their power and treat the administrator or liquidator as the taxable person, the administrator or liquidator becomes liable for dealing with the VAT compliance and accounting for VAT. However, as a result of a decision in *Sargent v Customs and Excise Commissioners* [1995] STC 398, HMRC's power is only exercisable against an administrator or liquidator where they have control of the management of the whole of the undertaking of the company. Accordingly, power cannot be exercised against an LPA receiver.

20.30   In the case of an LPA receiver, the case of *Sargent* followed an earlier decision in *Re John Willment (Ashford) Ltd* [1979] 2 All ER 615, the effect of which is that although an LPA receiver is not responsible for dealing with the general VAT compliance and liability of the business that owned the asset, there is a mechanism in the VAT regulations whereby they can and must account for VAT collected on the sale of an asset. The issue that arose in that case was whether the LPA receiver had to account for an amount representing VAT to HMRC or whether the amount could be paid to the chargeholder who had appointed the receiver? However, the court held that where a third party paid an amount in respect of VAT, the LPA receiver had to account to HMRC for that VAT rather than to the chargeholder. The LPA receiver can either have invoices issued through the trader or must issue the equivalent of an invoice under the VAT Regs 1985, reg 13(2), a statement to HMRC under the VAT Regs 1985, reg 27 for which HMRC have a form VAT 833. The VAT must be paid with the form VAT 833 within 21 days of the sale (VAT Regs 1985, reg 27).

20.31 Where an administrator or liquidator has to account for and deal with the VAT of a company in administration, if the supplies fall below the registration limit, currently £65,000 the administrator or liquidator can apply to deregister the company for VAT. Deregistration may be preferable in order to save on the cost of VAT obligations. However, deregistration has two significant consequences, namely:

(1) any continuing input tax that is incurred cannot be recovered except under special rules for tax incurred for supplies made before the deregistration which were taxable supplies (VAT Regs 1985, reg 111(5));

(2) the deregistration gives rise to a deemed supply of all of the goods which form part of the assets of the business at the time of the deregistration (VATA 1994, Sch 4, para 8). If that deemed supply is a taxable supply then any pre-deregistration input tax recovered can be retained, whereas if the supply is an exempt supply, then any pre-registration input tax recovered may be repayable. There is a de minimis exception namely that rule does not apply where the value of the deemed supply would be less than or equal to £1,000 (VATA 1994, Sch 4, para 8(1)(c)).

SALE OF PROPERTY

20.32 The principal taxes an insolvency practitioner is likely to encounter on the sale of property are VAT, corporation tax and in the case of trustees in bankruptcy CGT. The insolvency practitioner should establish whether the property was held as a fixed asset or as trading stock. Developers normally hold land as trading stock the gains from which are taxed as income profits. Any person who acquired land with a view to its sale at a profit would hold it as trading stock. The accounts of the company in question should show whether the land is treated as trading stock or as a fixed asset.

20.33 The insolvency practitioner would need to establish whether the sale will give rise to a gain. A certain level of due diligence will be required to ascertain whether or not there will be a taxable gain. As mentioned above, the capital gain arising on the disposal is an expense of the administration or liquidation which would have to be accounted for by the administrator. In the case of an LPA receiver, as the sale will be made by the LPA receiver as agent for the owner, the sale may trigger a gain in the hands of the owner.

20.34 Where a gain arises, a liquidator or administrator needs to establish whether there are any reliefs available which will reduce the tax cost. As mentioned above an administrator or liquidator will be in a new accounting period, therefore, only any brought forward capital losses may be available, or any trading profits arising in the same accounting period, for set-off against the capital gains. If an administrator or liquidator has access to the company's books it ought to be possible to calculate the tax exposure although that is not always easy.

VAT

20.35 An insolvency practitioner disposing of commercial property must always consider whether or not it needs to charge VAT on the disposal. As a general rule all transactions in commercial property are exempt unless the landowner had exercised the option to tax or the building is new and was completed within the previous 3 years, in which case VAT must be charged at the standard rate of 17.5%. If VAT should have been charged but was not, any consideration received will be deemed to be inclusive of VAT which will broadly mean that 14.89% of the sale proceeds will represent VAT. Where the land in question is an asset being sold as part of a business sale or it is an investment property being sold subject to leases, the transfer of going concern (TOGC) relief should be considered and steps taken to ensure that it is available. Where an insolvency practitioner is selling new or partly completed residential properties built by an insolvent developer the sales should be zero-rated. The disposal may involve mixed supplies, some of which are taxable or exempt. An example in point is the disposal of a building (which is not new) comprising of retail units with residential accommodation above. Where the option to tax has been exercised the consideration attributable to the commercial part is subject to VAT, whereas the consideration attributable to the residential accommodation is exempt. Other features of the property may add to complications such that careful planning may be required.

Option to tax

20.36 An option to tax in respect of land mentioned above must be notified in writing to HMRC within 30 days of its being made for it to be valid. Administrators and liquidators who effectively step into the shoes of the company in question are bound by its option. An LPA receiver is also bound by the option to tax of the landowner. In such cases a new option to tax would not be necessary. Where, however, the owner has not exercised the option to tax the insolvency practitioner should consider whether the option to tax should be exercised.

20.37 A number of detailed issues can arise with respect to options, but key points to note are as follows:

- an insolvency practitioner who cannot establish whether or not an option to tax has been exercised should contact HMRC's Option to Tax National Unit. Names (and any former names) combined with the VAT registration number of the owner should enable HMRC to advise whether or not an option to tax has been made;

- where the company in question was part of a group of companies, the option to tax may have been exercised by another group company, which binds the landowner company and consequently the insolvency practitioner. There are detailed rules on 'relevant associates' on which advice should be taken;

- in certain circumstances an option to tax may have needed consent and it may be necessary to establish whether the appropriate consent was obtained or was available under HMRC's published guidance.

20.38 The significance of the option to tax is not only that it enables the insolvency practitioner to decide whether or not to charge VAT on the disposable consideration, but it also determines the ability of the insolvency practitioner, or as appropriate the owner, to recover related input tax.

Liability to VAT

20.39 As mentioned above, where a liquidator or administrator charges VAT on the disposal consideration, following the decision in the case of *Sargent*, the insolvency practitioner effectively acts as tax collector and must account for the VAT to HMRC. In the case of the sale by LPA receiver, VAT regulations provide for a document equivalent to a VAT invoice that must be issued to both the buyer and copies sent to HMRC with the appropriate VAT payment. The VAT accounting is dealt with by an ad hoc procedure rather than the LPA receiver filing a VAT return for the owner.

20.40 A question remains over whether the *Sargent* case extends to a situation where VAT is not added to the disposable consideration but is deemed to be inclusive in the price as mentioned above. The point may be distinguished from the *Sargent* case on the basis that the insolvency practitioner will not have consciously charged VAT on the disposal. However, if the buyer specifically requests that the VAT is inclusive there is an underlying statutory presumption that part of the consideration represents VAT if due, and it is up to the LPA receiver to determine whether the disposal triggers a VAT liability.

Transfer of going concern

20.41 Where business assets are sold as part of a TOGC the transaction does not involve any supply for VAT purposes and is outside the scope of VAT. The buyer does not have to pay VAT and the seller does not have to account for it. The conditions for a TOGC relief under the Value Added Tax (Special Provisions) Order 1995, SI 1995/1268, art 5 are as follows:

- the transfer must put the purchaser in possession of a business which can be operated as such, and is a going concern at the time of transfer;

- the assets in question are intended to be used by the purchaser for carrying on the same kind of business as the seller;

- where the seller is a taxable person, the purchaser either is or will become as a result of the transfer a taxable person;

- there must not be a series of immediately consecutive transfers of the business;

- there must be no significant break in trading before or immediately after the transfer;

- where only part of the business has been sold it must be capable of operating separately.

20.42 Where the TOGC involves land or buildings and the option to tax had been exercised by the original owner, or exceptionally the insolvency practitioner, for the transfer to qualify as a TOGC the buyer must also exercise the option to tax before the relevant date. The relevant date is the exchange of contracts if the buyer pays a deposit to be held by the seller's solicitor as agent for the seller and completion if the buyer pays the deposit to be held as stakeholder. Suitable provisions should be made in the sale contract to ensure that the buyer complies with its obligations to enable the TOGC relief to be secured. Where there is uncertainty as to whether or not the TOGC relief is available, provisions may be required as to how to deal with the uncertainty. The insolvency practitioner should consider requesting an amount being placed in a stakeholder account on account of VAT such that when it is determined whether or not VAT is due, then it can be paid over to the insolvency practitioner if VAT is due or returned to the buyer. The sale contract should also contain provisions as to how to establish the final position and the terms on which the escrow account is operated.

20.43 It is possible to secure an advance ruling from HMRC on whether or not a TOGC relief is available in certain circumstances (see para 9.1 of the HMRC Notice 700/9/08 on the TOGC relief). HMRC, in their published guidance, state that an application should state why there is any doubt over the question whether the TOGC relief is available. Where uncertainty arises owing to missing facts, such as whether or not an option to tax has been made and even HMRC cannot determine whether or not it has, HMRC are unlikely to give a definitive view.

20.44 Where the going concern is let property, the following points are worth noting:

- a going concern may exist even where a tenant is not in place but active steps are being taken to secure a tenant; and

- where the property is partly let the whole of the sale can be a going concern if the intention remains that the balance of the property should be let. If the insolvency practitioner cannot determine whether or not the original owner had that intention that could give rise to difficulties.

Surrender of a lease

20.45 As discussed in chapter 7, a liquidator or trustee in bankruptcy has the power to disclaim property he considers to be onerous (IA 1986, s 178 for liquidators; IA 1986, s 315 for trustees in bankruptcy). The disclaimer operates as a surrender (*Re Levy, ex p Walton* (1881) 17 Ch D 746). Insolvency practitioners should establish whether or not the option to tax has been made. If there is no actual consideration for the disclaimer there should be no VAT in respect of the surrender. If there is any consideration, actual or latent (such as the assumption of liabilities by the landlord) then VAT could be due on the disclaimer, although the situation is rare in practice.

20.46 Where, however, rather than disclaiming a lease the insolvency practitioner negotiates a surrender of the lease, again VAT needs to be considered. If the surrender is made for actual consideration given by the landlord and again the owner had exercised the option to tax, the insolvency practitioner must charge VAT. Where it is appropriate, the insolvency practitioner is able to and pays a reverse premium to the landlord to accept a surrender if the landlord has exercised the option to tax then the landlord would charge VAT on the reverse premium. In such events the insolvency practitioner should insist that any reverse premium is inclusive of VAT. The insolvency practitioner should, however, demand, as it is entitled to do, a VAT invoice as it may be able to recover the related VAT.

RATES

20.47

Corporation tax			
Year ending:	31/03/ 2008	31/03/ 2009	31/03/ 2010
Taxable profits			
£0 – £300,000	20%	21%	22%
£300,001 – £1,500,000	32.50%	29.75%	29.50%
£1,500,000+	30%	28%	28%

Value added tax		
	2007/08	2008/09
Standard rate	17.5%	17.5%
Reduced rate*	5%	5%
Annual registration limit	£64,000	£67,000
Past 12 months sales reviewed	monthly	monthly
Deregistration limit	£62,000	£65,000

*Fuel and power, installation of energy saving material, certain housing refurbishment work

Capital gains tax		
	2007/08	2008/09
Rates of tax		
Individuals – added to income	10/20/40%	18%
Companies – added to income	0/20/30%	0/21/28%

Entrepreneurs' relief (disposals on or after 6/4/2008)	
Chargeable gains on qualifying business assets	*Effective rate of tax*

within lifetime allowance of £1m		10%
excess above lifetime allowance		18%
Reliefs	2007/08	2008/09
Annual gains exemption for individuals and personal representatives	£9,200	£9,600

Stamp Duty Land Tax

Transfers of land and buildings

Consideration	*Residential outside disadvantaged areas*	*Non-residential or residential in disadvantaged areas*
£	%	%
£125,001 – £150,000*	1	Nil
£150,001* – £250,000	1	1
£250,001 – £500,000	3	3
over £500,000	4	4

Lease Duty**: Net Present Value of Rent

Rate	*Residential*	*Non-residential*
Zero	£0 – £125,000	£0 – £150,000
1%	Over £125,000	Over £150,000

*£175,000 for transactions in residential land taking place in the period 3 September 2008 to 2 September 2009
**Premium charged as for land above with special rules where rent exceeds £600 per annum

Part 6

APPENDICES

Appendix 1

THE OPTIONS FOR LANDLORDS WITH INSOLVENT TENANTS

Type of insolvency

Type of action	IVA – during moratorium 14 days	IVA – after moratorium when IVA approved by creditors	Post-IVA new debt (subject always to express terms of the IVA)	Bankruptcy	CVA – during moratorium small companies only (28 days)	During CVA approved by creditors (all companies)	Post-CVA new debt (subject always to express terms of the CVA)	Administrative / LPA receivership	Administration	Members' / creditors' or voluntary liquidation	Compulsory liquidation
Peaceable re-entry	Not without the leave of the court	Yes, but exceptions	Yes	Yes	Not without the leave of the court	Yes, but exceptions	Yes	Yes	Not without the administrator's consent or the leave of the court	Yes, but liquidator can apply under IA 1986, s 112	Not without the liquidator's consent or the leave of the court
Distress for rent or CRAR	Not without the leave of the court	No	Yes	Yes for the 6 months' rent due before the bankruptcy order only	Not without the leave of the court	No	Yes	Yes	Not without the administrator's consent or the leave of the court	Yes	Not without the administrators consent or the leave of the court
Pursuit of guarantors and/or previous tenants	Yes for the whole of the arrears	Yes for the whole of the arrears	Yes for the whole of the arrears	Yes for the whole of the arrears	Yes for the whole of the arrears	Yes for the whole of the arrears	Yes for the whole of the arrears	Yes for the whole of the rent	Yes for the whole amount of the debt	Yes for the whole amount of the debt	Yes for the whole amount of the debt

	1	2	3	4	5	6	7	8	9	10
Section 6 notice on subtenants or s 81 under the new Act	Yes for the amount of the sub-rent	Yes for the amount of the sub-rent	Yes for the amount of the sub-rent	Yes for the amount of the sub-rent	Yes for the amount of the sub-rent	Yes for the amount of the sub-rent	Yes for the amount of the sub-rent	Yes for the amount of the sub-rent	Yes for the amount of the sub-rent	Yes for the amount of the sub-rent
Removal of funds from rent deposit (may depend on nature of deposit). See Chapter 6 re deposits structured as collateral security agreements	Not without the leave of the court	Yes	Yes	Not without the leave of the court	Yes	Yes	Yes	Not without the administrator's consent or the leave of the court	Yes	Not without the leave of court
Can the lease be disclaimed by the insolvency practitioner	No	No	Yes	No	No	No	No	No	Yes	Yes

Appendix 2

NOTICE UNDER SECTION 146 OF THE LAW OF PROPERTY ACT 1925

Law of Property Act 1925

Notice under Section 146 of the Law of Property Act 1925

TO: [   ] ('the Tenant') or such other person being the tenant of the premises situated at and known as [   ] under a lease made between [   ] (1) and [   ] (2) ('the Lease').

WE, [   ] ('the Landlord'), the landlord of the premises under the Lease:

GIVE YOU NOTICE AS FOLLOWS:

1   The Lease contains a proviso for re-entry on the tenant in the following terms:

     [INSERT PROVISION FROM LEASE ENTITLING FORFEITURE FOR INSOLVENCY EVENT AND/OR FOR OTHER BREACHES OF COVENANT]

2   [A meeting has been convened to take place during the week commencing [   ] for the purpose of considering a resolution for the winding up of the Tenant and in consequence the lease is liable to forfeiture.]

3   The breach of this proviso is incapable of remedy. You are required to make payment pursuant to clause [   ] of the Lease all expenses properly incurred (including solicitors' costs and surveyors' fees and any VAT payable on them) by the Landlord incidental to or in contemplation of the preparation and service of this Notice.

4   The aforementioned breach of condition is incapable of remedy. Accordingly on [INSERT DATE] the Landlord shall exercise its right of re-entry under the Lease and also claim damages.

DATED this [   ] day of [   ] 20[   ]

. . . .

Name:

Company:

Position:

Address:

REF:

For and on behalf of the Landlord

Appendix 3

NOTICE OF DISCLAIMER

Form 4.55

(Rule 4.192)

Notice of Intended Disclaimer to
Interested Party

                       No   **of**   .

IN THE

IN THE MATTER of

(Registered No.   **)**

AND IN THE MATTER of the Insolvency Act 1986

(a) Insert full particulars of property

I intend to disclaim [a]

If you claim an interest in this property, you must declare to me the nature and extent of your claim within 14 days of receiving this notice

If you fail to do so, I am entitled to assume that you do not have any interest in the property which will prevent or impede my disclaimer

Dated

Signed

                                   Liquidator

Name in BLOCK LETTERS

Appendix 4

NOTICE TO ELECT – LIQUIDATION

Form 4.54

(Rule 4.191)   **Notice to Elect**

No   **of**   .

IN THE

Re

(a) Insert name,

address and

particulars of

interest in

property

(e g landlord etc)

I (a)

(b) Insert details

of property comprising (b)

require the liquidator to decide within 28 days of receiving this notice whether he will disclaim the above property or not and to notify me of his decision.

Dated

Signed

Name in BLOCK LETTERS

To the liquidator of the above-named company

Address

Appendix 5

NOTICE OF DISCLAIMER UNDER SECTION 178 OF THE INSOLVENCY ACT 1986

Form 4.53

(Rule 4.187, 4.188,4.189)

Notice of Disclaimer under section 178 of the Insolvency Act 1986

No   of   .

IN THE

IN THE MATTER of

AND IN THE MATTER of the Insolvency Act 1986

PART 1

(a) Insert name of liquidator

I, (a)   , the liquidator of the above-named company, disclaim all the company's interest in:

(b) Insert full particulars of property

(b)

Dated

Signed

Name in BLOCK LETTERS

Address

PART 2

NOTE:

(c) Insert name of court

This is a copy of a notice filed at (c)   Court

(d) Insert date that notice filed in court

On (d)

Seal of the Court

**PART
3**

(e) Insert name
and address of
person to be
sent copy
notice under
Rule 4.188 or
4.189

To: (e)

This is a copy of a notice of disclaimer filed by the liquidator in the above matter at (c)   Court.

NOTE:

1. Part 1 is to be completed by the liquidator and filed in court with a copy

    Part 2 is to be completed by the court and returned to the liquidator

    Part 3 is to be completed by or on behalf of the liquidator when sending out copy notice under Rule 4.188 or 4.189

2. The attention of a recipient of this notice is drawn to sections 178–182 of the Insolvency Act 1986

3. Where the property concerned consists of land or buildings the nature of the interest should also be stated (e g whether leasehold, freehold, etc)

Appendix 6

NOTICE OF INTENDED DISCLAIMER TO INTERESTED PARTY

Form 6.63

(Rule 6.184)   **Notice of Intended Disclaimer to Interested Party**

No   of   .

IN THE

In Bankruptcy

Re:

(a) Insert full particulars of property

I intend to disclaim (a)

If you claim an interest in this property, you must declare to me the nature and extent of your claim within 14 days of receiving this notice

If you fail to do so, I am entitled to assume that you do not have any interest in the property which will prevent or impede my disclaimer

Dated

Signed

                                        Trustee

Address

Name in BLOCK LETTERS

Appendix 7

NOTICE TO ELECT – BANKRUPTCY

Form 6.62

Notice to Elect

(Rule 6.183)

No   of   .

IN THE

In Bankruptcy

Re

(a) Insert name, address and particulars of interest in property (e g landlord etc)

I (a)

(b) Insert details

of property comprising (b)

require the trustee to decide within 28 days of receiving this notice whether he will disclaim the above property or not and to notify me of his decision.

Dated

Signed

Name in BLOCK LETTERS

To the trustee of the above-named bankrupt's estate

Address

Appendix 8

NOTICE OF DISCLAIMER UNDER SECTION 315 OF THE INSOLVENCY ACT 1986

Form 6.61

(Rule 4.187, 4.188,4.189)

Notice of Disclaimer under section 315 of the Insolvency Act 1986

No   of   .

IN THE

In Bankruptcy

Re

PART 1

(a) Insert name

of trustee

I, (a)

the trustee of the above-named bankrupt's estate, disclaim all my interest in:

(b) Insert full

particulars of

property

(b)

Dated

Signed

Name in BLOCK LETTERS

Address

PART 2

(c) Insert name

of court

(d) Insert date

that notice filed

in court

NOTE:

This is a copy of a notice filed at (C)   Court

On (d)

Seal of the Court

PART 3

To: (e)

This is a copy of a notice of disclaimer filed by the trustee in the above matter at (c)   Court.

NOTE:

1.   Part 1 is to be completed by the trustee and filed in court with a copy

Part 2 is to be completed by the court and returned to the trustee

Part 3 is to be completed by or on behalf of the trustee when sending out copy notice under Rule 6.179 or 6.180

2.   The attention of recipient of this notice is drawn to sections 315–321 of the Insolvency Act 1986.

3.   Where the property concerned consists of land or buildings the nature of the interest should also be stated (e g whether leasehold, freehold, etc).

Appendix 9

PROOF OF DEBT – GENERAL FORM

Form 4.25

Rule 4.73   **PROOF OF DEBT – GENERAL FORM**

No   of   .

IN THE

IN THE MATTER OF

AND IN THE MATTER OF THE INSOLVENCY ACT 1986

Date of Winding-up order/Resolution for voluntary winding-up

1   Name of Creditor (if a Company please also give company registration number).

2   Address of Creditor for correspondence.

3   Total amount of claim, including any Value Added Tax and outstanding uncapitalised interest as at the date of the bankruptcy order.

- [£   ] Rent and other obligations arising prior to the commencement of liquidation [generally ordinary unsecured debt].

- [£   estimated] Damages for dilapidations [Particularly where lease has come to an end – see below attach evidence such as schedules of dilapidations and if appropriate a valuation pursuant to the Landlord and Tenant Act 1927, s 18 – also consider any other unliquidated claim arising under the terms of the lease]

- [£   ] Rent and other obligations arising after the commencement of liquidation [generally ordinary unsecured debt unless an expense]:

  - [£   ] Where they have fallen due (generally ordinary debt).

  - Where such sums have not yet fallen due (generally ordinary debt).

  - All rights are reserved in relation to any such sums which are payable as an *expense* of the liquidation.

  - Damages (following a disclaimer –if appropriate attach evidence of loss see below).

4   Details of any documents by reference to which the debt can be substantiated. (Note: There is no need to attach them now but the trustee may call for any document or evidence to substantiate the claim at his discretion as may the official receiver whilst acting as receiver and manager, or the chairman or convenor of any meeting.)

The following documents are attached

Schedule of dilapidations dated [   ]

Valuation of [   ] dated [   ]

[list and attach evidence supporting unliquidated claims above]

5   If amount in 3 above includes outstanding uncapitalised interest please state amount.

£ [include interest on sums due under the lease]

6   Particulars of how and when debt incurred.

[recite details of lease and relevant clauses]

7   Particulars of any security held, the value of the security, and the date it was given.

[declare rent deposit details and other security]

8   Particulars of any reservation of title claimed in respect of goods supplied to which the claim relates.

9   Signature of creditor or person authorised to act on his behalf.

Name in BLOCK LETTERS

Position with or relation to creditor

Address of person signing (if different from 2 above)

Date signed

Admitted to vote for

£

Date

Official Receiver/Trustee

Admitted for dividend for

£

Date

Trustee

Appendix 10

WITNESS STATEMENT

IN THE HIGH COURT OF JUSTICE   No. [   ] of [   ]

CHANCERY DIVISION

COMPANIES COURT

IN THE MATTER OF [*company name in liquidation*]

AND IN THE MATTER OF THE INSOLVENCY ACT 1986

[   ]

Applicant

and

[   ]

Respondents

WITNESS STATEMENT OF [   ]

I, AB of [address] [occupation] make this statement in support of the Applicant:

1   I am [Director of AB the Applicant]. I am duly authorised to make this witness statement on its behalf which I do from documents and information within my own knowledge and which I believe to be true. I make the witness statement in support of the application dated .... 20... for an order under Section 130(2) of the Insolvency Act 1986 for permission to distrain [or permission to exercise Commercial Rent Arrears Recovery pursuant to Section 71 of the Tribunals Courts and Enforcement Act 2007] upon goods of the Company at [address of demised premises].

2   The Applicant is the freehold owner of premises at [address] and has been at all material times. The Company is the lessee of the premises under the terms of a lease dated (insert all material terms of lease).

3   Over the term of the lease arrears of rent have accrued due and remain unpaid.

4   On .... 20... I therefore instructed [County Bailiff Company] certificated bailiffs of [address] to distrain upon the goods of the Company at the premises, which they did. I refer to a copy of a notice of seizure of goods and inventory pursuant to the Distress for Rent Rules 1988 [or to serve a notice of enforcement pursuant to paragraph 7

of Schedule 12 to the Tribunals Courts and Enforcement Act 2007 and then to take control over the goods of the Company at the premises by exercising Commercial Rent Arrears Recovery] [exhibit copies].

5   [County Bailiff Company] entered into a form of walking possession agreement with the Company [or a Controlled Goods Agreement],[exhibit copies].

6   A winding-up petition was presented against the Company on [   ] by [   ].

7   On [   ] a winding-up order was made. Notwithstanding repeated requests for facilities and arrangements for them to be removed the goods still remain at the Company's premises and the Liquidator of the Company, refuses to agree to [County Bailiff Company] removing them.

8   I request that the Court allow the Applicant to complete the distress by removal and sale of the goods described pursuant to Section 130(2) of the Insolvency Act 1986

Statement of Truth

This witness statement was made and signed at (address) on .... 20... by me, [state name].

I believe that the facts stated in this witness statement are true.

. . . .

Signed   Date

Appendix 11

APPLICATION NOTICE

IN THE HIGH COURT OF JUSTICE   No. [   ] of [   ]
CHANCERY DIVISION
COMPANIES COURT
IN THE MATTER OF [   ]
AND IN THE MATTER OF THE INSOLVENCY ACT 1986

[   ]

Applicant

and

[   ]

Respondents

APPLICATION NOTICE

TAKE NOTICE that the above named Applicant intends to apply to the Registrar on:

Date:

Time:

Place:

For an Order in the following terms:

1   A direction that pursuant to paragraph 43(6) of Schedule B1 of the Insolvency Act 1986, the Applicant be given permission to commence proceedings against the Respondents for a declaration that the rents that have accrued between [INSERT DATES] pursuant to a Lease made between [INSERT PARTIES] dated [INSERT DATE] ('the Lease'), [the term of which is currently vested in the [   ] Respondent, and the reversionary interest of which is vested in the Applicant, be paid forthwith as an expense of the administration of the [   ] Respondent pursuant to Rule 2.67(1)(a) or alternatively Rule 2.67(1)(f) of the Insolvency Rules 1986.

2   An order that the Respondents pay interest on the sums referred to in paragraph 1 above at such rate and for such period as the Court deems appropriate.

3   The Applicant be given leave pursuant to paragraph 43(4)(b) of Schedule B1 of the Insolvency Act 1986 to forfeit the lease by peaceable re-entry.

4   The grounds upon which the above directions are sought are set out in the Witness Statement of [   ] dated [   ].

Dated this [   ] day of [   ] 200[   ]

....

Solicitor for the Applicant

Address for service is:

[INSERT ADDRESS]

Appendix 12

LICENCE TO OCCUPY

DATE OF LICENCE TO OCCUPY   **2008**

PARTIES

(1)   [   ] (IN ADMINISTRATION) (Company
        Number [   ]) whose registered office is [
                              ] ("Licensor") acting by the Administrators

(2)   [   ] and [   ] both of [
                              ] ("Administrators") *[the administrators are
        included as a party to the licence to take the benefit of the exclusions of
        liability contained at clause 15. Arguably they provide no consideration
        for these exclusions, thereby necessitating the execution of the licence as
        a deed].*

(3)   [   ] (Company Number [   ]) whose
        registered office is at [   ]("Licensee")

THIS DEED WITNESSES THAT:

1   DEFINITIONS AND INTERPRETATION

1.1   In this Licence the following words and expressions have the following
        meanings unless the context otherwise provides:

        "Business Day" means a day other than Saturday or Sunday on which
        banks are open for business in London.

        "Landlord" means the Landlord specified in the Leases which shall
        include any person or persons entitled to the reversion immediately or
        mediately expectant on the determination of the Leases.

        "Leases" means the Leases specified in this Licence and all other deeds
        and documents supplemental thereto.

        "Licence Fee" means a sum equal to the Rent as defined in the Leases
        payable by the Licensor pursuant to the Leases on a pro-rata day-to-day
        basis to be paid on the first Monday in each week, or the next Business
        Day thereafter if that day is not a Business Day. For the avoidance of
        doubt if the Licence ceases to relate to part of the Premises the Licence
        Fee shall as from such determination date only be payable in respect of
        the remaining Lease *[Note that there is a risk for administrators if licence
        fees are not paid as the rent falling due under the Lease over the licence
        period will almost certainly be payable as an expense of the administration
        – see **2.80**.]*

        "Permitted Use" means such use as is defined in the Leases.

"Premises" means all the land property and buildings demised by the Leases.

"Statute" means any Act of Parliament already or hereinafter to be passed and any regulation order byelaw or other subordinate legislation already or hereafter to be made under or in pursuance of any Act of Parliament.

"VAT" means value added tax payable by virtue of the Value Added Tax Act 1994.

1.2   Reference to "Licensor", "Licensee" and/or "Administrators" includes the parties to this Licence respectively referred to above by those names and their successors in title and in the case of an individual his personal representatives and whilst the Administrators are appointed administrators of the Licensor "Licensor" shall mean the Licensor acting by the Administrators.

1.3   If the Licensor, Licensee and/or Administrators are at any time more than one person any reference to such party in this Licence shall include each such person and any covenants and/or obligations expressed or implied shall be joint and several covenants and obligations of such persons.

1.4   Words importing one gender include any other gender, words importing the singular include the plural and vice versa and any reference to a person includes a reference to an individual, company, authority, board, department or any other body.

1.5   The paragraph headings are for ease of reference only and shall not be taken into account in the construction or interpretation of this Licence.

1.6   Reference to clauses and schedules are to the clauses and schedules contained in this Licence unless expressly stated otherwise.

2   LICENCE

Subject to the clauses and paragraphs contained below, the Licensor hereby licences and authorises the Licensee and its employees so far as it may lawfully do (subject to the provisions of clause 11) in common with the Licensor and all those authorised by the Licensor to use the Premises for the Permitted Use and for no other purpose whatsoever. [*Consider whether such grant will constitute a breach of the alienation provisions in the lease, and in particular any prohibition on sharing occupation or parting with possession*]

3   TERM OF LICENCE

This Licence shall commence on the date hereof and shall automatically determine on [   ] unless determined earlier in accordance with the provisions of clause 11. [*Consider whether the licence should be contracted out of the provisions of the Landlord and Tenant Act 1954 if for more than 6 months, or if the purchaser/occupier is carrying on the same business as was carried on by the Company for a period exceeding 12 months.*]

4   LICENCE FEE

4.1   As from the date hereof and for so long as this Licence shall continue the Licensee shall pay the Licence Fee to the Licensor on the date specified above.

4.2   The Licensee shall also pay all sums referred to in clauses 8.15 and 8.17 and any other sums payable under the terms of this Licence within 10 working days of the Licensor's written request.

Provided that the Licensee shall only be responsible for the payments detailed in 4.1 and 4.2 above in so far as they relate to and are incurred in respect of the period after the date hereof in respect of the Licence period and in so far as the Licensor has not already discharged the same.

All outgoings accruing and payments referred to above which are referable to a period and partly before and partly after the date hereof shall be apportioned as at the date hereof. Any disputes shall be resolved in accordance with the mechanism set out in clause 11 of the Sale and Purchase Agreement between the parties of even date with this Licence.

5   RULES

The Licensee shall observe and perform and comply with all reasonable rules and regulations made from time to time by the Licensor acting reasonably and in the interests of good estate management for the general management and control of the Premises.

6   LICENSOR'S RIGHTS

The Licensee must not impede the Licensor or its servants, agents or other person so authorised by the Licensor in the exercise of its rights of possession and control of the Premises and every part of the Premises.

7   LICENSOR'S OBLIGATIONS

So long as the Licensee is not in breach of any of its obligations under this Licence, the Licensor shall not interfere with the Licensee's use of the Premises for the Permitted Use.

8   LICENSEE'S OBLIGATIONS

The Licensee agrees and undertakes with the Licensor as follows:

8.1   At all times to ensure that the Premises are kept in a clean and tidy condition and free from all offensive or noisome matter or things;

8.2   To keep the Premises in no worse a state of repair and decoration as they are at the date of the commencement of this Licence;

8.3   To be responsible for any repairs and decorations which may be required as a result of the Licensee's use of the Premises or access to them and not to cause any damage to the Premises;

8.4   Not to do any act or things by which any insurance of the Premises may become void or voidable or by which the insurance premium might be increased and to reimburse the Licensor for any such increase on demand;

8.5   Not to do cause or permit to be done any act or thing on or about or near to the Premises which may be or become a nuisance or inconvenience or cause damage or annoyance to any other occupiers of the Premises (if any) or to the occupiers of any adjoining or neighbouring property;

8.6   Not to make any alterations or additions to the Premises;

8.7   Not to use the Premises for any illegal or immoral purpose or in such a way as to cause nuisance annoyance inconvenience or cause damage to any other person or neighbouring property;

8.8   Not to allow anyone to sleep in the Premises;

8.9   To keep clean and free from obstruction and not to damage any conducting media in or serving the Premises;

8.10   To keep all goods and chattels from time to time at the Premises fully insured to the Licensor's reasonable satisfaction;

8.11   To keep the Premises fully secured at all times;

8.12   At its own expense to comply with all Statute and regulations made under them in relation to the Premises and their use and any requirements of local or other public authorities and statutory undertakers;

8.13   To use the Premises in accordance with the Permitted Use and for no other purpose;

8.14   To pay the Licence Fee at the time and in the manner specified in clause 4;

8.15   To defray all rates taxes charges and other outgoings in respect of the Premises incurred during the period of this Licence (but not further or otherwise) including any charges incurred by the Licensor or for which the Licensor shall be responsible to discharge for insuring the Premises and in the event of the same not being directly assessed on the Licensee to pay a fair proportion of such matters to the Licensor (such proportion to be certified by the Licensor and such certification to be conclusive save in the case of manifest error) but excluding any payments due in respect of dilapidations save insofar as those payments relate to any act or omission of the Licensee during the term of this Licence;

8.16   Not to obstruct or cause to be obstructed the passageways stairways lifts or other common parts of the Premises, nor to prevent or in any way inhibit the Licensor's movement in the Premises;

8.17   To pay promptly for all electricity water gas telephone calls and rental and any other supplies and utilities consumed on the Premises during this Licence;

8.18   Not to damage any of the Licensor's fixtures fittings equipment or chattels at the Premises and to ensure that at the end of this Licence they are in the same condition as at its commencement; [*may not be relevant where purchaser is acquiring the entirety of the Company's property. Also note that it may be appropriate to include a provision whereby if there is a default by the Licensee the Licensor will be given the right to recover possession and the title to the fixtures, fittings and chattel assets remaining on site will be deemed to revert back to the Licensor, or alternatively a right granted to the Licensor to sell any assets left on site on the expiry of a specified period*]

8.19 To pay to the Licensor interest on a daily basis at four per centum (4%) over the base rate from time to time of Barclays Bank plc both before as well as after judgment on any sums payable by the Licensee under this Licence (which are over 14 days late in payment) calculated from the due date to the date of actual payment; and

8.20 Not to do or permit to be done anything in or in relation to the Premises which may constitute a breach of the terms of the Leases.

9   AGREEMENT AND DECLARATION

It is agreed and declared that:

9.1 This Licence shall not give the Licensee any right of exclusive occupation of the Premises. [*The administrator should think carefully whether the landlord's consent is required to grant the licence (it invariably will be) – see* **8.24.**]

9.2 Notwithstanding the terms and provisions of this Licence the legal possession and control of the Premises shall at all times remain vested in the Licensor.

9.3 This Licence shall be temporary only and personal to the Licensee who shall not be at liberty to assign it or otherwise deal with it or to authorise any person to enter or occupy the Premises other than the Licensee's servants customers or agents in the usual course of the Licensee's business.

9.4 The Licensee shall occupy the Premises at its own risk and the Licensee shall fully indemnify the Licensor from and against all claims losses demands expenses or liabilities made:

(a)   in connection with any damage loss or injury to any goods or to any person arising out of the Licensee's occupation of the Premises however any such damage loss or injury may be caused;

(b)   in connection with any breach of any undertaking agreement or covenant on the part of the Licensee contained in this Licence.

9.5 It is not the intention of either the Licensor or Licensee to create between them the relationship of landlord and tenant and this Licence shall not in any way confer or impose on either of them any of the rights or obligations of a landlord or tenant or any other rights or obligations save those expressed or implied by law in this Licence [*note the requirements of documents purporting to create licences – see* **4.4**].

9.6 All rents and other payments receivable in respect of the Premises after the date hereof shall belong to the Licensee.

9.7 All payments receivable referred to in clause 9.6 above which are referable to a period partly before and partly after the date hereof shall be apportioned as at the date hereof. All and any amounts due from the Licensor to the Licensee shall be agreed and paid within [] Business Days of the Licensee's written request. [Any disputes shall be resolved in accordance with the mechanism set out in the sale and purchase agreement between the parties of even date] [*if there is one, failing which provision for the resolution of disputes will have to be made in the licence itself*].

10   NO WARRANTY

No warranty is implied in this Licence that the Premises are:

10.1   Fit for the Permitted Use; or

10.2   Comply with any Statute or derivative regulations or orders; or

10.3   That the Licensor may lawfully grant the same and the Licensee acknowledges to the Licensor that it has entered into this Licence having already inspected the Premises and the terms of the Leases and entirely at the Licensee's risk.

11   TERMINATION

This Licence may be determined at any time in any one or more of the following events:

11.1   If the Licensee shall fail to observe and perform any of its obligations howsoever arising under this Licence on its part;

11.2   If the Licensee is more than [   ] days in arrears in payment of any sums due under this Licence (whether formally demanded or not) [*a very short period is recommended in light of the risk that unpaid licence fees could create a liability for the administrator to pay rents under the Leases as an expense – see* **2.80**];

11.3   If any landlord takes proceedings to forfeit either of the Leases or eject the Licensee, or seeks the Administrators' consent to commence such proceedings;

[Provided that in respect of clauses 11.1 to 11.3 above, the right to terminate shall only apply in respect of the Premises affected.] [*in cases where there are multiple sites*]

11.4   If the Licensee:

(a)   is the subject of a proposal for a voluntary arrangement made under Part I of the Insolvency Act 1986 or the directors of the Licensee resolve to make a proposal for one;

(b)   if a petition for an administration order is made or a notice of intention to appoint an administrator is filed under the provisions contained within Schedule B1 of the Insolvency Act 1986 or the directors of the Licensee resolve to present such a petition or file a notice of intention to appoint or an administrator is appointed pursuant to paragraph 14 or paragraph 22 of Schedule B1 of the Insolvency Act 1986;

(c)   if a resolution for the Licensee's voluntary winding up is passed under Part IV of the Insolvency Act 1986 or a meeting of its creditors is called for the purpose of considering that it be wound up voluntarily (in either case, other than a voluntary winding up whilst solvent for the purposes of and followed by a solvent reconstruction or amalgamation);

(d)   if a petition for a winding up order is made under Part IV or by virtue of Part V of the Insolvency Act 1986 and advertised in accordance with Rule 4.11 of the Insolvency Rules 1986 or a resolution is passed that it be wound up by the court;

(e) if an application is made under Section 895 of the Companies Act 2006 or a proposal is made which could result in such an application;

(f) if it enters or proposes to enter into any arrangement, moratorium or composition (other than any referred to above) with its creditors;

(g) if it is dissolved or is removed from the Register of Companies or ceases to exist (whether or not capable of reinstatement or reconstruction); or

(h) if the Licensee suffers any distress [or commercial rent arrears recovery] or process of execution to be levied against it [or notice is served pursuant to paragraph 7 of Schedule 12 of the Tribunals Courts Enforcement Act 2007 [once in force]

and in any of the said cases the Licensor may give the Licensee [ ] days' notice [*the administrator will want as short a period as possible given the potential risks with the landlord – see 4.11*] to vacate the Premises and upon the expiration of such notice the Licensee shall immediately vacate the Premises and this Licence shall then immediately determine but without prejudice to any accrued rights of the Licensor against the Licensee in respect of any breach of the conditions and the Licensee on such determination shall not be entitled to any refund of the Licence Fee or other sums paid in advance.

11.5 The Licensee shall have the right to terminate this Licence in its entirety or in respect of [either] Premises on giving not less than [ ] written notice at any time.

11.6 This Licence shall determine automatically in the event that the Leases are assigned to the Licensee but this shall be without prejudice to the Licensor's right to recover all and any sums falling due or otherwise accruing under the terms of this Licence up to the date of determination.

11.7 In so far as any part or parts of the Premises are not specified by the Licensor or Licensee (as applicable) as being subject to determination pursuant to this clause, this Licence shall remain in full force and effect for the remainder of the Term in respect of the remainder of the Premises [*in respect of multiple sites*].

12 REMOVAL OF GOODS

On the determination or expiry of this Licence for whatever reason the Licensee shall immediately vacate the Premises and shall remove all its goods and effects from the Premises and shall leave the Premises in a condition as is required pursuant to the terms of this Licence and shall make good any damage caused to the Premises as a result of its occupation of the Premises.

13   INDEMNITY

The Licensee agrees to indemnify and keep indemnified the Licensor and the Administrators and each of them in respect of all actions claims costs demands and expenses whatsoever and whensoever arising of third parties (including any landlord) relating to actions or omissions of the Licensee during the period of the Licence hereby granted whether relating to the state of repair and condition of the Premises the use of the Premises and any activities carried out (including [any occupation in breach of the Leases and/or] in contravention of any planning statutes or regulations). For the avoidance of doubt the Licensee shall have no right of action against the Licensor and the Administrators or either of them in respect of any use or activity of the Premises or the state of repair and condition of the Premises during the period of occupation under the Licence.

14   EXCLUSION OF SECURITY OF TENURE

[*Administrators will often wish to contract out of the security of tenure provisions provided by the Landlord and Tenant Act 1954, in which case this clause could be adopted (notwithstanding this document purports to be a licence and may be for less than 6 months)*].

14.1   [The Licensor has served on the Licensee a notice dated [   ] in the form, or substantially in the form, set out in Schedule 1 to the Regulatory Reform (Business Tenancies) (England and Wales) Order 2003 in relation to this Licence.

14.2   The Licensee, or a person duly authorised by the Licensee, has made a statutory declaration dated 24 October 2008 in a form complying with the requirements of Schedule 2 to the Regulatory Reform (Business Tenancies) (England and Wales) Order 2003 in relation to the notice described in clause 14.

14.3   Where the declaration referred to in clause 14 was made by a person other than the Licensee, the Licensee confirms the declarant was duly authorised by the Licensee to make the declaration on the Licensee's behalf.

14.4   The Licensor and Licensee confirm that the notice and declaration referred to in clauses 14 and 14.2 were respectively served on and made by or on behalf of the Licensee before the Licensee became contractually bound to enter into the Licence under an agreement dated 24 October 2008 made between the Licensor acting by the Administrators (1) and the Licensee (2).

14.5   The Licensor and Licensee agree that the provisions of Sections 24 to 28 of the Landlord and Tenant Act 1954 are excluded in relation to this Licence.

15   EXCLUSION OF ADMINISTRATORS' PERSONAL LIABILITY

15.1   The Licensee acknowledges and agrees that in the negotiation and completion of this agreement the Administrators are acting only as agents of the Licensor and that notwithstanding that this Licence shall have been executed by the Administrators on behalf of the Licensor it is expressly agreed and declared that:

(a)   no personal liability under or in connection with this Licence shall fall on the Administrators or their firm, partners or employees and the Licensee shall indemnify the Administrators on a full indemnity basis against all and any Liabilities arising under or in connection with this Licence;

(b)   the Administrators are party to this Licence in their personal capacities only for the purpose of receiving the benefit of this sub-clause and the exclusions, limitations, undertakings, covenants and indemnities in their favour in this Licence; and

(c)   the Licensee hereby waives any claim in tort as well as under contract against the Administrators.

16   VAT [IF APPLICABLE]

All consideration and other sums in this Licence are expressed to be exclusive of Value Added Tax and the Licensee shall forthwith pay to the Licensor Value Added Tax on the same in the event of it being payable and on the Licensor presenting the Licensee with a valid VAT invoice for the same.

17   NOTICES

For the purpose of service of all notices in this Licence or by Statute authorised to be served the provisions contained in Section 196 of the Law of Property Act 1925 as amended by the Recorded Delivery Service Act 1962 shall be deemed to be incorporated.

18   EXCLUSION OF THIRD PARTY RIGHTS

This Licence does not create any right enforceable by a person not party to it and a person who is not a party to this licence shall have no rights under the Contracts (Rights of Third Parties) Act 1999 to enforce any term of this licence.

THIS LICENCE is executed as a deed and is delivered and takes effect on the date stated at the beginning of it.

SCHEDULE

Leases

Date	Document	Parties	Term	Short Description of Property Demised by the Leases

EXECUTED (but not delivered until the date hereof) **AS A DEED**, by **THE LICENSOR** (in administration) by [
], pursuant to powers conferred under the Insolvency Act 1986 in the presence of:

Witness

Signature

Name

Occupation

Address

> ....
>
> [SIGN IN NAME OF LICENSOR AND THE ADMINISTRATOR], its administrator

SIGNED (but not delivered until the date hereof) **AS A DEED** by [   ] for and on behalf of the Administrators] in the presence of:

Witness

Signature

Name

Occupation

Address

> ....
>
> [SIGNATURE OF JOINT ADMINISTRATOR]

EXECUTED (but not delivered until the date hereof) **AS A DEED** by **THE LICENSEE** acting by, Director and, [Director/Secretary]:

Director

Signature

Name

Director/Secretary

Signature

Name

Appendix 13

DEED OF APPOINTMENT OF RECEIVER UNDER LAW OF PROPERTY ACT 1925

THIS DEED OF APPOINTMENT OF RECEIVER is made the [   ] day of
[   ] 20[   ] by [   ] of [INSERT ADDRESS/REGISTERED
OFFICE ADDRESS] ("the Mortgagee")

BACKGROUND

1   By Legal Charge ("the Charge") short particulars of which are set out in
    the Schedule to this Deed the property described in the Schedule ("the
    Property") is charged to the Mortgagee to secure the monies and
    liabilities mentioned in the Schedule.
2   Demand for payment of the monies due to the Mortgagee and secured
    by the Charge has been made and default has been made in such
    payment and the power to appoint a Receiver and Manager of the
    Property pursuant to the Charge has arisen and become exercisable.

OPERATIVE PROVISIONS

1   In exercise of the powers contained in the Charge and of all other
    powers conferred on it by statute (or otherwise) the Mortgagee hereby
    appoints [   ] and [   ] ("the Receivers") of [   ] to be the Receivers and
    Managers of the Property with power to exercise with regard to it all
    powers and authorities contained by the Law of Property Act 1925
    ("the Act") and by the Charge and otherwise and where more than one
    party is appointed they shall have power to act severally as well as
    jointly.
2   The Mortgagee hereby directs the Receivers after providing for the
    matters specified in the first three paragraphs of sub-section (8) of
    Section 109 of the Act to apply all monies received by him in or towards
    the discharge of the principal monies and interest secured by the
    Charge.
3   The Receivers are hereby directed to insure the Property assets and
    rights over which they are appointed in such sum as he may consider
    appropriate having regard to current prudent commercial practice.
4   The Mortgagee shall delegate to the Receivers any of the powers
    conferred on the Mortgagee by statute and the Charge as it shall
    determine.
5   The Receivers acknowledge that they shall not take possession of the
    Property (other than as agent of the mortgagor) without the written
    instructions from the Mortgagee.
6   The Receivers shall be entitled to remuneration for the performance of
    their duties and for the reimbursement of all charges and expenses

correctly incurred by them in the manner now or from time to time agreed in writing between the Mortgagee and the Receivers.

DELIVERED as a deed on the date of this document.

SCHEDULE

Date of Charge	Mortgagor (and Company Number)	Property (including Title Number if registered)

COMMON SEAL OF

...

Was affixed in the presence of:

...

Director

...

Secretary

Appendix 14

WRITTEN ACCEPTANCE OF APPOINTMENT BY RECEIVER

**Form
3.1**

Rule 3.1

(TITLE)

(a) Insert name and address of person making appointment	To: (a)
(b) Insert full name and address of appointee	(b) Hereby accepts appointment as receiver of
(c) Insert name of company	(c)
(d) Insert date	In accordance with the instrument of appointment received on (d)
(e) Insert time	At (e)

Date:

Time:

Signed:

Name of Signatory:

(BLOCK LETTERS)

(by or on behalf of the appointee)

Appendix 15

DEED OF INDEMNITY TO RECEIVERS

THIS DEED OF INDEMNITY is given the [   ] date of [   ] 20[   ]

PARTIES

1. [   ] ("the Mortgagee") of [INSERT ADDRESS OR REGISTERED OFFICE ADDRESS]

2. [   ] ("the Receivers") of [INSERT ADDRESS]

BACKGROUND

(i) Under the powers contained in a Legal Charge dated [ ] ("the Charge") granted by [   ] ("the Mortgagor") to the Mortgagee by which the Mortgagor charged in favour of the Mortgagee the property referred to in the Schedule to this Deed ("the Property") the Mortgagee has by a Deed of Appointment ("the Appointment") dated [   ] and made between the Mortgagee and the Receivers the Mortgagee appointed the Receivers and receivers of the Property.

(ii) The Mortgagee has agreed to provide the Receivers with an indemnity in the terms as hereafter appears.

INDEMNITY

In consideration of your accepting appointment as Receivers of the undertaking, Property and assets comprised in the Charge at our request under an appointment made by the Mortgagee under the Charge, the Mortgagee now undertakes to indemnify the Receivers and keep them indemnified from and against all losses, liabilities, proceedings, claims, damages, costs and expenses incurred by the Receivers in the proper and reasonable conduct of such receivership and to pay the Receivers reasonable remuneration for the work performed notwithstanding any defect invalidity or irregularity in the Charge or any registration of it or in the Receivers' appointment for any reason whatsoever *(or)* incurred:

1   by reason of any defect, invalidity or irregularity in the Charge or any registration of it or in the Receivers' appointment for any reason whatsoever; or

2   by reason of any inability to recover and retain in full such sums as are required to discharge all reasonable remuneration due to the Receivers for work done in respect of such receivership and all costs expenses and liabilities incurred in the proper and reasonable conduct of it; or

3   by reason of any acts effected on the Mortgagee's instructions or with the Mortgagee's agreement

And so that this indemnity shall remain in force notwithstanding the termination or conclusion of the Receivers' office or functions under the Appointment.

Provided always that the above indemnity:

1   shall not render the Receivers the Mortgagee's agent for any purpose whatsoever; and
2   shall not apply to any losses, liabilities, proceedings, claims, damages, costs or expenses to the extent to which the Receivers are able to be indemnified or reimbursed out of the assets comprised in the Charge or from any other source or which the Receivers may incur by reason of their failure to exercise their powers or perform their duties with the degree of care, prudence and diligence required or expected of them as receivers accepting appointment as joint receivers for valuable consideration. This indemnity is in addition to any other rights of indemnity to which the Receivers are entitled by law or otherwise and it shall remain in full force notwithstanding the making of distributions to the Mortgagee in respect of the receivership or its termination.

DELIVERED as a deed on the date of this document . . . .

INDEX

References are to paragraph numbers.